THE NEW TESTAMENT IN GREEK IV
THE GOSPEL ACCORDING TO ST. JOHN

VOLUME ONE

THE PAPYRI

NEW TESTAMENT TOOLS AND STUDIES

EDITED BY

BRUCE M. METZGER, Ph.D., D.D., L.H.D., D. Theol., D. Litt.
Professor of New Testament Language and Literature, Emeritus
Princeton Theological Seminary
and
Corresponding Fellow of the British Academy

AND

BART D. EHRMAN, Ph.D.
Associate Professor, Department of Religious Studies
University of North Carolina at Chapel Hill

VOLUME XX

THE NEW TESTAMENT IN GREEK IV
THE GOSPEL ACCORDING TO ST. JOHN

EDITED BY

THE AMERICAN AND BRITISH COMMITTEES
OF THE INTERNATIONAL
GREEK NEW TESTAMENT PROJECT

VOLUME ONE

THE PAPYRI

EDITED BY

W.J. ELLIOTT AND D.C. PARKER

E.J. BRILL
LEIDEN · NEW YORK · KÖLN
1995

The paper in this book meets the guidelines for permanence and durability of the Committee on Production Guidelines for Book Longevity of the Council on Library Resources.

ISSN 0077-8842
ISBN 90 04 09940 9

PRINTED IN THE NETHERLANDS

CONTENTS

PREFACE

The American and British committees of the International Greek New Testament Project published their edition of The Gospel according to St Luke in two parts, one in 1984 and the other in 1987. In 1987 the two committees decided to regroup and to continue work, this time on the Gospel of St. John. A full critical apparatus to the Fourth Gospel is now under way. As one of its tasks the British Committee agreed to undertake the collating of Greek papyrus and majuscule manuscripts. With the agreement of the North American Committee, the British Committee decided to publish independently a volume on the Greek papyri containing St. John's Gospel. It seemed sensible to deal separately with the papyri, since these fragmentary manuscripts often require special treatment and different presentation because of the distinctive problems they pose when being deciphered. Partly as a consequence of this, a number of innovations have been made in the presentation of the material. The bulk of the work has been undertaken and organized by the two co-editors, Dr W.J. Elliott and Dr D.C. Parker, under the auspices of the British Committee. Dr Parker wrote the introductory matter and prepared the camera-ready copy submitted to the press.

J.K. Elliott
Secretary to the British Committee
April, 1995

COMMITTEES AND CONTRIBUTORS

1. The British Committee

The following members have served on the committee:

J.K. Elliott (1977 to date; Executive Editor 1977-87; Secretary 1987 to date)
W.J. Elliott (1980 to date; Co-Editor 1987 to date)
C.P. Hammond Bammel (1990 to date)
J.L. North (1975 to date)
D.C. Parker (1984 to date; Co-Editor 1987 to date)
T.S. Pattie (1972 to date; Secretary 1976-87; Treasurer 1976 to date; Chairman 1988 to date)
J.D. Thomas (1990 to date)

2. The American Committee

The American Committee was re-formed in 1988; the following members served on the committee:

J.A. Brooks (1988 to date; Secretary *pro tem.* 1994 to date)
B.D. Ehrman (1988 to date)
E.J. Epp (1968 to date)
G.D. Fee (1970 to date; Chair 1988 to date)
T.C. Geer, Jr. (1988-1994; Secretary 1988-1994)
M.W. Holmes (1988 to date; Editor 1988 to date)
P.R. McReynolds (1965 to date; Corresponding Secretary/Secretary 1965-1988)
B. Morrill (1992 to date)
C.D. Osburn (1988 to date; Vice Chair 1988 to date)
W.L. Petersen (1989 to date)

3. The International Steering Committee

This committee was formed in 1988, with the purpose of meeting every two years, to maintain links between the British and American Committees. The committee first met in 1989. The membership is as follows:

J.K. Elliott
G.D. Fee
C.D. Osburn
D.C. Parker

4. The Contributors

The following contributed by either collating or checking one or more papyrus:

P.W. Comfort[1]
J.K. Elliott
W.J. Elliott
G.D. Fee
E. Güting
M.W. Holmes
J.L. North
D.C. Parker
T.S. Pattie
C.J. Roetzel
R.B. Stone
J.D. Thomas
G.C. Whipple

Several papyri were collated for the Project in the sixties. Because of the new ground rules of this volume, we have not been able to use these collations.

---

[1] The following contributed to P.W. Comfort's work: D. Barrett, K. Berner, C. Brown, M. Ganly, A. Gerber, R. Harter, C. Hudson, R. Vishanoff.

The following assisted either by answering a query or by checking a collation against the papyrus itself:

B. Aland
R.S. Bagnall
J. Gascou
H. Harrauer
R. Pintaudi

INTRODUCTION

The question may be raised: what is the value in treating separately a collection of pieces dating from the second to the seventh centuries, of varying textual significance, some extremely fragmentary? There are three reasons. The first refers to the character of the material as a palaeographical problem, the second to its place in contemporary scholarship, the third (to which we shall turn later) to its coherence.

The problems of presenting the evidence accurately and fully, while doing justice to the unique skills of the papyrologist, require a different kind of edition. A presentation suited to traditional materials—that is, extensive parchment manuscripts—is not adequate to the task of setting fragmentary and sometimes scarcely legible papyri before textual critics. In preparing this edition, the editors and collators have time and again encountered the danger of leading the reader into a false dependence on their reconstruction of missing letters, words, and phrases. In the attempt to avoid this danger, the edition has taken on a quite distinctive shape. The following description both justifies the form (and the need to present this material separately), and guides the reader in its use.

The second reason is that, a century after the first New Testament Greek papyrus finds, and more than thirty years since the publication of the Bodmer papyri, the time has come to collect the material together in such a way that we can the more readily and the more scientifically evaluate it.

The edition falls into three parts: transcription of the papyri, *apparatus criticus* of readings, and photographs. Thus, the user has the information about the text of the papyri available in three forms. It is necessary to work with all three to make proper use of the edition and to achieve scientific accuracy.

The Transcriptions

In the first part, we provide a transcription of twenty-one of the twenty-three papyri of John's Gospel. The two exceptions are P^{66} and P^{75}, to which we will turn in a moment. All the transcriptions were made either from photographs, or (in the case of P^{5}, P^{22}, P^{45} and P^{90}) from the papyrus itself. (Only the portion of P^{45} containing

Chapters 10 and 11 was collated direct from the papyrus.) A collation was then made from the new transcription. Reference was not made to the previous editions at this stage. Each transcription and collation was then checked twice, and compared to earlier editions. At this point certain readings in the following papyri were checked in the original: P^{2}, P^{6}, P^{36}, P^{55}, P^{59} and P^{60}. In addition, the committee sought the aid of specialists in papyrology, one of whom joined the committee. The work was then entered on disk, and discussed by the editors. Finally, it was checked by reconstructing the text of each papyrus from the DEF and apparatus sections, and comparing the result with the transcription.

P^{66} and P^{75} were treated differently. No fresh transcription was made; instead, the collation was made directly from the photographs. Otherwise, precisely the same method was followed.

Particular problems arose with the two Colt papyri, P^{59} and P^{60}. Parts of these papyri that were available to the first editors are no longer extant (or at any rate, could not be found). We were able to obtain photographs of some of these parts. On the other hand, some fragments of which we could not obtain photographs turned out to be extant. For a detailed explanation of our treatment of these problems, the reader is referred to pp. 76-108.

Fragments A and B of P^{44} are by two separate hands (see p. 52). We have designated them P^{44A} and P^{44B}.

Our transcription of P^{84} is the *editio princeps*.

It should be noted that the editors' examination of P^{45} led them to depart significantly from Kenyon's transcription.

We may here briefly note that not all the papyri of John's Gospel were found in Egypt. P^{84} is from Judaea, P^{59} and P^{60} are from Nessana ('Auja el-Hafir, in the Negev).

The format of the transcriptions is as follows. At the top is given the number of the papyrus, contents in verses, and whether the fibres on the page run horizontally (→) or vertically (↓). The text follows, with line numbers in threes on the left, and verse numbers on the right. Brackets are placed around the verse number when the fragment or page lacks the beginning of it. The extant portion of the papyrus is printed in bold face majuscule type. Partially missing letters whose identity is not certain have a dot beneath them. The use of dots is not precisely that of a diplomatic transcript, but accepts that our knowledge of the text copied permits us to be fairly certain of a letter's identity even when little of it remains. Thus, the use of a dot beneath a blank space, to indicate that there are traces of ink which cannot be identified as a particular letter, is less frequent than it would be if we were providing a diplomatic transcript. The text is divided into words according to modern convention, regardless of the practice of the copyist.

Square brackets separate the extant text from the reconstruction of what is missing, which is provided in plain minuscule type. This reconstruction follows the text of the collating base, unless there is good reason to depart from it (usually, the reason is that the amount of space in the missing part of the papyrus does not correspond to the amount of text in the collating base). *Nomina sacra* are provided in the forms used by the papyrus, where they can be established, and in any case according to the amount of space available (for example, if there is room for $\overline{\alpha\nu\omega\nu}$ but not for ανθρωπων). In every transcription but that of P^{60}, we have departed from the collating base in the spelling of one proper name: πειλατοϲ replaces πιλατοϲ, for (with the exception of P^{60}) the papyri are consistent in their use of the diphthong. In addition, we follow the spelling of a papyrus where it appears consistent.

Corrections are given in the following form: the first reading is enclosed within braces { and }, and the correction is then placed within angle brackets < and >. For example, the scribe of P^{45} wrote γεινωϲκουϲι at 10:14; this was corrected by another hand to γεινωϲκει. The transcription reads **ΓЄΙΝѠϹΚ{ΟΥϹΙ} <ЄΙ>**. The manner of the correction is described in the notes. A correction made by the first hand is indicated by double braces {{ and }}.

The chapter and verse numbers are those of the United Bible Society's fourth edition. This differs from the collating base at 1:38-39 (where the collating base is ambiguous) and at 13:30-31.

Lunate sigma is used throughout, except in the notes to the transcriptions. There, the forms used by an edition being cited are preserved.

The transcription includes any page or leaf numbers, but not additional material such as the *hermeneiai* found in a number of Johannine papyri. Letters written above or below the line of writing by the first hand of a papyrus are transcribed in that position, unless such letters are a correction in which one or more letters are replaced.

Beneath the transcription are notes. For the most part these refer to places where the transcription differs from earlier ones. We do not indicate where we differ from them in the decision to place dots under letters; nor, generally, where we differ in the reconstruction of missing text. The notes also contain some comments on particular problems of decipherment.

The text is laid out so that a transcription and its accompanying notes are always visible at the same time. Only with P^{45} has this proved impossible. The material relating to each papyrus is laid out with as few page turns as possible. It is hoped that the user will nearly always be able to find the relevant information without needing to turn a page.

The Apparatus Criticus

The second part of the edition contains the collations. These, verse by verse, follow the basic format used in *The Gospel according to St Luke* (Oxford University Press; Vol. 1, 1984; Vol. 2, 1987). Beneath the chapter and verse number, is a list of papyri extant for some or all of the verse. Then comes the text of the collating base. This is given in lower case characters, without accents or breathings or iota subscript. The text of the collating base is the Oxford, 1873 reprint of the *Textus Receptus*, following *The Gospel according to St Luke.* For an explanation of the reasons for this, see D.C. Parker, 'The International Greek New Testament Project: the Gospel of John', *New Testament Studies* 36 (1990), 157-60, esp. p. 159. Here, we may remind the reader of the first of the general principles enunciated in *The Gospel according to St Luke*, Vol. 1, p. vi: 'The aim of the edition is to provide an objective presentation of the textual evidence, and not to construct a new text'.

Below the text of the collating base is the DEF section, which describes the contents of witnesses with lacunae. Most feature in this section. What is provided is precisely what is present in the papyrus (that is, the letters in bold face majuscule in the transcription), but without lectional signs—trema or diaeresis, accents, apostrophe, fillers, or punctuation (including spaces). Very rarely, a lectional sign is recorded: for example, it is all that has survived from a long lacuna in P^{75} at 12:4. *Nomina sacra* and other abbreviations are retained. A lacuna is indicated by a space within square brackets. The space is of one letter width if only one letter is missing, of two widths for all larger lacunae. Such a space is never divided at the end of a line. Where a large part of a verse survives, we have used ... in order to avoid having to provide the whole text. The dots do *not* mean that the text of the papyrus follows the collating base in what is not given in full. Sometimes, there is ambiguity because a letter or group of letters comes at several places in the verse (for example, P^{59} at 1:51). Since our reconstruction in the transcriptions provides our opinion, we only indicate the problem for P^{66} and P^{75}, by supplying a prompt in the form of a word from the collating base within the square brackets immediately preceding or following the problematical letter or letters. Of course, if there is a genuine question about the space available for text, it will be indicated in the collation.

The dots under incomplete letters and dots with no letter above are recorded only for P^{66} and P^{75}, since there would otherwise be no record of them. These two papyri are also treated differently in two other ways. The leaves of P^{75} containing parts of 6:19 and 33, and 12:48-15:8 could not be photographed. We are therefore dependent on the editor. Similarly, there are a few places in P^{66} where material at line ends that was available to the editor was destroyed. These are 3:21; 9:3, 16, 17, 26; 15:19, 20. We follow the editors of both papyri in including the material; the note '(teste ed. pr.)' is included in the DEF section as a reminder to the user of the source of the information.

Beneath is the collation. First, the text of the collating base; then, after the colon, the variants. We include all variants from the collating base: not only alteration of wording, but all spelling variants as well. Whilst it is not intended to keep all this information in future stages of *The Gospel according to St. John*, it is possible to include it in this relatively simple *apparatus*. It is hoped that this information will cause the present edition to contribute to our knowledge of scribal practice, and not only to questions of 'significant' readings. We have usually expanded *nomina sacra* and other abbreviations in the *apparatus*: to have kept them would have been to treat the abbreviated forms as variant readings; consistency would then demand that all be included. But the need for clarity has required us to retain the abbreviation occasionally—for example, if an abbreviated word is only partly extant.

Readings where there are lacunae do not attempt to prejudge the issue by suggesting what is possible or probable, by the use of the abbreviation *vid.*, or by containing the minuscule text from the transcription in square brackets. Instead, where there is a variant that requires a different wording in the lacuna, or where the space available is greater or less than the collating base text requires, we indicate the number of letter spaces available. Where the question of available space is not of significance, we leave the space between the square brackets blank (e.g. 6:46). As in the DEF section, the space is of one letter width if only one letter is missing, of two widths for all larger lacunae, and such a space is never divided by a line end. The reader may then compare this with our transcription, and make his or her own decision about the possible reading. Our opinion may be found in the transcription. It does not obtrude on the collation.

A slash (/) indicates the end of a line in the papyrus. Where it stands outside square brackets indicating a lacuna, the last letters of the line before the lacuna or the first letters after are it extant. Where it stands within the brackets, then the lacuna includes the end of one line and the beginning of the next. The reason for indicating this is that one has slightly more evidence for interpreting the papyrus if at least part of a margin is extant (especially if it is a line ending that has survived).

An example may help. At 8:21, there is a lacuna in P^{39} that begins in the middle of παλιν. The equivalent of the text of the collating base, αυτοιc ο ιηcουc, is missing. This page of the papyrus has a minimum of 11 and a maximum of 15 letters in a line. In fact, most have 13 or 14. Since five letters of this line (l. 18) are extant, the missing words are likely to have amounted to anything between 6 and 10 letters. The left margin is extant, so the beginning of the next line is certain. The *apparatus* indicates this as

παλιν αυτοιc ο ιηcουc: πα[6-10] /

It is therefore possible that the papyrus could have read παλιν ο $\overline{\text{ιηc}}$ (which would have been a line of 12 letters) or παλιν αυτοιc (14 letters). To indicate the more probable omission of ο ιηcουc would have been less satisfactory. Where deficient papyri have to be cited separately, but our reconstruction supposes them to have had the same text, we cross-reference the entries with '& cf.'.

Corrections in papyri are indicated as follows:

original reading: *
correction by scribe: ^{*c}
correction by another hand: ^{c}

Where a corrector introduces a divergence from the collating base, the first hand's agreement with the base is indicated by (for example) txt **P^{66*}**. Where a corrector brings the text into agreement with the collating base, this is indicated after the indication of the papyrus giving the variant by txt (papyrus number) ^{c}.

^{*c} has been used more sparingly than ^{c}, because we have not used it unless there is clear evidence for it. An erasure without any text supplied we always treat as ^{c}, even in P^{66}, where one would be justified in attributing it to the first hand. In fact, only two second hand corrections that consist of letters have been identified in P^{66}. One is at 13:19; the other, hitherto unnoticed, is at 14:22.

At 4:42 and 8:25 a correction in P^{66} is not certain of restoration. A dot will be found in the collation beneath the damaged letter.

The text is set out so that a left hand page always begins with a new verse—the evidence for a verse is never divided between a recto and a verso.

The Plates

The *editiones principes* of these papyri are scattered in time and place. Photographs of some may be found with the original edition. Some have never been published in photographic form. We have included here as much as we could. All but the two longest papyri are provided in their entirety. We have had to content ourselves with representative plates of P^{66} and P^{75}. The photographs are not all to scale, and our photographs were not always provided with a scale indicator.

We hope that the material will be of value to papyrologists and palaeographers. But we have also included the material because it supplements the other two forms in which we have provided the information. It does not provide an absolute check on our accuracy: one thing that this project has taught its editors is that the camera undoubtedly lies. But it encourages the user to treat the edition as an attempt to produce a printed representation of something very different, and so to study our work in the light of the original material.

The camera-ready copy was produced on Multi-Lingual Scholar, made by Gamma Productions of Santa Monica. The Greek fonts were developed for the edition, as were a number of the special symbols used.

We described at the beginning of this introduction two justifications of the present work. The third rejects the view that there is no coherence within the papyri. Rather than a miscellaneous collection that happen to be written all on one kind of material, they bear witness to two aspects of early Christianity and its texts. One group, consisting of pre-Constantinian material, is evidence of the textual materials used by the church before the general introduction of parchment codices in the fourth century. The second group consists of papyri of the fourth century and later. They are evidence of a copying that eschewed parchment. That is to say, the fact that the copies are on papyrus is a matter of significance for the character of the copies. It is therefore to be hoped that the material here presented will contribute, not only to purely textual concerns, but to the study of early Christianity's social and hermeneutical complexities.

ABBREVIATIONS AND SYMBOLS

APF	*Archiv für Papyrusforschung*
ANTF	*Arbeiten zur Neutestamentliche Textforschung*
DEF	the extant parts of manuscripts that are lacunose for this verse are as follows
ed. pr.	*editio princeps*
NTS	*New Testament Studies*
P. Oxy.	*Oxyrhynchus Papyri*, London, 1898-
Patr. Or.	*Patrologia Orientalis*
PSI	*Pubblicazioni della Società Italiana* (Papiri Greci e Latini), Florence, 1912-

*	the first hand of a papyrus
*c	a correction by the first hand of a papyrus
c	the corrector of a manuscript. A superscript number after differentiates between several correctors
+	the following words are added *or* (following a numeral) this number of letters or more
/	indicates a line ending in the witness

The apparatus criticus is written in Latin. The following terms and abbreviations merit explanation:

add.	added
aut	separates two possible readings
cj.	conjecture of
del.	deleted
eras.	erased
& cf.	and see, cross-referencing readings that are given separately but may be related (see p. 6)
legit	the witness reads as follows
OM	the witness omits these words
pro	instead of
ras.	erasure
rescript.	rewritten
txt	the witness(es) follow(s) the text of the collating base
vid.	refers to a reading that has had to be given in the previous verse

BIBLIOGRAPHY

This bibliography is not exhaustive. It cites the *editio princeps* and any other material which we have used, and the entry number in Van Haelst. The first (or only) entry for a papyrus is cited in the notes to the transcriptions as *ed. pr.* (*editio princeps*). The Oxyrhynchus papyri are cited by volume number and papyrus number (separated by a point), the year of publication of that volume in brackets, and the page numbers. For other papyri, we give volume and page number, followed by the number given to the papyrus by that editor in brackets. Entries for each papyrus are in chronological order, except that Van Haelst is always placed last.

GENERAL

Aland, 'Papyrus' K. Aland, Das Neuen Testament auf Papyrus, *Studien zur Überlieferung des Neuen Testaments und seines Textes* (ANTF 2), Berlin, 1967, pp. 91-136.

Cavallo G. Cavallo, *Ricerche sulla maiuscola biblica* (Studi e testi di papirologia 2), Florence, 1967.

Liste K. Aland, *Kurzgefasste Liste der griechischen Handschriften des Neuen Testaments* (ANTF 1), 2nd ed., Berlin, 1994.

Rep. K. Aland, *Repertorium der griechischen christlichen Papyri. I Biblische Papyri. Altes Testament, Neues Testament, Varia, Apokryphen* (Patristische Texte und Studien 18), Berlin and New York, 1976.

Seider R. Seider, *Paläographie der griechischen Papyri II*, Stuttgart, 1970. We cite the entry number.

Turner E.G. Turner, *The Typology of the Early Codex*, Pennsylvania, 1977.

Van Haelst J. Van Haelst, *Catalogue des papyrus littéraires Juifs et Chrétiens, Université de Paris IV Paris-Sorbonne. Série «Papyrologie»* 1, Paris, 1976. We cite the entry number.

EDITIONS AND STUDIES OF INDIVIDUAL PAPYRI

P^{2} E. Pistelli, 'Papiri evangelici', *Rivista di studi religiosi* 6 (1906), pp. 129-40 + plate (1); M. Naldini, *Documenti dell'Antichità cristiana. Papiri e pergamene greco-egizie della Raccolta Fiorentina*, Florence, 1965, pp. 1-8 + Plate 10 (13).
Van Haelst 455.

P^{5} B.P. Grenfell and A.S. Hunt, *P. Oxy.* 2.208 (1899), pp. 1-8; 15.1781 (1922), pp. 8-12.
C. Wessely, *Les plus anciens Monuments du christianisme écrits sur papyrus, Patr. Or.* 4 (1907), pp. 145-48 (10, = P. Oxy. 208); *ibid., Patr. Or.* 18 (1924), pp. 499-500 (Supplément, = P. Oxy. 1781) (the two parts have continuous pagination).
Van Haelst 428.

P^{6} F. Rösch, *Bruchstücke des ersten Clemensbriefes nach dem achmimischen Papyrus der Strassburger Universitäts- und Landesbibliothek*, Strasbourg, 1910, pp. X and 119-60 + plate.
Van Haelst 451.

P^{22} Grenfell and Hunt, *P. Oxy.* 10.1228 (1914), pp. 14-16.
Wessely, *op. cit., Patr. Or.* 18, pp. 451-2 (1).
Van Haelst 459.

P^{28} Grenfell and Hunt, *P. Oxy.* 13.1596 (1919), pp. 8-10.
Van Haelst 444.

P^{36} Pistelli, *PSI* 1 (1912), pp. 5-6 (3).
Naldini, *op. cit.*, p. 17 + Plate XI (14).
A. Carlini, 'Riesame di due frammenti Fiorentini del Vangelo di Giovanni (PSI 3)', *APF* 22/23 (1974), pp. 219-222 + Plate 13; reprinted in *Papiri letterari greci* (Biblioteca degli Studi classici e orientali 13), Pisa, 1978, pp. 193-199 + Plate 12 (28).
G.H.R. Horsley, 'Scribal Carelessness in P^{36} (Jn. 3.14-18, 31-35)?', *New Documents Illustrating Early Christianity* 3, Macquarie University, 1983, pp. 100-1.
Van Haelst 437.

P^{39} Grenfell and Hunt, *P. Oxy.* 15.1780 (1922), pp. 7-8.
Cavallo, p. 49.
Van Haelst 448.

P[44] (A and B) W.E. Crum and H.G. Evelyn White, *The Monastery of Epiphanius at Thebes, Metropolitan Museum of Art, Egyptian Exploration Publications* 4, New York, 1926, Vol. 1, p. 16; Vol. 2, pp. 120-1, 301 (583).
Van Haelst 365

P[45] F.G. Kenyon, *The Chester Beatty Biblical Papyri. Descriptions and Texts of Twelve Manuscripts on Papyrus of the Greek Bible. Fasciculus II, The Gospels and Acts. Text*, London, 1933; *Plates*, London 1934.
Cavallo, p. 119.
Seider 43.
T.C. Skeat and B.C. McGing, 'Notes on Chester Beatty Biblical Papyrus 1 (Gospels and Acts)', *Hermathena* 150 (1991), 21-25.
Van Haelst 371.

P[52] C.H. Roberts, *An Unpublished Fragment of the Fourth Gospel*, Manchester, 1935 (with plate); reprinted with slight alterations in *Bulletin of the John Rylands Library* 20 (1936), pp. 44-55; also in expanded form in C.H. Roberts, *Catalogue of the Greek and Latin Papyri in the John Rylands Library,* Vol. 3 (Manchester, 1938), pp. 1-3 (457).
A. Schmidt, 'Zwei Anmerkungen zu P.Ryl. III 457', *APF* 35 (1989), pp. 11-12.
Van Haelst 462.

P[55] P. Sanz, *Mitteilungen aus der Papyrussammlung der österreichischen Nationalbibliothek in Wien*, N.S. 4, Baden, 1946, pp. 58-9 (35).
Van Haelst 433.

P[59] L. Casson and E.L. Hettich, *Excavations at Nessana*, Vol. 2, *Literary Papyri*, Princeton, 1950, pp. 79-93 + Plates 4 and 5 (3).
C.J. Kraemer, *Excavations at Nessana*, Vol. 3, *Non-Literary Papyri*, Princeton, 1958, p. 9.
Van Haelst 429.

P[60] L. Casson and E.L. Hettich (see P[59]), pp. 94-111 (4).
C.J. Kraemer (see P[59]), p. 9.
Van Haelst 460.

P[63] O. Stegmüller, 'Zu den Bibelorakeln im Codex Bezae', *Biblica* 34 (1953), pp. 13-22.
Van Haelst 438.

P66 V. Martin, *Papyrus Bodmer II, Évangile de Jean*, chapters 1-14, Cologny-Geneva, 1956; *Supplément*, chapters 14-21, 1958; rev. ed. (with J.W.B. Barns), 1962 (of chapters 14-21 with plates of chapters 1-21). *Ed. pr.* here = 1956 and 1962 publications.

H. Hunger, 'Zur Datierung des Papyrus Bodmer II (P 66)', *Anzeiger der österreichischen Akademie der Wissenschaften in Wien, Philos.-Hist. Klasse*, 13 (1960), 12-23.

J.W.B. Barns, 'Papyrus Bodmer II, Some Corrections and Remarks', *Muséon* 75 (1962), pp. 327-9.

Cavallo, p. 23f.

G.D. Fee, *Papyrus Bodmer II (P66): Its Textual Relationships and Scribal Characteristics* (Studies and Documents 34), Salt Lake City, 1968, Appendix A, 'Annotated Corrections to the Editio Princeps of P66', pp. 85-97.

Seider 44.

M. Gronewald in M. Gronewald, K. Maresch and W. Schäfer, *Kölner Papyri (P. Köln)*, Vol. 5, Opladen, 1985, No. 214, pp. 73-6 + Plate VII (additional fragments of 19:8-11, 13-15, 18-20, 23-24).

E.G. Turner, *Greek Manuscripts of the Ancient World*, 2nd edition, edited by P.J. Parsons; Institute of Classical Studies, Bulletin Supplement 46, 1987, no. 63 (cited as *GMAW*).

Van Haelst 426.

P75 V. Martin and R. Kasser, *Papyrus Bodmer XIV-XV*, Cologny-Geneva, 1961, with complete plates.

Seider 49.

K. Aland, 'Neue neutestamentliche Papyri III', *NTS* 22 (1976), pp. 375-96, p. 381 (new fragments of 7:15, 31; 11.42, 54).

Van Haelst 406.

P76 H. Hunger, 'Zwei unbekannte neutestamentliche Papyrusfragmente der Österreichischen Nationalbibliothek', *Biblos* 8 (1959), pp. 7-12 + plate; 'Ergänzungen zu zwei neutestamentlichen Papyrusfragmenten der Österreichischen Nationalbibliothek', *Biblos* 19 (1970), pp. 71-5.

Van Haelst 442.

P80 R. Roca-Puig, 'Papiro del Evangelio de San Juan con «Hermeneia»', *Atti dell'XI Congresso Internazionale di Papirologia*, Milan, 1966, pp. 225-36 + plate.

Van Haelst 441.

P^{84} Unpublished; Van Haelst 387.

P^{90} T.C. Skeat, *P. Oxy.* 50.3523 (1983), pp. 3-8 + Plates I-II.

P^{93} G. Bastianini in M. Manfredi (ed.), *Trenta testi greci da Papiri letterari e documentari, in occasione del XVII Congresso Internazionale di Papirologia*, Florence, 1983, pp. 10-11 + Plate 3 (4).

P^{95} J. Lenaerts, 'Un Papyrus de l'Évangile de Jean: PL II/31', *Chronique d'Égypte* 60 (1985), pp. 117-20 + 2 plates.

ADDENDUM

T. Hirunuma, *The Papyri bearing the New Testament Text,* Vol. 1, Osaka, 1994.

We received this volume too late to be able to incorporate it into our notes. Volume 1 contains P^{1}-P^{45}. There are plates of P^{2} P^{28} and P^{45} (not of the fragment edited by Skeat and McGing). There are transcriptions of P^{2} P^{5} and P^{28}. There is an *apparatus criticus* throughout.

LIST OF THE PAPYRI

The following are the extant papyri of John. For each entry we list on the first line the Gregory-Aland number, the location and the shelf mark, followed below by the verses of John that are (fully or partially) extant.

P^{2} Florence, Museo Archeologico, Inv. 7134
12:12-15

P^{5} London, British Library, Pap. 782 and Pap. 2484 (P. Oxy. 208 and 1781)
1:23-31, 33-40; 16:14-30; 20:11-17, 19-25

P^{6} Strasbourg, Bibliothèque Nationale et Universitaire, Pap. Copt. 379, 381f, 384
10:1-2, 4-7, 9-10; 11:1-8, 45-52

P^{22} Glasgow, University Library, Ms General 1026/13 (P. Oxy. 1228)
15:25-16:2, 16:21-32

P^{28} Berkeley, Pacific School of Religion, Palestine Institute, Pap. 2
6:8-12, 17-22

P^{36} Florence, Biblioteca Laurenziana, PSI 3
3:14-18, 31-32, 34-36

P^{39} Rochester N.Y., Ambrose Swabey Library, Inv. 8864 (P. Oxy. 1780)
8:14-22

P^{44A} New York, Metropolitan Museum of Art, Inv. 14.1.527
10:8-14

P^{44B} New York, Metropolitan Museum of Art, Inv. 14.1.527
9:3-4; 12:12-13, 16-18

P^{45} Dublin, Chester Beatty Library, P. Chester Beatty 1
4:51-5:2, 5:21-25; 10:7-25, 29-11:11, 11:17-37, 42-57

P^{52} Manchester, John Rylands University Library, Gr. P. 457
18:31-33, 37-38

P^{55} Vienna, Österreichische Nationalbibliothek, Pap. G. 26214
1:31-33, 35-38

P^{59} New York, Pierpont Morgan Library, P. Colt 3
1:26, 28, 48, 51; 2:15-16; 11:40-52; 12:25, 29, 31, 35; 17:24-26; 18:1-2, 16-17, 22; 21:7, 12-13, 15, 17-20, 23

P^{60} New York, Pierpont Morgan Library, P. Colt 4
16:29-30, 32-33; 17:1-6, 8-9, 11-15, 18-25; 18:1-2, 4-5, 7-16, 18-20, 23-29, 31-37, 39-40; 19:2-3, 5-8, 10-18, 20, 23-26

P^{63} Berlin, Staatliche Museen, Ägyptische Abteilung, P. 11914
3:14-18; 4:9-10
P^{66} Cologny/Geneva, Fondation Bodmer, P. Bodmer II
Chapters 1-5; 6:1-11, 35-71; Chapters 7-13; 14:1-26, 29-30; 15:2-26; 16:2-7, 10-33; Chapters 17-19; 20:1-20, 22-23, 25-31; 21:1-9
P^{75} Cologny/Geneva, Fondation Bodmer, P. Bodmer XIV-XV
Chapters 1-10; 11:1-45, 48-57; 12:3-50; 13:1, 8-9; 14:8-29; 15:7-8
See also note below
P^{76} Vienna, Österreichische Nationalbibliothek, Pap. G. 36102
4:9, 12
P^{80} Barcelona, Fundació Sant Lluc Evangelista, P. Barc. 83
3:34
P^{84} Leuven, Bibliotheek Universiteit, P.A.M. Khirbet Mird 4, 11, 26, 27
17:3, 7-8
P^{90} Oxford, Ashmolean Museum, P. Oxy. 3523
18:36-19:7
P^{93} Florence, Istituto Papirologico 'G Vitelli', PSI Inv. 108
13:15-17
P^{95} Florence, Biblioteca Laurenziana PL II/31
5:26-29, 36-38

Note: Nestle-Aland[27] lists and cites material in P^{75} not published elsewhere. In the absence of photographs or a diplomatic transcription, we have not been able to cite it. The verses concerned are 13:1-10 (where we have only some evidence for verses 1, 8 and 9); 14:30-31; 15:1-6, 9-10.

DATES OF THE PAPYRI

The following are the dates that have been proposed for the various papyri. We have always given the date offered in the *editio princeps*. Amongst the other works which we have consulted, our use of the following needs some explanation:

Aland, *Liste* (the same dates are offered in Nestle-Aland[27], except for P^{52} and P^{75}, for which a less specific date is given).

Aland, *Repertorium*. This is a list of the opinions of others. We use the abbreviation *Rep.* to indicate that it names other writers than those whom we include in support of that date.

Turner and Turner (*GMAW*). Turner's dating in *Typology* is only given where he marks the entry with an asterisk.

Van Haelst. This writer is cited only where he offers his own opinion rather than listing those of others.

Other independent opinions not cited in *Rep.* are also included. Details of all these works are provided in the Bibliography.

The century is given in Roman numerals; a superscript number gives the half of the century; more precise dates are in Arabic numerals. Where no name follows, the date represents the consensus.

P^{2}	V-VI	Pistelli; *Rep.*
	VI	*Liste*; *Rep.*
	VI-VII	*Rep.*
P^{5}	III	*Liste*; *Rep.*; Turner
	III²	Grenfell & Hunt
	III-IV	*Rep.*
	IV	*Rep.*
P^{6}	IV	*Liste*; *Rep.*
	V end	Rösch
	V end-VI	*Rep.*
	VII-VIII	*Rep.*
P^{22}	III	*Liste*; *Rep.*
	III end	Grenfell & Hunt; *Rep.*
	c. 300	*Rep.*
	III-IV	*Rep.*
P^{28}	III	*Liste*; Turner
	IV¹	Grenfell & Hunt; *Rep.*
	IV	*Rep.*
P^{36}	after 400	Roberts & Skeat in Aland, 'Papyrus', p. 105, n.2
	VI	Pistelli; *Liste*; Turner; *Rep.*
	early VII	*Rep.*
P^{39}	III¹	Van Haelst
	III	*Liste*; *Rep.*
	late III	Cavallo; Turner
	IV	Grenfell & Hunt; *Rep.*
P^{44A}	VI-VII (before 650)	
P^{44B}	VI-VII (before 650)	
P^{45}	c. 250	*Rep.*
	III¹	Kenyon; *Rep.*
	III	*Liste*; Seider; Turner; *Rep.*
	III²	Cavallo; *Rep.*
P^{52}	II¹	Roberts; *Liste*; Turner; *Rep.*
	II middle	Cavallo
	II²	Schmidt
P^{55}	VI	Sanz; *Rep.*
	VI-VII	*Liste*; *Rep.*

P59	VII	Kraemer; Van Haelst; *Liste*; *Rep.*
	VII end	*Rep.*
	VII-VIII	Casson & Hettich
P60	VII	Kraemer; Van Haelst; *Liste*; *Rep.*
	VII end	*Rep.*
	VII-VIII	Casson & Hettich
P63	c.500	*Liste*; *Rep.*
	V-VI	Turner
	VI	Stegmüller
P66	II[1]	Hunger
	II middle	Seider, Cavallo
	c.200	Martin; *Liste*; *Rep.*
	III[1]	Turner; *GMAW*
P75	175-225	Martin & Kasser
	II-III	Seider
	225-275	Turner
	III[1]	*Liste*; *Rep.*
P76	after 400	Roberts in Aland, 'Papyrus', p. 106, n.3
	VI	Hunger; *Liste*; *Rep.*; Turner
P80	III[2]	Roca-Puig; *Liste*; *Rep.*
	III?-IV	*Rep.*
	early IV	Van Haelst
	V-VI	Turner
P84	VI	
P90	II	
P93	V	
P95	III[1]	Lenaerts
	III	*Liste*

THE PAPYRI EXTANT FOR EACH CHAPTER

Chapter One	P^{5} P^{55} P^{59} P^{66} P^{75}
Chapter Two	P^{59} P^{66} P^{75}
Chapter Three	P^{36} P^{63} P^{66} P^{75} P^{80}
Chapter Four	P^{45} P^{63} P^{66} P^{75} P^{76}
Chapter Five	P^{45} P^{66} P^{75} P^{84} P^{95}
Chapter Six	P^{28} P^{66} P^{75}
Chapter Seven	P^{66} P^{75}
Chapter Eight	P^{39} P^{66} P^{75}
Chapter Nine	P^{44B} P^{66} P^{75}
Chapter Ten	P^{6} P^{44A} P^{45} P^{66} P^{75}
Chapter Eleven	P^{6} P^{45} P^{59} P^{66} P^{75}
Chapter Twelve	P^{2} P^{44B} P^{59} P^{66} P^{75}
Chapter Thirteen	P^{66} P^{75} P^{93}
Chapter Fourteen	P^{66} P^{75}
Chapter Fifteen	P^{22} P^{66} P^{75}
Chapter Sixteen	P^{5} P^{22} P^{60} P^{66}
Chapter Seventeen	P^{59} P^{60} P^{66} P^{84}
Chapter Eighteen	P^{52} P^{59} P^{60} P^{66} P^{90}
Chapter Nineteen	P^{60} P^{66} P^{90}
Chapter Twenty	P^{5} P^{66}
Chapter Twenty-One	P^{59} P^{66}

OVERLAPS

A block ▪ represents a verse. The single vertical lines divide the chapters into groups of ten verses. The double vertical lines indicate the chapter endings.

Chapter One

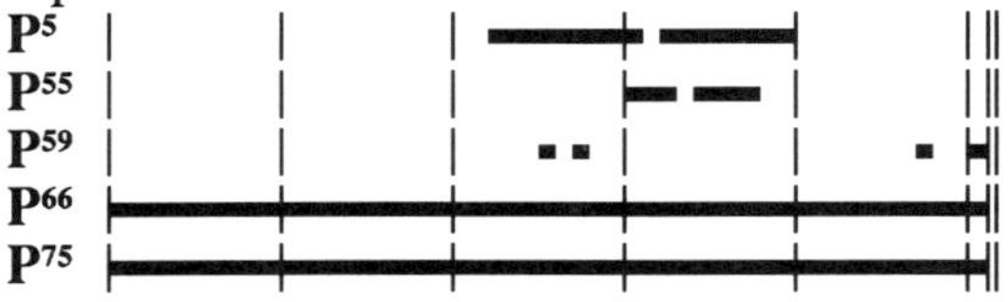

Chapter Two

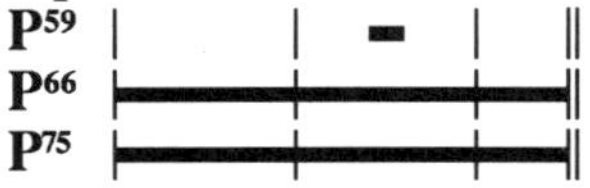

Chapter Three

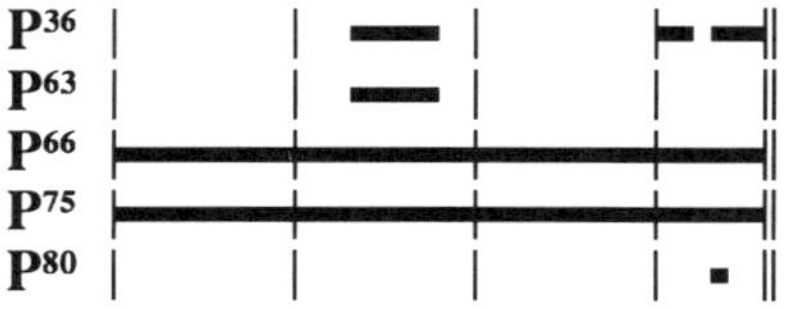

Chapter Four

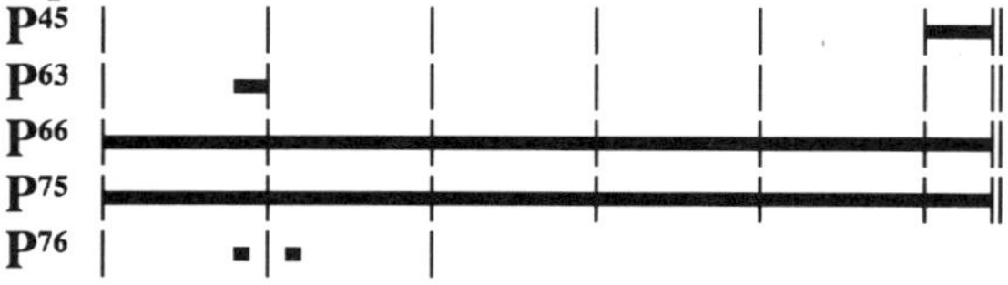

Chapter Five

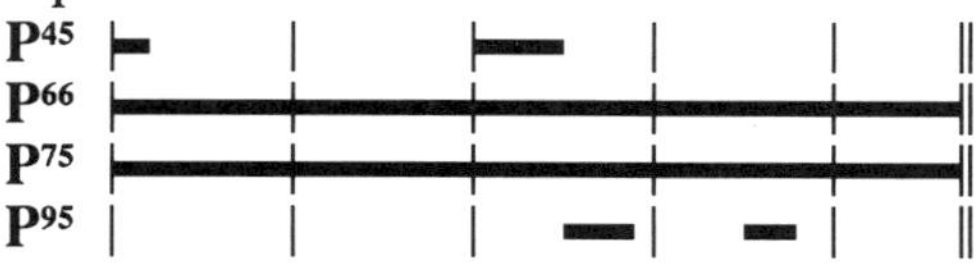

Chapter Six

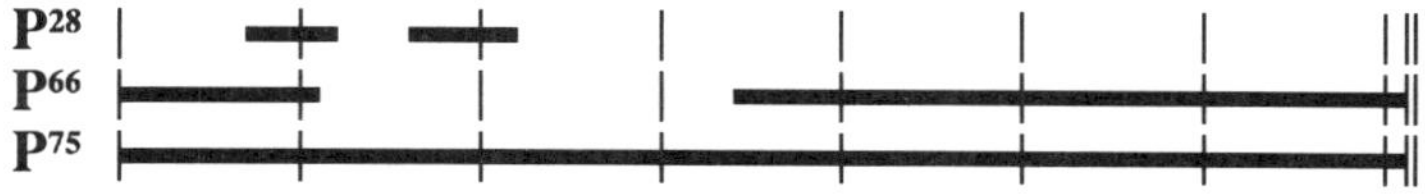

Chapter Seven

Chapter Eight

Chapter Nine

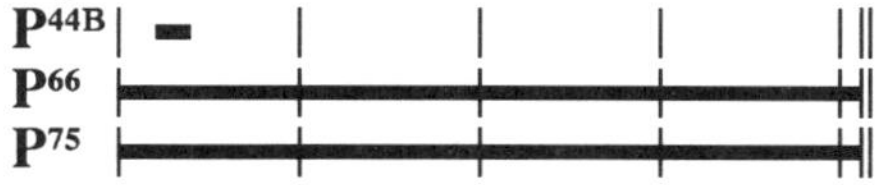

Chapter Ten

Chapter Eleven

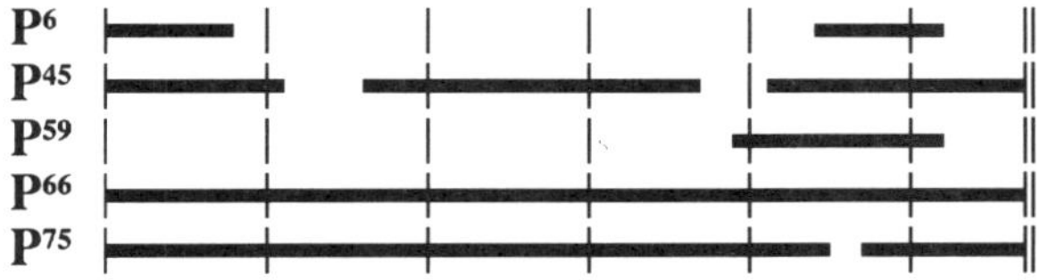

Chapter Twelve

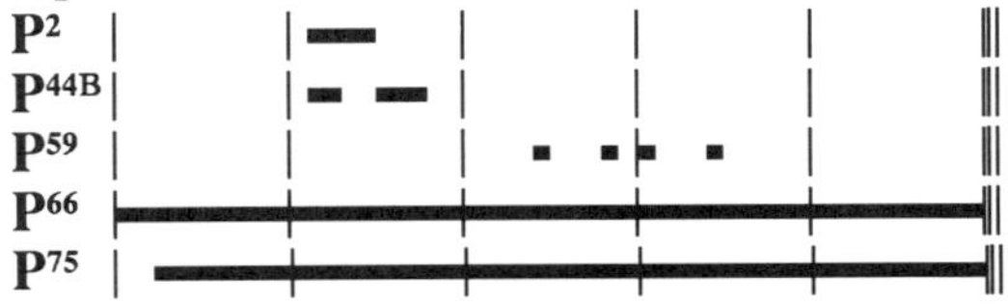

Chapter Thirteen

Chapter Fourteen

Chapter Fifteen

Chapter Sixteen

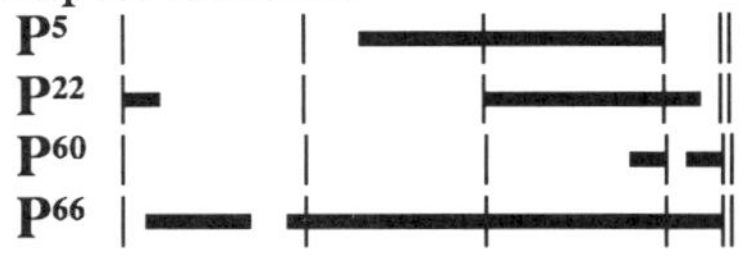

Chapter Seventeen

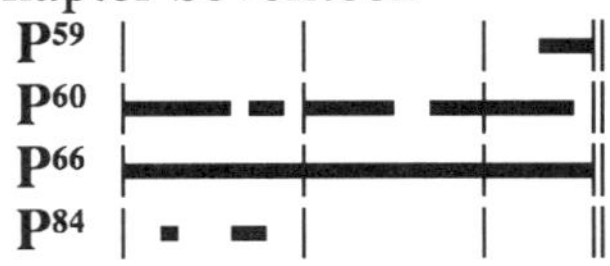

Chapter Eighteen

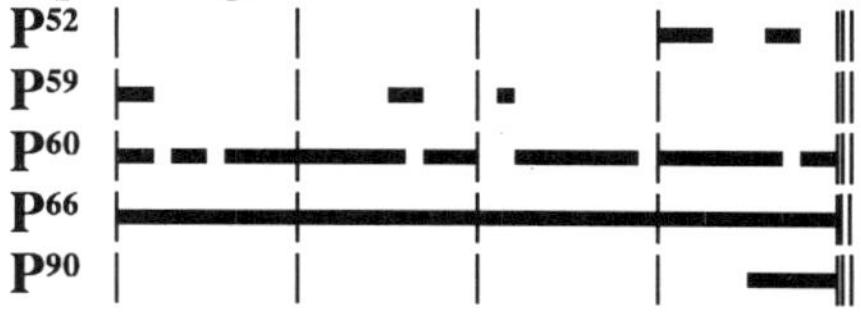

Chapter Nineteen

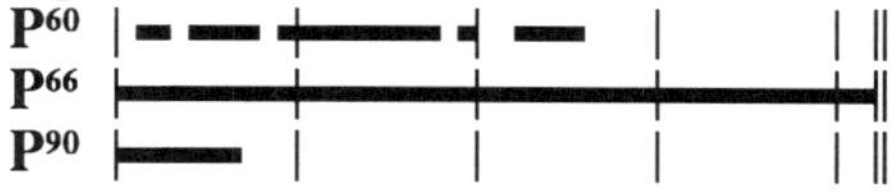

Chapter Twenty

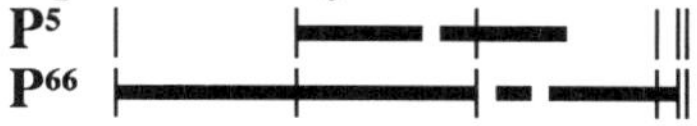

Chapter Twenty-One

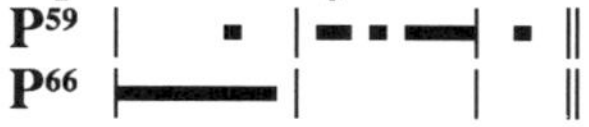

ACKNOWLEDGEMENTS

The plates are reproduced by kind permission of the following:

P^{2}	Soprintendenza alle Antichità - Florence
P^{5}	British Library, London
P^{6}	Bibliothèque Nationale et Universitaire, Strasbourg
P^{22}	The Librarian, Glasgow University Library
P^{28}	The Badè Institute of Biblical Archeology, Berkeley
P^{36} P^{95}	Biblioteca Medicea Laurenziana, Florence
P^{39}	The Ambrose Swabey Library, Colgate Rochester Divinity School, New York
P^{44}	The Metropolitan Museum of Art, Museum Excavations, 1913-14; Gogers Fund, 1914. (14.1.527), New York
P^{45}	The Trustees of the Chester Beatty Library, Dublin
P^{52}	The Director and University Librarian, the John Rylands University Library of Manchester
P^{55} P^{76}	Österreichische Nationalbibliothek, Vienna
P^{59} P^{60}	The Pierpont Morgan Library, New York (Colt Papyrus 3 and Colt Papyrus 4)
P^{63}	Staatliche Museen zu Berlin Preußischer Kulturbesitz, Papyrussammlung
P^{66} P^{75}	Bibliothèque Bodmer, Geneva
P^{80}	Fundació Sant Lluc Evangelista, Barcelona
P^{84}	Centrale Bibliotheek, Katholieke Universiteit Leuven
P^{90}	The Committee of the Egypt Exploration Society, London
P^{93}	Istituto Papirologico 'G. Vitelli', Florence

TRANSCRIPTIONS

P[2]

↓ (Jn 12:12-15)

Two lines of Coptic (Lk 7:50)

ЄΥΑΓΓЄΛ[ιον]
†ΤΗ̂ ЄΠΑΎΡΙΟΝ ΟΧ΄ΛΟϹ Π̣[ολυc ο ελθων ειc την 12
ЄΟΡΤΗΝ̀ ΑΚΟΎϹΑΝΤ̣[εc οτι ερχεται ο ι̅c̅
3 **ЄΙϹ ΪЄΡΟΥ**[cαλ]**Ή̣Μ̣ Є̣**[λαβον τα βαια των 13
ΦΟΙΝΙΚΩΝ̀ Κ[αι εξηλθον ειc υπαντηcιν αυτω
κα]**Ì ЄΚΡΑΎ**[γαζον ωcαννα ευλογημενοc
6 ο] **ЄΡΧΟΜ́Є**[νοc εν ονοματι κ̅υ̅ ο βαcιλευc
τ]**ΟΥ̂ ΪΗ̅Λ̅́ Є**[υρων δε ο ι̅c̅ οναριον εκαθιcεν 14
ε]**Π ΑΥΤ̣**[ο καθωc εcτι γεγραμμενον
9 μη]**`Φ̣**[οβου 15

Notes

It is manifest that this scribe is lax about the precise position of his accents. Our transcription shows where they are and not where they should be.

1. *ed. pr.* τη
2. *ed. pr.* εορτὴν
3. *ed. pr.* εὶς ϊερου[
4. *ed. pr.* φοινικων. [
6. *ed. pr.* ερχόμε

→ is Lk 7:22-26 in Coptic

P5

First page
First fragment (P. Oxy. 208)
↓ (Jn 1:23-31)

]Ω̣ ΦΩΝ[η] **Β̣Ο̣**[ωντος εν τη ερημω (23)
ευ]**Θ̣ΥΝΑΤ**[ε την οδον κ̅υ̅ καθως ει
3 π]**Ε̣Ν ΗΣΑ**[ιας ο προφητης και οι απεσ 24
τ]**Α̣ΛΜΕΝΟΙ** [ησαν εκ των φαρισαι
ω]**Ν̣ ΚΑΙ ΗΡ̣Ω̣**[τησαν αυτον τι ουν βα 25
6 **Π̣Τ̣ΙΖΕΙΣ ΕΙ** [συ ουκ ει ο χ̅ς̅ ουδε ηλιας
ΟΥΔΕ Ο ΠΡΟ[φητης απεκριθη αυτοις ο 26
ΙΩΑΝΝ[ης λεγων εγω βαπτιζω εν υ
9 **ΔΑΤΙ Μ**[εσος υμιν στηκει ον υμεις
ΟΥΚ ΟΙΔΑ[τε ο οπισω μου ερχομε 27
ν]**ΟΣ** [ο]**Υ Ο**[υκ ειμι αξιος ινα λυσω αυ
12 **ΤΟΥ ΤΟΝ** [ιμαντα του υποδηματος
ΤΑΥΤΑ ΕΝ̣ Β[ηθαβαρα εγενετο πε 28
ΡΑΝ ΤΟΥ ΪΟ[ρδανου οπου ην ο ιωαν
15 ν]**ΗΣ ΒΑΠΤΙ**[ζων τη επαυριον βλε 29
ΠΕΙ ΤΟΝ Ι̅Η̅Ν̅ [ερχομενον προς αυτον
ΚΑΙ ΛΕΓΕΙ [ιδε ο αμνος του θ̅υ̅ ο αιρων
18 **ΤΗΝ ΑΜΑΡ**[τιαν του κοσμου ουτος 30
ΕΣΤΙΝ ΫΠΕΡ̣ [ου εγω ειπον οπισω μου
ΕΡΧΕΤΑΙ Α[νηρ ος εμπροσθεν μου
21 **ΓΕΓΟΝ**[εν οτι πρωτος μου ην καγω 31
Ο̣ΥΚ Η̣Δ[ειν αυτον αλλ ινα φανερω
Θ̣Η̣ [τω ισραηλ δια τουτο ηλθον ε
24 **Γ̣**[

Notes

The transcriptions in Wessely reproduce *ed. pr.*, without dots below uncertain letters.

6. we read ουδε against ουτε in the collating base, since it appears in l. 7
8. *ed. pr.*, Wessely ϊωαννν

Second page
First fragment (P. Oxy. 208)
→ (Jn 1:33-40)

] **ΑΛΛ᾽ Ο Π̣**[εμ (33)
ψαϲ με βαπτιζειν εν υ]**ΔΑΤ**[ι] **Є̣**[κει
νοϲ μοι ειπεν εφ ον αν ι]**ΔΗϹ ΤΟ̣** [π̅ν̅α̅
καταβαινον και μεν]**ΟΝ ЄΠ ΑΥ**[τον
ουτοϲ εϲτιν ο βαπτιζ]**ΩΝ ЄΝ Π̅**[ν̅ι̅ α
γιω καγω εωρακα και μεμ]**ΑΡΤΥΡΗΚΑ Ο̣** 34
τι ουτοϲ εϲτιν ο υιο]**Ϲ̣ ΤΟΥ Θ̅Υ̅ ΤΗ Є̣** 35
παυριον ειϲτηκει ο ιωαν]**Ν̣ΗϹ ΚΑΙ ЄΚ**
των μαθητων αυτου δ]**Υ̣Ο̣ ΚΑΙ ЄΜ̣** 36
βλεψαϲ τω ι̅η̅υ̅ περιπατο]**ΥΝΤΙ ΛЄΓЄ**[ι
ιδε ο αμνοϲ του θ̅υ̅ και ηκο]**ΥϹΑΝ ÓΙ Δ̣Υ̣Ο̣** 37
μαθηται λαλουντοϲ και η]**ΚΟΛΟΥΘΗ**
ϲαν τω ι̅η̅υ̅ ϲτραφειϲ δ]**Є Ο Ι̅Η̅Ϲ̅ ΚΑΙ ΘЄ** 38
αϲαμενοϲ αυτουϲ ακ]**ΟΛΟΥΘΟΥΝΤΑϹ**
λεγει αυτοιϲ τι ζητει]**ΤЄ** {**ЄΙΠΑ̣Ν̣ ΑΥ**} <**ΟΙ ΔЄ ЄΙΠΑΝ**>
{τω} ραββι ο λεγεται ερ]**ΜΗΝЄΥΟΜЄ**
νον διδαϲκαλε που μεν]**ЄΙϹ ΛЄΓЄΙ** 39
αυτοιϲ ερχεϲθε και οψε]**ϹΘЄ ΗΛΘΑΝ**
και ειδαν που μενει κ]**ΑΙ ΠΑΡ ΑΥΤΩ**
εμειναν την ημεραν] **Є̣Κ̣Є̣Ι̣Ν̣Η̣Ν̣** [ω
ρα δε ην ωϲ δεκατη ην ανδ]**ΡЄΑϹ Ο Α** 40
δελφοϲ ϲιμωνοϲ ειϲ εκ των δ]**ΥΟ ΤΩΝ**
ακουϲαντων παρα ιωαννο]**Υ̣ ΚΑΙ Α**

Notes

15. the correction was effected by writing οι δε above the line and by placing points over αυ (and presumably τω on the next line)
19. we write ειδαν, against the collating base's ειδον, here and subsequently, to conform with the papyrus' text in l. 18
22. *ed pr.* prefers to read σιμωνος πετρου εις εκ δ]υο. In our judgment this is too long for the space available

Third page
Second fragment (P. Oxy. 1781)
→ (Jn 16:14-22)

]Δ̣Ι ΚΑΙ ΑΝΑ (14)
υγελει υμιν παντα οϲ]Δ̣ ЄΧЄΙ Ο Π̅Ρ̅ Є 15
μα εστι δια τουτο ειπο]Ν ΟΤΙ ЄΚ Τ[ου
εμου λημψεται και αναγ]Γ̣Є̣Λ̣Є̣Ι̣ ΥΜΙ̅
μεικρον και ου θεωρειτε με κ]ΑΙ 16
παλιν μεικρον κ]ΑΙ ΟΨЄϹΘЄ [με
ειπαν ουν εν των μ]ΑΘΗΤΩΝ ΑΥΤΟΥ 17
προϲ αλληλουϲ τι] ЄϹΤΙΝ ΤΟΥΤΟ Ο ΛЄ
γει ημιν μεικρον και ου θ]ЄΩΡЄΙΤ̣Є ΜЄ
και παλιν μεικρον και οψ]Є̣Ϲ̣Θ̣Є̣ Μ̣Є̣ Κ̣Α̣Ι̣ [οτ]Ι̣
εγω υπαγω προϲ τον] Π̅Ρ̅Α̅ ЄΛЄΓΟΝ Ο̣Υ̣Ν 18
τουτο τι εστιν] Μ̣ЄΙΚΡΟΝ Ο̣Υ̣Κ̣ ΟΙΔΑ
μεν τι λαλει εγ]ΝΩ <Ο> Ι̅Η̅Ϲ̅ ΟΤΙ Η̣[θ]Є̣ΛΟΝ 19
αυτον ερωταν] Κ̣ΑΙ ЄΙΠЄΝ ΑΥΤ[ο]ΙϹ
περι τουτου ζητ]Є̣ΙΤЄ ΜЄΤ ΑΛΛΗΛΩ[ν
οτι ειπον μεικρ]ΟΝ ΚΑΙ ΟΥ ΘЄΩΡЄΙ[τε
με και παλιν μεικρο]Ν ΚΑΙ ΟΨЄϹΘЄ Μ[ε
αμην αμην λεγ]Ω ΫΜЄΙΝ ΟΤ[ι κ]ΛΑ[υ 20
ϲετε και θρηνηϲ]ЄΤЄ ΫΜЄΙϹ Ο ΔЄ
κοϲμοϲ χαρηϲετ]ΑΙ ΫΜЄΙϹ ΛΟΥΠΗΘΗ
ϲεϲθε αλλ η λυπ]Η ΫΜΩΝ ЄΙϹ ΧΑΡΑΝ
γενηϲεται η γυν]Η ΟΤΑΝ ΤΙΚΤΗ Λ{ΟΙ}<Υ> 21
πην εχει οτι ηλθεν] Η̣ ΩΡΑ ΑΥΤΗϹ
οταν δε γεννηϲη το] Π̣ΑΙΔ[ι]ΟΝ ΟΥΚ Є̣
τι μνημονευει τηϲ θλ]ЄΙΨ[ε]ΩϹ ΔΙ
α την χαραν οτι εγενν]ΗΘ̣Η ΑΝΘΡΩ
ποϲ ειϲ τον κοϲμον] ΚΑΙ [υ]ΜЄΙϹ ΟΥΝ 22

Notes

1. *ed. pr.*, Wessely αναγ
4. *ed. pr.*, Wessely γ̣γ̣ελει ϋμεῑ
5. we read μεικρον, against the collating base, here and subsequently, to conform with the papyrus' usage in l. 12
6-7. *ed. pr.*, Wessely]αι οψεσθε [με ειπα]ν
9. *ed. pr.*, Wessely θεωρει[τ]ε
11. *ed. pr.*, Wessely read a space after π̅ρ̅α̅
13. *ed. pr.*, Wessely ε]γνω
   ed. pr., Wessely do not refer to a correction. The omicron was added above the line
   ed. pr., Wessely ηθελον
17. *ed. pr.*, Wessely με [
20. *ed. pr.*, Wessely λ⟦ο⟧υπηθη
22. the correction was made by striking through the omicron and changing iota to upsilon
24. *ed. pr.*, Wessely π]αιδιον
27. *ed. pr.*, Wessely ϋμεις

Fourth page
Second fragment (P. Oxy. 1781)
↓ (Jn 16:22-30)

ΝΥΝ ΜЄΝ[λυπην εχετε παλιν δε (22)
ΟΨΟΜΑΙ Ϋ̇Μ[ας και χαρηϲεται υμων
Η̣ ΚΑΡΔΙΑ [και την χαραν υμων ου
ΔЄΙϹ ΑΡЄΙ [αφ] **Υ̣**[μων και εν εκεινη 23
Τ[η] **ἭΜЄΡ̣**[α εμ]**Є̣** [ουκ ερωτηϲετε
ΟΥΔЄΝ [α]**ΜΗΝ Α̣**[μην λεγω υμειν οτι οϲα
ΑΝ ΤΙ ΑΙΤΗ[ϲ]**Η̣ΤЄ** [τον π̄ρ̄α̅ δωϲει υμειν
ЄΝ ΤѠ ΟΝ[ομ̣]**ΑΤ̣**[ι μου αιτειτε και 24
ΛΗΜΨЄϹΘЄ Ϊ[να η χαρα υμων η
Π̣ЄΠΛΗΡѠ[μενη ταυτα εν παροι 25
Μ̣ΙΑ[ι]**Ϲ ΛЄΛΑΛΗΚΑ** [υμειν αλλ ερχεται
Ѡ̣Ρ̣Α̣ ΟΤЄ Ο̣ΥΚ ЄΤ[ι εν παροιμιαιϲ λα
ΛΗϹѠ ΫΜЄΙΝ ΑΛ[λα παρρηϲια περι
ΤΟΥ Π̅Ρ̅Ϲ̅ Α̣ΠΑΓΓЄ[λω υμειν εν ε 26
ΚЄΙΝΗ ΤΗ ἭΜЄΡΑ [εν τω ονοματι
Μ̣ΟΥ ΑΙΤΗϹ̣ЄϹΘЄ [και ου λεγω υμειν
ο]**ΤΙ ЄΓѠ Є̇ΡѠΤΗϹ**[ω τον π̄ρ̄α̅ αυτοϲ 27
γ]**ΑΡ Ο Π̅Ρ̅ ΦΙΛЄΙ ΫΜ**[αϲ οτι υμειϲ εμε
ΠЄΦΙΛΗΚ̣Α̣ΤЄ̣ ΚΑΙ [πεπιϲτευκατε
ΟΤΙ ΠΑΡΑ Θ̅Υ̅ ЄΞΗΛΘ[ον εξηλθον 28
ΠΑΡΑ ΤΟΥ Π̅Ρ̅Ϲ̅ ΚΑΙ Є[ληλυθα ειϲ τον
Κ̣Ο̣Ϲ̣ΜΟΝ ΠΑΛΙΝ Α̣[φιημι τον κοϲμον
ΚΑΙ ΠΟΡЄΥΟΜΑΙ Π̇ΡΟ[ϲ τον π̄ρ̄α̅ λε 29
Γ̣Ο̣Υ̣Ϲ̣ΙΝ <ΑΥΤѠ> ΟΙ Μ[αθηται αυτου ιδε νυν
ΠΑΡΡΗ̣ϹΙΑ Λ[αλειϲ και παροιμιαν ου
ΔЄΜΙΑΝ Λ[εγειϲ νυν οιδαμεν 30
ΟΤΙ ΟΙΔΑϹ ΠΑ̣[

<**ЄΝ ΤѠ ΟΝΟΜΑΤΙ** [μου εωϲ αρτι ουκ ητηϲατε ουδεν εν
Τ[ω ονοματι μου]>

Notes

5. *ed. pr.*, Wessely τη ἡμερ[α] ε[μ]ε̣
6. *ed. pr.*, Wessely αμην α[
8. *ed. pr.*, Wessely ον[ο]ματ[
10. *ed. pr.*, Wessely πεπληρω[μ]ε̣[ν]η̣
11. *ed. pr.*, Wessely μιαις λελ[α]ληκα
14. *ed. pr.* απαγ'γε[(Wessely αππαγ'γε[)
24. the correction was made by adding αυτω above οι
the addition in the bottom margin is to l.8

Fifth page
First fragment (P. Oxy. 208)
→ (Jn 20:11-17)

ΜΝΗΜ[ειον κλαιουcα εξω ωc ουν εκλαιεν (11)
ΠΑΡΕΚΥ[ψεν ειc το μνημειον και θεω 12
3 **ΡΕΙ ΔΥΟ** [αγγελουc εν λευκοιc καθεζομε
Ν[ουc ενα προc τη κεφαλη και ενα προc
Τ[
Three lines missing
9 **ΜΟΥ** [και ουκ οιδα που εθηκαν αυτον και
ΤΑΥΤΑ [ειπουcα εcτραφη ειc τα οπι 14
CΩ ΚΑΙ [θεωρει τον ι̅η̅ν̅ εcτωτα και ου
12 **Κ ΗΔΕΙ** [οτι ο ι̅η̅c̅ εcτι λεγει αυτη ο ι̅η̅c̅ 15
ΓΥΝΑΙ [τι κλαιειc τινα ζητειc εκεινη
ΔΟΚΟΥ[cα οτι ο κηπουροc εcτι λεγει
15 **ΑΥΤΩ** [κ̅ε̅ ει cυ εβαcταcαc αυτον ειπε
ΜΟΙ Π[ου αυτον εθηκαc καγω αυτον
ΑΡΩ [λεγει αυτη ο ι̅η̅c̅ μαρια cτραφει 16
18 cα εκεινη λεγει αυτω εβραιcτι ραβ
Β[ουνι ο λεγεται κ̅ε̅ λεγει αυτη ο ι̅η̅c̅ 17
Ṃ[η μου απτου ουπω γαρ αναβεβηκα προc
21 **Ṭ**[

Notes

The line lengths on this page are larger than on the others. The average number of letters according to our reconstruction is almost 29, the numbers varying between 26 and 31; there are 7 lines with 28.

19. we follow *ed. pr.* in conjecturing κ̅ε̅ for διδαcκαλε. διδαcκαλε would give a line of 35 letters. There is support for the readings κ̅ε̅ διδαcκαλε and διδαcκαλε κ̅ε̅ as well as κ̅ε̅ alone

Sixth page
First fragment (P. Oxy. 208)
↓ (Jn 20:19-25)

] **Ḥ**[λθεν ο (19)
ι̅η̅c̅ και εcτη ειc το μεcο]**Ν** {**ΛЄΓЄΙ**} {{**ΚΑΙ ΛЄΓЄΙ**}}
3 αυτοιc ειρηνη υμιν και τ]**ΟΥΤ᾽ ЄΙΠ̅Ω̅** 20
εδειξεν ταc χειραc και την πλε]**Υ**
ραν αυτου εχαρηcαν ουν οι μαθητ]**ΑΙ Ϊ**
Three lines lost
9]**Ν̅Α̅ Α**
γιον αν τινων αφητε ταc αμ]**ΑΡΤΙΑC** 23
αφιενται αυτοιc αν τινων] **ΚΡΑΤΗΤЄ**
12 κεκρατηνται θωμαc δε ειc εκ τω]**Ν ΔΩ** 24
δεκα ο λεγομενοc διδυμοc ου]**Κ ΗΝ**
μετ αυτων οτε ουν ηλθ]**ЄΝ Ι̅Η̅C̅**
15 ελεγον αυτω οι μαθηται εω]**ΡΑΚΑ** 25
μεν τον κ̅ν̅ ο δε ειπεν αυτοι]**C ЄΑΝ**
μη ιδω εν ταιc χερcιν τον τυ]**Π̣Ọ Ṇ**

Notes

This page has between 22 (line 14) and 29 (line 5) letters to the line. The average is 26, but four have 25, including the last three.
1. *ed. pr.* ηλθ]ε̣ν̣ [ο
2. και is added above the line
6-9. the 140 letters of the collating base are too long for this space. If we calculate three times the minimum and three times the maximum number of letters in any line on the page, plus the space available in line 9, we find a probable range of between 89 and 111 letters missing
14. the collating base reads μετ αυτων οτε ηλθεν. This is too short. If we suppose a space after αυτων and ουν after οτε, the space is adequately filled. *Ed. pr.* supplies ουν but not the space

P6

First Page
↓ (Jn 10:1-2, 4-7, 9-10)

αμη]**Ν ΑΜΗΝ ΛЄΓΩ** [υμιν ο μη εις 1
ερ]**ΧΟΜЄΝΟϹ ΔΙΑ̣** [της θυρας εις
3 τη]**Ν ΑΥΛΗΝ ΤΩ**[ν προβατων αλ
λ]**Α̣ ΑΝΑΒ**[αινων αλλαχοθεν εκει
ν]**Ο̣Ϲ ΚΛЄ̣**[πτης εστι και ληστης
6 ο δ]**Є Є**[ισερχομενος 2
Six lines missing
Π̣[ορευεται και τα προβατα αυτω (4)
ΑΚ[ολουθει οτι οιδασι την φωνην
15 **ΑΥΤ̣Ο̣Υ̣ Α̣**[λλοτ]**Ρ̣**[ι]**Ω Δ̣**[ε ου μη ακολουθη 5
ϹΩϹΙΝ Α̣[λλα] **ΦЄ**[υξονται απ αυτου
Ο̣ΤΙ ΟΥΚ ΟΙ[δα]**ϹΙ Τ**[ην φωνην των αλλο
18 **ΤΡΙΩΝ: ΤΑ**[υτ]**ΗΝ** [την παροιμιαν ειπεν 6
ΑΥΤ̣ΟΙϹ Ο ΙϹ [ε]**Κ̣**[εινοι δε ουκ εγνωσαν
ΤΙ ΗΝ Α̂ [ελαλει αυτοις ειπεν ουν πα 7
21 **ΛΙΝ Ο ΙϹ** [αμην αμην λεγω υμιν οτι εγω
Є̣[ι]**Μ**[ι
Three lines missing
εαν τις εισελθ]**Η̣** [σωθησεται και εις (9)
27 ελευσεται και] **ЄΞЄΛ̣**[ευσεται και νο
μην ευρησει ο δ]**Є ΚΛ**[επτης ουκ ερχε 10
ται ει μη ινα κλ]**ЄΨΗ** [
Four lines of Coptic

Notes

15\. *ed. pr.* αυ[τ]ου α̣
16\. *ed. pr.* σωσιν αλλ̣[α] φευ̣
17\. *ed. pr.* ο̣τι
ed. pr. σι τη̣[ν
19\. *ed. pr.* [ε]κ̣ε̣[ινοι
20\. *ed. pr.* α̂
22\. *ed. pr.* ε̣[ι]μ̣ι̣
26-29. the line breaks are hypothetical.

Second page
→ (Jn 11:1-8)

P̅Δ̅
Eight lines of Coptic
]Ṇ Δ̣Ẹ ΤΙC ЄΚẸ[ι α]CΘ̣[ενων λαζαρος 1
Α̣ΠΟ ΒΗΘΑ̣Ṇ̣ΙΔ[c] Ẹ̣Κ Τ[ης κωμης μαριας
ΚΑΙ ΜΑΡΘ[ας] ΤΗC Α̣ΔЄ[λφης αυτης ην 2
ΔЄ ΜΑΡΙϨΑ[μ] Ḣ ΑΛ̣Ẹ[ιψασα τον κ̅ν̅
ΜΥΡѠΙ ΚΑ[ι] ЄΚΜ[αξασα τους ποδας
ΑΥΤΟΥ ΤΑΙ^C Θ̣ΡΙΞ̣Ι[ν αυτης ης ο αδελ
ΦΟC ΛΑΖΑΡΟC [η]CΘЄΝЄΙ. [απεστει 3
ΛΑΝ ΟΥΝ ΑΙ ΑΔẸΛΦΑ̣Ι ΠΡ[ος αυτον
ΛЄΓΟΥCΑ̣Ị Κ̅Є̅ ΪΔЄ [ο]Ν ΦΙΛЄ[ις ας
ΘЄΝЄΙ· [ακο]ΥCΑC Δ̣Ẹ [ο] Ι̅C̅ ЄΙΠ̣[εν αυ 4
Ṭ̣Η Ḣ Α̣[cθ]ЄΝЄΙΑ [ουκ] Ẹ̣Ç[τι προς
Θ̣[ανατο]Ν· ΑΛΛ [υπερ της δοξης
του θ̅]Υ̅ ΪΝΑ̣ Δ[οξασθ]Η Ο Υ.[ος
του θ̅υ̅ δ]Ι ΑΥṬḤ[c ηγαπ]Α ΔЄ [ο ι̅c̅ 5
την] ΜΑΡ[θαν και τη]Ν Μ[αριαμ την
αδε]Λ̣ΦΗΝ ΑΫ[της και] ΤΟΝ [λαζαρον
ως ου]Ν ΗΚΟΥCẸ[ν οτι ασθενει 6
τοτε με]Ν ЄΜЄΙ[νεν εν ω ην τοπω
δυο ημ]ЄΡΑC [επειτα μετα τουτο λε 7
γει τοις] ΜΑΘ[ηταις αγωμεν εις
την ιουδ]ΑΙΑṆ [παλιν λεγουσιν
αυτω οι μαθ]Ḥ[8

Notes

11. *ed. pr.* τη[ς α]δε
12. μαριϨα[μ]: Coptic ϨΟΡΙ
ed. pr. α[λ]ẹ[ιψασα
20. *ed. pr.* θ̣[ανατο]ṿ· αλλ· [υπερ της] δọ[ξης του]
21. *ed. pr.* [θεο]ῦ ϊνα̣ δ[οξασθη] ο υ[ιος του θε] . υς̣ cannot be read
22. *ed. pr.* [ου δ]ι αυτη[c ηγαπ]α δε [ο ι̅η̅c̅
23. *ed. pr.* την] μαρ[ιϨαμ και τη]ν μ[αρθαν την. See *apparatus criticus* (p. 281)
25-6 *ed. pr.* το] / [τε με]ν etc

Third page
→ (Jn 11:45)

P̅H̅
Twenty-seven lines of Coptic
ΠΟΛΛΟΙ ΟΥΝ ЄΚ ΤѠΝ ΪΟΥΔΑΙѠΝ ΟΙ 45
ЄΛΘΟΝΤЄϹ ΠΡΟϹ ΤΗΝ ΜΑΡΙΑΜ: ΚΑ[ι
ΘЄΑϹΑΜЄΝΟΙ Α ЄΠΟΙΗϹЄΝ ЄΠΙϹ

Notes

29. *ed. pr.* reads a single point: μαριαμ·

Fourth page
↓ (Jn 11:45-52)

Ρ̅Θ̅
τευcαν ειc αυτον τιν]**ЄC ΔЄ ЄΞ ΔΥ** (45) 46
των απηλθον προc τ]**Ο̣ΥC ΦΔΡΙCΔΙΟΥC**
και ειπον αυτοιc α] **ЄΠ̣Ο̣ΙΗCЄΝ Ι̅C̅**
cυνηγαγον ουν οι αρ]**ΧΙЄΡЄΙC** 47
και οι φαριcαιοι cυνεδριο]**Ν̣ ΚΔΙ ЄΛЄ**
γον τι ποιουμεν οτι ουτο]**C̣ Ο̣ ΔΝΘΡ̣**
ωποc πολλα cημεια ποιει] **ЄΔΝ** 48
αφωμεν αυτον ουτω]**C̣ ΠΔΝΤЄC**
πιcτευcουcιν ειc αυτον] **Κ̣ΔΙ ЄΛЄΥ**
cονται οι ρωμαιοι και αρου]**CΙΝ ΗΜΩ̅**
και τον τοπον και το εθνο]**C̣:** >
ειc δε τιc εξ αυτων καια]**ΦΔC** 49
αρχιερευc ων του ενιαυτο]**Υ̣ ЄΚЄΙΝ**[ου
ειπεν αυτοιc υ]**ΜЄ**[ιc ουκ] **ΟΙΔΔΤ**[ε
ουδεν ουδε λο]**Γ̣ΙΖЄ**[cθε ο]**Τ̣Ι CΥΜ** 50
φερει ημιν ι]**Ν̣**[α ειc αν]**ΘΡΩ**
ποc αποθανη] **Υ**[περ του λαο]**Υ**
και μη ολον το] **Є**[θ]**Ν̣**[οc απολη]**ΤΔ**[ι του 51
το δε αφ εαυτου] **ΟΥΚ Є̣**[ιπεν] **Δ̣ΛΛΔ̣**
αρχιερευc ων] **ΤΟΥ Є**[νια]**Υ̣ΤΟΥ ЄΚ̣**[ει
νου προεφητευcεν οτι ε]**ΜЄΛ̣Λ̣Є̣**[ν ο ι̅c̅
αποθνηcκειν υπερ το]**Υ̣ ЄΘ**[νουc
] . [ ] . [52
ινα και τα τεκ]**ΝΔ ΤΟΥ** [θ̅]**Υ̅** [τα
διεcκορπιcμενα] **CΥΝΔΓΔΓΗ Є̣ΙC ЄΝ̣**

Five lines of Coptic

Notes

1. *ed. pr.* τι]νες
6. *ed. pr.* ανθ̣ρ̣ω̣ / [πος
8. *ed. pr.* ουτως
11. *ed. pr.* εθνος]:
14. *ed. pr.* υμεις] με[ν ουκ] ο̣ιδατ[ε
15. there is unlikely to be room for διαλογιζεcθε
16. *ed. pr.* ι̣ν[α
21-2. *ed. pr.* η]μελ̣λ̣ε̣[ν] / [ι̅ς̅
23. *ed. pr.*] μ̣[ονον

P22

First fragment (Jn 15:25-16:2)

Τ̣ΩΝ ΓЄΓΡΑΜΜ[ενοϲ οτι εμιϲηϲαν με δωρεαν (25)
ΟΤΑΝ ЄΛΘΗ Ο ΠΑ̣[ρακλητοϲ ον εγω πεμψω υμ 26
ΙΝ ΠΑΡΑ ΤΟΥ Π̅Ρ̅Ϲ̅ [το π̅ν̅α̅ τηϲ αληθειαϲ ο παρα του
Π̅Ρ̅Ϲ̅ ЄΚΠΟΡЄ̣Υ̣Є̣[ται εκεινοϲ μαρτυρηϲει περι ε
Μ̣ΟΥ ΚΑΙ ΫΜ[ειϲ δε μαρτυρειτε οτι απ αρχηϲ μετ ε 27
Μ̣ΟΥ ЄϹΤЄ Τ[αυτα λελαληκα υμιν ινα μη ϲκανδ 16:1
ΑΛΙϹΘΗΤЄ [αποϲυναγωγουϲ ποιηϲουϲιν υμαϲ αλλ ε 2
Ρ̣ΧЄ̣[τ]**ΑΙ Ω**[

Notes

This papyrus is a roll, written on the ↓. Extant → is blank.
The lines have lost their beginning and end. Since they are so long (ranging from a probable 31 letters in line 2 to 39 in line 7), the line divisions cannot be determined. We have therefore followed the mechanical principle of putting the extant portion at the beginning of each line (except for lines 15, 17 and 22-9 of the second fragment).

1. *ed. pr.*, Wessely γεγραμμε
7. *ed. pr.* σκ]αδαλισθητε; Wessely σκ]ανδαλισθητε. There is no sign in the papyrus of the alleged αδ, still less of ανδ. One is led to suppose that Wessely was dependent on the *ed. pr.* (itself in error), which he falsely emended
8. *ed. pr.*, Wessely]ρχεται ωρ[

Second fragment (Jn 16:21-32)

]**Υ̣ΝΗ ΟΤΑΝ̣ ΤΙΚΤ̣Η̣ Λ̣Υ**[πην εχει οτι ηλθεν η ωρα αυ (21)
Τ̣Η̣Ϲ̣ Ο̣ΤΑΝ ΔΕ ΓΕΝ̣Ν̣Η[cη το παιδιον ουκ ετι μνημο
3 **ΝΕΥΕΙ ΤΗϹ ΘΛΕΙ̣ΨΕΩ̣**[c δια την χαραν οτι εγενν
Η̣ΘΗ Α̅Ν̅Ο̅Ϲ̅ ΕΙ̣Ϲ ΤΟΝ Κ̣[οcμον και υμειc ουν νυν μ 22
Ε̣Ν ΛΥΠΗΝ ΕΧΕΤ̣Ε Π̣[αλιν δε οψομαι υμαc και χαρη
6 **ϹΕΤΑΙ ΫΜΩΝ Η Κ̣ΑΡ**[δια και την χαραν υμων ου
Δ̣ΕΙϹ ΑΙΡΕΙ̣ ΑΦ [υ]**Μ̣Ω̣Ν** [και εν εκεινη τη ημερα εμε ου 23
Κ ΕΡΩΤΗϹΕΤ̣Ε̣ [ου]**Δ̣Ε**[ν αμην αμην λεγω υμιν ο
9 **Τ̣Ι ΕΑ̣Ν̣ ΑΙΤΗϹ̣**[η]**Τ**[ε τον π̅ρ̅α̅ εν τω ονοματι μου δωcει
ΫΜ̣Ε̣Ι̣Ν̣ ΕΩ̣[c αρ]**Τ̣Ι̣** [ουκ ητηcατε ουδεν εν τω ονο 24
Μ̣Α̣ΤΙ ΜΟ̣Υ ΑΙΤ[

Three lines missing

15 π̅]**Ρ̅Ϲ̅** [αναγγελ]**Ω** [(25)
. [(26)
εγ]**Ω** [ερωτηc]**Ω̣ Τ̣Ο̣Ν̣ Π̅Ρ̅Α̅** [περι υμων αυτοc γαρ ο 27
18 **Π̣̅Η̣̅**[ρ̅] **Φ**[ιλει] **ΫΜ**[αc] **Ο̣Τ̣Ι̣ ΫΜ̣**[ειc εμε πεφιληκατε κα
Ι Π̣[επιcτευ]**Κ̣Α̣Τ̣Ε ΟΤΙ ΕΓ**[ω παρα του θ̅υ̅ εξηλθο
Ν Ε[ξ]**Η**[λθο]**Ν ΠΑΡΑ** [τ]**ΟΥ Π̣̅**[ρ̅c̅] και εληλυθα ειc τ 28
21 **ΟΝ** [κοcμον] **ΠΑΛΙΝ Α**[φιημι τον κοcμον και
πορευομαι] **Π̣Ρ̣**[οc] **Τ̣**[ο]**Ν̣** [π̅ρ̅α̅ λεγουcιν αυτω
οι μαθηται αυ]**Τ**[ο]**Υ Ι̣Δ̣Ε** [νυν παρρηcια λαλειc και 29
24 παροιμιαν ου]**Δ̣ΕΜΙ̣**[αν] **Λ**[εγειc νυν οιδαμεν οτι 30
οιδαc πα]**ΝΤΑ Κ̣ΑΙ ΟΥ ΧΡΕΙ̣**[αν εχειc ινα τιc cε ερω
τα εν τ]**Ο̣ΥΤΩ** [πιc]**ΤΕΥΟ̣Μ̣**[εν οτι απο θ̅υ̅ εξηλθ
27 εc απ]**Ε̣ΚΡΙ**[θη] **ΑΥΤΟΙϹ Ι̣̅Η̣̅**[c̅] **Α̣**[ρτι πιcτευετε ιδου 31 32
ερχεται] **Ω̣ΡΑ** [και ε]**Λ̣Η̣Λ̣Υ̣ΘΕΝ̣** [ινα cκορπιcθητε
εκαcτοc ε]**Ι̣Ϲ̣** [τα ι]**Δ̣Ι̣Α̣ ΚΑ**[ι] **ΕΜ̣**[

Notes

1. *ed. pr.*, Wessely λυπ[ην
2. there is a space after τηc (recorded by *ed. pr.*, Wessely)
5. *ed. pr.*, Wessely εχετε [
6. *ed. pr.*, Wessely read a single dot over the upsilon in υμων
10. *ed. pr.*, Wessely εω[ς] αρτι
11. *ed. pr.*, Wessely ονο]ματι μου [
15. *ed. pr.*, Wessely π̅]ρ̅ς̅ [α]π̣[α]γ̣γ̣ε̣λ̣ω̣ [υμιν. The mark which could be part of the crossbar of π in απαγγελω is not clear enough to justify reconstruction
16. *ed. pr.*, Wessely ε]ν̣ τ̣ω̣ ο̣ν̣[οματ]ι̣ μ̣[ο]υ̣ α̣ι̣τ̣η̣[σεσθε
17. *ed. pr.*, Wessely ερω[τησ]ω
ed. pr., Wessely τ[ο]ν
18. the *pi* and *eta* are clear, but not the superline
ed. pr., Wessely π̅η̅[ρ̅ φιλει] ϋμα[ς ο]τι ϋμ[
19. *ed. pr.*, Wessely κα]ι π[επιστε]υκατ[ε] οτι εγ[ω
20. *ed. pr.*, Wessely εξηλθο]ν εξ[η]λθον παρα του π̅[ρ̅ς̅
23. *ed. pr.*, Wessely] ιδε [
25. *ed. pr.*, Wessely πα]ντ[α]
26. *ed. pr.*, Wessely [πισ]τευομε[ν
29. *ed. pr.*, Wessely ε]ις τ[α ι]δια κα[ι] εμ[ε

P[28]

→ (Jn 6:8-12)

14 lines lost

]**ΝΟϹ ΠΕΤΡΟ**[υ (8)
εϲτι παιδαριον εν ωδε ο ε]**Χ̣ΕΙ ΠΕΝΤΕ ΑΡΤΟΥϹ Κ̣**[ρι 9
θινουϲ και δυο οψαρια αλ]**ΛΑ ΤΑΥΤΑ ΤΙ ΕϹΤΙΝ ΕΙ̣**[ϲ
τοϲουτουϲ ειπε δε ο ι̅ϲ̅ ποιηϲ]**ΑΤΕ ΤΟΥϹ ΑΝΘΡΩΠΟΥ**[ϲ 10
αναπεϲειν ην δε χορτ]**Ο̣Ϲ ΠΟΛΥϹ ΕΝ ΤΩ̣ ΤΟΠ̣**[ω
ανεπεϲον ουν οι] **Α̣ΝΔΡΕϹ ΤΟΝ ΑΡΙΘ̣**[μον
ωϲει πεντακιϲ]**ΧΙΛΕ̣Ι̣**[ο]**Ι̣ Ε̣ΛΕΒΕΝ ΟΥ̣**[ν 11
τουϲ αρτουϲ ο ι̅ϲ̅ κα]**Ι ΕΥ̣ΧΑ̣ΡΙϹΤΗϹΑϹ ΕΔΩ̣**
κεν τοιϲ ανακειμ]**ΕΝΟΙϹ ΟΜΟΙΩϹ ΚΑΙ Ε**[κ
των οψαριων οϲο]**Ν ΗΘΕΛΟΝ ΩϹ ΔΕ** 12
ενεπληϲθηϲαν] **ΛΕΓΕΙ ΤΟΙϹ ΜΑΘΗΤΑΙϹ Α**[

Notes

16. *ed. pr.* [εστιν παιδαριον ωδε]
21. *ed. pr.*]χιλειοι
22. *ed. pr.* κ]αι

↓ (Jn 6:17-22)

13 lines missing
]**Ρ̣Α̣Ν̣ Τ̣**[ηϲ θαλαϲϲηϲ ειϲ καπερναουμ (17)
15 κα]**Ι ϹΚΟΤΙΑ ΗΔΗ̣ Є̣**[γε]**Γ̣**[ονει και ουκ
ε]**Λ̣ΗΛΥΘЄΙ Ο Ι̅Ϲ̅ Η ΤЄ Θ**[αλαϲϲα ανεμου μεγα 18
λο]**Υ ΠΝЄΟΝΤΟϹ ΔΙЄΓЄ**[ιρετο εληλακοτεϲ ουν 19
18 **Ω̣Ϲ ϹΤΑΔΙΟΥϹ ЄΙΚΟ̣Ϲ̣ΙΠ**[εντε η τριακοντα θεωρου
ϲι]**Ν Ι̅Ν̅ ΠЄΡΙΠΑΤΟΥ̣**[ντα επι τηϲ θαλαϲϲηϲ
κ]**ΑΙ ЄΝΓΥϹ ΤΟΥ ΠΛΟ**[ιου γινομενον και
21 **ЄΦΟΒΗΘΗϹΑΝ Ο̣ Δ**[ε λεγει αυτοιϲ εγω ειμι 20
ΜΗ ΦΟΒЄΙϹΘ̣Α̣Ι ΗΘ[ελον ουν λαβειν αυτον 21
ЄΙϹ ΤΟ ΠΛΟΙΟΝ ΚΑΙ Є[υθεωϲ το πλοιον εγενετο
24 **ЄΠΙ ΤΗϹ ΓΗϹ ЄΙϹ Η̣**[ν υπηγον τη επαυ 22
ΡΙΟΝ Ο ΟΧΛΟϹ Ο ЄϹΤ̣[ηκωϲ περαν τηϲ θαλαϲϲηϲ
ΪΔЄΝ ΟΤΙ ΠΛΟΙΑΡΙΟΝ [

Notes

15. *ed. pr.* κ]αι
ed. pr. εγ̣[ε]γ̣[ονει
16. *ed. pr.* reads a high point after ι̅ϲ̅
17. *ed. pr.* διεγει̣[ρετο
20. *ed. pr.* και
ed. pr. πλοι[ου
22. *ed. pr.* ηθε[λον
24. the papyrus has a space after γηϲ

P[36]

First fragment
→ (Jn 3:14-16)

ΛЄ̅
ΚΑΙ ΚΑΘΩϹ̣ [μωϲηϲ υψωϲε 14
ΤΟΝ ΟΦΙΝ [εν τη ερημω ουτωϲ
3 Υ̣ΨΩ̣Θ̣ΗΝ[αι δει τον υιον του α̅ν̅ο̅υ̅
ΙΝΑ ΠΑϹ Ο [πιϲτευων ειϲ αυτον 15
ЄΧΗ ΖΩΗΝ̣ [αιωνιον ουτω γαρ 16
6 ΗΓΑΠΗϹ[εν ο θ̅ϲ̅ τον κοϲμον ωϲ
Τ̣Є̣ ΤΟΝ ΥΙΟΝ̣ [αυτου τον μονογενη
Є̣Δ̣Ω̣Κ̣Є̣Ν̣ [ινα παϲ ο πιϲτευων επ
9 Α̣Υ̣ΤΩ ΜΗ [αποληται αλλ εχη
ΖΩΗΝ Δ[

Notes

Heading: Carlini, *New Doc.* λ̅ε̅
3. Carlini, *New Doc.* υ̣ψ̣ω̣θ̣η̣ν̣α̣ι̣
7. *ed. pr.*, Carlini, *New Doc.* [τον μονογενη. However, the line would be very short without αυτου
8. *ed. pr.* πιστευων **; Carlini, *New Doc.* πιστευων εν. This variant would be otherwise unattested

First fragment
↓ (Jn 3:17-18)

]**Ν̣ Ο Θ̅C̅ ΤΟΝ** (17)
υιον ειϲ τον κοϲ]**Μ̣ΟΝ ΪΝΑ**
κρινη τον κοϲμον αλ]**Λ̣ ΙΝΑ**
ϲωθη ο κοϲμοϲ δι αυτο]**Υ Ο ΠΙϹΤЄΥ** 18
ων ειϲ αυτον ου κρι]**Ν̣ΗΤΑΙ· Ο ΔЄ**
μη πιϲτευων {ειϲ] **ΤΟ ^{O}ΝΟΜΑ**}
ηδη κεκριται οτι μη πεπι]**ϹΤЄΥΚЄ**
ειϲ το ονομα του μο]**Ν̣ΟΓ̣ЄΝΟ^{ΥC}**

Notes

2. *ed. pr.*, *New Doc.* ινα
5. *ed. pr.* νεται (*ex errore*)
6-8. the dittography, shared with all previous editors, is based on line length. It appears the most obvious possibility with this wording. Of course, the possibility of a quite different wording cannot be excluded
6. *ed. pr.*] ονομα. The omicron added above the line could be by either the first or a second hand. We take it as the former. The words το ^{o}νομα (and, we infer, the missing ειϲ) have been deleted by the first hand with two horizontal strokes
8. the final two letters of the line are written over the omicron

Second fragment
↓ (Jn 3:31-2)

]Ρ̣Χ̣[ομενος επανω (31)
ΠΑΝ̣[των εϲτιν ο ων εκ τηϲ γηϲ
ЄΚ ΤΗ[ϲ γηϲ λαλει ο εκ του ο̅υ̅ν̅ο̅υ̅
ЄΡΧΟΜ̣[ενοϲ επανω παντων
ЄϹΤΙ Ο̣ [εωρακε και ηκουϲεν 32
ΤΟΥΤΟ Μ̣[

Notes

The reconstruction of this leaf by Carlini is identical in *APF* and *Papiri litterari greci.*

1. *ed. pr.* omits; Carlini, *New Doc.* ̣ ̣[
2. *ed. pr.* ε̣παν[ω παντων εστιν ο ων
3. *ed. pr.* εκ της [γης ο εκ του ουρανου
5. *ed. pr.*, Carlini, *New Doc.* εστιν [ο
6. *ed. pr.* τουτο μαρ̣[

Carlini reads a line 7, consisting of one unrecognizable letter

Second fragment
→ (Jn 3:34-6)

]Ṇ (34)
ο θ̅ς̅ τα ρηματα του] **ΘΥ**
3 λαλει ου γαρ εκ μετρου] **Δ̣Ι̣Δ̣Ω̣**
σιν το π̅ν̅α̅ ο π̅η̅ρ̅ αγαπα] **Ṭ Ō** 35
υιον και παντα δεδ]**Ω̣ΚΕ̣Ṇ**
6 εν τη χειρι αυτου ο π]**Ị Ϲ̣ Ṭ Ε̣**[36

Notes

The reconstruction of this leaf by Carlini is identical in *APF* and *Papiri litterari greci*.
Ed. pr. states that this page cannot be deciphered, and does not provide a transcription.

2. Carlini, *New Doc.* θ̅υ̅
6. Carlini, *New Doc.*] . .

P[39]

↓ (Jn 8:14-18)

] **Α̣ΥΤΟΙϹ** (14)
καν εγω μ]**Α̣ΡΤΥΡΩ**
3 περι εμαυτ]**ΟΥ Η ΜΑΡ**
τυρια μου] **Α̣ΛΗΘΗϹ**
εϲτιν οτι ο]**ΙΔΑ ΠΟ**
6 θεν ηλθο]**Ν ΚΑΙ ΠΟΥ**
υπαγω υ]**Μ̣ЄΙϹ ΔЄ**
ουκ οιδατ]**Є ΠΟΘЄΝ**
9 ερχομαι κα]**Ι̣ ΠΟΥ ΥΠΑ**
γω υμειϲ] **ΚΑΤΑ ΤΗ̄** 15
ϲαρκα κρι]**ΝЄΤЄ ЄΓΩ**
12 ου κριν]**Ω̣ ΟΥΔЄΝΑ**
και εαν κ]**ΡΙΝΩ ΔЄ** 16
εγω η κρ]**ΙϹΙϹ Η ЄΜΗ**
15 αληθηϲ ε]**ϹΤΙΝ Ο**
τι μονοϲ] **ΟΥΚ ЄΙ**
μι αλλ εγ]**Ω̣ ΚΑΙ Ο**
18 πεμψαϲ] **Μ̣Є Π̅Η̅Ρ̅**
και εν τω] **ΝΟΜΩ** 17
δε τω υμ]**ЄΤЄΡΩ**
21 γεγραπτ]**ΑΙ ΟΤΙ ΔΥ**
ο α̅ν̅ω̅ν̅ η] **ΜΑΡΤΥΡΙ**
α αληθηϲ] **ЄϹΤΙΝ Є** 18
24 γω ειμι ο] **ΜΑΡΤ̣ΥΡ̣**
ων περι] **ЄΜΑΥΤΟΥ**

Notes

According to this reconstruction, the number of letters in each line varies between 11 (lines 18-20) and 16 (line 9). 14 lines have 13 or 14 letters.

3. ed. pr.]του η μαρ
9. ed. pr. ερχομαι] η που υπα
11. ed. pr.]ινετε εγω
23. the papyrus has a space after εϲτιν

→ (Jn 8:18-22)

ΟΔ
ΚΑΙ Μ[αρτυρει περι (18)
ΕΜΟΥ [ο πεμψας με
Π̅Η̅Ρ̅ Ε[λεγον ουν 19
ΑΥΤΩ [που εστιν ο
Π̅Η̅Ρ̅ ΣΟ̣[υ απεκριθη ο
Ι̅Η̅Σ̅ ΟΥ[τε εμε οιδα
ΤΕ ΟΥΤ[ε τον π̅ρ̅α̅ μου
ΕΙ ΕΜΕ [ηδειτε και
ΤΟΝ Π̅Ρ̅[α̅ μου αν η
ΔΕΙΤΕ Τ̣[αυτα τα ρη 20
ΜΑΤΑ ΕΛ[αλησεν εν
ΤΩ ΓΑΖΟ[φυλακιω
ΔΙΔΑΣΚΩ̣[ν εν τω
ΪΕΡΩ ΚΑ[ι ουδεις
ΕΠΙΑΣ[εν αυτον ο
ΤΙ ΟΥΠ[ω εληλυθει
Η ΩΡΑ Α̣[υτου ειπεν 21
ΟΥΝ ΠΑ[λιν αυτοις
ΕΓΩ ΥΠ[αγω και ζη
ΤΗΣΕΤΕ Μ̣[ε και εν
τ]Η̣ ΑΜΑΡΤ̣[ια υμων
ΑΠΟΘΑΝ[εισθε ο
ΠΟΥ ΕΓΩ [υπαγω
υ]ΜΕ̣Ι̣Σ ΟΥ̣ [δυνασθε
ΕΛΘΕ[ι]Ν Ε̣[λεγον 22

Notes

Lines on this page have between 11 (line 23) and 15 letters. 16 lines have 13 or 14 letters.

3. the papyrus has a space after π̅η̅ρ̅
6. the papyrus has a space after ιης
11. *ed. pr.* ελα[λησεν
15. *ed. pr.* επιασε[ν
21. *ed. pr.* τη
24. *ed. pr.* υμεις
25. *ed. pr.* ελθειν ε[
the papyrus has a space after ελθε[ι]ν

P44A

Note: In our opinion, the pieces called Fragments A and B by *ed. pr.* are without doubt by different hands. The first editors write that 'A, B and C are all by the same hand, though in B the script is markedly larger' (p. 301).

↓ is Mt 17:1-3, 6-7; 18:15-17, 19

→ (Jn 10:8-14)

Ten lines of Mt 25:8-10, followed by a lacuna of about ten lines
] Π̣ΡΟ[βατα (8)
εγω ειμι η θυρα δι εμο]Υ̣ ЄΑ̣[ν τιϲ 9
3 ειϲελθη ϲωθηϲεται] Κ̣[
Three lines missing
]Λ̣Θ[ο]Ν̣. ΪΝΑ [ζωην (10)
εχωϲι κ]Α̣Ι̣ ΠЄΡΙ̣ϹϹÓΤ̣ЄΡΟΝ Є[χω
9 ϲιν εγω ε]Ι̣ΜΙ Ο Π[οιμην ο καλοϲ ο 11
ποιμην ο] ΚΑΛῺϹ [την ψυχην αυτου
τιθηϲιν υπ]Є̣Ρ̣ ΤΩ[ν προβατων ο
Four lines missing
Α̣ΡΠΑ[ζει αυτ]Α̣ [και ϲκορπιζει οτι (12) 13
17 ΜΙϹΘΩ̣[τοϲ εϲτι] ΚΑΙ̣ [ου μελει αυτω
περι των προβα]Τ̣ΩΝ· ЄΓΩ Є̣[ιμι ο ποι 14
μην ο καλοϲ κα]Ι ΓΙΝΏϹΚΩ [

Notes

The division into lines of lines 1-11 is purely hypothetical; *ed. pr.* has different divisions.

3. *ed. pr.* does not read anything for this line

8. *ed. pr.* κα]ι

9. the mark over o is odd. *Ed. pr.* represents it as a shallow cup shape. It is more likely to be the tail of rho in the line above

General note: *ed. pr.* does not record the detached parts of Fragments I and II, or any of Fragment III

Fragments I and II → (Jn 9:3-4)

ΟΥΤЄ Ọ!̣ Γ̣[ονειϲ αυτου αλλ ινα φανερω (3)
ΘΗ ΤΑ ЄΡΓ[α του θ̅υ̅ εν αυτω εμε δει εργα 4
ΖЄϹΘΑΙ Τ̣[α εργα το]**Υ Π̣**[εμψαντοϲ με ε
ΩϹ ΗΜ[ερα εϲτιν ε]**Ρ̣Χ**[εται νυξ οτε ουδειϲ
ΔΥΝΑΤ[

Fragment III ↓ (Jn 12:12-13)

] **ЄΡ̣**[χεται ο ι̅ϲ̅ ειϲ ιεροϲολυμα ελαβον τα (12) 13
β]**Α̣Ϊ Α̣** [

Notes (Fragment III)

→ contains part of a *nu* and traces of other letters

Fragments I and II ↓ (Jn 12:16-18)

]**Є̣**[ν]**Α̣ ΚΑΙ** [ταυ (16)
τα εποιηϲαν αυτω εμαρτυρει] **Ο̣ΥΝ Ο ΟΧΛΟ**[ϲ 17
ο ων μετ αυτου] **Ο̣ΤЄ̣** [τον λαζαρο]**Ν ЄΦΩΝ**[η
ϲεν εκ του μνημ]**ЄΙΟ̣**[υ και ηγειρ]**Є̣Ν ΑΥΤΟΝ**
εκ νεκρων δια τουτο και υπηντ]**ΗϹЄΝ Α̣**[18

Notes

1. *ed. pr.* γεγραμμεν]α και

Fragment C consists of two pieces, → and ↓, with fragments of sixteen lines of an unidentified text

P45

Note: These two fragments are not included in Kenyon's edition. They were first published by Skeat and McGing (see bibliography).

Fragments B → (Jn 4:51-53) and C → (Jn 4:54-5:2)

]**Η̣ΝΤ̣**[ηςαν αυτωι και απηγγειλαν (51)
λεγοντες οτι ο υ̅ς̅ ςου ζηι επυθ]**Ϲ̣ΤΟ ΟΥ**[ν παρ αυτων
την ωραν εν 52
ηι κομψοτερον εςχεν και ειπο]**Ν̣ ΟΤΙ Ϲ̣**[χθες
ωραν εβδομην αφη
κεν αυτον ο πυρετος εγνω ουν] **Ο Π̅Ρ̅ ΟΤ̣**[53
One line lost
] **Τ̣**[ο]**Υ̣**[το παλιν δευτερον ςημειον εποιηςεν ο ι̅η̅
ελθων εκ 54
της ι]**´ΟΥΔΑ̣**[ιας εις την γαλιλαιαν μετα ταυτα ην εορτη
των ιου 5:1
δαιω]**Ν· Κ̣Α̣Ι̣** [ανεβη ο ι̅η̅ εις ιεροςολυμα εςτιν δε εν τοις
ιεροςο 2
λυ]**Μ̣Ο̣Ι̣Ϲ̣** [
]**Ϲ̣**. . [

Notes

2. there does not appear to be sufficient space for παις. We therefore follow *ed. pr.* in conjecturing υ̅ς̅

3. the papyrus could have read either εςχεν και ειπο]ν or εςχεν ειπον ου]ν

7. the right hand dot of a diaeresis survives. We have ignored it in the apparatus

ου[ν in *ed. pr.* p. 22 is right against the reconstruction on p. 23

10. since the epsilon cannot be identified with one in the text (presumably it comes in v. 2) we have not included this line in the DEF section of the apparatus

Fragments B ↓ (Jn 5:21-23) and C ↓ (Jn 5:24-25)

]**Є̣Ρ Γ̣Α̣**[ρ ο π̅ρ̅ εγειρει τουϲ νεκρουϲ και ζω (21)
οποιει ουτωϲ και ο υ̅ϲ̅ ουϲ θε]**Λ̣ЄΙ ΖΩ̣**[οποιει ουδε γαρ
ο π̅ρ̅ κρινει 22
3 ουδενα αλλα την κριϲιν πα]**Ϲ̣ΑΝ ЄΔ̣**[ωκε τω υ̅ω̅ ινα
παντεϲ τι 23
μωϲι τον υ̅ν̅ καθωϲ τιμωϲι το]**Ν Π̅Ρ̅Α̣̅** [ο μη τιμων τον υ̅ν̅
ου τιμα
τον π̅ρ̅α̅ τον πεμψαντα αυτον αμην αμην λεγω υμιν οτι
ο]
Τ̣Ο̣Ν ΛΟ̣[γον 24
6 μου ακουων και πιϲτευων τωι πεμψαντι με εχει
ζωην] **Α̣ΙΩΝ**[ιον
και ειϲ κριϲιν ουκ ερχεται αλλα μεταβεβηκεν εκ
του] **Θ̣ΑΝΑ**[του
ειϲ την ζωην αμην αμην λεγω υμιν οτι ερχεται
ωρ]**Α̣ ΚΑ̣**[25

Notes

1-2. our reconstruction (with *ed. pr.*) provides 27 / 22 letters between the extant letters. This seems to be rather too many (the next two have 22 / 21 and 18 / 22). There is no obvious variant

2. *ed. pr.*]λ̣ει ζ[

2. *ed. pr.*]ον λο[

Note: The lines of the papyrus are too long to fit onto one of ours. We present them as a pair of left and right justified lines; the line and verse numbers include both of the pair.

F16v
↓ (Jn 10:7-25)

]Є[ν ουν] ΑΥΤΟΙϹ Ο ΙΗ̅ Α̣Μ̣[ην αμην λεγ]Ѡ̣ ΥΜΙΝ̣
[οτι] Є̣[γω] Є̣[ιμι η θυρα των (7)
Π̣ΡΟΒΑΤѠ̣Ν· ΠΑΝΤЄϹ ΟϹΟΙ̣ [ηλθον κλεπτ]Α̣Ι̣ ЄΙϹΙΝ
ΚΑΙ ΛΗϹΤΑΙ· Α[λλ ουκ η 8
ΚΟΥϹЄΝ ΑΥΤѠΝ ΤΑ ΠΡΟΒΑ̣ΤΑ [εγω ειμι η θ]Υ̣[ρ]Α·
ΔΙ ЄΜΟΥ ЄΑΝ̣ ΤΙϹ ЄΙϹ[ελθη cωθη 9
ϹЄΤΑΙ· ΚΑΙ ЄΙϹЄΛЄΥϹЄΤΑΙ· ΚΑΙ ЄΞ[ε]Λ[ε]ΥϹЄΤΑ̣Ι̣·
ΚΑΙ ΝΟΜΗΝ ЄΥΡΗϹЄΙ· [ο κλεπτης 10
ΟΥΚ ЄΡΧЄΤΑΙ ЄΙ ΜΗ ΪΝΑ ΚΛЄΨΗ· ΚΑΙ ΘΥϹΗ ΚΑΙ
ΑΠΟΛЄϹΗ· ЄΓѠ Δ[ε ηλθον
ΪΝΑ ΖѠΗΝ ЄΧѠϹΙ· ΚΑΙ ΠЄΡΙϹϹΟΝ ЄΧѠϹΙΝ· ЄΓѠ
ЄΙΜΙ Ο ΚΑΛΟϹ ΠΟΙ[μην 11
Ο ΚΑΛΟϹ ΠΟΙΜΗΝ. ΤΗΝ ΨΥΧΗΝ ΑΥΤΟΥ
ΔΙΔѠϹΙΝ ΫΠЄΡ ΤѠΝ ΠΡΟΒ[ατων ο 12
ΜΙϹΘѠΤΟϹ ΚΑΙ ΟΥΚ ѠΝ ΠΟΙΜΗΝ. ΟΥ ΟΥΚ
ЄϹΤΙΝ ΪΔΙΑ ΤΑ ΠΡΟΒΑΤΑ· Θ̣[εωρει
ΤΟΝ ΛΥΚΟΝ ЄΡΧΟΜЄΝΟΝ ΚΑΙ ΑΦЄΙΗϹΙΝ ΤΑ
ΠΡΟΒΑΤΑ· ΚΑΙ ΦЄΥΓЄΙ· ΚΑ̣[ι ο λυκος
ΑΡ̣[π]ΑΖЄΙ ΑΥΤΑ ΚΑΙ ϹΚΟΡΠΙΖЄΙ· ΟΤΙ ΜΙϹΘѠΤΟϹ
ЄϹΤΙΝ ΚΑΙ ΟΥ ΜЄΛЄ̣[ι αυτωι 13
ΠЄΡΙ ΤѠΝ ΠΡΟΒΑΤѠΝ· ЄΓѠ ЄΙΜΙ Ο ΠΟΙΜΗΝ Ο
ΚΑΛΟϹ ΚΑΙ ΓЄΙΝ[ωcκω τα 14
ЄΜΑ· ΚΑΙ ΓЄΙΝѠϹΚ{ΟΥϹΙ} <ЄΙ> ΜЄ ΤΑ ЄΜΑ·
ΚΑΙ ΚΑΘѠϹ ΓЄΙΝѠϹΚЄΙ [με ο π̅ρ̅ 15
ΚΑΓѠ ΓЄΙΝѠϹΚѠ ΤΟΝ Π̅Ρ̅Α̅· ΚΑΙ ΤΗΝ ΨΥΧΗΝ
ΜΟΥ ΔΙΔѠΜΙ ΫΠЄ̣[ρ των
ΠΡΟΒΑΤѠΝ· ΚΑΙ ΑΛΛΑ ΠΡΟΒΑΤΑ ЄΧѠ ΑΠЄΡ
ΟΥΚ ЄϹΤΙΝ ЄΚ ΤΗϹ [αυλης 16
ΤΑΥΤΗϹ. ΚΑΚЄΙΝΑ ΔЄΙ ΜЄ ΑΓΑΓЄΙΝ· ΚΑΙ ΤΗϹ
ΦѠΝΗϹ ΜΟΥ Α[κουcου
ϹΙΝ· ΚΑΙ ΓЄΝΗϹΟΝΤΑΙ ΜΙΑ ΠΟΙΜΝΗ· ЄΙϹ ΠΟΙΜΗΝ· ΔΙΑ
[τουτο ο π̅ρ̅ με 17
ΑΓΑΠΑ ΟΤΙ ЄΓѠ ΤΙΘΗΜΙ ΤΗ[ν] Ψ̣ΥΧΗΝ ΜΟΥ ΪΝΑ
ΠΑΛΙ[ν λαβω αυτην

18 ΟΥΔЄΙϹ ΗΡЄΝ ΑΥΤΗΝ ΑΠ ЄΜ[ου] Α̣ΛΛΑ ЄΓⲰ
ΤΙΘ̣ΗΜΙ ΑΥ[την απ εμαυτου 18
ЄΞΟΥϹΙΑΝ ЄΧⲰ ΘЄΙΝΑΙ ΑΥ[τ]Η̣Ν· ΚΑΙ ΠΑΛΙΝ
ЄΞ̣ΟΥ[cιαν εχω λαβειν
αυ]ΤΗΝ· ΤΑΥΤΗΝ ЄΛΑΒΟΝ [ε]ΝΤΟΛΗΝ Π̣ΑΡΑ ΤΟΥ
[π̅ρ̅c̅ μου cχιcμα ουν παλιν 19
21 εγ]ЄΝЄΤΟ ЄΝ ΤΟΙϹ ΪΟΥΔΑΙΟΙϹ Δ̣ΙΑ ΤΟΥϹ ΛΟΓΟΥϹ
ΤΟΥ[τουc ελεγον δε πολ 20
λο]Ι̣ ЄΞ ΑΥΤⲰΝ ΟΤΙ ΔΑΙΜΟΝ[ιο]Ν ЄΧЄΙ ΚΑΙ
ΜΑΙΝЄ[ται τι αυτου ακουετε
αλ]Λ̣ΟΙ ЄΛЄΓΟΝ ΤΑΥΤΑ ΤΑ ΡΗ[μ]Α̣ΤΑ ΟΥΚ ЄϹΤΙΝ
ΔΑ[ιμονιζομενου 21
24 μη δα]Ι̣ΜΟΝΙΟΝ ΔΥΝΑΤΑΙ ΤΥ̣[φ]Λ̣ⲰΝ ΟΦΘΑΛΜΟΥϹ
[ανοιγειν εγενετο 22
δε τα] ЄΝΚΑΙΝΙΑ ЄΝ ΪЄΡΟϹ[ολυμ]Ο̣ΙϹ· ΧЄΙΜⲰΝ ΔЄ
[ην και περιεπατει ο ι̅η̅ 23
ε]Ν ΤⲰΙ ΪЄΡⲰΙ ЄΝ ΤΗΙ ϹΤ̣[οα του c]ΟΛΟΜⲰΝΟϹ·
ЄΚ[υκλωcαν ουν αυτον 24
27 οι] ΪΟΥΔΑΙΟΙ ΚΑΙ Α̣Υ̣Τ̣[ωι ελεγον] ЄⲰ̣Ϲ ΠΟΤЄ ΤΗ[ν
ψυχην ημων αιρειc
ει] Ϲ̣Υ̣ ЄΙ [ο χ̅ρ̅c̅ ειπε ημιν παρρηcια κ]Α̣Ι̣ ΑΠЄ[25

Notes, F16v (Jn 10:7-25)

1. *ed. pr.* ι̅η̅ α[and [οτι εγω ειμι
2. *ed. pr.* κλεπτα]ι
3. *ed. pr.*] θ̣υ[ρ]α
5. *ed. pr.* has no point after κλεψη
   ed. pr. εγω η[λθον
6. *ed. pr.* πο[ιμην
7. *ed. pr.* has no point after ποιμην
8. *ed. pr.* [θεωρει
9. *ed. pr.* κ[αι
10. *ed. pr.* α[ρπ]αζει
   ed. pr. μελ[ει
12. the corrector has replaced ουcι by partly erasing it, and has written ει above
13. *ed. pr.* ϋπ[ερ
19. *ed. pr.* αυ[τη]ν
20. *ed. pr.* [π]αρα
   ed. pr. σχισμα παλι̅
21. *ed. pr.* [δ]ια
23. *ed. pr.* αλλ]οι
   ed. pr. ρη[μα]τα
24. *ed. pr.* δαι]μονιον
   ed. pr. τυ̣[φλ]ων
24-5. *ed. pr.* δε / τα
25. *ed. pr.* ϊεροσ[ολυμο]ις
27. *ed. pr.* [ελε]γ̣ο[ν αυτωι] ε[ω]ς
28. *ed. pr.*]υ̣ ει
   ed. pr. παρρησια·] απε[

F16r
→ (Jn 10:29-11:11)

]Є̣[ιροc το]Υ Π̣̅Ρ̣̅C̣̅ Μ̣Ο̣[υ εγω και ο π̅ρ̣̅ εν εcμ]Є̣Ν·
ЄΒΑCΤΑCΑ̣Ν ΛΙΘ[ουc οι (29) 30 31
ιουδ]ΑΙΟΙ ΪΝΑ ΛΙΘΑCѠC[ιν αυτον και α]ΠЄΚΡΙΘΗ
ΑΥΤΟΙC [ο] Ι̣̅Η̣̅ [πολλα 32
εργα κ]ΑΛΑ ЄΔЄΙΞΑ ΫΜΙΝ ЄΚ Τ[ου π̅ρ̅c̅ δια] Π̣ΟΙΟΝ
ΑΥΤѠΝ ЄΡΓΟΝ ЄΜЄ
λιθα]ΖЄΤЄ· ΑΠЄΚΡΙΘΗCΑΝ Α̣Υ̣Τ̣[ωι οι ι]Ο̣ΥΔΑΙΟΙ
ΠЄΡΙ ΚΑΛΟΥ ЄΡΓΟΥ ΟΥ Λ[ι 33
θαζο]ΜЄΝ CЄ· ΑΛΛΑ ΠЄΡΙ ΒΛΑCΦΗΜΙΑC· ΚΑΙ ΟΤΙ CΥ
ΑΝΘΡѠΠΟC ѠΝ
ποιε]ΙC CЄΑΥΤΟΝ Θ̅Ν̅· ΑΠЄΚΡΙΘΗ ΑΥΤΟΙC Ι̅Η̅ · ΟΥΚ
ЄCΤΙΝ ΓЄΓΡΑΜΜЄΝΟΝ 34
εν τη]Ι ΓΡΑΦΗΙ ЄΝ ΤѠΙ ΝΟΜѠΙ ΟΤΙ ЄΓѠ ЄΙΠΑ
ΘЄΟΙ ЄCΤЄ· ЄΙ ЄΚЄΙΝΟΥC Є[ι 35
πεν] ΘЄΟΥC ΚΑΙ ΟΥ ΔΥΝΑΤΑΙ ΛΥΘΗΝΑΙ ὉΝ Ο Π̅Ρ̅
ΗΓΙΑCЄΝ ΚΑΙ ΑΠЄCΤЄΙ 36
λεν ει]C ΤΟΝ ΚΟCΜΟΝ. ΫΜЄΙC ΛЄΓЄΤЄ ΟΤΙ
ΒΛΑCΦΗΜЄΙC ΟΤΙ ЄΙΠΟΝ Ὁ Υ̅C̣̅
του θ̅υ̅] ЄΙΜΙ· ЄΙ ΟΥ ΠΟΙѠ ΤΑ ЄΡΓΑ ΤΟΥ Π̅Ρ̅C̅ ΜΟΥ.
ΜΗ ΠΙCΤЄΥЄΤЄ ΜΟΙ: ЄΙ ΔЄ 37 38
ποιω] ΚΑΝ ЄΜΟΙ ΜΗ ΠΙCΤЄΥΗΤЄ. ΤΟΙC Є̣ΡΓΟΙC
ΠΙCΤЄΥCΑΤЄ· ΪΝΑ ΓΝѠΤЄ
και γ]Є̣Ν̣ѠCΚΗΤЄ ΟΤΙ ЄΝ ЄΜΟΙ Ο Π̅Ρ̅· ΚΑΓѠ ЄΝ
ΑΥΤѠΙ· ЄΖΗΤΟΥΝ ΔЄ ΑΥΤΟΝ 39
πιαcαι] ΚΑΙ ЄΞΗΛΘЄΝ ЄΚ ΤΗC ΧЄΙΡΟC ΑΥΤѠΝ· ΚΑΙ
ΑΠΗΛΘЄΝ ΠΑΛΙΝ ΠЄ 40
ραν το]Υ ΪΟΡΔΑΝΟΥ Є̣ΙC ΤΟΝ ΤΟΠΟΝ ὉΠΟΥ ΗΝ
ΪѠΑΝΝΗC ΤΟ ΠΡΟΤЄΡΟΝ ΒΑ
πτιζ]ѠΝ· ΚΑΙ ЄΜЄΙΝЄΝ ЄΚЄΙ· ΚΑΙ ΠΟΛΛΟΙ ΗΛΘΟΝ
ΠΡΟC ΑΥΤΟΝ· ΚΑΙ ЄΛЄ̣ 41
γον οτι] ΪѠΑΝΝΗC ΜЄΝ CΗΜЄΙΟΝ ЄΠΟΙΗCЄΝ ΟΥΔЄ
ЄΝ· ΠΑΝΤΑ ΔЄ ὉCΑ̣
ϊωανν]ΗC ЄΙΠЄΝ ΠЄΡΙ ΤΟΥΤΟΥ ΑΛΗΘΗ ΗΝ· ΚΑΙ
ΠΟΛΛΟΙ ЄΠΙCΤЄΥCΑΝ ЄΙ[c 42
αυτον ην] ΔЄ ΤΙC [α]CΘЄΝѠΝ ΛΑΖΑΡΟC ΑΠΟ
ΒΗΘΑΝΙΑΜ᾿ ЄΚ ΤΗC ΚѠΜΗ[c
11:1
μαριαc] ΚΑΙ ΜΑΡΘΑC ΤΗC ΑΔЄΛΦ̣Η̣C ΑΥΤΗC· ΗΝ ΔЄ
ἈΥΤΗ Η ΜΑΡ[ια η 2

αλειψαcα το]Ν K̄N̄ ΜΥΡΩΙ ΚΑΙ ЄΚΜ[αξαc]Α ΤΟΥC
ΠΟΔΑC ΑΥΤΟΥ ΤΑΙC ΘΡΙ
21 ξιν αυτηc ηc] Ο ΑΔЄΛΦΟC ΛΑΖΑΡ Η[cθε]ΝЄΙ·
ΑΠЄCΤЄΙΛΑΝ [ο]Υ̣Ν̣ ΑΙ ΑΔЄ̣[λφαι 3
προc αυτον λεγ]ΟΥCΑΙ· K̄Є̄ ΪΔЄ ΌΝ Φ[ι]Λ̣ЄΙC ΑCΘЄΝЄΙ·
ΑΚΟΥCΑC ΔЄ̣ [ο] ̣ [ι̅η̅ 4
ειπεν αυτη η] Α̣CΘЄΝЄ̣ΙΑ ΟΥΚ ЄC̣[τ]ΙΝ ΠΡΟC
ΘΑΝΑΤΟΝ· ΑΛΛ [ϋπερ
24 τηc δοξηc το]Υ̣ Θ̄Ȳ ΪΝΑ ΔΟΞΑCΘΗ [ο] Ȳ̄C̄ ΑΥΤΟΥ ΔΙ
ΑΥΤΗC· ΗΓΑΠΑ̣ [δε 5
ο ι̅η̅ την μαρθαν] ΚΑΙ ΤΗΝ ΑΔЄΛΦΗ[ν] ΑΥΤΗC ΚΑΙ
ΤΟΝ ΛΑΖΑΡΟΝ Ω[c ουν 6
ηκουcεν οτι] ΑCΘЄΝЄΙ. ΤΟΤЄ ΜЄ̣[ν] Є̣ΜЄΙΝЄΝ ЄΠΙ
Τ̇ΩΙ ΤΟΠ[ωι δυο
27 ημεραc επειτα] ΜЄΤΑ ΤΟΥΤΟ ΛЄΓЄ̣[ι αγ]ΩΜЄΝ ЄΙC
ΤΗΝ ΪΟΥΔΑΙ̣[αν πα 7
λιν λεγουcιν α]ΥΤΩΙ ΟΙ ΜΑΘΗΤΑ[ι ραβ]ΒЄΙ ΝΥΝ
ЄΖΗΤΟΥΝ CЄ Λ[ιθαcαι οι 8
ϊουδαιοι και π]ΑΛΙΝ ΫΠΑΓЄΙC [εκει α]ΠЄΚΡΙΘΗ Ο Ι̅Η̅
ΟΥΧΙ ΔΩ[δεκα 9
30 ειcιν ωραι τηc] ΗΜЄΡΑC· ЄΑΝ [τιc εν τηι] Η̣ΜЄΡΑ
ΠЄΡΙΠΑΤΗ [ου προc
κοπτει οτι το φ]ΩC ΤΟΥ Κ[ο]C̣[μου τουτου βλεπει εαν
δε τ]Ι̣C̣ ΠЄΡΙΠ̣[ατη 10
εν τη νυκτι προcκοπτει οτι το φωc ουκ εcτιν εν αυτωι
τα]Υ[11

Notes, F16r (Jn 10:29-11:11)

1. *ed. pr.* has nothing before]εν·
2. *ed. pr.* λιθασωσι [αυτον α]
   ed. pr. [ο ι̅η̅ πολλα. There are minute traces of ink after ιη
3. *ed. pr.* [του
4. *ed. pr.* [αυτωι
   ed. pr. ου λι
8. *ed. pr.* πεν θ]εους
9-10. *ed. pr.* υ̅[ι̅ / ος θ̅υ̅. But there are clear traces of sigma after upsilon
10. *ed. pr.* has no point after μου, and a single point after μοι
12. *ed. pr.* γ]εινωσκητε
14. *ed. pr.* οπου
15. *ed. pr.* πτιζω]ν·
18. *ed. pr.* ασθενων
   we follow *ed. pr.* βηθανιαμ' εκ, although the apostrophe is actually written as a complete circle
19. *ed. pr.* αδελ[φ]ης
21. *ed. pr.* [ου]ν
21-2. *ed. pr.* αδε[λ / φαι
22. *ed. pr.* προς αυτον λεγο]
   ed. pr. φ[ιλ]εις
   ed. pr. δ[ε ο ι̅η̅ . The superline is partly visible, but no part of the letter iota survives
23. *ed. pr.* α]σθενεια
24. *ed. pr.* ηγαπ[α δε
25. *ed. pr.* [ως ουν
26. *ed pr.* με[ν ε]μεινεν
26-7. *ed. pr.* τοπ[ωι / β̅ ημερας
27. *ed. pr.* ϊουδα[ιαν
28-9. *ed. pr.* λ[ιθασαι / οι
31. *ed. pr.* κ[οσμου... τις]
32. *ed. pr.* records nothing for this line

F17r
→ (Jn 11:17-37)

] . . [ ] Ḥ**Μ**[ερας ηδη εχοντα εν τωι μνημειωι
ην δε η βηθα (17) 18
νια εγγυς] **Ṭ**Ω̣**Ν Ϊ Є**[ροcολυμων ωc απο cταδιων
δ]**Є̣Κ̣Α̣ΠЄΝΤЄ· ΠΟ**[λλοι δε 19
3 **Є̣Κ̣ ΤΩΝ̣ Ϊ̣Ο̣Υ̣Δ̣ΑΙΩΝ ЄΛΗΛΥΘ**[ειcαν προc ταc π]**Є̣ΡΙ**
ΜΑΡΘΑΝ ΚΑΙ Μ[αριαν
ΪΝΑ ΠΑΡΑΜΥΘΗCΩΝΤΑΙ ΑΥ[ταc] **ΠΕΡ̣Ι̣ ΤΟΥ**
ΑΔЄΛΦΟΥ Η ΟΥΝ ΜΑΡΘΑ ΩC̣ 20
η]**ΚΟΥCЄΝ ΟΤΙ Ι̅Η̅ ЄΡΧЄΤΑΙ ΫΠΗ**[ν]**ΤΗCЄ̣Ν̣ ΑΥΤΩΙ·**
ΜΑΡΙΑ ΔЄ ЄΝ ΤΩΙ ΟΙΚΩ̣[ι
6 **ЄΚΑΘЄΖЄΤΟ· ЄΙΠЄΝ ΟΥΝ ΜΑΡΘ**[α] **Π̣ΡΟC ΤΟΝ Ι̅Η̅ Κ̅Є̅**
ЄΙ ΗC ΩΔЄ Ο Α[δελ 21
ΦΟC ΜΟΥ ΟΥΚ ΑΝ ΑΠЄΘΑΝЄΝ̣· ΑΛΛ̣[α κα]**Ι ΝΥΝ**
ΟΙΔ̣Α ΟΤΙ ΟC[α] **ΑΝ ΑΙΤΗ̣** 22
CΗC ΤΟΝ Θ̅Ν̅ ΔΩCЄΙ COI Ο Θ̅C̅· Λ[ε]**ΓЄΙ Α**[υτηι ο ι̅η̅
αν]**Α̣CΤΗCЄ̣**[τ]**Α̣Ι̣ Ο̣ ΑΔЄΛ̣Φ̣**[οc 23
9 **COY· ΛЄΓЄΙ ΑΥΤΩΙ ΜΑΡΘΑ· ΟΙΔΑ** [οτι αναcτηc]**ЄΤΑΙ**
ЄΝ Τ[ηι αναcτα 24
CЄΙ ЄΝ ΤΗΙ ЄCΧΑΤΗΙ ΗΜЄΡΑ ЄΙΠ[εν αυτηι ο ι]**Η̅ ЄΓΩ**
ЄΙΜ[ι η αναcτα 25
CIC· Ο ΠΙCΤЄΥΩΝ ЄΙC ЄΜЄ Κ̣ΑΝ Α̣[ποθανη ζη]**C̣ЄΙ·**
ΚΑ[ι παc ο ζων 26
12 **ΚΑΙ ΠΙCΤЄΥΩΝ ЄΙC ЄΜЄ ΟΥ Μ̣Η ΑΠ**[οθανη ειc τον
αιωνα πιcτευειc
ΤΟΥΤΟ· ΛЄΓЄΙ ΑΥΤΩΙ ΝΑΙ Κ̅Є̅ ЄΓΩ Π[επιcτευκα οτι
cυ ει ο χ̅c̅ ο υ̅c̅ του 27
Θ̅Υ̅ Ό ЄΙC ΤΟΝ ΚΟCΜΟΝ ЄΡ[χ]**ΟΜЄΝΟ**[c και ταυτα
ειπουcα απηλθεν και 28
15 **ЄΦΩΝΗCЄΝ ΜΑΡΙΑΝ ΤΗΝ ΑΔЄΛΦ**[ην αυτηc λαθρα
ειπουcα ο δι]**Δ**[α
CΚΑΛ̣ΟC ΠΑΡЄCΤΙΝ· ΚΑΙ ΦΩΝЄΙ CЄ [εκεινη ωc
ηκουcεν εγ]**Є̣ΙΡЄ** 29
ΤΑΙ ΤΑΧΥ· ΚΑΙ ЄΡΧЄΤΑΙ ΠΡΟC Α̣[υ]**ΤΟΝ· Ο**[υπω δε
εληλυθει ο ι]**Η̣̅ ЄΙC̣ Ṭ**[ην 30
18 **ΚΩΜΗΝ ΑΛΛ᾽ ΗΝ ЄΠΙ ΤΩ̣**[ι] **Ṭ̣ΟΠΩΙ** [οπου
υπηντηcεν αυ]**ΤΩΙ Μ**[αρ
ΘΑ· ΟΙ ΟΥΝ ΪΟΥΔΑΙΟΙ Ό̣Ι ΟΝΤ[εc] **ΜЄΤ᾽ Α**[υτηc εν τηι
οικια και] **ΠΑΡΑΜ̣**[υ 31

ΘΟΥΜΕΝΟΙ ΑΥΤΗΝ ΪΔΟΝΤ[εc τ]**ΗΝ Μ**[αριαν οτι
ταχεως ανεc]**ΤΗ ΚΑ**[ι
ε]**ΞΗΛΘΕΝ. ΗΚΟΛΟΥΘΗC**[αν αυτηι λεγον]**ΤΕC̣** [ο]**Ṭ**[ι
εις το μν]**Ḥ̣ΜΕΙΟ**[ν
υ]**ΠΑΓΕΙ ΪΝΑ ΚΛΑΥCΗ ΕΚΕ̣**[ι η ουν μαρ]**ΙΑ ΩC Η**[λθεν
οπου] **ΗΝ Ο Ι̅Η̅** 32
κα]**Ị ΪΔΟΥCΑ ΑΥΤΟΝ ΕΠΕC**[εν προς το]**ΥC ΠΟΔ**[α]**C**
Λ̣[εγουcα αυτωι
κ̅]**Ε̣̅ ΕΙ ΗC ΩΔΕ ΟΥΚ ΑΝ ΑΠ̣**[εθανεν μου ο αδελ]**Φ̣Ọ̣C̣·**
Ι[η̅ ουν ως ειδεν 33
αυ]**ΤΗΝ ΚΛΑΙΟΥCΑΝ ΚΑ**[ι τους ϊουδαιους κλαιο]**Ṇ̣ΤΑC**
Τ[ους cυνεληλυ
Θ̣ΟΤΑC ΑΥΤΗΙ ΕΤΑΡΑΧ̣[θη τωι π̅ν̅ι̅ ως
ενβριμ]**ΟΥΜΕṆO**[c και ειπε 34
π]**ΟΥ ΤΕΘΕΙΚΑΤΕ ΑΥ**[τον λεγουcιν αυτω κ̅ε̅ ερχου και
ιδε εδρακυcεν 35
ο] **Ι̅Η̅ · ΕΛΕΓΟΝ ΟΥ̣**[ν οι ϊουδαιοι ϊδε πως εφιλει αυτον τινες
δε 36 37
εξ α]**ΥṬ**[

Notes, F17r (Jn 11:17-37)

1. *ed. pr.* only records ink marks for this line
2. *ed. pr.*]ν ϊε[
   δεκα]πεντε πο[
3. *ed. pr.* εκ] των [ιου]δαιων εληλυ[θεισαν προς τας περ]
4. *ed. pr.* πε[ρι τ]ου
   ed. pr. ω[ς
5. *ed. pr.* ηκ]ουσεν
   ed. pr. ϋπη[ν]τησ[εν]
   ed. pr. οικ[ωι
7. *ed. pr.* αλ[λα
   ed. pr. οι[δ]α
   ed. pr. αιτ[η
8. *ed. pr.* λεγει
   ed. pr. αν]αστησ[εται ο]
9. *ed. pr.* has no point after μαρθα
   ed. pr. αναστη]σεται
11. *ed. pr.* [κ]αν [αποθανη ζησ]ει· κα[
14. *ed. pr.* ερχομενο[ς
15. *ed. pr.* αδελ[φην
15-16. the scrap of papyrus containing the few letters near the end of the line is reversed in the plate of *ed. pr.*, so that δ and ειρε are read on F17v
16. *ed. pr.* has δε after εκεινη. But there is not enough room
17. *ed. pr.* has no point after ταχυ
   ed. pr. [αυ]τον·
   ed. pr. ι̅η̅]
18. *ed. pr.* κωμην·
   ed. pr. τ[ωι] τοπωι
21. *ed. pr.* omits the point after [ε]ξηλθεν
   ed. pr. δοξαν]τε[ς οτι
22. *ed. pr.* εκ[ει
23. *ed. pr.* . .] ϊδουσα
   ed. pr. επεσ[εν αυτου προς το]
   ed. pr. ποδ[ας] λ̣εγουσ̣[α αυτωι (we do not consider this tiny piece of fragment to have been correctly placed, since the ↓ reading of *ed. pr.* cannot be correct)
24. κ̅]ε̅: only the end of the superline remains
25-6. the fragment of papyrus containing the final letters of the lines is misaligned
26. *ed. pr.* θ]οτας
   ed. pr. εταρα[χθη

28. *ed. pr.* ῑ]η̅
29. *ed. pr.* does not record this line

F17v
↓ (Jn 11:42-57)

] Ṇ [(42)
] . [ ]ΤΕΙΛΑϹ̣ Κ̣[αι] ΤΑΥΤΑ [ειπων 43
3 φω]ΝΗΙ ΜΕΓΑ[ληι εκραυγα]Ϲ̣ΕΝ [λαζ]Α̣Ρ̣[ε] ΔΕΥΡΟ
ΕΞ̣Ω̣· ΕΞΗΛ[θεν ο 44
τεθ]ΝΗΚΩϹ ΔΕΔΕ̣Μ̣Ε̣Ṇ[ο]Ϲ̣ [το]ΥϹ Π[οδ]Α̣Ϲ ΚΑΙ ΤΑϹ
ΧΕΙΡΑϹ ΚΗΡΙΔΙϹ ΚΑΙ
η ο]ΨΙϹ ΑΥΤΟΥ ϹΟΥΔΑ̣ΡΙΩΙ ΕΔΕ̣ΔΕΤΟ Λ̣[ε]Γ̣ΕΙ
Α̣ΥΤΟΙϹ Ο Ι̅Η̅ ΛΥϹΑΤΕ ΑΥΤΟΝ Κ[α]Ι
6 α]ΦΕΤΕ ΑΥΤΟΝ ΫΠΑΓΕΙΝ· ΠΟΛ[λ]Ο̣Ι ΕΚ [τ]ΩΝ
ΪΟΥΔΑΙΩΝ Ο̉Ι ΕΛΘΟΝΤΕϹ ΠΡΟϹ 45
τ]ΗΝ Μ[α]ΡΙΑΝ ΕΩΡΑΚΟΤΕ[ϲ] Α [ε]ΠΟΙΗ̣Ϲ̣ΕΝ
ΕΠΙϹΤΕΥϹΑΝ ΕΙϹ ΑΥΤΟΝ ΤΙ 46
ν]ΕϹ ΔΕ Ε̣[ξ αυ]ΤΩṆ Α̣ΠΗ̣[λθον] ΠΡΟϹ [τ]Ο̣ΥϹ
ΦΑΡΕΙϹΑΙΟΥϹ ΚΑΙ ΕΙΠΟΝ ΑΥ
9 τοιϲ α] Ε̣[π]Ο̣ΙΗϹΕΝ [ο ι̅η̅ ϲυνηγ]Α̣ΓΟΝ [ο]ΥΝ ΟΙ
ΑΡΧΙΕΡΕΙϹ ΚΑΙ ΟΙ ΦΑΡΕΙϹΑΙ 47
οι ϲυνε]Δ̣ΡΙΟΝ ΚΑΙ [ελεγον τι π]ΟΙ{ΗϹΟ} <ΟΥ> ΜΕΝ·
Ο̉ΥΤΟϹ Ο̉ ΑΝΘΡΩΠΟϹ ΠΟΛ
λα ποιει] ϹΗΜΕΙΑ̣ [εαν αφω]Μ̣ΕΝ ΑΥΤΟΝ ΟΥΤΩϹ.
ΠΑΝΤΕϹ ΠΙϹΤΕΥ 48
12 ϲουϲιν ειϲ] Α̣Υ̣Τ̣[ον και ελευϲοντ]Α̣Ι̣ ΟΙ Ρ̣Ω̣ΜΑΙΟΙ· ΚΑΙ
ΑΡΟΥϹΙΝ ΗΜΩΝ
και τον τοπον και το εθνοϲ] ΕΊϹ ΔΕ Τ̣ΙϹ ΕΞ ΑΥΤΩΝ
ΚΑΪΦΑϹ Α̣ΡΧΙΕ 49
ρευϲ ων του ενιαυτου εκειν]ΟΥ ΕΙΠΕ̣Ν ΑΥΤΟΙϹ ΫΜΕΙϹ
ΟΥΚ ΟΙΔΑΤΕ {Α}<Ο>Υ
15 δεν ουδε λογιζεϲθε οτι ϲυμ]ΦΕΡΕΙ ΥΜΙΝ ΪΝΑ ΕΊϹ
ΑΝΘΡΩΠΟϹ ΑΠΟ 50
θανη υπερ του λαου και μη ολ]ΟΝ ΤΟ ΕΘ̣ΝΟϹ
ΑΠΟΛΗΤΑΙ· ΤΟΥΤΟ̣ ΔΕ ΑΦ Ε 51
α]ΥΤΟ̣Υ̣ [ουκ ειπεν αλλα αρχι]ΕΡΕΥ[ϲ ω]Ν
ΕΠΡΟΦΗΤΕΥϹΕΝ ΟΤΙ ΗΜΕΛ
18 λ]ΕΝ Ι̅Η̣̅ [αποθνηϲκειν υπερ] ΤΟΥ Ε[θν]ΟΥϹ ΚΑΙ
{Υ}<Ο>ΥΧ ΥΠΕΡ̣ ΤΟ̣Υ ΕΘΝΟ[υϲ 52
μ]ΟΝΟ̣[ν αλλ ινα και τα τεκν]Α̣ ΤΟΥ [θ̅υ̅] Τ̣Α
ΕϹΚΟΡΠΙϹΜΕΝΑ ϹΥΝΑΓΑ[γη
ε]ΙϹ ΈΝ [απ εκεινηϲ ουν] Τ̣ΗϹ Η̣[μ]Ε̣ΡΑϹ
ΕΒΟΥΛΕΥϹΑΝΤΟ ΪṆ[α 53
21 Α̣ΠΟΚΤ̣[εινωϲιν αυτον ι̅η̅ ου]Ṇ [ουκ ετι] ΠΑΡΗϹΙΑ
ΠΕΡΙΕΠΑΤΕΙ̣ [εν 54

τ]**Ọ̣ΙϹ̣ ̣̈ΟΥ̣**[δαιοις αλλ]**Α ΑΠΗ**[λθεν εις τη]**Ν ΧΩΡΑΝ**
ЄΓΓΥϹ ΤΗϹ Є[ρη
μου εις ε]**Φ̣**[ραιμ] **Λ̣ЄΓΟΜЄ**[νην πολιν] **ΚΑΚЄΙ**
ΔΙЄΤΡЄΙΒЄΝ ΜЄ̣[τα
24 των μαθητ]**ΩΝ: Η**[ν δε εγγυς το π̣α̣σχ]**Α ΤΩΝ**
ΪΟΥΔΑΙΩΝ· ΚΑΙ Α̣[νε 55
βησαν πολ]**Λ̣ΟΙ ЄΙϹ** [ιεροσολυμα εκ της χ]**ΩΡΑϹ ΠΡΟ**
ΤΟΥ ΠΑϹΧΑ ΪΝ̣[α
αγνισω]**ϹΙΝ ЄΑΥΤ̣**[ους εζητουν ουν τον ι̅]**Η̅ ΚΑΙ ЄΛЄΓΟΝ**
ΜЄΤ [αλ 56
27 ληλων εν τω ιερω εστηκοτες τι δοκει υ]**Μ̣ΙΝ ΟΤΙ ΟΥ ΜΗ**
ЄΛΘ[η
εις την εορτην δεδωκεισαν δε οι αρχιερεις] **Κ̣ΑΙ ΟΙ ΠΡЄϹ**[57
]**Ϲ̣Η̣** [

Notes, F17v (Jn 11:42-57)

1. *ed. pr.* does not record this line
2. *ed. pr.*]ειλα[ς]
3. *ed. pr.* μεγα[λη ι εκραυγασεν λαζαρε] δευρο ε̣λ̣θ̣ε̣ ε̣ξ̣ω̣ κ[αι εξηλθεν ο
4. *ed. pr.* δεδε[μενος του]ς
   ed. pr. κειριαις
5. *ed. pr.* εδ[εδ]ετο [λε]γει
   ed. pr. και
6. *ed. pr.* υπαγειν πολ[λο]ι
   ed. pr. [τω]ν
7. *ed. pr.* μαριαν
   ed. pr. [ε]ποι[ησ]εν
8. *ed. pr.* [εξ αυ]τω[ν απηλθον
   ed. pr. [το]υς
9. *ed. pr.* τοισ α επ]
   ed. pr. has no ο before ι̅η̅
   ed. pr. συνηγα]γον
11. *ed. pr.* αφωμ]εν α[υ]τον
    ed. pr. has no point after ουτως
12. *ed. pr.* σουσιν... ελευσοντα]ι
    ed. pr. [ρω]μαιοι·
13. *ed. pr.* does not record the breathing over εις
    ed. pr. [τ]ις
14. *ed. pr.* ειπ[ε]ν
    ed. pr. does not record the correction. The scribe wrote alpha and then wrote omicron over it
15. the papyrus has a hole where a diaeresis over upsilon in υμιν would be
16. *ed. pr.* ε̣[θ]νος
17. see note to F17r, ll. 15-16, for the reversal of the fragment containing υτου
    ed. pr. ὁτι
18. *ed. pr.* has a point after ε[θν]ους
    ed. pr. does not record the correction. The scribe wrote upsilon and then wrote omicron over it
    the papyrus has a hole where a diaeresis over upsilon in υπερ would be
    ad fin. ed. pr. τ[ο]υ
19. *ed. pr.* θ̄[ῡ] τ̣α
20. *ed. pr.* η[με]ρας
    ed. pr. ϊ[να
21. *ed. pr.* α]ποκ[τεινωσιν
    ed. pr. ουν ουκετι]
    ed. pr. περιεπατε[ι εν
22. *ed. pr.* το]ις ιο[. The diaeresis over the initial letter is present, but there

is no trace of an iota

23. *ed. pr.* μ[ετα

24. *ed. pr.* των μ]αθητων· η[ν (see note on 17r, l. 23)
ed. pr. [ανε

25. *ed. pr.* βησαν] πολλοι εις [

26-28. *ed. pr.* does not attempt to supply what is lost beyond partly extant words

27. *ed. pr.* υμ]ιν

29. *ed. pr.* does not record this line

P[52]

→ (Jn 18:31-33)

ΟΙ ΪΟΥΔΑΙ[ο]**Ι̣ ΗΜЄ**[ιν ουκ εξεϲτιν αποκτειναι (31)
ΟΥΔЄΝΑ ΪΝΑ Ο Λ[ογοϲ του ι̅υ̅ πληρωθη ον ει 32
ΠЄΝ ϹΗΜΑΙΝΩ[ν ποιω θανατω ημελλεν απο
ΘΝΗϹΚЄΙΝ ΙϹ[ηλθεν ουν παλιν ειϲ το πραιτω 33
ΡΙΟΝ Ο Π[ειλατοϲ και εφωνηϲε τον ι̅ν̅
ΚΑΙ ЄΙΠ[εν αυτω ϲυ ει ο βαϲιλευϲ των ιου
δ]**ΑΙΩ**[

↓ (Jn 18:37-38)

Υ̣ΤΟ Γ[ε]**Γ̣Є̣ΝΝ̣Η̣ΜΑΙ** (37)
και εληλυθα ειϲ τον κο]**Ϲ̣ΜΟΝ ΪΝΑ ΜΑΡΤΥ̣**
ρηϲω τη αληθεια παϲ ο ων] **Є̣Κ̣ ΤΗϹ ΑΛΗΘЄ**[ι
αϲ ακουει μου τηϲ φωνηϲ] **Λ̣ЄΓЄΙ ΑΥΤΩ** 38
ο πειλατοϲ τι εϲτιν αληθεια κ]**Α̣Ι ΤΟΥΤΟ̣**
ειπων παλιν εξηλθε προϲ] **Τ̣ΟΥϹ ΙΟ̣**[υ
δαιουϲ και λεγει αυτοιϲ εγω ουδ]**ЄΜΙ**[

Notes (↓)

2. *ed. pr.* και <εις τουτο> εληλυθα... , with the note 'most probably we should reckon with the omission of the repeated εἰς τοῦτο' (p. 29)

P[55]

→ (Jn 1:31-33)

]**Ο̣Ν̣** (31)
αλλ ινα φανερωθη τω] **Ι̣Η̅Λ̅**
3 δια τουτο ηλθον εγω ε]**Ν̣ ΫΔΑ**
τι βαπτιζων] **Κ̣ΑΙ Є̣ΜΑΡΤΥ** 32
ρηcεν ιωανν]**Η̣C ΛЄΓΩΝ**
6 οτι τεθεαμαι τ]**Ο̣ Π̅Ν̅Α̅ ΚΑΤΑ**
βαινον ωc] **Π̣ЄΡΙCΤЄΡΑ̣Ν̣**
εξ ουρανου κ]**Α̣Ι ЄΜЄΙΝЄΝ**
9 επ αυτον κα]**ΓΩ ΟΥΚ ΗΔ̣Є̣Ι̣Ν** 33
αυτον αλλ ο] **Π̣ЄΜΨΑ̣C ΜЄ̣ Β̣Α̣**
πτιζειν εν] **Ϋ̣ΔΑΤΙ ЄΚЄ̣Ι̣ΝΟ̣**[c
12 μοι ειπεν ε]**Φ ΟΝ ΑΝ ΪΔ̣ΗC**
το π̅ν̅α̅ κατα]**Β̣ΑΙΝΟΝ̣ ΚΑΙ**
μενον επ α]**Υ̣ΤΟ̣Ν Ο̣ΥΤ̣ΟC̣**
15 εστιν ο βαπτιζων] **Є̣Ν Π̣̅**[ν̅ι̅

Notes

1. *ed. pr.* αυτο]ν̣
7. *ed. pr.* ως π]ερι̣στεραν
10-11. *ed. pr.* π̣εμψας με̣ [βα / πτιζειν εν υ]δατι εκε̣ι̣νος
15. *ed. pr.* ε]ν̣ π̅[τι (sic)

↓ (Jn 1:35-38)

Ṭ[η επαυριον παλιν ειϲτηκει 35
Ο Ι̣ΩΔ[ννηϲ και εκ των μα
Θ̣Η̣Τ̣Ω̣[ν αυτου δυο και εμβλε 36
ΨΑϹ ΤΩ Ι̅Υ̅ Π̣[εριπατουντι λε
ΓΕΙ ΕΙΔΕ̣ Ο̣ Α̣[μνοϲ του θ̅υ̅ και 37
ΗΚΟΥϹΑΝ Ο[ι δυο μαθηται αυ
ΤΟΥ ΛΑΛΟΥΝ[τοϲ και ηκολου
ΘΗϹ̣ΑΝ ΤΩ Ι̅Υ̅ [ϲτραφειϲ δε 38
Ο̣ Ι̅Ϲ̅ ΚΑΙ ΘΕΑϹ̣[αμενοϲ αυτουϲ
Α̣ΚΟΛΟΥΘΟΥΝ[ταϲ λεγει αυ
Τ̣ΟΙϹ ΤΙ ΖΗΤ[ειτε

Hermeneia beneath

Notes

The line length varies between 18 (line 2) and 23 (line 1) letters. Lines 3-7 all have 21 letters

3. *ed. pr.* θ̣η̣τ̣ω̣[ν] α̣[υτου
4. *ed. pr.* [περιπατουντι
8-9. *ed. pr.* ο] / ι̅ϲ̅

only the heading of the hermeneia is legible

P59

Fragments I & II

Note: We were unable to obtain photographs of these fragments. But the original has been consulted, and the *ed. pr.* compared with it.

Fragment I
→ (Jn 1:26)

] **Ι̣ΩΑ̣Ν̣**[νηc
λεγων εγω βα]**Π̣ΤΙΖΩ̣**
3 εν υδατι με]**C̣Ο̣C Ŷ M**[ων εc
τηκεν ον υμει]**C ΟΥ̣**[

Notes

1. *ed. pr.*]ωα̣ν̣[

↓ (Jn 1:28)

]**Α̣ ЄΝ ΒΗ̣**[θα
βαρα εγενετ]**Ο ΠЄΡ**[αν του
3 ιορδανου οπο]**Υ̣ Η̣Ν̣** [

Fragment II

Note: Although present, this fragment is out of place in its frame and partly obscured.

↓ (Jn 1:48)

]**Ϲ̣Ι̣Ϲ̣ ΑΠϹΚ̣**[ριθη
ο ι̅ϲ̅ προ] **Τ̣ΟΥ ϹϹ̣ Φ**[ιλιπ
πον φων]**Η̣ϹΑΙ ΟΝΤ̣**[α υπο την
ϲυκην ειδ]**Ο̣Ν** [

→ (Jn 1:51)

]**Α̣Ι̣Ν̣**[οντας επι τον
υιον] **ΤΟΥ Α̅Ν̅**[ο̅υ̅

Fragment III

↓ (Jn 2:15-16)

]̣ ̣[...] ̣ [(15)
]**Ϲ̣Τ̣Ω̣Ν̣** [εξεχεε
τα κερμ]**Α̣Τ̣Α ΚΑΙ̣ Τ̣Α̣**[ϲ τραπε
ζαϲ αυτ]**ΩΝ ΚΑΤ̣Ϲ̣**[ϲτρεψε
και τοιϲ] **Τ̣ΑϹ̣ Π̣ϹΡ̣Ι̣**[ϲτεραϲ 16
πωλουϲι]**Ν̣ ϹΙ̣Π̣**[εν αρατε
ταυτα ε]**Ν̣ΤϹΥ̣Θ̣**[εν μη
ποιειτε] **ΤΟΝ ΟΙ**[κον του
π̅ρ̅ϲ̅ μου] **ΟΙΚΟΝ̣** [

Notes (Fragment III)

3. *ed. pr.* μα]τ̣α
4. *ed. pr.* κατ̣[ε]σ[τρ

→ contains a line with traces of ink, a second transcribed by *ed. pr.* as
] ̣ υ̣[ ]τ̣ο[
and traces of a hermeneia. We have ignored it.

Fragment IV (a)
↓ (Jn 11:40-43)

Note: *Ed. pr.* records letters which cannot now be located at the end of lines 1-4. We record them, without bold face or upper case, and include them in the collation.

Λ̅ЄΓЄΙ ΑΥ̣[τη ο ι̅ϲ̅ ουκ ειπον ϲο]ι 40
ΟΤΙ ЄΑΝ̣ [πιϲτευϲηϲ οψ]η
ΤΗΝ Δ[οξαν του θ̅υ̅ ηρ]α̣ν 41
ου]**Ν Τ̣**[ον λιθον ηρεν] ο̣ ι̅[ϲ̅
ΤΟΥ̣[ϲ οφθαλμουϲ ανω
ΚΑΙ Є̣[ιπε π̅ρ̅ ευχαριϲτω
ϹΟΙ ΟΤ[ι ηκουϲαϲ μου
ЄΓΩ [δ]**Є̣ ΗΔΙ**[ν οτι παν 42
ΤΟΤЄ ΜΟΥ ΑΚ[ουειϲ αλλα δια
ΤΟΝ ΟΧΛΟΝ ΤΟ[ν περιεϲτω
ΤΑ ЄΙΠΟΝ ΙΝΑ [πιϲτευϲω
ϹΙΝ ΟΤ[ι] **ϹΥ Μ̣Є̣** [απεϲτειλαϲ
ΚΑΙ ΤΑΥΤΑ̣ [ειπων εκραυ 43
ΓΑϹЄΝ ΛΑΖ̣Α̣Ρ̣[

Hermeneia beneath

Notes

11. *ed. pr.* ι̂να. There is nothing visible over iota
12. *ed. pr.* οτι̣

Fragment IV (b)
→ (Jn 11:44-46)

Note: *Ed. pr.* records letters which cannot now be located at the beginning of lines 1-3. We record them, without bold face or upper case, and include them in the collation.

Εξ[ηλθεν ο τεθνη]**ΚΩC** 44
δε̣[δεμενος τους] **Π̣ΟΔΑC**
3 κα[ι τας χειρας κειρι]**ΑΙC**
και η οψιc αυτου cου]**ΔΑΡ̣**[ιω
περιεδεδε̲τ̲ο και λεγε]**Ι**
6 αυτοιc ο ι̅c̅ λυcατε] **Κ̣ΑΙ**
αφετε αυτον υπ]**Α̣Γ̣ΙΝ**
πολλοι ου]**Ν ЄΚ Τ̇**[ων] **ÎΟΥ** 45
9 δαιων οι ε]**ΛΘΟΝΤЄC ΠΡΟC**
την μαρια]**Μ ΚΑΙ ΘЄΑCΑ**
μενοι α ε]**Π̣ΟΙΗCЄΝ ЄΠΙ**
12 cτευcαν ειc α]**Υ̣Τ̣Ο̣Ν ΤΙ** 46
νεc δε εξ αυτ]**Ω̣Ν ΑΠΗΛ**
θον προc] **ΤΟΥ**[c] **ΦΑΡΙCΑΙ**
15 ουc και ειπο]**Ν** [α]**Υ̣ΤΟΙC**
α εποιηcεν] **Ο̣** [ ] . .

Hermeneia beneath

Notes

1. *ed. pr.* Εξ[ηλθεν ο τεθν]η̣κως
6. *ed. pr.* [αυτοις λυσατε αυτον]
16. *ed. pr.* [α εποιησ]ε̣[ν] ι̅ς̣̅. There are either one or two letters lost in the lacuna after **Ο̣**. The two subsequent letters would therefore need to be the beginning of verse 47

Fragment IV (c)
→ (Jn 11:47-48)

Note: Although we were able to obtain a photograph of the whole fragment, lines 1-5 could not be located for checking. In addition, *ed. pr.* records letters which cannot now be located in lines 9-10. We record them, without bold face or upper case, and include them in the collation.

C̄ ΥṆ[ηγαγον ουν οι αρχιε 47
ΡΙC Κ[αι οι φαριcαιοι cυνε
ΔΡ̣ΙΟ[ν και ελεγον τι ποι
ΟΥ[μεν οτι ουτος ο α̅ν̅ο̅c̅
Π[ολλα cημεια ποιει εαν
ΑΦ[ωμεν αυτον ουτω 48
ΠΑ̣[ντεc πιcτευcουcιν
ЄΙC̣ [αυτον και ελευcον
ΤЄ̣ [οι ρωμαιοι] κ̣αι ερ[ουcιν
ΗΜ[ων και το]ν̣ τ̣ο̣[πον
ΚΑΙ Τ̣[ο εθνοc

Notes

5. *ed. pr.* ποιει σημεια
ed. pr. records a hermeneia beneath the text. There appears to be a trace of ink visible below the last line

Fragment IV (d) (i) and (ii)
↓ (Jn 11:49-52) (lines 1-11 = (i) and 12-17 = (ii))

Note: Although we were able to obtain a photograph of the whole fragment, lines 1-5 could not be located for checking. In addition, *ed. pr.* records letters which cannot now be located in lines 5, 8-9 and 12. We record them, without bold face or upper case, and include them in the collation.

ειc δε τιc εξ αυτων] **ΚΑΙ̂ΑΦΑC** 49
αρχιερευc ων του] **Є̣ΝΙΑΥΤΟ̣Υ**
εκεινου ειπεν αυ]**Τ**[ο]**Ι̣C̣ Υ**
μειc ουκ οιδατε ου]**ΔЄΝ**
ουδε λογιζεcθε] **ΟΤΙ̣** 50
cυμφερει ημιν ι]**Ν̣Α ЄΙC**
α̅ν̅ο̅c̅ αποθανη υπε]**Ρ ΤΟΥ**
λαου] κ̣αι μ̣[η ολον το εθ]**ΝΟC**
απο]λητ[αι τουτο δε α]**Φ ЄΑΥ** 51
του ουκ ειπεν αλλα αρ]**ΧΙЄΡЄΥ̣C**
ων του ενιαυτου] **ЄΚΙ̣ΝΟΥ̣**
προεφητευcεν] **Ο̣ΤΙ ΜЄ̣**[λλει] ι̅c̅
αποθνηcκειν υ]**Π̣ЄΡ ΤΟΥ**
εθνουc και ουχ υ]**Π̣ЄΡ ΤΟΥ Є̣** 52
θνουc μονο]**Ν ΑΛΛ ΙΝΑ Κ̣ΑΙ**
τα] **Τ̣Є̣Κ̣ΝΑ̣ Τ̣ΟΥ Θ̣̅Υ̅ ΤΑ̣ Δ̣**[ιεc]**Κ̣ΟΡ**
ΠΙCΜЄΝΑ CΥΝΑΓΑΓΗ ЄΙC Є̣[ν

Hermeneia beneath

Notes

3. *ed. pr.* αυ]το̣ις υ̂
5. *ed. pr.* ουδε λογιζεσθα]ι οτι
6. *ed. pr.* υμιν
12. *ed. pr.* επροφητευσεν] ο̣τι μ̣ε̣λ̣[..] ι̅ς̅. This part of the papyrus is now obscured in its frame
13-14. *ed. pr.* υ]π̣ερ το̣υ ε̣-/[θνους

Fragment V
↓ (Jn 12:25)

] . [
] ΖΩΗΝ ΑΙΩΝ̣[
3] . [ ] . . [

→ (Jn 12:29)

]Η̣ΚΩϹ Κ̣[αι
ακουϲαϲ ελ]ΕΓΕΝ ΒΡΟΝΤΗ̣̅

Fragment VI
→ (Jn 12:31)

] Ε̣ϹΤΙΝ ΤΟΥ[

↓ (Jn 12:35)

ΕΙΠΕΝ ΟΥΝ̣ [αυτοιϲ ο ι̅ϲ̅ ετι
μι]Κ̣Ρ̣Ο̣[

Notes (Fragment VI ↓)

2. *ed. pr.* [μι]κ̣ρ̣[ον

Fragment VII

Although we were able to obtain a photograph, the fragment could not be located for checking.

↓ (Jn 17:24-26)

(24)
]Ω̣Ϲ̣Ι̣
την δοξαν την ε]**Μ̣ΗΝ**
ην εδωκαϲ μοι] **Ο̣Τ̣Ι̣ Η**
γαπηϲαϲ με] **Π̣ΡΟ ΚΑΤΑ**
βοληϲ κοϲ]**Μ̣ΟΥ ΠΕ̣Ρ ΔΙ** 25
καιε και ο κο]**Ϲ̣Μ̣Ο̣Ϲ̣ Ϲ̣Ε̣ Ο̣Υ̣Κ̣**
εγνω εγ]**Ω̣ ΔΕ** [ϲε] **ΕΓΝΩ**
οτι με απ]**ΕϹΤ̣**[ει]**ΛΑϹ ΚΑΙ** 26
] . . [ ] . . .

Notes

1. *ed. pr.* ωϲι](ν). We see no traces of this line in the photograph
2. *ed. pr.* θεωρ]ω̣ϲ̣ι̣(ν)
4. *ed. pr.* δεδωκας
9. *ed. pr.* [6-7 απ]

→ (Jn 18:1-2)

ΧΕΙ[μαρρου των κεδρων (1)
ΟΠΟ[υ ην κηποϲ ειϲ ον
ΕΙϹΗ[λ]**Θ̣**[εν αυτοϲ και οι μα
ΘΗΤΑΙ ΑΥΤ̣[ου ηδει δε 2
ΚΑΙ Ι̂ΟΥΔΑϹ Ο̣ [παραδιδουϲ
ΑΥΤΟΝ ΤΟΝ [τοπον οτι
ΠΟΛΛΑΚΙϹ Ϲ̣[υνηχθη ο ιϲ
Ε̣ΚΙ ΜΕΤ̣Α ΤΩ̣[ν μαθητων
Α̣[υ]**Τ̣Ο̣**[

Notes

1. *ed. pr.* χειμ̣[αρρου
3. *ed. pr.* ειϲη[λθεν
9. *ed. pr.* α̣[υ]τ̣[ου

Fragment VIII

Note: We were unable to obtain photographs of this fragment. But the *ed. pr.* has been compared with the original, and we therefore print it in bold uppercase characters.

→ (Jn 18:16-17)

]. . .[(16)
] **Κ̣ΑΙ ЄΙΠ̣**[ε
τη θυρωρ]**Ω̣ ΚΑΙ ЄΙ**[cηγ
αγε τον π]**Є̣ΤΡΟΝ** [λεγει 17
ουν τω πε]**Τ̣ΡΩ Η̣** [παι
δicκη η θ]**Υ̣Ρ̣ΩΡ̣**[oc μη
και cυ εκ τ]**Ω̣Ν Μ̣**[

Fragment VIII ↓ contains part of the heading ερμενεια

Fragment IX
↓ (Jn 18:22)

] Є̣Ι̣Ϲ̣ Τ̣Ω̣
παρεστωτων υ]Π̣ЄΡΔΙ
3 των ε]Δ̣Ω̣Κ̣ЄΝ ΡΑΠЄΙ
σμα τω] Ι̅Υ̅ ЄΙΠΩΝ ΟΥΤΩϹ
αποκρ]Ι̣ΝΗ ΤΩ ΑΡΧΙЄΡЄΙ

Hermeneia beneath

Notes
1. *ed. pr.*]α̣δ̣ ̣ ̣ ̣
there is no extant trace of a superscript line over omega
2. *ed. pr.* [7-9 υ]π̣ε̣ρα̣ι̣-

Fragment IX → contains part of a Hermeneia

Fragment X (a)
→ (Jn 21:7)

Ζ̣Ω̣[

Notes

For the location of this fragment, see *ed. pr*., p. 79f

Fragment XI
↓ (Jn 21:12-13)

]**Ξ̣**[ετασαι αυτον̲ cυ τις ει (12)
ЄΙΔ[οτες οτι ο κ̅c̅ εcτιν
ЄΡΧ̣[13

→ (Jn 21:15)

] . [. .] .
] **ΠΛΙ**
ον τουτων λεγει αυτω ναι] **Κ̅Є̅ CΥ**

Fragment XII
→ (Jn 21:17)

ΛΕΓΕΙ ΑΥΤ[ω το τριτον
ϹΙ̣ΜΩΝ [ιωαννου φι
ΛΕΙϹ ΜΕ ΕΛ[υπηθη ο πε
ΤΡΟϹ̣ ΟΤΙ Ε̣[ιπεν αυτω το
ΤΡΙ̣[τον ειπεν αυτω κ̅ε̅
ΠΑ̣[ντα ϲυ οιδαϲ ϲυ γι
Ν̣Ω̣[ϲκειϲ οτι φιλω
ϹΕ̣ Λ̣[εγει αυτω ο ι̅ϲ̅ βο
Ϲ̣[

Notes

3. *ed. pr.* ελυ[πηθη
5. *ed. pr.* τρι̣[τον 10-11. In a note, it suggests τρι[τον και ειπεν κ̅ε̅

↓ (Jn 21:18)

]**Ν̣ ΛΕΓΩ ϹΟΙ**
οτε ηϲ νεω]**Τ̣ΕΡΟϹ ΕΖΩ̅**
νυεϲ ϲεαυτο]**Ν̣ ΚΑΙ ΠΕΡΙ**
επατειϲ οπου] **Η̣Θ̣Ε̣Λ̣ΕϹ Ο**
ταν δε γηραϲηϲ εκ]**ΤΕΝΕΙϹ**
ταϲ χειραϲ ϲου και] **ΑΛΛΟΙ**
ϲε ζωϲουϲιν και α]**Π̣ΟΙϹΟΥ**
] . . [

Fragment X (c)
↓ (Jn 21:19-20)

ΚΑΙ ΤΟ̣[υ]**Τ̣**[ο ειπων λεγει αυ (19)
ΤΩ ΑΚΟΛ[ουθει μοι επι
CΤΡΑ̣ΦЄ̣ΙC Δ̣[ε ο πετροc βλε 20
ΠΙ ΤΟΝ ΜΑ[θητην ον η
ΓΑΠΑ Ο̣ Ι̣̅C̣̅ [ακολουθουντα οc
ΚΑΙ Α̣[νεπεcεν εν τω δει
ΠΝΩ̣ [επι το cτηθοc
Ι̣Υ̣ Κ̣[

Fragment X (d)
→ (Jn 21:23)

]**Ν̣ Ο̣ ΛΟ̣Γ̣Ο̣C**
ουτοc ειc το]**Υ̣C ΑΔЄΛ**
φουc οτι ο] **Μ̣Α̣ΘΗΤΗC**
εκεινοc ο]**Υ̣Κ̣ Α̣ΠΟΘ̣ΝΗ**
cκει ο̣υ̣κ ει]**Π̣Є̣Ν̣ ΔЄ ΑΥ**
τω ο ι̅c̅ οτι ουκ απο]**Θ̣ΝΗ**
cκει αλλ εαν αυτον] **ΘЄ**
λω μενειν εωc ε]**ΡΧΟ**

Notes

4. *ed. pr.* ου]κ̣
6. *ed. pr.* ο]υ̣κ̣ α̣[π]ο̣θνη

P[60]

General notes:

1. The papyrus has deteriorated considerably since its first publication. There are two problems, which we have handled in two quite separate ways. The first problem is that some parts of the fragments are no longer present, either in the frame or in our photographs. When this has occurred, we have adopted the reading of *ed. pr.*, printing its letters without bold face or upper case, and including them in the collation. The second problem is that there are a number of places where the papyrus is no longer legible. On these occasions we record only what can be seen, not what was read by *ed. pr.*

2. We consider various dots found in the papyrus to be accidental, and not punctuation (e.g. Fragment V→, line 5 after κοcμου).

Fragment I

Note: This fragment can no longer be located. We were able to obtain a photograph of the lower part of it. We record the fragment as it is transcribed in *ed. pr.*

↓ (Jn 16:29-30)

        ]ε̣ ν̣[υν εν παρρη (29)
    cια λαλ]ειc [και παροιμιαν
3   ουδεμι]αν [λεγειc νυν 30
    ο̣ι̣**Δ̣ΑΜ̣Є̣**ν [

Notes

1. the line seems unduly short without εν (not in our collating base), although we do not know the exact position of the extant letters above line 2

4. *ed. pr.* was able to read the whole of οιδαμεν. Only four letters are present in our plate

→ (Jn 16:32)

        ] ω̣ρ̣α̣ κ̣αι ε̣λ̣η̣[λυ
    θεν ινα cκορπι]c̣θ̣η̣[τε
3   εκαcτοc] ε̣ι̣c̣ **Τ̣Α Ι̣ΔΙΑ**
    καμε μονον] **ΑΦ**[

Fragment II
→ (Jn 16:33)

] . . . . . [
] **Є̣**[ι]**Ρ̣Η̣Ν̣**[ην εχητε
3 εν τ]**Ω̣ ΚΟϹΜ̣**[ω θλιψιν
εξε]**ΤΑΙ ΑΛΛΑ̣** [θαρϲειτε
Ν̣ЄΝΙΚΗΚΑ Τ̣[

Notes

2. *ed. pr.* ε̣ι̣ρ̣η̣ν̣[ην

↓ (Jn 17:1-2)

] **Ο̣ Ι̣̅Ϲ̅ ΚΑ̣**[ι (1)
επηρε τουϲ οφθα]**ΛΜΟ̣Υ̣Ϲ̣**
3 αυτου ειϲ τον ουρα]**ΝΟΝ** [και
ειπε π̅ε̅ρ̅ εληλυ]**Θ̣ЄΝ Η ΩΡΑ̣**
δοξαϲον ϲου] **ΤΟ̣Ν Υ̅Ν̅ Î Ν**[α
6 ο υ̅ϲ̅ δοξαϲη ϲ]**Є ΚΑΘΩ**[ϲ 2
εδωκαϲ αυτω ε]**Ξ̣ΟΥϹΙΑΝ̣**
παϲηϲ ϲαρκο]**Ϲ̣** [ι]**Ν̣**[α] **Π̣Α̣**[

Fragment III

↓ (Jn 17:3-4)

Note: *Ed. pr.* recorded two lines at the top which cannot now be located.

]ε̣ ε[cτιν (3)
] . [
3 τον μο]**ṆOṆ** [αληθινον θ̅ν̅
και] **ỌN ΑΠ̣**[εcτειλαc ι̅ν̅ χ̅ν̅
ε]**Γ̣Ω CЄ ЄΔΟ**[ξαcα επι τηc 4
6 γ]**HC TO Є̣**[ργον ετελειωcα
ο] **Δ̣Є̣ΔΩ̣**[

Notes

5. *ed. pr.* εγ]ω

→ (Jn 17:5-6)

Note: *Ed. pr.* recorded two lines at the top of this fragment, one at the end and letters throughout which cannot now be located.

] μ̣ε c̣[υ] π̣[ε]ρ̣ (5)
παρα cεαυτω] τ̣η δο̣[ξ]η̣
3 η ειχον] **Π̣Ρ̣Ο̣ Τ̣Ο̣Υ̣** τον
κοcμον ειν]α̣ι̣ **ΠΑΡΑ̣** cο ̣
εφανε]ρ**ΩCΑ COỴ** το̣ 6
6 ονομα το]**Ι̣C̣ Α̣̅Ν̅Ο̅Ι̅C̅ ΟΥC** δ̣[ε
δωκαc μο]ι̣ ε̣**Κ̣ Τ̣Ο̣Υ̣ Κ̣**[οc
μου cοι ηcα]ν̣ κ̣α̣μ̣[

Notes

1. no trace of a superline was visible to *ed. pr.*
4. *ed. pr.* states that the letter after σο cannot be iota, and is most likely to be upsilon

Fragment IV

→ (Jn 17:8-9)

] **Τ̣Α̣ ΡЄΙΜΑΤ**[α α δεδωκας (8)
μοι δ]**ЄΔΩΚΑ Α̣**[υτοις και αυ
3 τοι] **Є̣ΛΑΒΟΝ ΚΑ̣**[ι εγνωσαν
ΑΛΗΘΩϹ ΟΤΙ Π̣[αρα σου εξηλ
θ]**Ο̣Ν̣ ΚΑΙ ЄΠΙϹΤ̣**[ευσαν οτι συ
6 μ]**Є̣ ΑΠЄϹΤΙΛΑ**[ς εγω περι του
κο]**Ϲ̣ΜΟΥ ЄΡΩΤ̣**[ω αλλα περι 9
ων] **Δ̣ЄΔΩΚ**[

Notes

6. *ed. pr.* α̣πεστιλα̣ς̣

↓ (Jn 17:11)

]**ΙΜΙ ЄΝ Τ̣Ω̣** [κοσμω και
ουτοι εν τ]**Ω ΚΟϹΜΩ** [εισι και
3 εγω προς] **ϹЄ ЄΡΧΟΜЄ̣** [περ
αγιε τηρ]**Η̣ϹΟΝ ΑΥΤΟΥ̣Ϲ Є̣Ν̣**
τω ονομ]**Α̣ΤΙ ϹΟΥ Ω Δ̣ЄΔ̣**[ω
6 κας μοι ιν]**Α ΩϹΙΝ ЄΝ Κ̣Α̣**[

Notes

4. *ed. pr.* τηρη]σον

Fragment V

↓ (Jn 17:12-13)

]**ΤЄ ΗΜΗΝ Μ̣**[ετ αυτων (12)
εγω] **ЄΤΗΡΟ̣Υ̣**[ν αυτους εν
Τ̣[ω] **Ο̣ΝΟΜΑΤΙ** [cου ους δεδω
ΚΑC ΜΟΙ ΚΑΙ [εφυλαξα και
Ο̣Υ̣ΔЄ̣ΙC ЄΞ̣ ΑΥΤ̣[ων απωλε
το ε]**Ι̣ ΜΗ Ο Υ̣**[c̄ της απω
λ]**Є̣Ι̣Α̣C̣ ΙΝΑ Γ̣**[ραφη πλη
ρω]**Θ̣Η̣ ΝΥΝ** [δε προς cε 13
ερχομαι] **ΚΑ̣**[

Notes

3. *ed. pr.* τ̣ω ονοματ[ι
6. there is no visible trace of a line over υ, though there is a diagonal stroke above the space to its right. *Ed. pr.* reads υ[ιος
7. *ed. pr.* λει]α̣ς ι̣̂να η [
9. *ed. pr.* [. . .] . . . κα̣[ι

→ (Jn 17:14-15)

]**Α̣ ΑΥΤΟ**[ι]**C̣ Τ̣ΟΝ̣** (14)
λογον cου] **Κ̣Α̣Ι Ο ΚΟCΜΟC̣** [εμι
cηcεν αυτ]**ΟΥC ΟΤΙ ΟΥ**[κ ε]**Ι̣CΙ̣**[ν
εκ του κ]**Ο̣C̣ΜΟΥ ΚΑΘΩC ЄΓΩ**
ουκ ειμι] **Є̣Κ̣ ΤΟΥ ΚΟCΜΟΥ**
ουκ ερω]**Τ̣Ω ΙΝΑ ΑΡΗC Α̣Υ̣** 15
τους εκ το]**Υ̣ ΚΟC̣ΜΟΥ** [α]**Λ̣**[λ ινα
τηρηc]**Η̣C̣ Α̣ΥΤΟΥ̣**[

Notes

1. *ed. pr.* αυτο̣ι̣ς
2-7. the papyrus is now too darkened and shredded to be read. Our reconstruction is offered on the evidence of the photographs
2. *ed. pr.* σο]υ̣ κ̣α̣ι
3. *ed. pr.*] α̣υ̣τ̣ους
4. *ed. pr.* κο]σ̣μ̣ου
5. *ed. pr.* ειμ]ι̣ ε̣κ̣
6. *ed. pr.* ερ]ω̣τ̣ω ι̂να

7. *ed. pr.* εκ] τ̣ο̣υ̣ κοσ̣μ̣ου αλλ [

Fragment VI
→ (Jn 17:18-20)

]ΩϹ ЄΜЄ̣ Α̣Π̣[εϲτειλαϲ ειϲ (18)
Τ̣Ο̣Ν̣ ΚΟϹΜΟΝ [καγω απεϲτει
3 ΛΑ Α̣ΥΤΟΥϹ ЄΙϹ Τ̣Ο̣Ν̣ [κοϲμον
ΚΑ̣Ι̣ Υ̂ΠЄΡ ΑΥΤ̣Ω̣Ν̣ [εγω 19
ΑΓΙΑΖΩ ЄΜΑΥΤ̣Ο̣[ν ινα
6 ΩϹΙΝ ΚΑΙ ΑΥΤ̣Ο̣Ι̣ Η̣[γιαϲμε
ΝΟΙ ЄΝ ΑΛΗΘЄΙΑ̣ [ου πε 20
Ρ̣Ι̣ ΤΟΥ[τ]ΩΝ Δ̣Є̣ [ερωτω
9 μονον] Α̣ΛΛΑ Κ̣Α̣[

↓ (Jn 17:21-23)

] Π̣ΙϹΤЄΥϹΗ Ο̣[τι (21)
ϲυ με απεϲ]Τ̣Ι̣Λ̣ΑϹ ΚΑΓΩ [την 22
3 δοξαν ην] Δ̣ЄΔΩΚΑϹ Μ̣Ο̣Ι̣
δεδωκ]Α̣ Α̣ΥΤΟΙϹ Ι̂ΝΑ ΩϹ̣[ι]Ν
εν καθωϲ] Η̣ΜΙϹ ЄΝ ЄΓΩ Є̣[ν 23
6 αυτοιϲ κ]Α̣Ι ϹΥ ЄΝ ЄΜΟΙ Ι̂ΝΑ
ωϲιν τε]Τ̣ЄΛΙΩΜЄΝΟΙ
ειϲ εν ινα] Γ̣ΙΝΩ[ϲκ]Η Ο ΚΟϹ
9 μοϲ οτι ϲυ με] Α̣Π̣[εϲ]Τ̣ΙΛΑ[ϲ
και ηγαπ]Η̣ϹΑ̣[

Notes

5. *ed. pr.* εγω ε̣ν
6. *ed. pr.* κ̣αι
8. *ed. pr.* ιν]α γ̣ινωσ̣[κ]η
9. *ed. pr.* α]π̣[εσ]τ̣ιλ[ας

Fragment VII

↓ (Jn 17:24-25)

]**Ρ̣ Ο ΔЄΔѠ̣**[κας μοι θελω (24)
ι]**Ν̣**[α] **ΟΠΟΥ̣ Є̣Ι̣Μ̣**[ι εγω κακει
ν]**Ο̣Ι ѠCΙΝ ΜЄΤ̣**[εμου ινα
ΘЄѠΡΟΥCΙΝ Τ[ην δοξαν
ΤΗΝ ЄΜΗΝ ΗΝ̣ [εδωκας
ΜΟΙ ΟΤΙ ΗΓΑΠ[ηcαc με προ
ΚΑΤΑΒ̣Ο̣ΛΗC [κοcμου περ
δ]**ΙΚΑ̣Ι̣**[ε] **Κ̣Α̣Ι̣ Ο** [κοcμοc 25
cε] **ΟΥΚ̣** [εγ]**ΝѠ̣**[

Notes

8. *ed. pr.* δ]ι̣κ̣α̣[ιε κ]α̣ι̣

→ (Jn 18:1-2)

]**Ν̣ Ο̣ Ι̣С̣̅** **ЄΞΗΛΘ**[ε (1)
cυν τοιc μαθ]**Η̣ΤЄC Α̣ΥΤ̣**[ου
περαν τ]**Ο̣Υ̣ ΧΙΜΑΡΡΟΥ**
των κε]**Δ̣Ρ̣ѠΝ ΟΠΟΥ ΗΝ**
κηποc ει]**C̣ Ο̣Ν̣ ЄΙCΗΛΘЄΝ**
αυτοc και οι] **ΜΑΘΗΤЄ**
αυτου ηδει] **ΔЄ ΚΑΙ Ι̂ΟΥ** 2
δαc ο παρα]**Δ̣ΙΔ̣**[ου]**C Α̣ΥΤ̣Ο**[ν
τον τοπο]**Ν̣ ΟΤ̣**[

Fragment VIII
→ (Jn 18:4-5)

] Ο̣Υ̣Ν Ε̣ΙΔ̣[ωc παντα τα ερ (4)
Χ̣[ο]Μ̣Ε̣ΝΑ̣ [επ αυτον εξηλ
ΘΕΝ ΕΞΩ Κ̣[αι ειπεν αυτοιc
ΤΙΝΑ ΖΗΤΙΤΕ̣ [απεκριθηcαν αυτω 5
Ι̅Ν̅ ΤΟΝ ΝΑΖΩΡ̣[αιον λεγει
ΑΥΤΟΙC ΕΓΩ Ε̣[ιμι ειcτηκει
ΔΕ ΚΑΙ Ι̂ΟΥΔΑ̣C̣ [

Notes

7. *ed. pr.* records nothing for this line. This is evidently an error, for the letters are clear

↓ (Jn 18:7-9)

]ΩΤΗ̣C[εν (7)
αυτουc τινα ζ]ΗΤΙΤΕ Ο̣Ι ΔΕ̣
ειπον ι̅ν̅] ΤΟ̣Ν ΝΑΖΩΡΕ̣Ο̣Ν̣
απεκριθη] Ι̣̅C̣̅ Ε̣ΙΠΟΝ Υ̂ΜΙΝ 8
οτι εγω ει]Μ̣Ι ΕΙ ΟΥΝ ΕΜΕ̣
ζητειτε αφ]Ε̣ΤΕ ΤΟΥΤΟΥC
υπαγειν ινα] Π̣Λ̣Η̣Ρ̣ΩΘΗ Ο̣ 9
λογοc ον ειπε]Ν ΟΤ[ι ο]Υ̣C̣ Δ̣Ε̣Δ̣[

Notes

7. *ed. pr.* π̣λ̣[η]ρ̣ω̣θη̣ ο λ̣[ο

Fragment IX
↓ (Jn 18:10-11)

]Μ̣ⲰΝ̣ ΟΥΝ Π̣[ετρος εχων 10
ΜΑΧΑΙΡΑΝ ΗΛΚΥ̣[cεν αυτην
ΚΑΙ ЄΠЄCЄΝ ΤΟΝ̣ [του αρχιε
ΡЄⲰC ΔΟΥΛΟΝ ΚΑ̣[ι απεκοψεν
ΑΥΤΟΥ ΤΟ ⲰΤΑΡ[ιον το δε
ΞΙΟΝ ΗΝ ΔЄ ΟΝΟ[μα τω δου
λ]Ⲱ ΜΑΛΧΟC Є̣Ι̣Π̣[εν ουν ο ι̅c̅ 11
τ]Ⲱ̣ ΠЄΤΡ̣Ⲱ Β̣Α̣[λε την μα
χα]Ι̣Ρ̣Α̣Ν̣ Є̣[ι]C̣ Τ̣Η̣Ν̣ [

Notes

1. *ed. pr.* σ̣[ι]μ̣ω̣ν̣

→ (Jn 18:12-14)

]α̣ ΚΑΙ Ο Χ̣Ι̣Λ̣Ι̣Αρχο[c (12)
και οι υπηρε]ΤЄ ΤⲰΝ̣ ΙΟΥ̣
δαιων cυ]ΝЄΛΑΒΟΝ ΤΟΝ Ι̅Ν̅
και εδηc]Α̣Ν ΑΥΤΟΝ ΚΑΙ Α 13
πηγαγον] ΠΡΟC ΑΝΝΑΝ
πρω]Τ̣ΟΝ ΗΝ ΓΑΡ ΠЄΝΘЄ
ρος του κ]ΑΙ̂ΑΦΑ ΟC ΗΝ ΑΡΧ
ιερευc ην] Δ̣Є ΚΑΙ̂ΑΦΑC C̣ΥΜ̣ 14
βουλευcac] Τ̣Ο̣Ι̣C̣ ΙΟΥΔΑ[

Notes

1. a piece of papyrus has been lost from each end of this line
3. *ed. pr.* σ]υ̣ν̣ε̣λαβο̣ν
4. *ed. pr.* εδησα]ν

Fragment X
→ (Jn 18:15-16)

ḤKỌΛOỴΘI Δ̣Ϲ̣ [τω ι̅υ̅ ϲιμων 15
ΠϹTPOϹ Ḳ ΔI Ọ [αλλοϲ μαθη
THϹ O ΔϹ MΔΘḤ[τηϲ εκεινοϲ
ḤN ΓNΩϹTOϹ Ṭ Ω̣ [αρχιερει και
Ϲ̣YNIϹ̣HΛΘϹN Ṭ Ω̣ [ι̅υ̅ ειϲ την
ΔYΛHN TOY Δ̣P̣X̣[ιερεωϲ
o] ΔϹ ΠϹTPOϹ̣ Ị[ϲτηκει προϲ 16
τ]Ḥ ΘYPΔ̣ Ϲ̣ΞΩ̣ Ϲ̣Ξ̣[

Notes

2. *ed. pr.* κ̣α̣ι̣ α̣λ̣λ̣ο̣[ς
3. *ed. pr.* μαθη̣τ̣η̣[ς
7. *ed. pr.* ι̣σ̣[τηκει

↓ (Jn 18:18)

]Ị ΔOYΛOI KΔI O[ι
υπηρεται ανθ]P̣ΔKIΔN ΠϹ
ποιηκοτεϲ ο]Ṭ I ΨYXOϹ HN KΔI
εθερμαινοντο] HN ΔϹ KΔI O
πετροϲ μετ] ΔYTΩN ϹϹTΩϹ̣
και θερμαινο]MϹNOϹ

Fragment XI

↓ (Jn 18:19-20)

] **ΟΥΝ ΑΡΧΙ̣Ε̣Ρ̣**[ευϲ ηρωτηϲε (19)
τ]**ΟΝ Ι͞Ν͞ ΠΕΡ**[ι] **Τ̣**[ων μαθητων
α]**ΥΤΟΥ ΚΑΙ ΠΕΡ**[ι τηϲ διδαχηϲ
α]**ΥΤΟΥ ΑΠΕΚΡΙ**[θη αυτω ο ι͞ϲ͞ 20
ε]**ΓΩ ΠΑΡΡΗϹΙ̣Α̣** [ελαληϲα τω
κ]**ΟϹΜΩ ΕΓΩ Π̣**[αντοτε εδι
δ]**ΑΞΑ ΕΝ ϹΥΝ**[αγωγη και εν
τω] **Ι̣̂ΕΡΩ** [ο]**Π̣Ο̣**[υ παντοτε οι ιου
δαιοι] **Ϲ̣Υ̣Ν̣**[

Notes

6. *ed. pr.* κ̣οϲμω

→ (Jn 18:23-25)

] **Ι̣Ϲ̣ ΕΙ ΚΑΚΩ̣**[ϲ (23)
ελαληϲα μαρ]**ΤΥΡΗϹΟΝ ΠΕ̣**
ρι του κακ]**Ο̣Υ ΕΙ ΔΕ ΚΑΛΩϹ**
τ̅ι̅ με δερει]**Ϲ̣ ΑΠΕϹΤΙΛΕΝ Ο̣Υ̣**[ν 24
ι̅ν̅ ο ανναϲ δε]**ΔΕΜΕΝΟΝ ΠΡ̣**[οϲ
τον καιαφαν] **Τ̣Ο̣Ν ΑΡΧΙΕΡΕΑ** [ην 25
δε ϲιμων πετ]**Ρ̣ΟϹ ΜΕΤ ΑΥΤ**[ου
εϲτωϲ και θε]**Ρ̣ΜΕΝΟΜ**[

Notes

4-5. *ed. pr.* δερει]ς... ο̣υ̣[ν] / [ca. 10] ̣ δεμενον
5-6. *ed. pr.* π̣ρ̣[ος] / [ca. 10] τ̣ο̣ν̣
7. *ed. pr.* πε]τ̣ρ̣ος

Fragment XII
→ (Jn 18:26-27)

Λ̣ΕΓΕΙ ΕΙϹ ΕΚ ΤΩ̣[ν δουλων 26
ΤΟΥ ΑΡΧΙΕΡΕΩϹ [ϲυγγενηϲ
3 ΩΝ ΟΥ ΑΠΕΚΟΨ̣[ε πετροϲ
Τ̣Ο ΩΤΙΟΝ ΟΥΚ̣ Ε̣[γω ϲε ειδον
Ε̣Ν ΤΩ ΚΗΠΩ̣ [μετ αυτου
6 Π̣ΑΛΙΝ ΟΥΝ Η̣[ρνηϲατο 27
ο] ΠΕΤΡ̣[ο]Ϲ̣ ΚΑ̣[ι ευθεωϲ
αλ]Ε̣Κ̣[

Notes

6. *ed. pr.* η̣ρ̣[νησατο

↓ (Jn 18:28-29)

]Ν ΤΟΝ Ι̅Ν̅ ΑΠΟ ΤΟ[υ (28)
καιαφα ει]Ϲ̣ ΤΟ ΠΡΑΙΤΩΡ̣Ι̣Ο̣[ν
3 ην δε πρ]Ω̣Ι̣ ΚΑΙ ΑΥΤΟΙ ΟΥΚ̣
ειϲηλθο]Ν̣ ΕΙϹ ΤΟ ΠΡΑΙΤΩ
ριον ινα] Μ̣Η̣ ΜΙΑΝΘΩϹΙΝ
6 αλλ ινα φα]Γ̣ΩϹΙ ΤΟ ΠΑϹΧ̣[α
εξηλθε]Ν̣ ΟΥΝ̣ Ο̣ ΠΙΛΑ[τοϲ 29
] . . [

Notes

1. *ed. pr.* ο]υ̣ν̣
8. *ed. pr.* ... αυτου]ς κ̣[αι

Fragment XIII

↓ (Jn 18:31)

ЄΙΠЄΝ ΟΥΝ̣ Α̣Υ̣[τοιϲ ο πιλα
ΤΟϹ ΛΑΒЄΤЄ [αυτον υμειϲ
3 ΚΑΙ Κ̣ΑΤΑ ΤΟΝ̣ [νομον
ΗΜΩΝ ΚΡΙΝ[ατε αυτον
ЄΙΠΟΝ ΟΥΝ Α̣[υτω οι ιου
6 Δ̣ΑΙΟΙ Η̣̂[μ]Ι̣Ν [
] . . [

Notes

6. *ed. pr.* η̣̂[μ]ι̣ν ο̣[υκ
7. *ed. pr.* [α]π̣[ο]κ̣τ̣[ειναι ουδενα ινα]

→ (Jn 18:32-33)

] Τ̣ΟΥ Ι̅Υ̅ ΠΛΗΡΩΘΗ̣ (32)
ον ειπε] Ϲ̣ΗΜЄΝΩΝ
3 ποιω θα]ΝΑΤΩ ΗΜЄΛΛЄ[ν
αποθν]Η̣ϹΚΙΝ ЄΞΗΛΘЄΝ̣ 33
ουν ειϲ] ΤΟ ΠΡΑΙΤΩΡΙ̣[ον
6 παλιν κ]Α̣Ι ЄΙ̣Π̣ЄΝ ΑΥΤ̣[ω ϲυ
ει ο βαϲι]Λ̣Є̣[υϲ] Τ̣ΩΝ Ι̣Ο̣[

Notes

3. *ed. pr.* θ]α̣ν̣ατω
5. *ed. pr.* πραιτωρι̣ο̣[ν

Fragment XIV
→ (Jn 18:34-35)

]ЄΚΡΙΘΗ̣ Ο̣ [ι̅ϲ̅ αφ εαυ (34)
Τ̣Ο̣Υ̣ ΤΟΥΤ̣Ο̣ [λεγειϲ η αλ
λ]Ο̣Ι Ϲ̣ΟΙ ЄΙ̣ΠΟ̣Ν̣ [περι εμου
ΑΠЄΚ̣ΡΙΘ[η ο πιλατοϲ 35
Μ̣Η̣[τ]Ι̣ Є̣γω̣ [ιουδαιοϲ ειμι
Τ̣Ο ЄΘΝ̣[ο]ϲ̣ το̣ ϲ̣[

Notes

5-6. a piece of papyrus has been lost. We follow *ed. pr.*
ed. pr. recorded illegible ink marks in a seventh line

↓ (Jn 18:36)

] Η̣ ΒΑϹΙΛЄΙ[α η ε (36)
μη ουκ εϲτ]ΙΝ ЄΚ ΤΟΥ̣ [κοϲ
μου του]Τ̣Ο̣Υ̣ ЄΙ ЄΚ ΤΟ[υ
κοϲμου του]ΤΟΥ ΗΝ Η ΒΑ[ϲι
λεια η εμη ο]ι ΥπΗ̣Ρ̣ЄΤЄ
οι εμοι ηγω]ν̣ι̣ζο̣ν̣ΤΟ ΑΝ̣
ινα μη παρ]α̣δ̣ο̣[θ]Ω ΤΟ̣[
] . [

Notes

5. *ed. pr.* ῦπ̣ηρ̣ετε
5-7. a piece of papyrus has been lost. We follow *ed. pr.*
8. *ed. pr.*] β̣[α

Fragment XV
↓ (Jn 18:37)

]**Π̣ЄΚΡΙΘΗ Ι̣**[c̄ cυ λεγειc οτι
βαcι]**ΛЄΥϹ ЄΙΜ̣**[ι εγω ειc του
3 **Τ̣Ο Γ̣ЄΓЄΝΝΗ̣**[μαι και ειc του
ΤΟ ЄΛΗΛΥΘ̣[α ειc τον κοcμον
Ι̣Ν̣Α̣ Μ̣[α]**Ρ̣Τ̣**[υρηcω τη αλη
6 **ΘЄΙΑ Π̣**[α]**Ϲ Ο Ω̣**[ν εκ τηc
αλ]**Η̣ΘЄΙ**[

Notes

ed. pr. recorded traces of ink in two lines at the beginning of this fragment
1. *ed. pr.* απ]εκρ̣ιθη ι̣ς̄
2. *ed. pr.* βασ]ι̣λευς
5. *ed. pr.* ῑ̣ν̣α̣ μ̣α̣ρ̣τ̣[

→ (Jn 18:39-40)

]**Ν̣ΗΘΙΑ Υ̂Μ**[ιν (39)
απολε]**Ϲ̣ΘΑΙ ΤΟ Π**[αcχα
3 βουλεc]**Θ̣Α̣Ι̣ ΟΥΝ ΑΠΟ**
λυcω υμιν το]**Ν ΒΑϹΙΛЄΑ**
των ιουδα]**Ι̣Ω̣Ν̣ Є̣**[κραυ 40
6 γαcαν ουν] **ΠΑΛ̣**[ι]**Ν̣ ΛЄ**
γοντεc μη τουτο]**Ν̣ ΑΛ**[

Notes

ed. pr. recorded traces of ink in a line at the top of this fragment
5. we follow *ed. pr.* Nothing is legible now

Fragment XVI

→ (Jn 19:2-3)

]Ị ΟΙ CΤΡ[ατιωται πλε (2)
Ξ̣[α]**Ν̣**[τε]**C CΤ̣**[εφανον εξ α
3 **ΚΑΝΘΩΝ** [επεθηκαν
Α̣Υ̣ΤΟΥ Τ̣Η̣ [κεφαλη και πορ
φυ̣**Ρ̣Ο̣Υ̣Ν̣** ῑ̣μ̣[ατιον πε
6 **ΡΙЄΒΑ**[λ]ο̣ν α̣[υτον και ηρ 3
Χ̣Ο̣[

Notes

2. *ed. pr.* ξα̣ν̣[τ̣]ες
4. *ed. pr.* τ[η
5-6. we follow *ed. pr.*, which found letters no longer present

↓ (Jn 19:5-6)

]ΞΩ ΦΟ̣[ρων (5)
τον ακανθινο]**Ν CΤЄΦ**[ανον
3 και το πορφυ]**Ρ̣ΟΥ̣Ν Ι̣Μ̣Α̣Τ̣**[ιον
και λεγει αυτοις] **Ι̣̂ΔΟΥ Ο ΑΝΟ̅**[c̄
οτε ουν ειδο]**Ν̣ Α̣ΥΤ**[ο]**Ν̣** [οι αρχ 6
6 ιερεις και οι υπηρε]**ΤЄ̣ Є̣**
κραυγασαν λεγον]**Τ̣ЄC CΤ̣**[

Notes

2. *ed. pr.* ακανθιν]ο̣ν
3. *ed. pr.* πορφ]υ̣ρουν̣ ῑ̣μ̣α̣τ̣[ιον
5. *ed. pr.*]ν αυτ[ο]ν̣ ο̣ι̣ [
6. *ed. pr.*] υ̣πη̣ρ̣ε̣τε

Fragment XVII

↓ (Jn 19:7-8)

]ΚΡΙΘΗϹ̣Α̣[ν αυτω οι ιου (7)
ΔΑ̣[ιο]**Ι̣ Η̣ΜΙϹ Ν**[ομον εχομεν
3 **ΚΑΙ̣ Κ̣Α̣ΤΑ Τ**[ο]**Ν̣** [νομον ημων
ο]**ΦΙΛΙ ΑΠ**[οθανειν οτι υ̅ν̅ του
Θ̣Υ Ε[α]**ΥΤΟΝ Ε̣**[ποιηϲεν οτε 8
6 ο]**Υ̣Ν ΗΚ̣Ο̣Υ̣Ϲ̣Ε̣**[ν ο πιλατοϲ
το]**ΥΤΟ**[

Notes

2. *ed. pr.* δ̣α̣[ιοι]
3. *ed. pr.* τ̣ο̣ν
5. *ed. pr.* ε̣π̣[οιηϲεν

→ (Jn 19:10-11)

] **Π̣ΙΛΑΤΟ̣**[ϲ εμοι ου (10)
λαλειϲ ουκ] **Ο̣ΙΔΑϹ̣ Ο̣ΤΙ̣** [ε]**Ξ̣ΟΥ̣**
3 ϲιαν εχω απ]**Ο̣Λ̣ΥϹΕ ϹΑ̣Ι ΚΑ**[ι εξ
ουϲιαν εχω] **Ϲ̣ΤΑΥΡΩ̣ϹΕ̣** [ϲε
απεκριθη αυ]**ΤΩ Ο Ι̅Ϲ̣̅** [ουκ ειχεϲ 11
6 εξουϲιαν κατ] **Ε̣ΜΟΥ̣** [ου
δεμιαν ει μη ην δ]**Ε**[

Notes

2. *ed. pr.* ο̣τ̣[ι ε]ξου̣-
3. *ed. pr.* ϲ̣.ι̣
7. *ed. pr.* δ̣ε̣[δ-

Fragment XVIII
→ (Jn 19:12-13)

Ọ[ι] Δ̣[ε ε]**ΚΡΔΥ̣Γ̣**[αζον λεγοντες (12)
ЄΔṆ ṬỌỤṬΟΝ Δ̣[πολυcηc
ΟΥΚ Ι ΦΙΛΟC Τ[ου καιcαροc
ΠΔ[c] **Ο ΒΔCΙ**[λεα αυτον
ΠΟΙ̣ѠΝ ΔΝΤ[ιλεγει τω καιcα
Ρ̣Ι Ο ΟΥΝ ΠΙΛ̣[ατοc ακου 13
cα]**C ΤѠΝ** [λ]**Ọ**[γων τουτων
ηγαγ]**Є̣Ṇ** [

Notes

4. *ed. pr.* πα̣ς̣

↓ (Jn 19:14-15)

]**ΟΥΔΔ**[ιοιc 14
ιδε ο βαcιλευ]**C Ŷ̂ΜѠ**[ν] **ỌỊ Δ̣Є** 15
εκραυγαcαν] **ΛЄΓΟΝṬЄC**
αρον αρον c]**ṬΔΥΡѠC**[ο]**Ν ΔΥΤỌ̄**
λεγει αυτοι]**C̣ Ο ΠΙΛΔΤΟC**
τον βαcιλε]**Δ̣ ŶΜѠΝ CΤΔ**[υ
ρωcω απεκ]**ΡỊ**[θ]**ΗCΑΝ Ọ**[ι
αρχιερειc ο]**ΥΚ Є̣Χ̣**[

Notes

1. *ed. pr.*] ι̣̂ουδα[ιος
6. *ed. pr.* σταυ̣-
7. *ed. pr.* [οι]

Fragment XIX

↓ (Jn 19:16-18)

] **ΔЄ** π̣α̣**Ρ̣**[αλαβοντεϲ τον ι̅ν̅ (16)
Α̣π̣[η]**Γ̣Α̣ΓΟ̣Ν Κ̣**[αι βασταζων 17
εαυ**ΤΩ ΤΟΝ C**[ταυρον εξηλ
θεν **ЄΙC ΤΟΝ** [λεγομενον
κρ**ΑΝΙΟΥ Τ**[οπον οϲ λεγε
τ̣α̣**Ι̣ ЄΒΡΑΪ̂CΤ̣**[ι γολγοθα οπου 18
α]**Υ̣ΤΟΝ ЄC**[ταυρωϲαν και
με]**Τ̣ ΑΥ**[

Notes

1-6. we include letters no longer present, read by *ed. pr.*

→ (Jn 19:20)

] τ̣ο̣**Ν Τ**ι̣τ**Λ**[ον
πολλοι ανε]**ΓΝΩC**α̣ν̣ τ̣ων
ιουδαιων] ο̣**ΤΙ** ε**ΓΓΥC ΗΝ**
ο τοποϲ τηϲ] **ΠΟΛЄΩC**
οπου εϲταυ]**ΡΩΘΗ Ο Ι̣̅C̅**
και ην γεγρα]**ΜΜЄΝΟ**[ν
εβραιϲτι ρωμα]**Ι̂CΤ**[

Notes

1-3. we include letters no longer present, read by *ed. pr.*
7. there is nothing to allow us to determine the order of the words εβραιϲτι ελληνιϲτι ρωμαιϲτι, except that there is insufficient space for ελληνιϲτι to have come first or second

Fragment XX
→ (Jn 19:23)

Ο̣[ι ο]**Υ̣Ν** [cτρατιωται οτε ε
Ϲ̣ΤΑΥ̣ΡΩϹ̣Α̣Ν̣ [τον ι̅ν̅ ελα
3 **ΒΟΝ ΤΑ Ι̣Μ̣Α̣Τ̣**[ια αυτου και
επο]**Ι̣Η̣Ϲ̣Α̣**[ν τεccαρα μερη
εκαc]**ΤΩ ϹΤ̣**[ρατιωτη με
6 ρο]**Ϲ̣ ΚΑΙ̣ ΤΟΝ** [χιτωνα ην
δε] **Ο̣ ΧΙΤ̣**[

Notes

3. *ed. pr.* ι̣̑μ̣α̣τ̣

↓ (Jn 19:24-26)

]**Α̣Ι̣ Τ**[αυτα ε (24)
ποιηcαν ει]**ϹΤΗ̣Κ̣ΙϹΑΝ** [δε 25
3 παρα τω] **Ϲ̣Τ̣Α̣Υ̣ΡΩ ΤΟΥ** [ι̅υ̅ η
μ̅η̅ρ̅ αυτου κ]**Α̣Ι̣ Η̣ Α̣**[δε]**Λ̣**[φη
τηc μ̅ρ̅c̅ α]**Υ̣ΤΟΥ** [μαρια
6 η μαγδαλη]**ΝΗ Ι̅Ϲ̅** [ουν ι 26
δων την μ̅ρ̅]**Α̣ ΚΑΙ** [

P63

First Page
→ (Jn 3:14-15)

ΡΙΒ

ΚΑΘΩ̣Ϲ̣ Μ̣ΩΫϹΗϹ ΫΨΩ 14
ϹΕΝ ΤΟΝ ΟΦΙΝ Ε̣Ν ΤΗ ΕΡΗ̣
ΜΩ ΟΥΤΩϹ ΫΨΩΘΗΝΑΙ
ΔΕΙ ΤΟΝ ΥΙΟΝ ΤΟΥ ΑΝΘ̣Ρ̣Ω̣
ΠΟ̣[υ ινα] ΠΑϹ Ο Π[ιϲτευ 15
Ω[ν ειϲ] Α̣ΥΤΟΝ ΜΗ ΑΠΟ
ΛΗ̣Τ̣[αι αλ]Λ᾽ ΕΧ̣Η̣ ΖΩΗΝ
ΑΙΩΝΙΟΝ

Hermeneia beneath

Notes

1. *ed. pr.* καθω[ς Μ]ωῡσης
7. *ed. pr.* λ[ηται αλλ]α εχη

Second Page
↓ (Jn 3:16-18)

Ρ̅Ι̅Γ̅

ΟΥΤⲰϹ ΓΑΡ ΗΓΑ[πη]**ϹЄΝ Ο ΘЄ** 16
Ο̣Ϲ ΤΟΝ ΚΟϹΜΟΝ Ⲱ̣Ϲ̣[τε] **ΤΟΝ ΥΙ**
Ο̣Ν ΑΥΤΟΥ ΤΟΝ̣ [μονογ]**Є̣**[νη] **ЄΔⲰ**
ΚЄΝ ЄΙϹ ΤΟ[ν κοϲμ]**ΟΝ ΪΝΑ Ο̣ ΠΙ**
ϹΤЄΥⲰΝ ЄΙϹ [αυ]**Τ̣**[ο]**Ν̣ ΜΗ ΑΠΟΛΗ**
ΤΑΙ ΑΛΛ᾽ Є[χη] **ΖⲰ**[ην] **ΑΙⲰΝΙΟΝ**
ου] . . . . [πεϲτειλεν] **Ο̣ Θ̣ЄΟϹ ΤΟΝ** 17
ΥΙΟΝ ΑΥΤΟΥ ЄΙϹ ΤΟ̣[ν κ]**Ο̣Ϲ̣Μ**[ον
ΑΛΛ ΪΝΑ Ϲ̣Ⲱ̣Θ̣[η ο] **ΚΟ**[ϲμ]**ΟϹ Δ̣Ι ΑΥ**
ΤΟΥ Ο ΠΙϹΤЄ̣ΥⲰΝ ЄΙϹ ΑΥΤΟΝ ΟΥ 18
ΚΡΙΝЄΤΑΙ Ο ΔЄ ΜΗ ΠΙϹΤЄΥⲰΝ
ΗΔΗ ΚΑΙΚΡ[ι]**ΝЄΤΑΙ ΟΤΙ ΜΗ ΠЄ**
ΠΙϹΤ[ευ]**ΚЄΝ ЄΙϹ ΤΟ ΟΝΟΜΑ ΤΟΥ**
ΜΟΝΟΓЄΝΟΥϹ ΥΙΟΥ ΤΟΥ Θ̅Υ̅

Hermeneia beneath

Notes

1. *ed. pr.* ηγαπ̣η̣σεν
2. *ed. pr.* ωσ̣τ̣ε̣ τ̣ο̣ν
3. *ed. pr.* [μονογενη]
5. *ed. pr.* α̣υ̣τ̣ο̣ν̣
6. *ed. pr.* εχ̣η
7. *ed. pr.* [ου γαρ απεστειλεν]
8. *ed. pr.* τ[ον κ]οσμ[ον]
9. *ed. pr.* αλλ᾽ ῑνα
   ed. pr. σωθ̣η [ο κοσ]μ̣ος δι
12. *ed. pr.* και κρ̣ινεται (2 words)

Third Page
↓ (Jn 4:9)

Ρ̅Κ̅[β̅]

ΛΕΓΕΙ ΟΥΝ ΑΥΤΩ Η ΓΥΝΗ Η ΣΑ
ΜΑΡ̣Ε̣Ι̣Τ̣Ι̣Σ̣ ΠΩΣ ΣΥ ΪΟΥΔΑΙΟΣ
ΩΝ ΠΑΡ ΕΜΟΥ ΠΕΙΝ ΑΙΤΕΙΣ
ΓΥΝΑΙΚΟΣ ΣΑΜΑΡΙΤ̣ΙΔΟΣ
ΟΥΣΗΣ̣ ΟΥ ΓΑΡ ΣΥΝΧΡΩΝ
ΤΑΙ ΪΟΥΔΑΙΟΙ ΣΑΜΑΡΕΙ
ΤΑΙΣ

Hermeneia beneath

Fourth Page
→ (Jn 4:10)

Ρ̅Κ̅Γ̅

ΑΠΕΚΡΙΘΗ Ο Ι̅Σ̅ ΚΑΙ ΕΙΠ̣[ε]Ν̣ ΑΥΤ[η
ΕΙ ΗΔΕΙΣ ΤΗΝ ΔΩΡΕΑΝ ΤΟΥ Θ̅Υ̅ ΚΑΙ
ΤΙΣ ΕΣΤΙΝ Ο ΛΕΓΩΝ ΣΟΙ Δ[ο]Σ ΜΟΙ
ΠΕΙΝ ΣΥ Α̣Ν ΗΤΗΣΑΣ [α]ΥΤ̣ΟΝ ΚΑΙ
ΕΔΩΚ̣Ε̣Ν ΑΝ ΣΟΙ {{ΖΩ}} Υ̣Δ̣ΩΡ
ΖΩΝ

Hermeneia beneath

Notes

1. *ed. pr.* ειπ̣ε̣ν̣
   ed. pr. αυ[τη]
3. *ed. pr.* δος
4. *ed. pr.* α̣υ̣τον
5. *ed. pr.* [υδ]ωρ

P[76]

↓ (Jn 4:9)

]**Ṭ̣ΙΔΟC** [ουcηc (9)
ου γαρ] **CΥΝΧ̣Ρ̣**[ωνται
3 ιου]**ΔΑΙΟΙ CΑ**[

Hermeneia beneath

Notes

1. *ed. pr.* ο̣[υσης

→ (Jn 4:12)

] **ΜΙΖΩ̣**[ν ει του (12)
πρ]**C ΗΜΩΝ̣** [ιακωβ
3 οc]**ΤΙC ЄΔΩ̣**[κεν ημιν
τ]**Ο̣ ΦΡЄ̣Α̣Ρ·** [και] **Α̣**[υτος
ε]**Ξ̣ ΑΥΤΟΥ ЄΠΙЄ̣**[ν και
6 τ]**Α̣ ΘΡЄ̣Μ̣ΜΑΤΑ** [

Hermeneia beneath

Notes

2. *ed. pr.* π̅ρ̅]ς̅
4. *ed. pr.* φρεαρ· α̣[υτος και

P^{80}

↓ (Jn 3:34)

] **Ρ̣**[ημα]**Ṭ**[α του θεου λαλει
ου] **ΓΑΡ ЄΚ ΜЄΡΟΥ**[c διδωcιν ο θεοc
3 **ΤΟ ΠΝЄΥΜΑ >-**

Hermeneia beneath

Notes

2. *ed. pr.* ο]ῦ̣ γαρ

P84

First fragment (P.A.M. Kh. Mird 11)
↓ Heading to Jn 5:5ff (see notes)

Second fragment (P.A.M. Kh. Mird 26)
→ (Jn 17:3)

ΓΙΝΩCΚ̣[ωcι
C̣[ε] ΤΟ̣Ṅ Μ̣[

Third fragment (P.A.M. Kh. Mird 26B)
↓ of second fragment (Jn 17:7-8)

]Ρ̣Α COY ЄΙCῙ (7)
οτ]Ι̣ Τ̣Α̣ Ρ̣[ηματ]Α̣ 8

Notes

First fragment:
The heading reads
περι του τριακ]ΟΝΤΑ ΚΑΙ
οκτω ετη] Є̣ΧΟΝΤΟC
3 εν τη αcθε]Ν̣ΙΑ

P[90]

→ (Jn 18:36-19:1)

]ΙΛΕ̣ΙΑ Η ΕΜ̣[η οι υπηρεται οι εμοι (36)
ηγ]Ω̣ΝΙΖ[ο]ΝΤΟ [αν ινα μη παραδοθω
3 Τ̣ΟΙϹ ΙΟΥ̣[δα]ΙΟ̣ΙϹ [νυν δε η βαϲιλεια η
ΕΜΗ ΟΥΚ̣ [ε]Ϲ̣ΤΙΝ̣ [εντευθεν ειπεν 37
Ο̣ΥΝ ΑΥΤΩ [ο π]Ε[ιλατοϲ ουκουν βαϲι
6 ΛΕΥϹ ϹΥ ΕΙ Α[πεκριθη ο ι̅ϲ̅ ϲυ λεγειϲ
ΟΤΙ ΒΑϹ̣Ι̣Λ̣Ε̣ΥϹ̣ [ειμι εγω ειϲ τουτο
ΓΕ̣Γ̣Ε̣Ν̣Ν̣[ημαι και ειϲ τουτο εληλυ
9 θα] ΕΙϹ Τ̣[ον κοϲμον ινα μαρτυρη
Ϲ̣Ω̣ [τ]Η Α̣Λ̣[ηθεια παϲ ο ων εκ τηϲ
ΑΛ̣[η]Θ̣Ε̣Ι̣[αϲ ακουει μου τηϲ φωνηϲ
12 ΛΕΓ̣ΕΙ ΑΥ̣[τ]Ω̣ Ο̣ Π̣[ειλατοϲ τι εϲτιν 38
ΑΛΗΘΕΙΑ ΚΑΙ Τ[ουτο ειπων παλιν
ΕΞΗΛΘΕΝ Π̣ΡΟϹ Τ[ουϲ ιουδαιουϲ
15 κ]ΑΙ ΛΕΓΕΙ ΑΥΤΟΙϹ [εγω ουδεμιαν
ευρ]ΙϹΚΩ Ε̣Ν̣ ΑΥΤ̣[ω αιτιαν εϲτι 39
δε] ϹΥΝΗΘ[ε]ΙΑ ΫΜ[ιν ινα ενα απο
18 λυ]ϹΩ ΫΜΕΙΝ [εν τω παϲχα βουλε
ϹΘΕ ΟΥΝ Ι̣ΝΑ̣ [υμιν απολυϲω τον
ΒΑϹΙΛΕΑ Τ̣[ων ιουδαιων εκραυγ 40
21 ΑϹΑΝ̣ [ο]ΥΝ Π̣[αλιν παντεϲ λεγοντεϲ μη
ΤΟ̣Υ̣[το]Ν̣ Α[λλα τον βαραββαν ην
ΔΕ Ο ΒΑΡΑΒΒ̣[αϲ ληϲτηϲ τοτε ουν 19:1
24 ΛΑΒΩΝ Ο ΠΕΙΛ[ατοϲ τον ι̅ν̅ εμα

Notes

2. *ed. pr.* ηγ]ω̣νιζο̣ντο α̣[ν
6. *ed. pr.* απ̣[εκριθη
8. *ed. pr.* γε̣γ̣ε̣ν̣ν̣η̣[μαι
9. *ed. pr.* θ̣α εις τ̣[
10. *ed. pr.* τη
12. *ed. pr.* αυ̣τ̣ω̣
13. *ed. pr.* το̣[υτο
16. *ed. pr.* ευ]ρ̣ισκω εν αυ[τω
17. *ed. pr.* υμε[ιν
21. *ed. pr.* ου̣ν
22. *ed. pr.* αλ̣[λα

↓ (Jn 19:1-7)

στιγωσε και οι στ]**ΡΑΤΙΩ̣ΤΑΙ Π̣**[λε (1) 2
ξαντες στεφανο]**Ν ЄΞ̣ Α̣ΚΑΝΘ**[ων
επεθηκαν αυτ]**ΟΥ̣ ΤΗ** [κε]**ΦΑΛΗ ΚΑ̣**[ι
ιματιον πορφυρ]**Ο̣Υ̣**[ν] **Π̣Є̣ΡΙЄΒΑ**
λον αυτον και ηρ]**Χ**[ο]**Ν̣Τ̣Ο ΠΡΟϹ ΑΥ** 3
τον και ελεγον] **ΧΑΙ̣ΡЄ Ο ΒΑϹΙΛЄΥ**[ϲ
των ιουδαιων κ]**ΑΙ ЄΔ̣**[ιδ]**ΟϹΑΝ ΑΥ**
τω ραπισματα ε]**Ξ**[ηλ]**ΘЄΝ ΠΑΛΙΝ** 4
ο πειλατος και λεγει] **ΑΥΤΟΙϹ Ϊ̣ΔЄ**
αγω υμιν αυτον εξ]**Ω̣ Ι̣Ν̣**[α γ]**ΝΩ̣**
τε οτι αιτιαν ε]**Ν** [αυτω] **ΟΥΧ Є̣**[υρ]**ΙϹ**
κω εξηλθεν ο]**ΥΝ** [ο] **ΙϹ̅ ЄΞΩ̣ ΦΟ̣**> 5
ρων τον ακαν]**ΘΙΝΟΝ ϹΤЄΦΑΝΟΝ**
και το πορφυρ]**ΟΥΝ ΙΜΑΤΙΟΝ Κ**[αι
λεγει αυτοις ι]**Δ̣ΟΥ Ο Α̣ΝΘΡΩΠΟ**[ϲ
οτε ουν ειδον α]**Υ̣ΤΟΝ Ο**[ι] **ΑΡΧΙЄΡЄ̣**[ιϲ 6
και οι υπηρεται] **Є̣ΚΡΑΖΑΝ Λ**[εγον
τες σταυρωσον α]**Υ**[τον] **ΛЄΓЄ**[ι αυ
τοις ο πειλατος λαβ]**ЄΤ̣Є Ϋ̣ΜЄΙϹ**
αυτον και σταυρωσ]**Α̣Τ̣Є ЄΓΩ̣ ΓΑΡ**
ουχ ευρισκω εν αυτ]**Ω̣ ΑΙ̣ΤΙΑΝ**
απεκριθησαν οι ιουδ]**ΑΙΟΙ ΗΜ̣ЄΙϹ̣** 7
νομον εχομεν κα]**Ι ΚΑΤΑ ΤΟΝ**

Notes

2. *ed. pr.* α̣κανθω̣[ν
3. *ed. pr.* κα̣ι̣
7. *ed. pr.* κ̣αι εδ̣[ι]δ̣οσαν
8. *ed. pr.* ε̣ξ[ηλ]θεν
10. *ed. pr.* ι̣ν̣α̣
11. *ed. pr.* ε]ν̣ αυ̣[τω] ουχ ευ̣ρ̣ις
12. *ed. pr.* ο̣

P93

→ (Jn 13:15-17)

ḲẠỊ [υμειc ποιητε αμην αμην (15) 16
ΛЄΓω ÍṂ[ιν ουκ εcτι δουλοc μιζων
3 **ΤΟΥ ΚΥΡ**[ιου αυτου ουδε αποcτολοc
ΜΙΖωΝ [του πεμψαντοc αυτον
Ị ΤΑΥΤẠ [οιδατε μακαριοι εcτε εαν 17
6 **ΠΊΤЄ** [

Notes

1. *ed. pr.* ḳạị ụṃ[εις

↓ blank

P^{95}

→ (Jn 5:26-29)

]**ΑΥΤΩ ΚΑ**[ι (26) 27
αυτω τω υιω εξ]**Ο̣ΥϹΙΑΝ̣ ЄΔ**[ω
κεν κριϲιν π]**ΟΙЄΙΝ ΟΤΙ ΫΙΟ̣**[ϲ
ανθρωπου εϲτι]**Ν ΜΗ ΘΑΥΜ**[α 28
ζετε τουτο ο]**ΤΙ ЄΡΧЄΤΑΙ** [ω
ρα εν η παντεϲ οι ε]**Ν** [τ]**ΟΙϹ ΜΝ̣**[η
μειοιϲ ακουϲαντ]**ЄϹ ΤΗϹ** [φω
νηϲ αυτου και εκ]**ΠΟΡЄΥϹ**[ον 29
ται οι τα αγαθα ποι]**ΗϹΑ̣**[

Notes

1-2. *ed. pr.* [εξ]
2-3. *ed. pr.* εδ[ω/κεν αυτω κρισιν π]
4. *ed. pr.* θαυμα̣
6. *ed. pr.* ο]ι̣ ε̣ν
7. *ed. pr.* φ̇[ω. The trace of ink does not seem compatible with any probable letter. There is no extant phi for comparison

↓ (Jn 5:36-38)

]**Ω̣ϹΩ ΑΥΤΑ̣ Τ̣**[α εργα α̲ εγω ποιω (36)
μαρ]**Τ̣ΥΡЄΙ ΠЄΡΙ ЄΜ̣**[ου οτι ο π̅ρ̅ με
απε]**Ϲ̣ΤΑΛΚЄΝ ΚΑ**[ι ο πεμψαϲ με 37
π̅ρ̅ ε]**ΚЄΙΝΟϹ ΜЄΜ̣**[αρτυρηκε
πε]**ΡΙ ЄΜΟΥ ΟΥ**[τε φωνην αυ
το]**Υ̣ Π̣ΩΠ**[ο]**Τ̣**[ε ακηκοατε ου
τε] **ЄΙ̣ΔΟϹ Α̣**[υτου εωρακατε και 38
το]**Ν ΛΟΓ̣**[

Notes

1. *ed. pr.* (which reads αυτα τ̣[α) notes Pintaudi's suggestion of αυταυ̣[τα (haplography for αυτα αυτα)
5. *ed. pr.* π]ε̣ρι

APPARATUS CRITICUS

CHAPTER ONE

P^{5} P^{55} P^{59} P^{66} P^{75}

Superscription ευαγγελιον κατα ιωαννην **P^{66}**; ευαγγελιον κατα ιωανην **P^{75}**

1:1

P^{66} P^{75}

1: εν αρχη ην ο λογος και ο λογος ην προς τον θεον και θεος ην ο λογος.

DEF: **P^{66}** εν... το[ ] και...

1:2

P^{66} P^{75}

2: ουτος ην εν αρχη προς τον θεον.

DEF: **P^{66}** ουτος... προς [

1:3

P^{66} P^{75}

3: παντα δι αυτου εγενετο και χωρις αυτου εγενετο ουδε εν ο γεγονεν.

DEF: **P^{66}** ... χωρις α[ ] εγενετο...

ουδε εν: ουδεν **P^{66}**

1:4

P^{66} **P**^{75}

4: εν αυτω ζωη ην και η ζωη ην το φως των ανθρωπων.

DEF: **P**^{66} ... ζω[ ] η[ ] και...

εν: OM **P**^{66}
ζωη ην^{1}: ζωην **P**^{75*}; txt **P**^{75*c}

1:5

P^{66} **P**^{75}

5: και το φως εν τη σκοτια φαινει και η σκοτια αυτο ου κατελαβεν.

σκοτια^{1}: σκοτεια **P**^{75}
σκοτια^{2}: σκοτεια **P**^{75}

1:6

P^{66} **P**^{75}

6: εγενετο ανθρωπος απεσταλμενος παρα θεου ονομα αυτω ιωαννης.

DEF: **P**^{66}]γενετο...

ιωαννης: ιωανης **P**^{75}

1:7

P^{66} **P**^{75}

7: ουτος ηλθεν εις μαρτυριαν ινα μαρτυρηση περι του φωτος ινα παντες πιστευσωσι δι αυτου.

μαρτυριαν: μαρτυριον **P**^{75}
πιστευσωσι: πιστευσωσιν **P**^{66} **P**^{75}

1:8

P66 P75

8: ουκ ην εκεινος το φως αλλ ινα μαρτυρηση περι του φωτος.

DEF: **P66** ... μαρτυρης[ ] περι...

1:9

P66 P75

9: ην το φως το αληθινον ο φωτιζει παντα ανθρωπον ερχομενον εις τον κοσμον.

παντα: πανταν **P66***; txt **P66*c**

1:10

P66 P75

10: εν τω κοσμω ην και ο κοσμος δι αυτου εγενετο και ο κοσμος αυτον ουκ εγνω.

ην: ηηεν (sic) **P75*c**; txt **P75***

1:11

P66 P75

11: εις τα ιδια ηλθε και οι ιδιοι αυτον ου παρελαβον.

DEF: **P66** ... ηλθ[ ] και...

ηλθε: ηλθεν **P75**

1:12

P66 P75

12: οσοι δε ελαβον αυτον εδωκεν αυτοις εξουσιαν τεκνα θεου γενεσθαι τοις πιστευουσιν εις το ονομα αυτου.

DEF: **P66** οσο[ ] δε...

1:13

P^{66} P^{75}

13: οι ουκ εξ αιματων ουδε εκ θεληματοc cαρκοc ουδε εκ θεληματοc ανδροc αλλ εκ θεου εγεννηθηcαν.

DEF: **P^{66}** οι [ ]κ εξ... θελημ[ ] cαρκοc... αν[ ] αλλα...
P^{75} ... ανδροc̣...

αλλ: αλλα **P^{66}**
εγεννηθηcαν: εγενηθηcαν **P^{75}**

1:14

P^{66} P^{75}

14: και ο λογοc cαρξ εγενετο και εcκηνωcεν εν ημιν και εθεαcαμεθα την δοξαν αυτου δοξαν ωc μονογενουc παρα πατροc πληρηc χαριτοc και αληθειαc.

DEF: **P^{66}** και [ ]αρξ... ημ[ ] και... αυτου [ ]ξαν... πληρ[ ] χαριτοc...

αληθειαc: αληθιαc **P^{66}**

1:15

P^{66} P^{75}

15: ιωαννηc μαρτυρει περι αυτου και κεκραγε λεγων ουτοc ην ον ειπον ο οπιcω μου ερχομενοc εμπροcθεν μου γεγονεν οτι πρωτοc μου ην.

DEF: **P^{66}** ιωαννηc μα[ ]τυρι... και κ[ ]εκραγεν λεγ[ ] ουτοc... ερχ[ ]μενοc... γεγονεν [ ]τι...

ιωαννηc: ιωανηc **P^{75}**
μαρτυρει: μα[ ]τυρι **P^{66}**
κεκραγε: κ[1]εκραγεν **P^{66}** (littera (κ aut ρ) eras. inter κ et ε)
ο: OM **P^{66*}**; txt **P^{66*c}**

1:16

P^{66} **P**^{75}

16: και εκ του πληρωματος αυτου ημεις παντες ελαβομεν και χαριν αντι χαριτος.

DEF: **P**^{66} ... ελαβ[ ]μεν...
P^{75} ... π̣ληρωματος ...

και^{1}: οτι **P**^{66} **P**^{75}

1:17

P^{66} **P**^{75}

17: οτι ο νομος δια μωςεως εδοθη η χαρις και η αληθεια δια ιηςου χριςτου εγενετο.

DEF: **P**^{66} οτι ο [ ]μος... χαρ[ ] δε και... εγενετ[

μωςεως: μωυςεως **P**^{66} **P**^{75}
και: δε και **P**^{66}
αληθεια: αληθια **P**^{66}

1:18

P^{66} **P**^{75}

18: θεον ουδεις εωρακε πωποτε ο μονογενης υιος ο ων εις τον κολπον του πατρος εκεινος εξηγηςατο.

DEF: **P**^{66} ... πωποτε μ[ ]νογενης... κολπον τ[ ] πατρος...

εωρακε πωποτε: πωποτε εορακεν **P**^{75*}; εορακεν πωποτε **P**^{75*c}
εωρακε: εωρακεν **P**^{66}
πωποτε: πωποται **P**^{66}
ο^{1}: OM **P**^{66}
υιος: θεος **P**^{66} **P**^{75}
εκεινος: εκινος **P**^{66}

1:19

P^{66} P^{75}

19: και αυτη εστιν η μαρτυρια του ιωαννου οτε απεστειλαν οι ιουδαιοι εξ ιεροcολυμων ιερεις και λευιτας ινα ερωτηcωcιν αυτον cυ τις ει.

DEF: **P^{66}** και αυτη [ ] μαρτυρια... οτε απ[ ]cτιλαν... ιεροcολυμ[ ]ερειc... ερωτηc[ ]υτον...

ιωαννου: ιωανου **P^{75}**
απεστειλαν: απ[ ]cτιλαν **P^{66}**; απεcτειλεν **P^{75}**
λευιτας: λευειτας **P^{66} P^{75}**; ·/. post λευειτας **P^{66*c}** (et forsan προc αυτον scriptum in margine sinistro, qui nunc perditum est)
ερωτηcωcιν: ερωτηcουcιν **P^{75}**
cυ τις: cυc **P^{66*}**; txt **P^{66*c}**

1:20

P^{66} P^{75}

20: και ωμολογηcε και ουκ ηρνηcατο και ωμολογηcεν οτι ουκ ειμι εγω ο χριcτοc.

DEF: **P^{66}** και ωμολογηcεν κα[ ]υκ ηρνηcατο και ωμολογηcεν [ ]ι εγω...

ωμολογηcε: ωμολογηcεν **P^{66} P^{75}**
ουκ ειμι εγω: εγω ουκ ιμι **P^{66}**; εγω ουκ ειμι **P^{75}**

1:21

P^{66} P^{75}

21: και ηρωτηcαν αυτον τι ουν ηλιαc ει cυ και λεγει ουκ ειμι ο προφητηc ει cυ και απεκριθη ου.

DEF: **P^{66}** και ηρωτ[ ]ν αυτον... ηλειαc ει [ ] ουκ ειμι ο προφητηc ει cυ [ ] απεκριθη ου

τι: τιc **P^{66}**
ηλιαc ει cυ: cυ ηλειαc ει **P^{66} P^{75*c}**; cο ηλειαc ει **P^{75*}**

1:22

P[66] **P**[75]

22: ειπον ουν αυτω τις ει ινα αποκρισιν δωμεν τοις πεμψασιν ημας τι λεγεις περι σεαυτου.

ειπον: ειπαν **P**[66] **P**[75]
αυτω: + συ **P**[66*c] **P**[75]; txt **P**[66*]
περι: υπερ **P**[75*c]; txt **P**[75*]

1:23

P[5] **P**[66] **P**[75]

23: εφη εγω φωνη βοωντος εν τη ερημω ευθυνατε την οδον κυριου καθως ειπεν ησαιας ο προφητης.

DEF: **P**[5]]ω φων[ ] βο[ ]θυνατ[ ]εν ησα[

ευθυνατε: ευθυναται **P**[66]

1:24

P[5] **P**[66] **P**[75]

24: και οι απεσταλμενοι ησαν εκ των φαρισαιων.

DEF: **P**[5]]αλμενοι [ ]ν

οι: OM **P**[66] **P**[75]

1:25

P^{5} **P**^{66} **P**^{75}

25: και ηρωτηcαν αυτον και ειπον αυτω τι ουν βαπτιζειc ει cυ ουκ ει ο χριcτοc ουτε ηλιαc ουτε ο προφητηc.

DEF: **P**^{5} και ηρω[ ]πτιζειc ει [ ] ουδε ο προ[

ηρωτηcαν αυτον και ειπον αυτω τι ουν βαπτιζειc: ηρω[15-20] / πτιζειc **P**^{5}
ειπον: ειπαν **P**^{66} **P**^{75}
ουτε^{1}: ουδε **P**^{66} **P**^{75}
ηλιαc: ηλειαc **P**^{66*c} **P**^{75}; txt **P**^{66*}
ουτε^{2}: ουδε **P**^{5} **P**^{66} **P**^{75}

1:26

P^{5} **P**^{59} **P**^{66} **P**^{75}

26: απεκριθη αυτοιc ο ιωαννηc λεγων εγω βαπτιζω εν υδατι μεcοc δε υμων εcτηκεν ον υμειc ουκ οιδατε.

DEF: **P**^{5}] ιωανν[ ]δατι μ[ ] ουκ οιδα[
P^{59}] ιωαν[ ]πτιζω [ ]cοc υμ[ ]c ου[

ιωαννηc: ιωανηc **P**^{75*}; txt **P**^{75*c}
λεγων: OM **P**^{75}
μεcοc δε υμων εcτηκεν ον υμειc: μ[18-23] / **P**^{5}
δε: OM **P**^{59} **P**^{66} **P**^{75}
εcτηκεν: ιcτηκει **P**^{75}
26-27 οιδατε αυτοc εcτιν ο οπιcω μου ερχομενοc: οιδα[16-21 / 1]οc **P**^{5}
οιδατε: οιδαται **P**^{66}

1:27

P^{5} **P**^{66} **P**^{75}

27: αυτοc εcτιν ο οπιcω μου ερχομενοc οc εμπροcθεν μου γεγονεν ου εγω ουκ ειμι αξιοc ινα λυcω αυτου τον ιμαντα του υποδηματοc.

DEF: **P**^{5}]οc [ ]υ ο[ ]του τον [

P[66] ... ερχομενο[ ] ου ουκ... υποδηματος αυ

αυτος εστιν ο οπισω μου ερχομενος: cf. v. 26
αυτος εστιν: OM **P**[66] **P**[75]
ος εμπροσθεν μου γεγονεν: OM **P**[5] **P**[66] **P**[75]
εγω ουκ ειμι: ουκ ειμι **P**[5] **P**[66*] **P**[75]; ουκ ειμι εγω **P**[66*c]
αξιος: ικανος **P**[66] **P**[75]
27-28 αυτου τον ιμαντα του υποδηματος ταυτα: τον ιμαντα του υποδηματος αυ / ταυτα **P**[66*]; τον ιμαντα του υποδηματος αυṭ[ ] ταυτα **P**[66*c]

1:28

P[5] **P**[59] **P**[66] **P**[75]

28: ταυτα εν βηθαβαρα εγενετο περαν του ιορδανου οπου ην ιωαννης βαπτιζων.

DEF: **P**[5] ταυτα εν β[ ]ραν του ιο[ ]ης βαπτι[
P[59]]α εν βη[ ]ο περ[ ]υ ην [
P[66] ... περαν το[ ] ιορδανου... ιωαννης β[ ]πτιζων

εν βηθαβαρα εγενετο: εγενετο εν βηθανια **P**[66]; εν βηθανια εγενετο **P**[75]
ιωαννης: ο ιωαννης **P**[66] **P**[75]

1:29

P[5] **P**[66] **P**[75]

29: τη επαυριον βλεπει ο ιωαννης τον ιησουν ερχομενον προς αυτον και λεγει ιδε ο αμνος του θεου ο αιρων την αμαρτιαν του κοσμου.

DEF: **P**[5]]πει τον $\overline{\text{ιην}}$ [ ] και λεγει [ ] την αμαρ[
P[66] ... αιρων τη[ ]μαρτιαν...

ο ιωαννης: OM **P**[5] **P**[66] **P**[75]

1:30

P^{5} P^{66} P^{75}

30: ουτος εστι περι ου εγω ειπον οπισω μου ερχεται ανηρ ος εμπροσθεν μου γεγονεν οτι πρωτος μου ην.

DEF: **P^{5}**] εστιν υπερ [ ] ερχεται α[ ] γεγον[

εστι: εστιν **P^{5} P^{66} P^{75}**
περι: υπερ **P^{5} P^{66} P^{75}**

1:31

P^{5} P^{55} P^{66} P^{75}

31: καγω ουκ ηδειν αυτον αλλ ινα φανερωθη τω ισραηλ δια τουτο ηλθον εγω εν τω υδατι βαπτιζων.

DEF: **P^{5}**] ουκ ηδ[ ]θη [ ]γ[
P^{55}]ον [ ] $\overline{\text{ιηλ}}$ [ ]ν υδα[

τω^{2}: OM **P^{55} P^{66} P^{75}**

1:32

P^{55} P^{66} P^{75}

32: και εμαρτυρησεν ιωαννης λεγων οτι τεθεαμαι το πνευμα καταβαινον ωσει περιστεραν εξ ουρανου και εμεινεν επ αυτον.

DEF: **P^{55}** και εμαρτυ[ ]ης λεγων [ ]ο $\overline{\text{πνα}}$ κατα[ ] περιστεραν [ ]αι εμεινεν [

καταβαινων ωσει: κατα[8] **P^{55}** (& cf. **P^{75}**)
ωσει: ως **P^{75}** (& cf. **P^{55}**)

1:33

P^{5} P^{55} P^{66} P^{75}

33: καγω ουκ ηδειν αυτον αλλ ο πεμψας με βαπτιζειν εν υδατι εκεινος μοι ειπεν εφ ον αν ιδης το πνευμα καταβαινον και μενον επ αυτον ουτος εστιν ο βαπτιζων εν πνευματι αγιω.

DEF: **P**^{5}] αλλ ο π[ ]δατ[ ] ε[ ]δης το [ ]ον επ αυ[ ]ων εν π̅[
P^{55}]γω ουκ ηδειν [ ] πεμψας με βα[ ] υδατι εκεινο[ ]φ ον αν ιδης [ ]βαινον και [ ]υτον ουτος [ ] εν π̅[
P^{66} ... πεμψα[ ] με... εκεινο[ ] μοι... αυτον [ ]υτος
P^{75} ... π̅ν̅α̅ [ ]αταβαινον...

υδατι: τω υδατι **P**^{66}
ιδης: ειδης **P**^{66}

1:34

P^{5} **P**^{66} **P**^{75}

34: καγω εωρακα και μεμαρτυρηκα οτι ουτος εστιν ο υιος του θεου.

DEF: **P**^{5}]αρτυρηκα ο[ ]c του θ̅υ̅
P^{66} ... μεμαρτυρ[ ]κα...

καγω: + κα[ ] post κα **P**^{75*c}; txt **P**^{75*}
εωρακα: εορακα **P**^{75}

1:35

P^{5} **P**^{55} **P**^{66} **P**^{75}

35: τη επαυριον παλιν ειστηκει ο ιωαννης και εκ των μαθητων αυτου δυο.

DEF: **P**^{5} τη ε[ ]νης και εκ [ ]υο
P^{55} τ[ ] ο ιωα[ ]θητω[
P^{66}]η επαυριον... ιωα[ ]νης... αυτο[ ]υο

επαυριον παλιν ειστηκει ο ιωαννης: ε / [15-20]νης **P**^{5}
παλιν: OM **P**^{75}
ειστηκει: ιστηκει **P**^{66}; ειστηχει **P**^{75}
ο: OM **P**^{75}

1:36

P^{5} P^{55} P^{66} P^{75}

36: και εμβλεψας τω ιηcου περιπατουντι λεγει ιδε ο αμνος του θεου.

DEF: **P^{5}** και εμ[ ]υντι λεγε[
P^{55}]ψας τω ι̅υ̅ π[ ]γει ειδε ο α[
P^{66} ... περιπα[ ] λεγει... ο α[ ]ων... κοcμο[

ιδε: ειδε **P^{55}**
θεου: + ο α[ ]ων την αμαρτιαν του κοcμο[ ] **P^{66*}**; txt **P^{66*c}**

1:37

P^{5} P^{55} P^{66} P^{75}

37: και ηκουcαν αυτου οι δυο μαθηται λαλουντος και ηκολουθηcαν τω ιηcου.

DEF: **P^{5}**]υcαν οι δυο [ ]κολουθη[
P^{55}] ηκουcαν ο[ ]του λαλουν[ ]θηcαν τω ι̅υ̅
P^{66} ... μαθη[ ] λαλουντοc...

αυτου οι δυο μαθηται: ο[13 /]του **P^{55}**
αυτου οι δυο: οι δυο αυτου **P^{66} P^{75}**
αυτου: OM **P^{5}**

1:38

P^{5} P^{55} P^{66} P^{75}

38: cτραφειc δε ο ιηcουc και θεαcαμενοc αυτουc ακολουθουνταc λεγει αυτοιc τι ζητειτε οι δε ειπον αυτω ραββι ο λεγεται ερμηνευομενον διδαcκαλε που μενειc.

DEF: **P^{5}**]ε ο ι̅η̅c̅ και θε[ ]ολουθουνταc [ ]τε ειπαν
αυ[ ]μηνευομε[ ]ειc
P^{55}] ο ι̅c̅ και θεαc[ ] ακολουθουν[ ]τοιc τι ζητ[

ακολουθουνταc: + αυτω **P^{66}**
ζητειτε: ζητειται **P^{66}**
οι δε ειπον αυτω: ειπαν αυ[ ] **P^{5*}**; οι δε ειπαν **P^{5c}**

ειπον: ειπαν **P**[66] **P**[75]
ραββι: ραββει **P**[66] **P**[75]
λεγεται: λεγετε **P**[66]
ερμηνευομενον: μθερμηνευομενον **P**[66*]; μεθερμηνευομενον **P**[66*c] **P**[75]

1:39

P[5] **P**[66] **P**[75]

39: λεγει αυτοις ερχεcθε και ιδετε ηλθον και ειδον που μενει και παρ αυτω εμειναν την ημεραν εκεινην ωρα δε ην ως δεκατη.

DEF: **P**[5] λεγει [ ]cθε ηλθαν [ ]αι παρ αυτω [ ] εκεινην [

ερχεcθε: ερχεcθαι **P**[66]
ιδετε: [ ]cθε **P**[5]; οψεcθαι **P**[66]; οψεcθε **P**[75]
ηλθον: ηλθαν **P**[5]; ηλθαν ουν **P**[66] **P**[75]
ειδον: ειδαν **P**[66] **P**[75]
δε: OM **P**[66] **P**[75]

1:40

P[5] **P**[66] **P**[75]

40: ην ανδρεας ο αδελφος cιμωνος πετρου εις εκ των δυο των ακουcαντων παρα ιωαννου και ακολουθηcαντων αυτω.

DEF: **P**[5]]ρεαc ο α[ ]υο των [ ]υ και α[

αδελφος cιμωνος πετρου εις εκ των δυο: α / [18-24]υο **P**[5]
πετρου: πετρος **P**[75*]; txt **P**[75*c]
ακολουθηcαντων: ηκολουθηcαντων **P**[75]

1:41

P^{66} **P**^{75}

41: ευρισκει ουτος πρωτος τον αδελφον τον ιδιον σιμωνα και λεγει αυτω ευρηκαμεν τον μεσσιαν ο εστι μεθερμηνευομενον ο χριστος.

πρωτος: πρωτον **P**^{66} **P**^{75}
εστι: εστιν **P**^{66} **P**^{75}
ο^{2}: OM **P**^{66} **P**^{75}

1:42

P^{66} **P**^{75}

42: και ηγαγεν αυτον προς τον ιησουν εμβλεψας δε αυτω ο ιησους ειπε συ ει σιμων ο υιος ιωνα συ κληθηση κηφας ο ερμηνευεται πετρος.

και: OM **P**^{66*} **P**^{75}; ουτος **P**^{66*c}
δε: OM **P**^{66}
ειπε: ειπεν **P**^{66} **P**^{75}
ιωνα: ιωαννου **P**^{66} **P**^{75}

1:43

P^{66} **P**^{75}

43: τη επαυριον ηθελησεν ο ιησους εξελθειν εις την γαλιλαιαν και ευρισκει φιλιππον και λεγει αυτω ακολουθει μοι.

DEF: **P**^{75} ... αυτω̣...

ο ιησους: OM **P**^{66} **P**^{75}
ευρισκει: ευρισκι **P**^{66}
λεγει: λεγι **P**^{66}
αυτω: + ο ιησους **P**^{66} **P**^{75}

1:44

P^{66} P^{75}

44: ην δε ο φιλιπποϲ απο βηθϲαιδα εκ τηϲ πολεωϲ ανδρεου και πετρου.

DEF: **P^{75}** ... φι̣λιπποϲ...

βηθϲαιδα: βηθϲαιδαν **P^{66}**; βηδϲαιδα **P^{75*}**; txt **P^{75*c}**

1:45

P^{66} P^{75}

45: ευριϲκει φιλιπποϲ τον ναθαναηλ και λεγει αυτω ον εγραψε μωϲηϲ εν τω νομω και οι προφηται ευρηκαμεν ιηϲουν τον υιον του ιωϲηφ τον απο ναζαρετ.

DEF: **P^{75}** ... φιλι̣π̣ποϲ... λεγει̣ αυτω ο̣ν̣... προφη̣τ̣α̣ι̣... ιωϲ̣ηφ το̣ν απο ναζαρεθ̣

ευριϲκει: ευριϲκι **P^{66}**
εγραψε: εγραψεν **P^{66} P^{75}**
μωϲηϲ: μωυϲηϲ **P^{66} P^{75}**
τον^{2}: OM **P^{66} P^{75}**
ιωϲηφ: ιϲηφ **P^{66*}**; txt **P^{66*c}**
ναζαρετ: ναζαρεθ **P^{75}**

1:46

P^{66} P^{75}

46: και ειπεν αυτω ναθαναηλ εκ ναζαρετ δυναται τι αγαθον ειναι λεγει αυτω φιλιπποϲ ερχου και ιδε.

DEF: **P^{75}** ... α̣υτω̣... α̣γαθ̣ον... κ̣αι ιδε

ναζαρετ: ναζαρεθ **P^{75}**
αυτω^{2}: + ο **P^{66*c}**; + [1] **P^{75}**; txt **P^{66*}**
ιδε: ειδε **P^{66}**

1:47

P^{66} **P**^{75}

47: ειδεν ο ιηcουc τον ναθαναηλ ερχομενον προc αυτον και λεγει περι αυτου ιδε αληθωc ιcραηλιτηc εν ω δολοc ουκ εcτι.

DEF: **P**^{75} ... ερ̣χομενον...

ειδεν: ιδεν **P**^{75}
ιcραηλιτηc: ιcραηλειτηc **P**^{66} **P**^{75}
εcτι: εcτιν **P**^{66} **P**^{75}

1:48

P^{59} **P**^{66} **P**^{75}

48: λεγει αυτω ναθαναηλ ποθεν με γινωcκειc απεκριθη ο ιηcουc και ειπεν αυτω προ του cε φιλιππον φωνηcαι οντα υπο την cυκην ειδον cε.

DEF: **P**^{59}]ειc απεκ[ ] του cε φ[ ]ηcαι οντ[ ]ον [
P^{75} ... φωνηcαι [ ]ντα...

γινωcκειc: γεινωcκειc **P**^{75}
απεκριθη ο ιηcουc και ειπεν αυτω προ: απεκ[10-15] **P**^{59}
ο: OM **P**^{66} **P**^{75}

1:49

P^{66} **P**^{75}

49: απεκριθη ναθαναηλ και λεγει αυτω ραββι cυ ει ο υιοc του θεου cυ ει ο βαcιλευc του ιcραηλ.

ναθαναηλ και λεγει αυτω: αυτω ναθαναηλ **P**^{66} **P**^{75}
ραββι: ραββει **P**^{75}
ει^{1}: + αληθωc **P**^{66*}; txt **P**^{66*c}
ει ο βαcιλευc: βαcιλευc ει **P**^{75}

1:50

P[66] **P**[75]

50: απεκριθη ιηcουc και ειπεν αυτω οτι ειπον coι ειδον cε υποκατω τηc cυκηc πιcτευειc μειζω τουτων οψει.

coι: + οτι **P**[66] **P**[75]
υποκατω τηc cυκηc: υπο την cυκην **P**[66]
μειζω: μειζονα **P**[66]; μειζων **P**[75]
οψει: οψη **P**[66] **P**[75]

1:51

P[59] **P**[66] **P**[75]

51: και λεγει αυτω αμην αμην λεγω υμιν απ αρτι οψεcθε τον ουρανον ανεωγοτα και τουc αγγελουc του θεου αναβαινονταc και καταβαινονταc επι τον υιον του ανθρωπου.

DEF: **P**[59]]αιν[ ] του $\overline{\text{αν}}$[

απ αρτι: OM **P**[66] **P**[75]

CHAPTER TWO

P^{59} **P**^{66} **P**^{75}

2:1

P^{66} **P**^{75}

1: και τη ημερα τη τριτη γαμος εγενετο εν κανα της γαλιλαιας και ην η μητηρ του ιηcου εκει.

κανα: τη κανα **P**^{75}

2:2

P^{66} **P**^{75}

2: εκληθη δε και ο ιηcουc και οι μαθηται αυτου εις τον γαμον.

και^{1}: OM **P**^{66*}; txt **P**^{66*c}

2:3

P^{66} **P**^{75}

3: και υcτερηcαντοc οινου λεγει η μητηρ του ιηcου προc αυτον οινον ουκ εχουcι.

του: τω **P**^{66*}; txt **P**^{66*c}
εχουcι: εχουcιν **P**^{66} **P**^{75}

2:4

P^{66} **P**^{75}

4: λεγει αυτη ο ιηcουc τι εμοι και cοι γυναι ουπω ηκει η ωρα μου.

DEF: **P**^{75} ... μ̣ου

λεγει: και λεγει **P**^{66}

coι: cυ **P**^{75*c}; txt **P**^{75*}

2:5

P^{66} **P**^{75}

5: λεγει η μητηρ αυτου τοιc διακονοιc ο τι αν λεγη υμιν ποιηcατε.

αν: εαν **P**^{66} **P**^{75}
ποιηcατε: ποιηcαται **P**^{66}

2:6

P^{66} **P**^{75}

6: ηcαν δε εκει υδριαι λιθιναι εξ κειμεναι κατα τον καθαριcμον των ιουδαιων χωρουcαι ανα μετρηταc δυο η τρειc.

DEF: **P**^{75} ηcαν δ̣ε ε̣κει... καθαρ̣ιcμον...

υδριαι λιθιναι: λιθιναι υδριαι **P**^{66} **P**^{75}
κειμεναι κατα τον καθαριcμον των ιουδαιων: κατα τον καθαριcμον των ιουδαιων κειμεναι **P**^{66} **P**^{75} (sed ϊδαιων pro ιουδαιων **P**^{75})
χωρουcαι: χωρηcαι **P**^{75}
μετρηταc: μητραc **P**^{75}
τρειc: τριc **P**^{66}

2:7

P^{66} **P**^{75}

7: λεγει αυτοιc ο ιηcουc γεμιcατε ταc υδριαc υδατοc και εγεμιcαν αυταc εωc ανω.

DEF: **P**^{75} ... ι̣̅c̣̅... εχ̣ε̣μιcαν...

2:8

P^{66} P^{75}

8: και λεγει αυτοις αντλησατε νυν και φερετε τω αρχιτρικλινω και ηνεγκαν.

DEF: **P^{75}** ... αρχι[ ]ρ̣ι̣κ̣λεινω...

λεγει: λεγι **P^{66}**
αντλησατε: αντλησαται **P^{66}**
φερετε: φερεται **P^{66}**
αρχιτρικλινω: αρχιτρικλεινω **P^{66}**; αρχι[ ]ρικλεινω **P^{75}**
και^{3}: οι δε **P^{75}**

2:9

P^{66} P^{75}

9: ως δε εγευσατο ο αρχιτρικλινος το υδωρ οινον γεγενημενον και ουκ ηδει ποθεν εστιν οι δε διακονοι ηδεισαν οι ηντληκοτες το υδωρ φωνει τον νυμφιον ο αρχιτρικλινος.

DEF: **P^{75}** ως δε εγευ[ ]α̣τ̣ο̣... γ̣ε̣γενημενον... [ ]ς̣τιν... ηδειc̣αν...
ηντλη[ ]τ̣ε̣c... [ ] α̣ρ̣χ̣ι̣τρικλε̣ι̣ν̣οc

αρχιτρικλινοc^{1}: αρχιτρικλεινοc **P^{66} P^{75}**
και^{1}: οι δε **P^{66}**
ηδειcαν: ηcαν **P^{66*}**; txt **P^{66*c}**
αρχιτρικλινοc^{2}: αρχιτρικλεινοc **P^{66} P^{75}**

2:10

P^{66} P^{75}

10: και λεγει αυτω πας ανθρωπος πρωτον τον καλον οινον τιθησι και οταν μεθυσθωσι τοτε τον ελασσω συ τετηρηκας τον καλον οινον εως αρτι.

DEF: **P^{66}** και [ ]γει...
P^{75} και λεγε̣ι̣ αυτω πας α̣ν̣ο̣c̣ τον κα[ ]ο̣ν ο̣ι̣ν̣ον πρ̣[ ]τον
τιθηcιν και οταν μ̣ε̣θ̣υ̣c̣θωcι̣ν τον ελαccω c̣υ τετηρ̣η̣κ̣α̣c̣ τ̣ο̣ν
[ ]α̣[ ]ο̣ν οινον εως αρτι

πρωτον τον καλον οινον: τον κα[ ]ον οινον πρ[ ]τον **P^{75}**
τιθηcι: τιθηcιν **P^{66} P^{75}**
μεθυcθωcι: μεθυcθωcιν **P^{66} P^{75}**
τοτε: OM **P^{66} P^{75}**

2:11

P^{66} P^{75}

11: ταυτην εποιηcε την αρχην των cημειων ο ιηcουc εν κανα τηc γαλιλαιαc και εφανερωcε την δοξαν αυτου και επιcτευcαν ειc αυτον οι μαθηται αυτου.

DEF: **P^{75}** τα̣υ̣τ̣η̣ν̣ επ[ ]η̣c̣εν αρχην των cημει̣ω̣ν̣ ο̣ ι̣̅c̣̅ εν κανα τηc γαλιλαιαc και ε̣φα̣ν̣ε̣ρωc̣ε̣ν... ε̣π̣ι̣c̣τ̣ε̣υ̣c̣α̣ν̣ ε̣ιc... αυτο̣[

εποιηcε την αρχην: πρωτην αρχην εποιηcεν **P^{66*}**; εποιηcεν αρχην **P^{66*c}**; επ[ ]ηcεν αρχην **P^{75}**
τηc: τη **P^{66}**
γαλιλαιαc: γαλειλαιαc **P^{66}**
εφανερωcε: εφανερωcεν **P^{66} P^{75}**
αυτον: cαυτον **P^{66*}**; txt **P^{66c}**

2:12

P^{66} P^{75}

12: μετα τουτο κατεβη ειc καπερναουμ αυτοc και η μητηρ αυτου και οι αδελφοι αυτου και οι μαθηται αυτου και εκει εμειναν ου πολλαc ημεραc.

DEF: **P^{75}** ... ε̣ι̣c̣ κ̣αφαρναο̣υ̣[ ] αυτοc... οι α̣δ̣ε̣λφοι και οι μαθηται α̣υ̣τ̣[ ] κα̣ι εκ̣ε̣ι ε̣μ̣ειναν ου πολλαc ημ̣εραc

καπερναουμ: καφαρναουμ **P^{66}**; καφαρναου[ ] **P^{75}**
αυτου^{2}: OM **P^{66*} P^{75}**; txt **P^{66*c}**
εμειναν: εμεινιν **P^{66*c}**; txt **P^{66*}**

2:13

P66 P75

13: και εγγυς ην το πασχα των ιουδαιων και ανεβη εις ιεροσολυμα ο ιησους.

εγγυς: + δε **P66***; txt **P66c**
εις ιεροσολυμα ο ιησους: ο ιησους εις ιεροσολυμα **P66 P75**

2:14

P66 P75

14: και ευρεν εν τω ιερω τους πωλουντας βοας και προβατα και περιστερας και τους κερματιστας καθημενους.

βοας: τας βοας **P75**

2:15

P59 P66 P75

15: και ποιησας φραγελλιον εκ σχοινιων παντας εξεβαλεν εκ του ιερου τα τε προβατα και τους βοας και των κολλυβιστων εξεχεε το κερμα και τας τραπεζας ανεστρεψε.

DEF: **P59**]στων [ ]ατα και τα[ ]ων κατε[

ποιησας: + ως **P66 P75**
εξεχεε: εξεχεεν **P66 P75**
το κερμα: [ ]ατα **P59**; τα κερματα **P66*c P75**; txt **P66***
τας τραπεζας: τα[ ]ων **P59**
ανεστρεψε: κατε[ ] **P59**; ανετρεψεν **P66**; ανεστρεψεν **P75**

2:16

P59 P66 P75

16: και τοις τας περιστερας πωλουσιν ειπεν αρατε ταυτα εντευθεν μη ποιειτε τον οικον του πατρος μου οικον εμποριου.

DEF: **P59**] τας περι[ ]ν ειπ[ ]ντευθ[ ] τον οι[ ] οικον [

αρατε: αραται **P66**

εντευθεν: + και **P**^{66}
ποειτε: ποιειται **P**^{66}
οικον^{2}: οικου **P**^{75}

2:17

P^{66} **P**^{75}

17: εμνηcθηcαν δε οι μαθηται αυτου οτι γεγραμμενον εcτιν ο ζηλοc του οικου cου κατεφαγε με.

δε: OM **P**^{66} **P**^{75}
εcτιν: + οτι **P**^{66} **P**^{75}
κατεφαγε: κατεφαγετε **P**^{66}; καταφαγεται **P**^{75}

2:18

P^{66} **P**^{75}

18: απεκριθηcαν ουν οι ιουδαιοι και ειπον αυτω τι cημειον δεικνυειc ημιν οτι ταυτα ποιειc.

ειπον: ειπαν **P**^{66} **P**^{75}
cημειον: cημιον **P**^{66}
δεικνυειc: δικνυειc **P**^{66}
ημιν: OM **P**^{75}

2:19

P^{66} **P**^{75}

19: απεκριθη ο ιηcουc και ειπεν αυτοιc λυcατε τον ναον τουτον και εν τριcιν ημεραιc εγερω αυτον.

ο: OM **P**^{66} **P**^{75}
λυcατε: λυcαται **P**^{66}

2:20

$\mathbf{P}^{66}$ $\mathbf{P}^{75}$

20: ειπον ουν οι ιουδαιοι τεσσαρακοντα και εξ ετεσιν ωκοδομηθη ο ναος ουτος και cυ εν τριcιν ημεραις εγερεις αυτον.

ειπον: ειπαν $\mathbf{P}^{66}$ $\mathbf{P}^{75}$
τεσσαρακοντα: τεσσερακοντα $\mathbf{P}^{66}$
ωκοδομηθη: οικοδομηθη $\mathbf{P}^{66}$ $\mathbf{P}^{75}$
cυ: OM $\mathbf{P}^{66*}$; cοι $\mathbf{P}^{75*}$; txt $\mathbf{P}^{66*c}$ $\mathbf{P}^{75*c}$

2:21

$\mathbf{P}^{66}$ $\mathbf{P}^{75}$

21: εκεινος δε ελεγε περι του ναου του cωματος αυτου.

ελεγε: ελεγεν $\mathbf{P}^{66}$ $\mathbf{P}^{75}$

2:22

$\mathbf{P}^{66}$ $\mathbf{P}^{75}$

22: οτε ουν ηγερθη εκ νεκρων εμνηcθηcαν οι μαθηται αυτου οτι τουτο ελεγεν αυτοις και επιcτευcαν τη γραφη και τω λογω ω ειπεν ο ιηcουc.

αυτοις: OM $\mathbf{P}^{66}$ $\mathbf{P}^{75}$
ω: ον $\mathbf{P}^{66}$ $\mathbf{P}^{75}$

2:23

$\mathbf{P}^{66}$ $\mathbf{P}^{75}$

23: ωc δε ην εν ιεροcολυμοις εν τω πασχα εν τη εορτη πολλοι επιcτευcαν εις το ονομα αυτου θεωρουντες αυτου τα cημεια α εποιει.

DEF: $\mathbf{P}^{66}$ ... cημεια α επ[ ]ει

ιεροcολυμοις: τοις ιεροcολυμοις $\mathbf{P}^{66}$ $\mathbf{P}^{75}$
cημεια: cημια $\mathbf{P}^{66}$

2:24

P^{66} **P**^{75}

24: αυτος δε ο ιηcουc ουκ επιcτευεν εαυτον αυτοιc δια το αυτον γινωcκειν παντας.

ο: OM **P**^{66} **P**^{75}
εαυτον: OM **P**^{75}
γινωcκειν: γεινωcκειν **P**^{75}

2:25

P^{66} **P**^{75}

25: και οτι ου χρειαν ειχεν ινα τιc μαρτυρηcη περι του ανθρωπου αυτος γαρ εγινωcκε τι ην εν τω ανθρωπω.

DEF: **P**^{75} ... τ̣ου...

χρειαν: χριαν **P**^{66*}; txt **P**^{66*c}
του: OM **P**^{66*}; txt **P**^{66*c}
εγινωcκε: εγινωcκεν **P**^{66}; εγεινωcκεν **P**^{75}

CHAPTER THREE

P^{36} P^{63} P^{66} P^{75} P^{80}

3:1

P^{66} P^{75}

1: ην δε ανθρωπος εκ των φαρισαιων νικοδημος ονομα αυτω αρχων των ιουδαιων.

DEF: **P^{75}** ... νεικο̣δημος ο̣νο̣μα...

νικοδημος: νεικοδημος **P^{66} P^{75}**

3:2

P^{66} P^{75}

2: ουτος ηλθε προς τον ιησουν νυκτος και ειπεν αυτω ραββι οιδαμεν οτι απο θεου εληλυθας διδασκαλος ουδεις γαρ ταυτα τα σημεια δυναται ποιειν α συ ποιεις εαν μη η ο θεος μετ αυτου.

DEF: **P^{75}** ... προ̣ς... αυτο̣υ

ηλθε: ηλθεν **P^{66} P^{75}**
τον ιησουν: αυτον **P^{66} P^{75}**
ραββι: ραββει **P^{66} P^{75}**
ταυτα τα σημεια δυναται: δυναται ταυτα τα σημεια **P^{66} P^{75}** (σημια **P^{66}**)
σημεια: + α **P^{75*}**; txt **P^{75c}**
η: OM **P^{66*}**; txt **P^{66*c}**

3:3

P^{66} P^{75}

3: απεκριθη ο ιησους και ειπεν αυτω αμην αμην λεγω σοι εαν μη τις γεννηθη ανωθεν ου δυναται ιδειν την βασιλειαν του θεου.

ο: OM **P^{66} P^{75}**

λεγω: + υ̣μ̣ω̣ν̣ **P**^{66*}; txt **P**^{66c} (verbum eras.)
γεννηθη: γεννηθην **P**^{75*}; txt **P**^{75c}

3:4

P^{66} **P**^{75}

4: λεγει προς αυτον ο νικοδημος πως δυναται ανθρωπος γεννηθηναι γερων ων μη δυναται εις την κοιλιαν της μητρος αυτου δευτερον εισελθειν και γεννηθηναι.

λεγει: λεγι **P**^{66*}; txt **P**^{66*c}
ο: OM **P**^{66} **P**^{75}
ανθρωπος γεννηθηναι: γεννηθηναι ανθρωπος **P**^{66}
εισελθειν: εισελθιν **P**^{66}

3:5

P^{66} **P**^{75}

5: απεκριθη ο ιησους αμην αμην λεγω σοι εαν μη τις γεννηθη εξ υδατος και πνευματος ου δυναται εισελθειν εις την βασιλειαν του θεου.

ο: OM **P**^{66} **P**^{75}
βασιλειαν: βασιλιαν **P**^{66}

3:6

P^{66} **P**^{75}

6: το γεγεννημενον εκ της σαρκος σαρξ εστι και το γεγεννημενον εκ του πνευματος πνευμα εστι.

γεγεννημενον^{1}: γεγεγεννημενον **P**^{66}
εστι^{1}: εστιν **P**^{66} **P**^{75}
εστι^{2}: εστιν **P**^{66} **P**^{75}

3:7

$\mathbf{P}^{66}$ $\mathbf{P}^{75}$

7: μη θαυμασης οτι ειπον σοι δει υμας γεννηθηναι ανωθεν.

3:8

$\mathbf{P}^{66}$ $\mathbf{P}^{75}$

8: το πνευμα οπου θελει πνει και την φωνην αυτου ακουεις αλλ ουκ οιδας ποθεν ερχεται και που υπαγει ουτως εστι πας ο γεγεννημενος εκ του πνευματος.

πνευμα: πνευα $\mathbf{P}^{66*}$; ευ postea eras.
πνει: $\overline{\text{πνει}}$ $\mathbf{P}^{75}$
οιδας: οιδες $\mathbf{P}^{75}$
εστι: εστιν $\mathbf{P}^{66}$ $\mathbf{P}^{75}$
γεγεννημενος: γενημενος $\mathbf{P}^{66*}$; txt $\mathbf{P}^{66*c}$

3:9

$\mathbf{P}^{66}$ $\mathbf{P}^{75}$

9: απεκριθη νικοδημος και ειπεν αυτω πως δυναται ταυτα γενεσθαι.

3:10

$\mathbf{P}^{66}$ $\mathbf{P}^{75}$

10: απεκριθη ο ιησους και ειπεν αυτω συ ει ο διδασκαλος του ισραηλ και ταυτα ου γινωσκεις.

ο^{1}: OM $\mathbf{P}^{66}$ $\mathbf{P}^{75}$
γινωσκεις: γεινωσκεις $\mathbf{P}^{66}$ $\mathbf{P}^{75}$

3:11

$\mathbf{P}^{66}$ $\mathbf{P}^{75}$

11: αμην αμην λεγω σοι οτι ο οιδαμεν λαλουμεν και ο εωρακαμεν μαρτυρουμεν και την μαρτυριαν ημων ου λαμβανετε.

εωρακαμεν: εωρακεμεν $\mathbf{P}^{66*}$; εορακαμεν $\mathbf{P}^{75}$; txt $\mathbf{P}^{66*c}$

λαμβανετε: λαμβανεται **P66**

3:12

P66 P75

12: ει τα επιγεια ειπον υμιν και ου πιστευετε πως εαν ειπω υμιν τα επουρανια πιστευσετε.

επιγεια: επιγια **P66**
υμιν[1]: υμειν **P66**
υμιν[2]: υμειν **P66**
πιστευσετε: πιστευσεται **P66**; πιστευετε **P75**

3:13

P66 P75

13: και ουδεις αναβεβηκεν εις τον ουρανον ει μη ο εκ του ουρανου καταβας ο υιος του ανθρωπου ο ων εν τω ουρανω.

ουδεις: ουδις **P66**
ο ων εν τω ουρανω: OM **P66 P75**

3:14

P36 P63 P66 P75

14: και καθως μωσης υψωσε τον οφιν εν τη ερημω ουτως υψωθηναι δει τον υιον του ανθρωπου.

DEF: **P36** και καθως [ ] τον οφιν [ ] υψωθην[
P63 ... ανθρωπο[

και: OM **P63**
μωσης: μωυσης **P63 P66 P75**
υψωσε: υψωσεν **P63 P66 P75**

3:15

$\mathbf{P}^{36}$ $\mathbf{P}^{63}$ $\mathbf{P}^{66}$ $\mathbf{P}^{75}$

15: ινα πας ο πιστευων εις αυτον μη αποληται αλλ εχη ζωην αιωνιον.

DEF: $\mathbf{P}^{36}$ ινα πας ο [ ] εχη ζωην [
$\mathbf{P}^{63}$] πας ο π[ ]ω[ ] αυτον μη απολητ[ ]λ εχη ζωην αιωνιον

πιστευων εις αυτον μη αποληται αλλ: [12-18 /] $\mathbf{P}^{36}$; πιστευων επ αυτω $\mathbf{P}^{66}$; πιστευων εν αυτω $\mathbf{P}^{75}$

3:16

$\mathbf{P}^{36}$ $\mathbf{P}^{63}$ $\mathbf{P}^{66}$ $\mathbf{P}^{75}$

16: ουτω γαρ ηγαπησεν ο θεος τον κοσμον ωστε τον υιον αυτου τον μονογενη εδωκεν ινα πας ο πιστευων εις αυτον μη αποληται αλλ εχη ζωην αιωνιον.

DEF: $\mathbf{P}^{36}$] ηγαπησ[ ]τε τον υιον [ ] εδωκεν [ ] αυτω μη [ ] ζωην α[
$\mathbf{P}^{63}$ ... ηγα[ ]σεν ... κοσμον ωσ[ ] τον υιον αυτου τον [ ]ε[ ] εδωκεν εις το[ ]ον ινα ... εις [ ]τ[ ]ν μη ... αλλ ε[ ] ζω[ ] αιωνιον
$\mathbf{P}^{66}$ ... ηγαπ[ ]ησεν...

ουτω: ουτως $\mathbf{P}^{63}$ $\mathbf{P}^{66}$ $\mathbf{P}^{75}$
ηγαπησεν: ηγαπ[ ]ησεν $\mathbf{P}^{66*}$; littera (forsan ν) postea eras.
αυτου: OM $\mathbf{P}^{66}$ $\mathbf{P}^{75}$
εδωκεν: + εις το[5]ον $\mathbf{P}^{63}$
πας: OM $\mathbf{P}^{63}$
εις αυτον: [ ] αυτω $\mathbf{P}^{36}$; επ αυτον $\mathbf{P}^{75*}$; txt $\mathbf{P}^{75c}$

3:17

$\mathbf{P}^{36}$ $\mathbf{P}^{63}$ $\mathbf{P}^{66}$ $\mathbf{P}^{75}$

17: ου γαρ απεστειλεν ο θεος τον υιον αυτου εις τον κοσμον ινα κρινη τον κοσμον αλλ ινα σωθη ο κοσμος δι αυτου.

DEF: **P**[36]]ν ο θ̅ς̅ τον [ ]μον ινα [ ]λ ινα [ ]υ
P[63]] ο θεος ... εις το[ ]οσμ[ ] αλλ ινα σωθ[ ] κο[ ]ος δι αυτου

απεστειλεν: απεστιλεν **P**[66]
υιον αυτου εις τον κοσμον: [13-19 /]μον **P**[36]
αυτου[1]: OM **P**[66] **P**[75]
ινα κρινη τον κοσμον: OM **P**[63] **P**[66*]; txt **P**[66*c] (ν eras. sub κ in κοσμον)

3:18

P[36] **P**[63] **P**[66] **P**[75]

18: ο πιστευων εις αυτον ου κρινεται ο δε μη πιστευων ηδη κεκριται οτι μη πεπιστευκεν εις το ονομα του μονογενους υιου του θεου.

DEF: **P**[36] ο πιστευ[ ]νηται ο δε [ ] το ονομα [ ]στευκε [ ]νογενους [
P[63] ... ηδη καικρ[ ]νεται ... πεπιστ[ ]κεν ...

κρινεται: [ ]νηται **P**[36]
μη πιστευων ηδη κεκριται οτι μη πεπιστευκεν εις το ονομα του μονογενους: [13-20] το ονομα / [14-21]στευκε [/ 14-21]νογενους **P**[36*] (ο[1] in ονομα supra lineam); del. το ονομα **P**[36*c]
κεκριται: καικρ[1]νεται **P**[63]

3:19

P[66] **P**[75]

19: αυτη δε εστιν η κρισις οτι το φως εληλυθεν εις τον κοσμον και ηγαπησαν οι ανθρωποι μαλλον το σκοτος η το φως ην γαρ πονηρα αυτων τα εργα.

DEF: **P**[75] ... φως [ ]λ̣η̣λυθεν... ηγαπησαν [ ]ι α̅ν̅ο̅ι̅... ην [ ]αρ...

οτι το: οτι **P**[66]
οι ανθρωποι μαλλον: μαλλον οι ανθρωποι: **P**[66]
πονηρα αυτων: αυτων πονηρα **P**[66] **P**[75]

3:20

$\mathbf{P}^{66}$ $\mathbf{P}^{75}$

20: πας γαρ ο φαυλα πρασσων μισει το φως και ουκ ερχεται προς το φως ινα μη ελεγχθη τα εργα αυτου.

DEF: $\mathbf{P}^{66}$ ... εργα [ ]υτου...
$\mathbf{P}^{75}$ ... φαυλ̣α...

μισει: μειсι $\mathbf{P}^{66}$
τα εργα αυτου: αυτου τα εργα $\mathbf{P}^{75}$
αυτου: [ ]υτου ο̣τι πονηρα εστιν $\mathbf{P}^{66}$

3:21

$\mathbf{P}^{66}$ $\mathbf{P}^{75}$

21: ο δε ποιων την αληθειαν ερχεται προς το φως ινα φανερωθη αυτου τα εργα οτι εν θεω εστιν ειργασμενα.

DEF: $\mathbf{P}^{66}$ ... την [ ]ληθιαν... ινα [ ]ανερωθη... θεω [ ]στιν... (teste ed. pr.)

δε: OM $\mathbf{P}^{66*}$; txt $\mathbf{P}^{66*c}$
αληθειαν: [ ]ληθιαν $\mathbf{P}^{66}$
ειργασμενα: ηργασμενα $\mathbf{P}^{66}$

3:22

$\mathbf{P}^{66}$ $\mathbf{P}^{75}$

22: μετα ταυτα ηλθεν ο ιησους και οι μαθηται αυτου εις την ιουδαιαν γην και εκει διετριβε μετ αυτων και εβαπτιζεν.

DEF: $\mathbf{P}^{66}$]τα ταυτα... μαθη[ ]αι... και [ ]κει... και ε[ ]απτιζεν
$\mathbf{P}^{75}$ μ̣ετα...

διετριβε: δειετριβεν $\mathbf{P}^{66}$; διετρειβεν $\mathbf{P}^{75}$

3:23

$\mathbf{P}^{66}$ $\mathbf{P}^{75}$

23: ην δε και ιωαννης βαπτιζων εν αινων εγγυς του σαλειμ οτι υδατα πολλα ην εκει και παρεγινοντο και εβαπτιζοντο.

DEF: **P**[66] ... ιωαννης [ ]απτιζων... του [ ]αλειμ... εκει [ ]αι παρεγεινοντο και εβαπτι[ ]οντο

ιωαννης: ο ιωαννης **P**[66]
παρεγινοντο: παρεγεινοντο **P**[66]

3:24

P[66] **P**[75]

24: ουπω γαρ ην βεβλημενος εις την φυλακην ο ιωαννης.

DEF: **P**[66] ... βεβλημενος [ ]c την...

3:25

P[66] **P**[75]

25: εγενετο ουν ζητησις εκ των μαθητων ιωαννου μετα ιουδαιων περι καθαρισμου.

DEF: **P**[66] εγε[ ]ετο... μαθη[ ]ων... ιουδαιων [ ]ερι...

ιουδαιων: ιουδαιου **P**[75]

3:26

P[66] **P**[75]

26: και ηλθον προς τον ιωαννην και ειπον αυτω ραββι ος ην μετα σου περαν του ιορδανου ω συ μεμαρτυρηκας ιδε ουτος βαπτιζει και παντες ερχονται προς αυτον.

DEF: **P**[66] ... τον [ ]ωαννην... ραβ[ ]ει... ιορ[ ]ανου... ιδε [ ]τος...

ηλθον: ην **P**[66*]; ηλθαν **P**[75]; txt **P**[66*c]
ειπον: ειπαν **P**[66] **P**[75]
ραββι: ραβ[ ]ει **P**[66]; ραββει **P**[75]

3:27

P[66] **P**[75]

27: απεκριθη ιωαννης και ειπεν ου δυναται ανθρωπος λαμβανειν ουδεν εαν μη η δεδομενον αυτω εκ του ουρανου.

DEF: **P**[66] ... ιωαννη[ ] και...

ιωαννης: ιωανης **P**[75]
λαμβανειν: λαμβανει **P**[75]
ουδεν: ουδε εν **P**[66] **P**[75]
η: ην **P**[66]

3:28

P[66] **P**[75]

28: αυτοι υμεις μοι μαρτυρειτε οτι ειπον ουκ ειμι εγω ο χριστος αλλ οτι απεσταλμενος ειμι εμπροσθεν εκεινου.

μοι: OM **P**[75]
ειπον: + οτι **P**[66] **P**[75]
απεσταλμενος: απταλμενος **P**[66]; txt **P**[66*c]

3:29

P[66] **P**[75]

29: ο εχων την νυμφην νυμφιος εστιν ο δε φιλος του νυμφιου ο εστηκως και ακουων αυτου χαρα χαιρει δια την φωνην του νυμφιου αυτη ουν η χαρα η εμη πεπληρωται.

DEF: **P**[75] ... εcṭιν... ῃ ẹṃῃ...

την[1]: τη **P**[66*]; txt **P**[66*c]

3:30

P^{66} **P**^{75}

30: εκεινον δει αυξανειν εμε δε ελαττουcθαι.

DEF: **P**^{75} ... αυξανẹịṿ...

3:31

P^{36} **P**^{66} **P**^{75}

31 ο ανωθεν ερχομενος επανω παντων εστιν ο ων εκ της γης εκ της γης εστι και εκ της γης λαλει ο εκ του ουρανου ερχομενος επανω παντων εστι.

DEF: **P**^{36}]ρχ[ ] παν[ ] εκ τη[ ] ερχομ[ ] εστι
P^{75} ... ερ̣χ̣ο̣μενος...

ανωθεν ερχομενος: ανοθερχομενος **P**^{66*}; ανοθεν ερχομενος **P**^{66*c}
εκ της γης εστι και εκ της γης λαλει ο εκ του ουρανου: εκ τη[16-20 /] **P**^{36}
εστι[1]: εστιν **P**^{66} **P**^{75}
και εκ της γης λαλει: OM **P**^{66*}; [ ] ε̣κ τ̣ης γης λαλει **P**^{66*c} (in margine inferiore addita)
ο[3]: + ων **P**^{66*}; txt **P**^{66c} (ων postea eras.)
ερχομενος: OM **P**^{66*}; txt **P**^{66*c}
επανω παντων εστι: OM **P**^{75}
εστι[3]: εστιν **P**^{66}

3:32

P^{36} **P**^{66} **P**^{75}

32 και ο εωρακε και ηκουσε τουτο μαρτυρει και την μαρτυριαν αυτου ουδεις λαμβανει.

DEF: **P**^{36} ο [ ] τουτο μ[
P^{66} ... την μαρτυ[ ]αν...

και[1]: OM **P**^{36} **P**^{66} **P**^{75}
εωρακε: εωρακεν **P**^{75}
ηκουσε: ηκουσεν **P**^{75}

3:33

P[66] **P**[75]

33: ο λαβων αυτου την μαρτυριαν εσφραγισεν οτι ο θεος αληθης εστιν.

DEF: **P**[66] ο [ ]βων... εσφρα[ ]σεν...
P[75] ... μαρτυριαν...

μαρτυριαν: + ουτος **P**[66*c]; txt **P**[66*]

3:34

P[36] **P**[66] **P**[75] **P**[80]

34: ον γαρ απεστειλεν ο θεος τα ρηματα του θεου λαλει ου γαρ εκ μετρου διδωσιν ο θεος το πνευμα.

DEF: **P**[36]]ν [ ] θυ [ ] διδω[
P[66] ον γαρ [ ]πεστιλεν... θεου [ ]αλει... το [ ]να
P[80]] ρ[ ]τ[ ] γαρ εκ μερου[ ] το πνευμα

απεστειλεν: [ ]πεστιλεν **P**[66]
μετρου: μερου **P**[66*]; txt **P**[66*c]; μερου[ ] **P**[80]
(34-5) διδωσιν ο θεος το πνευμα πατηρ αγαπα: διδω[/ 16-20] **P**[36]
διδωσιν: διδωσι **P**[75]
ο θεος[2]: OM **P**[66] **P**[75]

3:35

P[36] **P**[66] **P**[75]

35 ο πατηρ αγαπα τον υιον και παντα δεδωκεν εν τη χειρι αυτου.

DEF: **P**[36]] το̅ [ ]ωκεν[
P[66] ... παν[ ] δεδωκεν...

ο πατηρ αγαπα: cf. v. 34

3:36

P^{36} P^{66} P^{75}

36 ο πιστευων εις τον υιον εχει ζωην αιωνιον ο δε απειθων τω υιω ουκ οψεται ζωην αλλ η οργη του θεου μενει επ αυτον.

DEF: **P^{36}**]ιστε[
P^{66} ο [ ]στευων... ζωην [ ]ωνιον... υ̅ω̅ [ ]υκ... του [ ]υ̅...

η: OM **P^{66*}**; txt **P^{66*c}**

CHAPTER FOUR

P^{45} **P**^{63} **P**^{66} **P**^{75} **P**^{76}

4:1

P^{66} **P**^{75}

1: ως ουν εγνω ο κυριος οτι ηκουςαν οι φαριςαιοι οτι ιηςους πλειονας μαθητας ποιει και βαπτιζει η ιωαννης.

DEF: **P**^{66}] ουν... οι [ ]αριςαιοι... μαθη[ ]ας...

κυριος: ι̅c̅ **P**^{66*}; txt **P**^{66*c}

4:2

P^{66} **P**^{75}

2: καιτοιγε ιηςους αυτος ουκ εβαπτιζεν αλλ οι μαθηται αυτου.

DEF: **P**^{66}]αιτοιγε... εβαπτιζεν [ ]λλ...

4:3

P^{66} **P**^{75}

3: αφηκε την ιουδαιαν και απηλθε παλιν εις την γαλιλαιαν.

DEF: **P**^{66} ... την [ ]ουδαιαν... παλιν [ ]ις...

αφηκε: αφηκεν **P**^{66} **P**^{75}
απηλθε: απηλθεν **P**^{66} **P**^{75}

4:4

P^{66} **P**^{75}

4: εδει δε αυτον διερχεςθαι δια της ςαμαρειας.

DEF: **P**^{66} ... αυτον δ̣ιερχεςθαι...

σαμαρειας: σαμαριας **P66**

4:5

P66 P75

5: ερχεται ουν εις πολιν της σαμαρειας λεγομενην συχαρ πλησιον του χωριου ο εδωκεν ιακωβ ιωσηφ τω υιω αυτου.

DEF: **P66** ερ[ ]εται... πλησιο̅ [ ]ου χωριου... ιακωβ [ ]ω ιωσηφ...

ερχεται: εερχεται (sic) **P75**
ουν εις πολιν της σαμαρειας: OM **P75***; txt **P75*c**
ο: ου **P66**
ιωσηφ: [ ]ω ιωσηφ **P66**; τω ιωσηφ **P75**

4:6

P66 P75

6: ην δε εκει πηγη του ιακωβ ο ουν ιησους κεκοπιακως εκ της οδοιποριας εκαθεζετο ουτως επι τη πηγη ωρα ην ωσει εκτη.

DEF: **P66** ην [ ] εκει...

ο: OM **P66***; txt **P66*c**
εκαθεζετο: εκαθιζετο **P66***; txt **P66*c**
πηγη: γη **P66***; txt **P66*c**
ωσει: ως **P66 P75**

4:7

P66 P75

7: ερχεται γυνη εκ της σαμαρειας αντλησαι υδωρ λεγει αυτη ο ιησους δος μοι πιειν.

σαμαρειας: σαμαριας **P66**
πιειν: πειν **P66 P75**

4:8

P^{66} P^{75}

8: οι γαρ μαθηται αυτου απεληλυθειcαν ειc την πολιν ινα τροφαc αγοραcωcι.

αγοραcωcι: αγοραcωcιν **P^{66} P^{75}**

4:9

P^{63} P^{66} P^{75} P^{76}

9: λεγει ουν αυτω η γυνη η cαμαρειτιc πωc cυ ιουδαιοc ων παρ εμου πιειν αιτειc ουcηc γυναικοc cαμαρειτιδοc ου γαρ cυγχρωνται ιουδαιοι cαμαρειταιc.

DEF: **P^{76}**]τιδοc [ ] cυνχρ[ ]δαιοι cα[

cαμαρειτιc: cαμαριτιc **P^{66*}**; txt **P^{66c}**
παρ εμου: παρα μου **P^{66*}**; txt **P^{66c}**
πιειν αιτειc: ετειc πειν **P^{66*}**; πειν αιτειc **P^{66*c}**
πιειν: πειν **P^{63} P^{75}**
ουcηc γυναικοc cαμαρειτιδοc: γυναικοc cαμαριτιδοc ουcηc **P^{63} P^{66}**; [ ]τιδοc [5 /] **P^{76}**
ουcηc γυναικοc: γυναικοc ουcηc **P^{75}**
cυγχρωνται: cυνχρωνται **P^{63} P^{66} P^{75} P^{76}** (cυνχρ[ ])
cαμαρειταιc: cαμαριταιc **P^{66}**

4:10

P^{63} P^{66} P^{75}

10: απεκριθη ιηcουc και ειπεν αυτη ει ηδειc την δωρεαν του θεου και τιc εcτιν ο λεγων cοι δοc μοι πιειν cυ αν ητηcαc αυτον και εδωκεν αν cοι υδωρ ζων.

DEF: **P^{63}** ... ειπ[ ]ν αυτ[ ] ει ... cοι δ[ ]c ... ητηcαc [ ]υτον ...

ιηcουc: ο $\overline{\text{ιc}}$ **P^{63}**
ει ηδειc: ει ειδειc **P^{66*}**; txt **P^{66c}**
πιειν: πειν **P^{63} P^{66} P^{75}**
υδωρ: ζω υδωρ **P^{63*}**; txt **P^{63*c}**

4:11

P^{66} **P**^{75}

11: λεγει αυτω η γυνη κυριε ουτε αντλημα εχεις και το φρεαρ εστι βαθυ ποθεν ουν εχεις το υδωρ το ζων.

DEF: **P**^{66} ... εχεις [ ]αι...

αυτω: αυτη **P**^{66*}; txt **P**^{66*c}
η γυνη: OM **P**^{75}
εστι: εστιν **P**^{75}
βαθυ: βα $\overline{\theta\upsilon}$ **P**^{66*}; txt **P**^{66*c}

4:12

P^{66} **P**^{75} **P**^{76}

12: μη συ μειζων ει του πατρος ημων ιακωβ ος εδωκεν ημιν το φρεαρ και αυτος εξ αυτου επιε και οι υιοι αυτου και τα θρεμματα αυτου.

DEF: **P**^{76}] μιζω[ ]ς ημων [ ]τις εδω[ ]ο φρεαρ [ ] α[ ]ξ αυτου επιε[ ]α θρεμματα [

μειζων: μιζω[ ] **P**^{76}
ος: [ ]τις **P**^{76}
εδωκεν: δεδωκεν **P**^{66} **P**^{75}
επιε και οι υιοι αυτου και τα θρεμματα: επιε[1-4 / 1]α θρεμματα **P**^{76}
επιε: επιεν **P**^{66} **P**^{75}
οι: OM **P**^{66*}; txt **P**^{66*c}

4:13

P^{66} **P**^{75}

13: απεκριθη ο ιησους και ειπεν αυτη πας ο πινων εκ του υδατος τουτου διψησει παλιν.

ο^{1}: OM **P**^{66} **P**^{75}
πας: πως **P**^{75*}; txt **P**^{75c}
πινων: πεινων **P**^{66} **P**^{75}

4:14

P^{66} **P**^{75}

14: οc δ αν πιη εκ του υδατοc ου εγω δωcω αυτω ου μη διψηcη εις τον αιωνα αλλα το υδωρ ο δωcω αυτω γενηcεται εν αυτω πηγη υδατοc αλλομενου εις ζωην αιωνιον.

DEF: **P**^{75} ... εγω δω[ ] αυτω ... αιωνα α̣λλο...

διψηcη: διψηcει **P**^{75}
αλλα: αλλο **P**^{75}
εν αυτω πηγη: πηγη εν αυτω **P**^{66}

4:15

P^{66} **P**^{75}

15: λεγει προc αυτον η γυνη κυριε δοc μοι τουτο το υδωρ ινα μη διψω μηδε ερχωμαι ενθαδε αντλειν.

διψω: διψηcω **P**^{66*}; txt **P**^{66c}
ερχωμαι: διερχωμαι **P**^{66}; διερχομαι **P**^{75}

4:16

P^{66} **P**^{75}

16: λεγει αυτη ο ιηcουc υπαγε φωνηcον τον ανδρα cου και ελθε ενθαδε.

ο ιηcουc: OM **P**^{66} **P**^{75}

4:17

P^{66} **P**^{75}

17: απεκριθη η γυνη και ειπεν ουκ εχω ανδρα λεγει αυτη ο ιηcουc καλωc ειπαc οτι ανδρα ουκ εχω.

DEF: **P**^{75} απεκριθ̣η... ανδρα λ̣εγει αυτη... ανδρα [ ]υκ εχω

ειπεν: λεγει **P**^{75}; + αυτω **P**^{66} **P**^{75}

4:18

P^{66} P^{75}

18: πεντε γαρ ανδρας εϲχεϲ και νυν ον εχειϲ ουκ εϲτι ϲου ανηρ τουτο αληθεϲ ειρηκαϲ.

εϲτι: εϲτιν **P^{66} P^{75}**
ειρηκαϲ: ειπαϲ **P^{75}**

4:19

P^{66} P^{75}

19: λεγει αυτω η γυνη κυριε θεωρω οτι προφητηϲ ει ϲυ.

4:20

P^{66} P^{75}

20: οι πατερεϲ ημων εν τουτω τω ορει προϲεκυνηϲαν και υμειϲ λεγετε οτι εν ιεροϲολυμοιϲ εϲτιν ο τοποϲ οπου δει προϲκυνειν.

τουτω τω ορει: τω ορει τουτω **P^{66} P^{75}**
λεγετε: λεγεται **P^{66}**
δει προϲκυνειν: προϲκυνειν δει **P^{66} P^{75}**

4:21

P^{66} P^{75}

21: λεγει αυτη ο ιηϲουϲ γυναι πιϲτευϲον μοι οτι ερχεται ωρα οτε ουτε εν τω ορει τουτω ουτε εν ιεροϲολυμοιϲ προϲκυνηϲετε τω πατρι.

γυναι πιϲτευϲον μοι: πιϲτευε μοι γυναι **P^{66} P^{75}**
ορει: κοϲμω **P^{66*}**; ορι **P^{66*c}**
προϲκυνηϲετε: προϲκυνηϲεται **P^{66}**

4:22

P66 P75

22: υμειϲ προϲκυνειτε ο ουκ οιδατε ημειϲ προϲκυνουμεν ο οιδαμεν οτι η ϲωτηρια εκ των ιουδαιων εϲτιν.

προϲκυνειτε: προϲκυνιται **P66**
οιδατε: οιδαται **P66**

4:23

P66 P75

23: αλλ ερχεται ωρα και νυν εϲτιν οτε οι αληθινοι προϲκυνηται προϲκυνηϲουϲι τω πατρι εν πνευματι και αληθεια και γαρ ο πατηρ τοιουτουϲ ζητει τουϲ προϲκυνουνταϲ αυτον.

αλλ: αλλα **P66 P75**
προϲκυνηϲουϲι: προϲκυνηϲουϲιν **P66**
αληθεια: αληθια **P66**
τοιουτουϲ: τοιου[ras.]τουϲ **P66**
προϲκυνουνταϲ: προϲκυνουταϲ **P66**
αυτον: αυτω **P66***; txt **P66*c**

4:24

P66 P75

24: πνευμα ο θεοϲ και τουϲ προϲκυνουνταϲ αυτον εν πνευματι και αληθεια δει προϲκυνειν.

αληθεια: αληθια **P66**

4:25

P66 P75

25: λεγει αυτω η γυνη οιδα οτι μεϲϲιαϲ ερχεται ο λεγομενοϲ χριϲτοϲ οταν ελθη εκεινοϲ αναγγελει ημιν παντα.

οιδα: οιδαμεν **P66*c**; txt **P66***
μεϲϲιαϲ: μεϲϲειαϲ **P75**
ημιν: ημειν **P66**
παντα: απαντα **P66 P75**

4:26

P66 P75

26: λεγει αυτη ο ιηcουc εγω ειμι ο λαλων cοι.

4:27

P66 P75

27: και επι τουτω ηλθον οι μαθηται αυτου και εθαυμαcαν οτι μετα γυναικοc ελαλει ουδειc μεντοι ειπε τι ζητειc η τι λαλειc μετ αυτηc.

εθαυμαcαν: εθαυμαζον **P66 P75**
ειπε: ειπειν **P75***; ειπεν **P75*c**

4:28

P66 P75

28: αφηκεν ουν την υδριαν αυτηc η γυνη και απηλθεν ειc την πολιν και λεγει τοιc ανθρωποιc.

4:29

P66 P75

29: δευτε ιδετε ανθρωπον οc ειπε μοι παντα οcα εποιηcα μητι ουτοc εcτιν ο χριcτοc.

ιδετε: ιδεται **P66***; txt **P66*c**
ειπε: ειπεν **P66 P75**

4:30

P66 P75

30: εξηλθον ουν εκ τηc πολεωc και ηρχοντο προc αυτον.

ουν: OM **P75**

4:31

P66 P75

31: εν δε τω μεταξυ ηρωτων αυτον οι μαθηται λεγοντες ραββι φαγε.

DEF: **P75** ẹν...

δε : OM **P66**
μεταξυ: μετοξυ **P66**
ραββι: ραββει **P66 P75**

4:32

P66 P75

32: ο δε ειπεν αυτοις εγω βρωσιν εχω φαγειν ην υμεις ουκ οιδατε.

4:33

P66 P75

33: ελεγον ουν οι μαθηται προς αλληλους μη τις ηνεγκεν αυτω φαγειν.

4:34

P66 P75

34: λεγει αυτοις ο ιηcουc εμον βρωμα εστιν ινα ποιω το θελημα του πεμψαντος με και τελειωσω αυτου το εργον.

ποιω: ποιηcω **P66 P75**
τελειωcω: τελιωcω **P66**

4:35

P66 P75

35: ουχ υμεις λεγετε οτι ετι τετραμηνον εστι και ο θερισμος ερχεται ιδου λεγω υμιν επαρατε τους οφθαλμους υμων και θεασασθε τας χωρας οτι λευκαι εισι προς θερισμον ηδη.

λεγετε: λεγεται **P^{66}**
ετι: OM **P^{75}**
τετραμηνον: τετραμηνος **P^{66} P^{75}**
εστι: εστιν **P^{66} P^{75}**
επαρατε: επαραται **P^{66}**; απαρατε **P^{75}**
εισι: εισιν **P^{66} P^{75}**

4:36

P^{66} P^{75}

36: και ο θεριζων μισθον λαμβανει και συναγει καρπον εις ζωην αιωνιον ινα και ο σπειρων ομου χαιρη και ο θεριζων.

και^{1}: OM **P^{66} P^{75}**
μισθον: μεισθον **P^{66}**
και^{3}: OM **P^{66} P^{75}**
σπειρων: σπιρων **P^{66}**
χαιρη: χαιρων **P^{75*}**; txt **P^{75c}**
ο^{3}: OM **P^{66}**

4:37

P^{66} P^{75}

37: εν γαρ τουτω ο λογος εστιν ο αληθινος οτι αλλος εστιν ο σπειρων και αλλος ο θεριζων.

OM totum versum **P^{75}**
αλλος: αλος **P^{66*}**; txt **P^{66c}**

4:38

P^{66} P^{75}

38: εγω απεστειλα υμας θεριζειν ο ουχ υμεις κεκοπιακατε αλλοι κεκοπιακασι και υμεις εις τον κοπον αυτων εισεληλυθατε.

απεστειλα: απεστιλα **P^{66}**
κεκοπιακασι: κεκοπιακασιν **P^{66} P^{75}** (ο sub α^{2} **P^{75}**, teste ed. pr.)
εισεληλυθατε: εισεληλυθαται **P^{66}**

4:39

P^{66} P^{75}

39: εκ δε της πολεως εκεινης πολλοι επιστευσαν εις αυτον των σαμαρειτων δια τον λογον της γυναικος μαρτυρουσης οτι ειπε μοι παντα οσα εποιησα.

σαμαρειτων: σαμαριτων **P^{66}**
μαρτυρουσης: ματυρουσης **P^{66*}**; ματυρ rescript. **P^{66*c}**
ειπε: ειπεν **P^{66} P^{75}**
οσα: α **P^{75}**
εποιησα: OM **P^{66*}**; txt **P^{66*c}**

4:40

P^{66} P^{75}

40: ως ουν ηλθον προς αυτον οι σαμαρειται ηρωτων αυτον μειναι παρ αυτοις και εμεινεν εκει δυο ημερας.

σαμαρειται: σαμαριται **P^{66}**
μειναι: μιναι **P^{66}**

4:41

P^{66} P^{75}

41: και πολλω πλειους επιστευσαν δια τον λογον αυτου.

πλειους: πλειον **P^{75}**

4:42

P^{66} P^{75}

42: τη τε γυναικι ελεγον οτι ουκετι δια την σην λαλιαν πιστευομεν αυτοι γαρ ακηκοαμεν και οιδαμεν οτι ουτος εστιν αληθως ο σωτηρ του κοσμου ο χριστος.

τε: δε **P^{66}**
ελεγον: ειπαν ελεγον **P^{75*}**; txt **P^{75c}**
σην λαλιαν: λαλιαν σου **P^{75}**
λαλιαν: λαλειαν **P^{66}**
ουτος: α̣υτος **P^{66*}**; txt **P^{66c}**

εϲτιν: ε rescript. **P66***
ο χριϲτοϲ: OM **P66 P75**

4:43

P66 P75

43: μετα δε ταϲ δυο ημεραϲ εξηλθεν εκειθεν και απηλθεν ειϲ την γαλιλαιαν.

και απηλθεν: OM **P66 P75**

4:44

P66 P75

44: αυτοϲ γαρ ο ιηϲουϲ εμαρτυρηϲεν οτι προφητηϲ εν τη ιδια πατριδι τιμην ουκ εχει.

ο: OM **P66 P75**

4:45

P66 P75

45: οτε ουν ηλθεν ειϲ την γαλιλαιαν εδεξαντο αυτον οι γαλιλαιοι παντα εωρακοτεϲ α εποιηϲεν εν ιεροϲολυμοιϲ εν τη εορτη και αυτοι γαρ ηλθον ειϲ την εορτην.

α: οϲα **P66 P75**

4:46

P66 P75

46: ηλθεν ουν ο ιηϲουϲ παλιν ειϲ την κανα τηϲ γαλιλαιαϲ οπου εποιηϲε το υδωρ οινον και ην τιϲ βαϲιλικοϲ ου ο υιοϲ ηϲθενει εν καπερναουμ.

DEF: **P75** ... γαλιλαιαϲ [ ]ου εποιηϲεν... ην τ̣ιϲ...

ο ιηϲουϲ: OM **P66 P75**
εποιηϲε: εποιηϲεν **P66 P75**
καπερναουμ: καφαρναουμ **P66 P75**

4:47

P^{66} P^{75}

47: ουτος ακουσας οτι ιησους ηκει εκ της ιουδαιας εις την γαλιλαιαν απηλθε προς αυτον και ηρωτα αυτον ινα καταβη και ιασηται αυτου τον υιον ημελλε γαρ αποθνησκειν.

ιησους: ο ιησους **P^{66*}**; txt **P^{66c}**
απηλθε: απηλθεν **P^{66} P^{75}**
προς αυτον: OM **P^{75}**
αυτον^{2}: OM **P^{66} P^{75}**
ιασηται: ιαση **P^{75*}**; txt **P^{75c}**
ημελλε: ημελλεν **P^{66} P^{75}**

4:48

P^{66} P^{75}

48: ειπεν ουν ο ιησους προς αυτον εαν μη σημεια και τερατα ιδητε ου μη πιστευσητε.

ουν: OM **P^{66*}**; txt **P^{66*c}**
αυτον: σαυτον **P^{66*}**; txt **P^{66c}**
σημεια: σημια **P^{66}**
πιστευσητε: πιστευσηται **P^{66}**

4:49

P^{66} P^{75}

49: λεγει προς αυτον ο βασιλικος κυριε καταβηθι πριν αποθανειν το παιδιον μου.

4:50

P^{66} P^{75}

50: λεγει αυτω ο ιησους πορευου ο υιος σου ζη και επιστευσεν ο ανθρωπος τω λογω ω ειπεν αυτω ο ιησους και επορευετο.

και^{1}: OM **P^{66} P^{75}**
ω: ον **P^{75}**
αυτω^{2}: OM **P^{75}**

4:51

P45 P66 P75

51: ηδη δε αυτου καταβαινοντος οι δουλοι αυτου απηντησαν αυτω και απηγγειλαν λεγοντες οτι ο παις cου ζη.

DEF: **P45**]ηντ[

51-52 απηντησαν αυτω και απηγγειλαν λεγοντες οτι ο παις cου ζη επυθετο: [ ]ηντ[18-22 / 23-26]ετο **P45** (& cf. **P66*c**)
απηντησαν: υπηντησαν **P66 P75**
και απηγγειλαν: OM **P75**
απηγγειλαν: απηγγιλαν **P66**
παις cου: παις αυτου **P66* P75**; υιος cου **P66*c** (& cf. **P45**)

4:52

P45 P66 P75

52: επυθετο ουν παρ αυτων την ωραν εν η κομψοτερον εcχε και ειπον αυτω οτι χθες ωραν εβδομην αφηκεν αυτον ο πυρετος.

DEF: **P45**]ετο ου[ ]ν οτι ε[

παρ αυτων την ωραν: την ωραν παρ αυτων **P66**
παρ αυτων: OM **P75**
ωραν: + εκεινην **P75**
κομψοτερον: κοψοτερον **P75***; txt **P75c**
εcχε: εcχεν **P66 P75**
και: OM **P66 P75**
ειπον: + ουν **P66*c P75**; txt **P66***
αυτω: OM **P45**
χθες: εχθες **P66 P75**; ε[ ] **P45**

4:53

P^{45} **P**^{66} **P**^{75}

53: εγνω ουν ο πατηρ οτι εν εκεινη τη ωρα εν η ειπεν αυτω ο ιηcουc οτι ο υιοc cου ζη και επιcτευcεν αυτοc και η οικια αυτου ολη.

DEF: **P**^{45}] ο π̅ρ̅ οτ[

πατηρ: + αυτου **P**^{66}
εν^{1}: OM **P**^{75}
οτι^{2}: OM **P**^{66} **P**^{75}

4:54

P^{45} **P**^{66} **P**^{75}

54: τουτο παλιν δευτερον cημειον εποιηcεν ο ιηcουc ελθων εκ τηc ιουδαιαc ειc την γαλιλαιαν.

DEF: **P**^{45} τ[ ]υ[ ]ουδα[

τουτο: + δε **P**^{66} **P**^{75}
δευτερον cημειον εποιηcεν: εποιηcεν δευτερον cημειον **P**^{75}

CHAPTER FIVE

P^{45} P^{66} P^{75} P^{84} P^{95}

5:1

P^{45} P^{66} P^{75}

1: μετα ταυτα ην εορτη των ιουδαιων και ανεβη ο ιηcουc ειc ιεροcολυμα.

DEF: **P^{45}**]ν και [

ο: OM **P^{66} P^{75}**

5:2

P^{45} P^{66} P^{75}

2: εcτι δε εν τοιc ιεροcολυμοιc επι τη προβατικη κολυμβηθρα η επιλεγομενη εβραιcτι βηθεcδα πεντε cτοαc εχουcα.

DEF: **P^{45}**]μοιc [

εcτι: εcτιν **P^{66} P^{75}**
επιλεγομενη: εcτιν λεγομενη **P^{66*}**; txt **P^{66*c}**
βηθεcδα: βηδcαιδαν **P^{66*}**; βηδcαιδα **P^{66c}**; βηθcαιδα **P^{75}**

5:3

P^{66} P^{75}

3: εν ταυταιc κατεκειτο πληθοc πολυ των αcθενουντων τυφλων χωλων ξηρων εκδεχομενων την του υδατοc κινηcιν.

πολυ: OM **P^{66} P^{75}**
εκδεχομενων την του υδατοc κινηcιν: OM **P^{66} P^{75}**

5:4

P^{66} P^{75}

4: αγγελος γαρ κατα καιρον κατεβαινεν εν τη κολυμβηθρα και εταραςςε το υδωρ ο ουν πρωτος εμβας μετα την ταραχην του υδατος υγιης εγινετο ω δηποτε κατειχετο νοςηματι.

OM totum versum **P^{66} P^{75}**

5:5

P^{66} P^{75} P^{84}

5: ην δε τις ανθρωπος εκει τριακονταοκτω ετη εχων εν τη αςθενεια.

DEF: **P^{84}** (cf. p. 115)

ανθρωπος εκει: εκει ανθρωπος **P^{66}**
τριακονταοκτω ετη: ετη $\overline{\lambda\eta}$ **P^{66*}**; $\overline{\lambda\eta}$ ετη **P^{66*c}**
ετη: OM **P^{75*}**; txt **P^{75c}**
αςθενεια: + αυτου **P^{66} P^{75}**

5:6

P^{66} P^{75}

6: τουτον ιδων ο ιηςους κατακειμενον και γνους οτι πολυν ηδη χρονον εχει λεγει αυτω θελεις υγιης γενεςθαι.

ιδων: ειδων **P^{66}**
πολυν: πολλυν **P^{75*}**; txt **P^{75c}**
ηδη χρονον εχει: χρονον ηδη εχει **P^{75}**; εχει χρονον **P^{66*}**; ηδη εχει χρονον **P^{66*c}**

5:7

P^{66} P^{75}

7: απεκριθη αυτω ο αςθενων κυριε ανθρωπον ουκ εχω ινα οταν ταραχθη το υδωρ βαλλη με εις την κολυμβηθραν εν ω δε ερχομαι εγω αλλος προ εμου καταβαινει.

DEF: **P^{75}** ... ταραχθη τ̣ο...

βαλλη: βαλη $\mathbf{P}^{66}$ $\mathbf{P}^{75}$
με: μαι $\mathbf{P}^{66}$

5:8

$\mathbf{P}^{66}$ $\mathbf{P}^{75}$

8: λεγει αυτω ο ιηcουc εγειραι αρον τον κραββατον cου και περιπατει.

εγειραι: εγιραι $\mathbf{P}^{66}$; εγειρε $\mathbf{P}^{75}$
8-9: inter περιπατει et και quattuor litterae eras. $\mathbf{P}^{66}$

5:9

$\mathbf{P}^{66}$ $\mathbf{P}^{75}$

9: και ευθεωc εγενετο υγιηc ο ανθρωποc και ηρε τον κραββατον αυτου και περιεπατει ην δε cαββατον εν εκεινη τη ημερα.

DEF: $\mathbf{P}^{75}$ ... ανθρωποc [ ]α̣ι ηρεν τον̣... και π̣εριεπατει...

ηρε: ηρεν $\mathbf{P}^{66}$ $\mathbf{P}^{75}$
κραββατον: κραβαττον $\mathbf{P}^{66}$

5:10

$\mathbf{P}^{66}$ $\mathbf{P}^{75}$

10: ελεγον ουν οι ιουδαιοι τω τεθεραπευμενω cαββατον εcτιν ουκ εξεcτι cοι αραι τον κραββατον.

οι: cοι $\mathbf{P}^{66*}$; txt $\mathbf{P}^{66c}$ (c eras.)
εcτιν: + και $\mathbf{P}^{66}$ $\mathbf{P}^{75}$
εξεcτι: εξεcτιν $\mathbf{P}^{66}$ $\mathbf{P}^{75}$
κραββατον: κραβαττον cου $\mathbf{P}^{66}$ $\mathbf{P}^{75}$

5:11

P66 P75

11: απεκριθη αυτοις ο ποιησας με υγιη εκεινος μοι ειπεν αρον τον κραββατον σου και περιπατει.

απεκριθη: ο δε απεκριθη **P66**; ος δε απεκριθη **P75**
μοι: ποι aut τοι aut σοι **P66**
αρον: αραν **P66***; txt **P66*c**
κραββατον: κραβαττον **P66 P75**
σου: σοι **P75***; txt **P75c**

5:12

P66 P75

12: ηρωτησαν ουν αυτον τις εστιν ο ανθρωπος ο ειπων σοι αρον τον κραββατον σου και περιπατει.

ουν: OM **P66**
αυτον: OM **P75**
τον κραββατον σου: OM **P66 P75**

5:13

P66 P75

13: ο δε ιαθεις ουκ ηδει τις εστιν ο γαρ ιησους εξενευσεν οχλου οντος εν τω τοπω.

γαρ: δε **P75**

5:14

P66 P75

14: μετα ταυτα ευρισκει αυτον ο ιησους εν τω ιερω και ειπεν αυτω ιδε υγιης γεγονας μηκετι αμαρτανε ινα μη χειρον τι σοι γενηται.

DEF: **P66** ... αυτω ι[ ]ε υγιης... αμαρτα[ ]ε ινα...

ευρισκει: ευρισκι **P66c**; txt **P66*** (ε² eras.)
τι σοι: σοι τι **P66 P75**

5:15

P^{66} P^{75}

15: απηλθεν ο ανθρωπος και ανηγγειλε τοις ιουδαιοις οτι ιησους εστιν ο ποιησας αυτον υγιη.

ανηγγειλε: ανηγγιλεν **P^{66}**; ανηγγειλεν **P^{75}**
τοις ιουδαιοις: τοις ιουδαιους **P^{75}**

5:16

P^{66} P^{75}

16: και δια τουτο εδιωκον τον ιησουν οι ιουδαιοι και εζητουν αυτον αποκτειναι οτι ταυτα εποιει εν σαββατω.

δια: fortasse + duae litterae postea eras. **P^{66}**
τον ιησουν οι ιουδαιοι: οι ιουδαιοι τον ιησουν **P^{66} P^{75}**
και εζητουν αυτον αποκτειναι: OM **P^{66} P^{75}**
οτι: τι **P^{66*}**; txt **P^{66*c}**
εποιει: εποιησεν **P^{75}**

5:17

P^{66} P^{75}

17: ο δε ιησους απεκρινατο αυτοις ο πατηρ μου εως αρτι εργαζεται καγω εργαζομαι.

ιησους: OM **P^{75}**

5:18

P^{66} P^{75}

18: δια τουτο ουν μαλλον εζητουν αυτον οι ιουδαιοι αποκτειναι οτι ου μονον ελυε το σαββατον αλλα και πατερα ιδιον ελεγε τον θεον ισον εαυτον ποιων τω θεω.

εζητουν αυτον οι ιουδαιοι: οι ιουδαιοι εζητουν αυτον **P^{66}**
αποκτειναι: αποκτιναι **P^{66}**
ελεγε: ελεγεν **P^{66} P^{75}**

5:19

P^{66} P^{75}

19: απεκρινατο ουν ο ιηcουc και ειπεν αυτοιc αμην αμην λεγω υμιν ου δυναται ο υιοc ποιειν αφ εαυτου ουδεν εαν μη τι βλεπη τον πατερα ποιουντα α γαρ αν εκεινοc ποιη ταυτα και ο υιοc ομοιωc ποιει.

ο ιηcουc: OM **P^{75}**
ειπεν: ελεγεν **P^{66} P^{75}**
εαυτου: ε fortasse add. postea **P^{75*}**
ουδεν: ουδε εν **P^{66}**
εαν: εα **P^{66*}**; txt **P^{66*c}**
αν: εαν **P^{66}**

5:20

P^{66} P^{75}

20: ο γαρ πατηρ φιλει τον υιον και παντα δεικνυcιν αυτω α αυτοc ποιει και μειζονα τουτων δειξει αυτω εργα ινα υμειc θαυμαζητε.

φιλει: φιλι **P^{66*}**; txt **P^{66*c}**
δεικνυcιν: δικνυcιν **P^{75}**
θαυμαζητε: θαυμαζηται **P^{66}**; θαυμαcητε **P^{75}**

5:21

P^{45} P^{66} P^{75}

21: ωcπερ γαρ ο πατηρ εγειρει τουc νεκρουc και ζωοποιει ουτω και ο υιοc ουc θελει ζωοποιει.

DEF: **P^{45}**]ερ γα[ ]λει ζω[
P^{75} ... και ζωοποι̣ει...

γαρ ο πατηρ εγειρει τουc νεκρουc και ζωοποιει ουτω και ο υιοc ουc θελει: γα[18-22 / 21-22]λει **P^{45}**
ουτω: ουτωc **P^{66} P^{75}**

5:22

P^{45} **P**^{66} **P**^{75}

22: ουδε γαρ ο πατηρ κρινει ουδενα αλλα την κρισιν πασαν δεδωκε τω υιω

DEF: **P**^{45}]cαν εδ[

ουδε: ου **P**^{66*}; txt **P**^{66*c}
κρινει: κρεινει **P**^{75*}; txt **P**^{75c}
δεδωκε: εδ[ ] **P**^{45}; δεδωκεν **P**^{66} **P**^{75} (τ sub δ^{1} **P**^{75})

5:23

P^{45} **P**^{66} **P**^{75}

23: ινα παντεc τιμωcι τον υιον καθωc τιμωcι τον πατερα ο μη τιμων τον υιον ου τιμα τον πατερα τον πεμψαντα αυτον.

DEF: **P**^{45}]ν $\overline{\text{πρα}}$ [
P^{75} ... καθωc τιμω[ ]ατερα ο μη τιμων .[ ] πατε̣ρ̣α̣ τον πεμ[

τιμωcι^{1}: τιμωcιν **P**^{75}
μη: OM **P**^{66*}; txt **P**^{66*c}

5:24

P^{45} **P**^{66} **P**^{75}

24: αμην αμην λεγω υμιν οτι ο τον λογον μου ακουων και πιcτευων τω πεμψαντι με εχει ζωην αιωνιον και ειc κριcιν ουκ ερχεται αλλα μεταβεβηκεν εκ του θανατου ειc την ζωην.

DEF: **P**^{45}] τον λο[ ] αιων[ ] θανα[
P^{75}]μην αμην... οτ[ ] τον [ ] μ̣ου... πιcτευω̣ν̣ τω [ ]αντι...
αιων̣[ ]ον [ ] κ̣ρ̣ιcιν [ ]κ̣ ερχεται αλλα μ[ ]τ̣αβ[ ]κ του...

εχει: εχι **P**^{66}

5:25

P^{45} **P**^{66} **P**^{75}

25: αμην αμην λεγω υμιν οτι ερχεται ωρα και νυν εϲτιν οτε οι νεκροι ακουϲονται τηϲ φωνηϲ του υιου του θεου και οι ακουϲαντεϲ ζηϲονται.

DEF: **P**^{45}]α κα[
P^{75} α̣[ ]μην λεγω... νυ̣[ ]τιν ο̣τε [ ]ι νεκροι... τηϲ [ ]ν̣η̣[ ] τ̣ο̣υ υιο̣υ̣... ακουϲαν[ ]ουϲιν

υμιν: υμειν **P**^{66}
ωρα: OM **P**^{75}
ακουϲονται: ακουϲωϲιν **P**^{66}; ακουϲουϲιν **P**^{75}
οι^{2}: OM **P**^{66}
ζηϲονται: ζηϲουϲιν **P**^{66}; [ ]ουϲιν **P**^{75}

5:26

P^{66} **P**^{75} **P**^{95}

26: ωϲπερ γαρ ο πατηρ εχει ζωην εν εαυτω ουτωϲ εδωκε και τω υιω ζωην εχειν εν εαυτω.

DEF: **P**^{75} ... εχει [ ]ην εν... εδω[ ] ζωην...
P^{95}]αυτω

εχει: εχι **P**^{66}
εδωκε και τω υιω: και τω υιω εδωκεν **P**^{66}; και τω υιω εδω[ ] **P**^{75}

5:27

P^{66} **P**^{75} **P**^{95}

27: και εξουϲιαν εδωκεν αυτω και κριϲιν ποιειν οτι υιοϲ ανθρωπου εϲτι.

DEF: **P**^{75} και εξο̣υ̣ϲιαν [ ]ωκεν α[ ]τω... ποιειν ο[ ] υιοϲ $\overline{\text{ανου}}$ εϲτι̣ν̣
P^{95} κα[ ]ουϲιαν εδ[ ]οιειν οτι υιο[ ]ν

και εξουϲιαν: κα[1 / 11-12]ουϲιαν **P**^{95}
εδωκεν αυτω και κριϲιν ποιειν: εδ[1 / 10-12]οιειν **P**^{95}
και^{2}: OM **P**^{66} **P**^{75}

εστι: εστιν **P66** **P75**; [ ]ν **P95**

5:28

P66 **P75** **P95**

28: μη θαυμαζετε τουτο οτι ερχεται ωρα εν η παντες οι εν τοις μνημειοις ακουσονται της φωνης αυτου.

DEF: **P75** μη θαυμαζ[ ]το οτι... παντες [ ] τοις... τη̣[ ]νης αυτου
P95 μη θαυμ[ ]τι ερχεται [ ]ν [ ]οις μν[ ]ες της [

θαυμαζετε: θαυμαζεται **P66**
οι: OM **P66***; σοι **P66*c**; txt **P66c**
τοις μνημειοις: τω ερημω **P66***; txt **P66*c**
ακουσονται: ακουσωσιν **P66**; ακουσουσιν **P75**; [ ]ες **P95**

5:29

P66 **P75** **P95**

29: και εκπορευσονται οι τα αγαθα ποιησαντες εις αναστασιν ζωης οι δε τα φαυλα πραξαντες εις αναστασιν κρισεως.

DEF: **P75** και εκπορευσοντα[ ] αγαθα... αναςτ̣[ ] οι δε τα φαυ̣λ̣α πραξαντες̣ [ ] κρισεω[
P95]πορευσ[ ]ησα[

εκπορευσονται: εκπορευσωνται **P66***; txt **P66*c**
οι δε: και οι **P66***; οι **P66c**

5:30

P^{66} P^{75}

30: ου δυναμαι εγω ποιειν απ εμαυτου ουδεν καθωc ακουω κρινω και η κριcιc η εμη δικαια εcτιν οτι ου ζητω το θελημα το εμον αλλα το θελημα του πεμψαντοc με πατροc.

DEF: **P^{75}** ... ποι̣ε̣[ ]αυτου... κ̣ρι[ ] κ̣α̣ι η κρι̣[ ]ιc εμη̣ [ ]τιν
ο̣[ ] θελημα το εμον α[ ]λα τ[ ]λη[ ] πεμψαντοc με

δυναμαι: δυνομαι **P^{66}**
ουδεν: ουδε εν **P^{66}**
αλλα: αλλο **P^{75*}**; txt **P^{75*c}**
πατροc: OM **P^{66} P^{75}**

5:31

P^{66} P^{75}

31: εαν εγω μαρτυρω περι εμαυτου η μαρτυρια μου ουκ εcτιν αληθηc.

DEF: **P^{75}**]ν̣ ε̣[ ]τυ[ ]ρι εμαυτου η μαρ[ ]cτι̣ν̣ α̣λ̣η̣θ̣ηc

5:32

P^{66} P^{75}

32: αλλοc εcτιν ο μαρτυρων περι εμου και οιδα οτι αληθηc εcτιν η μαρτυρια ην μαρτυρει περι εμου.

DEF: **P^{75}** αλ[ ]c εc̣τιν [ ]ρ̣ι... αλη̣[ ]α̣ρτυρια ην μαρτυρε̣[

μαρτυρει: μαρτυρι **P^{66}**

5:33

P^{66} **P**^{75}

33: υμεις απεσταλκατε προς ιωαννην και μεμαρτυρηκε τη αληθεια.

DEF: **P**^{75} υμẹị[ ] απ̣[ ] και μ̣[

υμεις: υμις **P**^{66*}; txt **P**^{66*c}
απεσταλκατε: απεσταλκαται **P**^{66}
μεμαρτυρηκεν: εμεμαρτυρηκεν **P**^{66*}; ε^{1} postea eras.
αληθεια: αληθια **P**^{66}

5:34

P^{66} **P**^{75}

34: εγω δε ου παρα ανθρωπου την μαρτυριαν λαμβανω αλλα ταυτα λεγω ινα υμεις σωθητε.

DEF: **P**^{75}] δẹ ọυ̣ π̣α̣[ ] . . [ ]ρ̣τυριαν α[ ]ω̣ ịνα υμεις cωθητε

μαρτυριαν λαμβανω αλλα: [ ]ρτυριαν α[ ] **P**^{75} (ordo verborum mutatus nihilo omisso, ut videtur)

5:35

P^{66} **P**^{75}

35: εκεινος ην ο λυχνος ο καιομενος και φαινων υμεις δε ηθελησατε αγαλλιασθηναι προς ωραν εν τω φωτι αυτου.

DEF: **P**^{75}]υ̣χνος ο καιομ̣ẹṿος κα̣[ ]λ̣ηcα[ ] αγαλλị[ ] . [ ]τ̣ị α[

ηθελησατε: ηθελησαται **P**^{66}
αγαλλιασθηναι: αγαλλιαθηναι **P**^{66}

5:36

P^{66} P^{75} P^{95}

36: εγω δε εχω την μαρτυριαν μειζω του ιωαννου τα γαρ εργα α εδωκε μοι ο πατηρ ινα τελειωσω αυτα αυτα τα εργα α εγω ποιω μαρτυρει περι εμου οτι ο πατηρ με απεσταλκε.

DEF: **P^{75}**] μ̣ε̣[ ]ω̣α̣γ̣[ ]ρ̣[ ]ε[ ]τα εργ[ ]οιω μ[ ]τι ο πατηρ με απε̣[ ]αλ[
P^{95}]ωcω αυτα τ[ ]τυρει περι εμ[ ]cταλκεν

μειζω: μειζων **P^{66}**
α: OM **P^{66*}**; α **P^{66*c}**
εδωκε: δεδωκεν **P^{66}**
κ postea eras. post δεδωκεν **P^{66}**
τελειωσω: τελιωcω **P^{66}**
αυτα^{2}: OM **P^{95}**; ταυτα **P^{66*}** (τ^{1} partim eras.)
εργα α εγω ποιω: εργ[3]οιω **P^{75}**
εγω^{2}: OM **P^{66}**
μαρτυρει: μαρτυρι **P^{66}**
ο^{2}: OM **P^{66}**
απεσταλκε: απεασταλκεν **P^{66}** (α^{2} postea eras.); [ ]cταλκεν **P^{95}**

5:37

P^{66} P^{75} P^{95}

37: και ο πεμψας με πατηρ αυτος μεμαρτυρηκε περι εμου ουτε φωνην αυτου ακηκοατε πωποτε ουτε ειδος αυτου εωρακατε.

DEF: **P^{75}**]μψαc... εκει[ ]οc μ[ ]κεν πε̣ρι ε̣μου [ ]η̣ν αυτου πωποτ̣[ ]ου̣[ ]ε ειδ[ ]c αυτ̣ου εορ̣ακατε
P^{95} κα[ ]κεινος μεμ[ ]ρι εμου ου[ ]υ πωπ[ ]τ[ ] ειδος α[

αυτος: εκει[ ]οc **P^{75}**; [ ]κεινος **P^{95}**
μεμαρτυρηκε: μεμαρτυρηκεν **P^{66}**; μ[ ]κεν **P^{75}**
ακηκοατε πωποτε: ποτε ακηκοατε **P^{66*}**; πωποτε ακηκοατε **P^{66*c}**; πωποτ[9] **P^{75}**; πωπ[ ]τ[9-11] **P^{95}**
εωρακατε: εωρακαται **P^{66}**; εορακατε **P^{75}**

5:38

P^{66} P^{75} P^{95}

38: και τον λογον αυτου ουκ εχετε μενοντα εν υμιν οτι ον απεστειλεν εκεινος τουτω υμεις ου πιστευετε.

DEF: **P^{75}**]ν̣ λο[ ]ν̣ αυτου ουκ εχετε εν [ ] μεν̣[ ]ντα οτι ον απεστειλεν [ ]οc τ[ ]υ̣τω...
P^{95}]ν λογ[

εχετε: εχεται **P^{66}**
μενοντα εν υμιν: εν υμιν μενοντα **P^{66}**; εν [ ] μεν[ ]ντα **P^{75}**
απεστειλεν: απεστιλεν **P^{66}**
πιστευετε: πιστευεται **P^{66}**

5:39

P^{66} P^{75}

39: ερευνατε τας γραφας οτι υμεις δοκειτε εν αυταις ζωην αιωνιον εχειν και εκειναι ειcιν αι μαρτυρουcαι περι εμου.

DEF: **P^{75}**]ατε̣ τ̣αc... υμε̣ι̣[ ] δοκε̣ι̣[ ] ε̣ν̣... εχειν [ ]αι εκειναι...

ερευνατε: εραυναται **P^{66}**
rasura inter και et εκειναι **P^{66}**

5:40

P^{66} P^{75}

40: και ου θελετε ελθειν προc με ινα ζωην εχητε.

DEF: **P^{75}** κ̣αι... ελθ̣ειν̣ π̣ρ̣ο̣c̣...

θελετε: θελεται **P^{66}**
εχητε: εχηται **P^{66}**

5:41

P^{66} **P**^{75}

41: δοξαν παρα ανθρωπων ου λαμβανω.

DEF: **P**^{75} δοξαν παρ̣[ ] α̣νων̣...

5:42

P^{66} **P**^{75}

42: αλλ εγνωκα υμας οτι την αγαπην του θεου ουκ εχετε εν εαυτοις.

DEF: **P**^{75} ...υμ̣[ ] την... εα[ ]τοιc

αλλ: αλλα **P**^{75}
ουκ: ουχ **P**^{66*}; txt **P**^{66*c}

5:43

P^{66} **P**^{75}

43: εγω εληλυθα εν τω ονοματι του πατρος μου και ου λαμβανετε με εαν αλλος ελθη εν τω ονοματι τω ιδιω εκεινον λημψεcθε.

DEF: **P**^{75} ... τ̣ω̣ ονομ̣ατι̣ τ̣[ ]ρ̣ο̣ς̣... λαμ[ ]ν̣ετε με ε̣α̣ν [ ] ε̣λθη...
ιδιω [ ]ον λημψεcθε

εγω: + δε **P**^{66*}; txt **P**^{66c}
λημψεcθε: λημψεcθε **P**^{66} **P**^{75}

5:44

P^{66} **P**^{75}

44: πως δυνασθε υμεις πιστευσαι δοξαν παρα αλληλων λαμβανοντες και την δοξαν την παρα του μονου θεου ου ζητειτε.

DEF: **P**^{75} πωc δυναcθε [ ]c πιcτευcαι... αλλη[ ]μβανοντεc...
δοξαν [ ]υ̣ μονου ου ζητειτε

δυναcθε: δυναcθαι **P**^{66}

θεου: OM **P**^{66} **P**^{75}
ζητειτε: ζητιται **P**^{66*}; ζητειται **P**^{66*c}

5:45

P^{66} **P**^{75}

45: μη δοκειτε οτι εγω κατηγορησω υμων προς τον πατερα εστιν ο κατηγορων υμων μωσης εις ον υμεις ηλπικατε.

DEF: **P**^{75} μη [ ] εγω κατηγορη̣σω υμιν [ ] τον... κατη̣[ ]ορων [ ]ν μω̣υσης... ηλπι[

δοκειτε: δοκιτε **P**^{66*}; txt **P**^{66*c}
υμων^{1}: υμιν **P**^{75*}; txt **P**^{75*c}
μωσης: μωυσης **P**^{66} **P**^{75}
ηλπικατε: ηλπικαται **P**^{66}

5:46

P^{66} **P**^{75}

46: ει γαρ επιστευετε μωση επιστευετε αν εμοι περι γαρ εμου εκεινος εγραψεν.

DEF: **P**^{75} ει γα[ ] . . .]υ̣[ ]τε μωυσει επι[ ]ετε [ ]ν̣... εμ[ ]ρ̣α̣[ ]ν

επιστευετε: επιστευεται **P**^{66}
μωση: μωυσει **P**^{66} **P**^{75}

5:47

P^{66} **P**^{75}

47: ει δε τοις εκεινου γραμμασιν ου πιστευετε πως τοις εμοις ρημασι πιστευσετε.

DEF: **P**^{75} ... εκειν̣[γρα]μ̣[ ]ιστευετε πως τ̣[εμοι]ς̣ [ ]ιστευ[ ]ε̣

εκεινου: εκινου **P**^{66}
πιστευετε: πιστευεται **P**^{66}
ρημασι: ρημασιν **P**^{66}
πιστευσετε: πιστευετε **P**^{66}; πιστευε[ ]ε **P**^{75*}; πιστευσε[ ]ε **P**^{75c}

CHAPTER SIX

$\mathbf{P}^{28}$ $\mathbf{P}^{66}$ $\mathbf{P}^{75}$

6:1

$\mathbf{P}^{66}$ $\mathbf{P}^{75}$

1: μετα ταυτα απηλθεν ο ιηcουc περαν τηc θαλαccηc τηc γαλιλαιαc τηc τιβεριαδοc.

DEF: $\mathbf{P}^{75}$ μ̣ε̣τα̣ τ̣α̣[ ]α̣ [ ] ι̣̅c̣̅ περαν τ̣ηc θαλαccηc τη̣c [ ]c τιβεριαδοc

τηc τιβεριαδοc: OM $\mathbf{P}^{66*}$; txt $\mathbf{P}^{66*c}$

6:2

$\mathbf{P}^{66}$ $\mathbf{P}^{75}$

2: και ηκολουθει αυτω οχλοc πολυc οτι εωρων αυτου τα cημεια α εποιει επι των αcθενουντων.

DEF: $\mathbf{P}^{75}$ ηκολουθ[ ]ι εθεωρ̣ω[ ]ου̅[ ]ν

και ηκολουθει: ηκολουθι δε $\mathbf{P}^{66}$; ηκολουθ[ ] $\mathbf{P}^{75}$ (habet lacunam 2 / 21 litterarum inter ηκολου[ ] et ι εθεωρω[ ])
εωρων αυτου τα cημεια α εποιει επι των αcθενουντων: εθεωρω[1 / 26]ου̅[2]ν $\mathbf{P}^{75}$
εωρων: εθεωρουν $\mathbf{P}^{66*c}$; εθεωρω[ ] $\mathbf{P}^{75}$; txt $\mathbf{P}^{66*}$
αυτου: OM $\mathbf{P}^{66}$
cημεια: cημια $\mathbf{P}^{66}$

6:3

$\mathbf{P}^{66}$ $\mathbf{P}^{75}$

3: ανηλθε δε ειc το οροc ο ιηcουc και εκει εκαθητο μετα των μαθητων αυτου.

DEF: $\mathbf{P}^{75}$ ανη̣[ ] κ̣[ ]ι εκει εκαθητ[ ]θητων αυτου

ανηλθε: ανηλθεν **P**^{66}
ο: OM **P**^{66}
εκαθητο: εκαθεζετο **P**^{66}

6:4

P^{66} **P**^{75}

4: ην δε εγγυc το παcχα η εορτη των ιουδαιων.

DEF: **P**^{75} ηṿ [ ]cχα η εορτη τω[

6:5

P^{66} **P**^{75}

5: επαραc ουν ο ιηcουc τουc οφθαλμουc και θεαcαμενοc οτι πολυc οχλοc ερχεται προc αυτον λεγει προc τον φιλιππον ποθεν αγοραcομεν αρτουc ινα φαγωcιν ουτοι.

DEF: **P**^{66} ... ερχετẹι...
P^{75}] τουc οφθαλμ̣ο̣[ ]τι πολ̣[ ] λεγει π[ ] φ[ ]π̣[ ]ωcιṿ
[ ]τ[ ]α̣ φαγ[

ο ιηcουc τουc οφθαλμουc: τουc οφθαλμουc ο ι̅c̅ **P**^{66}
πολυc οχλοc: οχλοc πολυc **P**^{66*}; txt **P**^{66*c}
ερχεται: ερχετει **P**^{66*}; txt **P**^{66*c}
προc τον: π[3-4] **P**^{75}
τον: OM **P**^{66}
αγοραcομεν: αγοραcωμεν **P**^{66}; [ ]ωcιν **P**^{75}

6:6

P^{66} **P**^{75}

6: τουτο δε ελεγε πειραζων αυτον αυτοc γαρ ηδει τι εμελλε ποιειν.

DEF: **P**^{75}]γε[ ]ειραζ[ ]δει τι εμελλ̣[

ελεγε: ελεγεν **P**^{66}; [ ]γε[1] **P**^{75}
πειραζων: πιραζων **P**^{66}
εμελλε: ημελλεν **P**^{66}

6:7

$\mathbf{P}^{66}$ $\mathbf{P}^{75}$

7: απεκριθη αυτω φιλιπποϲ διακοϲιων δηναριων αρτοι ουκ αρκουϲιν αυτοιϲ ινα εκαϲτοϲ αυτων βραχυ τι λαβη.

DEF: $\mathbf{P}^{75}$] αυτω φιλιπ[ ]ω̣ν̣ [ ]αριων αρτοι ου[ ]υτο[ ]να [ ]α̣ϲτοϲ βραχυ λαβη

απεκριθη: + ουν $\mathbf{P}^{66}$
φιλιπποϲ: ο φιλιπποϲ $\mathbf{P}^{66}$
δηναριων: δηριων $\mathbf{P}^{66*}$; txt $\mathbf{P}^{66*c}$
αυτοιϲ: αυτουιϲ $\mathbf{P}^{66*}$; txt $\mathbf{P}^{66*c}$
αυτων: OM $\mathbf{P}^{66}$ $\mathbf{P}^{75}$
τι: OM $\mathbf{P}^{75}$

6:8

$\mathbf{P}^{28}$ $\mathbf{P}^{66}$ $\mathbf{P}^{75}$

8: λεγει αυτω ειϲ εκ των μαθητων αυτου ανδρεαϲ ο αδελφοϲ ϲιμωνοϲ πετρου.

DEF: $\mathbf{P}^{28}$]νοϲ πετρο[
$\mathbf{P}^{66}$ ... αδελφοϲ [ ] πετρου
$\mathbf{P}^{75}$ λεγει αυτω [ ] ε̣κ̣ [ ]ν̣ μαθητων αυτου ανδρεαϲ ο αδελ[ ]μ̣ωνοϲ πετρου

6:9

$\mathbf{P}^{28}$ $\mathbf{P}^{66}$ $\mathbf{P}^{75}$

9: εϲτι παιδαριον εν ωδε ο εχει πεντε αρτουϲ κριθινουϲ και δυο οψαρια αλλα ταυτα τι εϲτιν ειϲ τοϲουτουϲ.

DEF: $\mathbf{P}^{28}$]χει πεντε αρτουϲ κ[ ]λα ταυτα τι εϲτιν ει[
$\mathbf{P}^{75}$ εϲτιν παιδαριον ωδε [ ]χει ε̅ αρτουϲ κριθινουϲ και β̅ οψαρ̣ια αλ[ ] ταυτα...

εϲτι: εϲτιν $\mathbf{P}^{66}$ $\mathbf{P}^{75}$
εν: OM $\mathbf{P}^{66}$ $\mathbf{P}^{75}$
ωδε ο εχει: ωδε [3]χει $\mathbf{P}^{75}$
ο: οϲ ο $\mathbf{P}^{66*}$; οϲ $\mathbf{P}^{66*c}$
ταυτα τι εϲτιν: τι εϲτιν ταυτα $\mathbf{P}^{66*}$; txt $\mathbf{P}^{66*c}$

6:10

P^{28} P^{66} P^{75}

10: ειπε δε ο ιηcουc ποιηcατε τουc ανθρωπουc αναπεcειν ην δε χορτοc πολυc εν τω τοπω ανεπεcον ουν οι ανδρεc τον αριθμον ωcει πεντακιcχιλιοι.

DEF: **P^{28}**]ατε τουc ανθρωπου[ ]οc πολυc εν τω τοπ[ ] ανδρεc τον αριθ[ ]χ̣ι̣λει[ ]ι
P^{75}]ιπεν [ ] ι̣c̄... αναπε[ ]ε̣ι̣ν̣ η̣[ ]ρ̣τ̣[ ]ν̣ [ ] τοπω α̣νεπε̣[ ]ν̣ ωc πεντ[

ειπε: ειπεν **P^{66}**; [ ]ιπεν **P^{75}**
δε ο: [1] **P^{75}**
δε: ουν **P^{66}**
ποιηcατε: ποιηcαται **P^{66}**
αναπεcειν: αναπεcιν **P^{66}**
ανεπεcον: ανεπεcαν **P^{66}**
οι: OM **P^{66*}**; txt **P^{66*c}**
ωcει: ωcι **P^{66}**; ωc **P^{75}**
πεντακιcχιλιοι: πεντακιcχειλιοι **P^{66*c}**; [ ]χιλει[ ]ι **P^{28}**; txt **P^{66*}**

6:11

P^{28} P^{66} P^{75}

11: ελαβε δε τουc αρτουc ο ιηcουc και ευχαριcτηcαc διεδωκε τοιc μαθηταιc οι δε μαθηται τοιc ανακειμενοιc ομοιωc και εκ των οψαριων οcον ηθελον.

DEF: **P^{28}** ελεβεν ου[ ]ι ευχαριcτηcαc εδω[ ]ενοιc ομοιωc και ε[ ]ν ηθελον
P^{66} ... ομοιωc [
P^{75}] τουc [ ]ρ̣τ̣ου̣[ ] δ̣[ ]ε̣δωκ̣εν τ[ ]ιc ομοιω̣c και [ ]κ̣ τω̣[ ] οcον ηθελο[

ελαβε: ελεβεν **P^{28}**; ελαβεν **P^{66}**
δε: ου[**P^{28}**; ουν **P^{66}**
διεδωκε τοιc μαθηταιc οι δε μαθηται τοιc ανακειμενοιc: εδω[/ 12-15]ενοιc **P^{28}**
διεδωκε: εδωκεν **P^{66}**; δ[ ]εδωκεν **P^{75}**
τοιc μαθηταιc οι δε μαθηται τοιc ανακειμενοιc: τ[13]ιc **P^{75}**
μαθηταιc οι δε μαθηται τοιc: OM **P^{66}** (& cf. **P^{28} P^{75}**)

6:12

P^{28} **P**^{75}

12: ωc δε ενεπληcθηcαν λεγει τοιc μαθηταιc αυτου cυναγαγετε τα περιccευcαντα κλαcματα ινα μη τι αποληται.

DEF: **P**^{28} ωc δε [ ] λεγει τοιc μαθηταιc α[
P^{75} ωc δ̣ε̣ [ ]π̣[ ]ει τοιc μαθη[ ]ου cυναγαγε[ ]ε̣ρ̣ιccευ̣[ ]α κλα[ ]ματα...

6:13

P^{75}

13: cυνηγαγον ουν και εγεμιcαν δωδεκα κοφινουc κλαcματων εκ των πεντε αρτων των κριθινων α επεριccευcε τοιc βεβρωκοcιν.

DEF: **P**^{75} ... αρτων τ̣[ ]ιθινων [ ] ε̣περιccευcαν το̣ι̣c̣ β̣[ ]ρ̣[ ]ο̣cιν

επεριccευcε: επεριccευcαν **P**^{75}

6:14

P^{75}

14: οι ουν ανθρωποι ιδοντεc ο εποιηcε cημειον ο ιηcουc ελεγον οτι ουτοc εcτιν αληθωc ο προφητηc ο ερχομενοc ειc τον κοcμον.

DEF: **P**^{75} οι [ ]ν α̅ν̣̅[ ] ιδο̣ντεc α εποιηcεν [ ]ημεια ελεγον [ ]τι...

ο: α **P**^{75}
εποιηcε: εποιηcεν **P**^{75}
cημειον: [ ]ημεια **P**^{75}
ο ιηcουc: OM **P**^{75}

6:15

P^{75}

15: ιηcουc ουν γνουc οτι μελλουcιν ερχεcθαι και αρπαζειν αυτον ινα ποιηcωcιν αυτον βαcιλεα ανεχωρηcε παλιν ειc το οροc αυτοc μονοc.

DEF: **P**^{75} ... καị α̣ρ̣[ ]α̣ζειν α̣υ̣τον ινα π[ ]ι̣ηcωcιν βαc̣ιλεα α̣νεχωρηcεν παλιν̣ ειc το [ ]ρ̣ο̣c̣...

αυτον^{2}: OM **P**^{75}
ανεχωρηcε: ανεχωρηcεν **P**^{75}

6:16

P^{75}

16: ωc δε οψια εγενετο κατεβηcαν οι μαθηται αυτου επι την θαλαccαν.

DEF: **P**^{75} ωc... κα̣[ ]η̣c̣α̣ν... την̣ [

6:17

P^{28} **P**^{75}

17: και εμβαντεc ειc το πλοιον ηρχοντο περαν τηc θαλαccηc ειc καπερναουμ και cκοτια ηδη εγεγονει και ουκ εληλυθει προc αυτουc ο ιηcουc.

DEF: **P**^{28}]ραν τ[ ]ι cκοτια ηδη ε[ ]γ[ ]ληλυθει ο ι̅c̅
P^{75} και... ηρχ[ ]ραν... καφαρν̣[ ] cκοτια... εγεγονει̣ και ηδη̣
[ ]ω̣ προc αυτουc εγεγον[ ] ο ι̅c̅

το: OM **P**^{75}
καπερναουμ: καφαρν[ ] **P**^{75}
ουκ: ηδη [3] **P**^{75*}; [3]ω **P**^{75*c}
εληλυθει προc αυτουc: προc αυτουc εγεγον[ ] **P**^{75}
προc αυτουc: OM **P**^{28}

6:18

P^{28} P^{75}

18: η τε θαλαccα ανεμου μεγαλου πνεοντοc διηγειρετο.

DEF: **P^{28}** η τε θ[ ]υ πνεοντοc διεγε[
P^{75} η δ[ ]λ̣αccα ανεμο̣υ̣... δ̣[ ]ατ̣ο

τε: δ[ ] **P^{75}**
διηγειρετο: διεγε[ ] **P^{28}**; δ[5-6]ατο **P^{75}**

6:19

P^{28} P^{75}

19: εληλακοτεc ουν ωc cταδιουc εικοcιπεντε η τριακοντα θεωρουcι τον ιηcουν περιπατουντα επι τηc θαλαccηc και εγγυc του πλοιου γινομενον και εφοβηθηcαν.

DEF: **P^{28}**] ωc cταδιουc εικοcιπ[ ]ν ι̅ν̅ περιπατου[ ]αι ενγυc
του πλο[ ] εφοβηθηcαν
P^{75} εληλακοτε̣c̣ ο̣υ̣[ ] ω̣c cταδιο̣υ̣[ ] η λ̅ θεωρουcι τ[ ]
π̣ε̣ριπατου[ ] την θαλαcc[ ] ε̣γγυc του [ ]νομενο̣ν̣
κ̣α̣[ ]βηθηcα[(teste ed. pr.)

εικοcιπεντε η τριακοντα θεωρουcι τον: εικοcιπ[10-20 / 2]ν **P^{28}**
τηc θαλαccηc: την θαλαcc[ ] **P^{75}**
εγγυc: ενγυc **P^{28}**

6:20

P^{28} P^{75}

20: ο δε λεγει αυτοιc εγω ειμι μη φοβειcθε.

DEF: **P^{28}** ο δ[ ] μη φοβειcθαι
P^{75}]γει αυτοιc εγω ε[ ]η φοβ[

φοβειcθε: φοβειcθαι **P^{28}**

6:21

P[28] **P**[75]

21: ηθελον ουν λαβειν αυτον εις το πλοιον και ευθεως το πλοιον εγενετο επι της γης εις ην υπηγον.

DEF: **P**[28] ηθ[ ] εις το πλοιον και ε[ ] επι της γης εις η[
P[75]]λον ουν λαβειν α[ ]τοṿ ẹις το πλ̣[ ] και ευθẹ[ ]ετο ṭο
πλοιọṿ [τ]ῃ[ ] ṿ[ ]ῃγον

το πλοιον εγενετο: [ ]ετο το πλοιον **P**[75]

6:22

P[28] **P**[75]

22: τη επαυριον ο οχλος ο εστηκως περαν της θαλασσης ιδων οτι πλοιαριον αλλο ουκ ην εκει ει μη εν εκεινο εις ο ενεβησαν οι μαθηται αυτου και οτι ου συνεισηλθε τοις μαθηταις αυτου ο ιησους εις το πλοιαριον αλλα μονοι οι μαθηται αυτου απηλθον.

DEF: **P**[28]]ριον ο οχλος ο εστ[ ] ιδεν οτι πλοιαριον [
P[75] τ[ ]χ̣λος ο ẹ[ ]ω̣[ ]ς ειδο[ ] π̣λοι[ ]υκ ην εκει ε[ ]ν καị
[ ]εισηλθεν [ ]ταις αυ[ ] εις το πλοιο[ ] μ̣ονοι οι [ ] α̣π̣ηλθον

ιδων: ιδεν **P**[28]; ειδο[ ] **P**[75]
εκεινο εις ο ενεβησαν οι μαθηται αυτου: OM **P**[75]
πλοιαριον αλλο: πλοιο[5] **P**[75]
συνεισηλθε: [ ]εισηλθεν **P**[75]

6:23

P[75]

23: αλλα δε ηλθε πλοιαρια εκ τιβεριαδος εγγυς του τοπου οπου εφαγον τον αρτον ευχαριστησαντος του κυριου.

DEF: **P**[75] ... εκ̣... οπου [ ]φ[ ]γον... ευχαριστησαντ[ ]ṿ κυ

δε: OM **P**[75]
ηλθε: ηλθεν **P**[75]
πλοιαρια: πλοια **P**[75]

6:24

P^{75}

24: οτε ουν ειδεν ο οχλος οτι ιηcουc ουκ εcτιν εκει ουδε οι μαθηται αυτου ενεβηcαν και αυτοι ειc τα πλοια και ηλθον ειc καπερναουμ ζητουντεc τον ιηcουν.

DEF: **P**^{75} ... ι̅c̅ [ ]κ̣ εcτιν... αυτ[ ] ανεβηcαν... πλοιαρια κα[ ]
η̣λθον ειc καφ[ ]ν̣α̣[ ] ι̣̅ν̣̅

ενεβηcαν: ανεβηcαν **P**^{75}
και^{1}: OM **P**^{75}
πλοια: πλοιαρια **P**^{75}
καπερναουμ: καφ[ ]να[ ] **P**^{75}

6:25

P^{75}

25: και ευροντεc αυτον περαν τηc θαλαccηc ειπον αυτω ραββι ποτε ωδε γεγοναc.

DEF: **P**^{75} και ευρο̣[ ]αλαc̣cηc ειπ[ ]δ̣ε γεγοναc

6:26

P^{75}

26: απεκριθη αυτοιc ο ιηcουc και ειπεν αμην αμην λεγω υμιν ζητειτε με ουχ οτι ειδετε cημεια αλλ οτι εφαγετε εκ των αρτων και εχορταcθητε.

DEF: **P**^{75} α̣π̣[ ]κ̣ρ̣[ ]π̣ε̣ν̣ αμην αμην λεγω υ̣[ ]ε̣ ουχ οτ̣ι̣ ειδε̣τε
cημεια α[ ]τε εκ [ ]των και εχο[

6:27

P^{75}

27: εργαζεcθε μη την βρωcιν την απολλυμενην αλλα την βρωcιν την μενουcαν ειc ζωην αιωνιον ην ο υιοc του ανθρωπου υμιν δωcει τουτον γαρ ο πατηρ εcφραγιcεν ο θεοc.

DEF: $\mathbf{P}^{75}$]θ̣ε̣ μη̣ [ ]ν̣ βρωc[ ]ν̣ απολλυμενη̣[ ] αλλα... ο̣ υ̣̅c̣̅ τ̣ου... τουτον [ ]ατηρ...

6:28

$\mathbf{P}^{75}$

28: ειπον ουν προς αυτον τι ποιουμεν ινα εργαζωμεθα τα εργα του θεου

DEF: $\mathbf{P}^{75}$ ειπον ουν̣ [ ]υτον... εργαζωμεθα... εργα τ̣[ ]υ̣ θ̅υ̅

ποιουμεν: ποιωμεν $\mathbf{P}^{75}$

6:29

$\mathbf{P}^{75}$

29: απεκριθη ο ιηcουc και ειπεν αυτοιc τουτο εcτι το εργον του θεου ινα πιcτευcητε ειc ον απεcτειλεν εκεινοc.

DEF: $\mathbf{P}^{75}$ α̣π̣εκρ[ ]θη... τουτ[ ] ε̣cτιν το ερ[ ]ν του... απ̣[ ]ιλεν εκεινοc

ο: OM $\mathbf{P}^{75}$
εcτι: εcτιν $\mathbf{P}^{75}$
πιcτευcητε: πιcτευητε $\mathbf{P}^{75}$

6:30

$\mathbf{P}^{75}$

30: ειπον ουν αυτω τι ουν ποιειc cυ cημειον ινα ιδωμεν και πιcτευcωμεν cοι τι εργαζη.

DEF: $\mathbf{P}^{75}$ ... ι̣δωμεν και πιcτευcωμεν̣...

6:31

P^{75}

31: οι πατερεc ημων το μαννα εφαγον εν τη ερημω καθωc εcτι γεγραμμενον αρτον εκ του ουρανου εδωκεν αυτοιc φαγειν.

DEF: **P^{75}** οι πατερεc η[ ]ν το... εν τη [ ]ωc εcτιν γεγραμμενον [ ]κ̣ τ̣ου... αυτοιc φ[

εcτι: εcτιν **P^{75}**

6:32

P^{75}

32: ειπεν ουν αυτοιc ο ιηcουc αμην αμην λεγω υμιν ου μωcηc δεδωκεν υμιν τον αρτον εκ του ουρανου αλλ ο πατηρ μου διδωcιν υμιν τον αρτον εκ του ουρανου τον αληθινον.

DEF: **P^{75}** ... αμην αμ̣[ ]εγω... δεδωκεν υμι̣[ ]ο̣ν αρτον̣... πα[ ] μου διδω̣cιν υμιν τον αρτον τ̣ο̣ν [ ] τ̣ου ουραν̣[ ]υ̣ τον̣ α̣ληθ̣ινον

μωcηc: μωυcηc **P^{75}**
αρτον^{2}: + τον **P^{75}**

6:33

P^{75}

33: ο γαρ αρτοc του θεου εcτιν ο καταβαινων εκ του ουρανου και ζωην διδουc τω κοcμω.

DEF: **P^{75}** ο [ ]c̣ το̣υ θ̅υ̅ ε[ ]α̣ταβαινων [ ]ρανου και ζ[ ] διδουc τω κο[(teste ed. pr.)

6:34

P^{75}

34: ειπον ουν προc αυτον κυριε παντοτε δοc ημιν τον αρτον τουτον.

DEF: **P^{75}**]πον ουν [ ]υ̣τον κ̅ε̅ παν[ ] ημιν τ̣[ ]τ̣ον τουτον

6:35

P^{66} P^{75}

35: ειπε δε αυτοιc ο ιηcουc εγω ειμι ο αρτοc τηc ζωηc ο ερχομενοc προc με ου μη πειναcη και ο πιcτευων ειc εμε ου μη διψηcη πωποτε.

DEF: **P^{66}**] ειc...
P^{75} ει[ ]υ̣τοιc ο ι̅[ ] ε̣γω [ ]ι̣μι ο αρτοc τηc [ ] ο ερχομενοc [ ]c εμε̣ ο̣υ̣ μη [ ]α̣c̣η και [ ]ι̣c̣τ̣[ ]με ου [ ] π̣ω̣[

ειπε δε αυτοιc: ει[4]υτοιc **P^{75}**
με: εμε **P^{75}**
διψηcη: διψηcει **P^{66}**
πωποτε: πωποται **P^{66}**

6:36

P^{66} P^{75}

36: αλλ ειπον υμιν οτι και εωρακατε με και ου πιcτευετε.

DEF: **P^{75}**]μ̣ι̣ν̣ [ ]ρ̣ακα[ ] και ου π[

υμιν: υμειν **P^{66}**
πιcτευετε: πιcτευεται **P^{66}**

6:37

P^{66} P^{75}

37: παν ο διδωcι μοι ο πατηρ προc εμε ηξει και τον ερχομενον προc με ου μη εκβαλω εξω.

DEF: **P^{75}**]δ̣ωcι̣ν̣ [ ] πατη[ ]ρ̣[ ] κ̣αι το[ ]ν προc εμ[ ]βαλω εξ[

διδωcι: διδωcιν **P^{66}**; [ ]δωcιν **P^{75}**
με: εμε **P^{66}**; εμ[ ] **P^{75}**

6:38

P^{66} P^{75}

38: οτι καταβεβηκα εκ του ουρανου ουχ ινα ποιω το θελημα το εμον αλλα το θελημα του πεμψαντος με.

DEF: **P^{75}**]α̣ταβεβηκα [ ]υρανου̣ [ ] π̣οιω... του π[ ]τος με

εκ: απο **P^{66}**

6:39

P^{66} P^{75}

39: τουτο δε εστι το θελημα του πεμψαντος με πατρος ινα παν ο δεδωκε μοι μη απολεσω εξ αυτου αλλα αναστησω αυτο εν τη εσχατη ημερα.

DEF: **P^{75}** τουτ̣ο̣... του π̣[ ]ψαντος... μη απ̣[ ]λεσω εξ...

δε: OM **P^{75}**
εστι: εστιν **P^{66} P^{75}**
πατρος: OM **P^{66} P^{75}**
δεδωκε: δεδωκεν **P^{66}**; εδωκεν **P^{75}**
εν: OM **P^{66} P^{75}**

6:40

P^{66} P^{75}

40: τουτο δε εστι το θελημα του πεμψαντος με ινα πας ο θεωρων τον υιον και πιστευων εις αυτον εχη ζωην αιωνιον και αναστησω αυτον εγω τη εσχατη ημερα.

τουτο δε εστι το θελημα: OM **P^{66*}**; τουτο γαρ ε[7]ελημα **P^{66*c}**
δε: OM **P^{75}**
εστι: εστιν **P^{75}**
πεμψαντος με: πατρος μου **P^{66} P^{75}**
πιστευων: πιστεων **P^{66*}**; txt **P^{66*c}**
εχη: εχει **P^{66*c}**; txt **P^{66*}**
εγω: OM **P^{66}**
τη: εν τη **P^{66}**

6:41

P^{66} P^{75}

41: εγογγυζον ουν οι ιουδαιοι περι αυτου οτι ειπεν εγω ειμι ο αρτος ο καταβας εκ του ουρανου.

αρτος: littera eras. inter ρ et τ **P^{66}**

6:42

P^{66} P^{75}

42: και ελεγον ουχ ουτος εστιν ιηcουc ο υιος ιωcηφ ου ημεις οιδαμεν τον πατερα και την μητερα πως ουν λεγει ουτος οτι εκ του ουρανου καταβεβηκα.

ουχ: οτι **P^{66*}**; ουχι **P^{75}**; txt **P^{66*c}**
τον πατερα: txt **P^{66*}**; OM **P^{66c}**
μητερα: μητεραν **P^{66*}**; txt **P^{66c}**
ουν: νυν **P^{75}**
ουτος^{2}: OM **P^{66} P^{75}**

6:43

P^{66} P^{75}

43: απεκριθη ουν ο ιηcουc και ειπεν αυτοιc μη γογγυζετε μετ αλληλων.

DEF: **P^{75}** απεκ[ ]ị θ̣ η̣ ι̣̅c̣̅ [ ]α̣[ ] ειπεν αυτο[ ]γγυζ[ ]λων

ουν: OM **P^{66} P^{75}**
ο: OM **P^{75}**
γογγυζετε: γογγυζεται **P^{66}**

6:44

P^{66} **P**^{75}

44: ουδειc δυναται ελθειν προc με εαν μη ο πατηρ ο πεμψαc με ελκυcη αυτον και εγω αναcτηcω αυτον τη εcχατη ημερα.

DEF: **P**^{75} ουδειc [ ]υ̣[ ]αι ελθειν [ ] εαν... με [ ]λκυ̣c̣η̣... αυτο̣ν...
τη εcχατ̣η ημερ[

πατηρ: + μου **P**^{66}
και εγω: καγω **P**^{66} **P**^{75}
αυτον: + εν **P**^{66*}; txt **P**^{66*c}

6:45

P^{66} **P**^{75}

45: εcτι γεγραμμενον εν τοιc προφηταιc και εcονται παντεc διδακτοι του θεου παc ουν ο ακουcαc παρα του πατροc και μαθων ερχεται προc με.

DEF: **P**^{75}]τιν γεγρ̣αμμενον εν τοιc [ ]φητα[ ] κ̣αι εcονται
παν̣[ ]εc διδακτο̣[ ] π̣αc ο ακ̣[ ]υcαc... π̣̅[ ]c̅ και μαθω̣[ ]ται
πρ[ ] εμε

εcτι: εcτιν **P**^{66}; [ ]τιν **P**^{75}
διδακτοι του θεου: διδακτοι [1 / 2-3] **P**^{75}
του[1]: OM **P**^{66}
ουν: OM **P**^{66} **P**^{75}
με: εμε **P**^{75}

6:46

P^{66} **P**^{75}

46: ουχ οτι τον πατερα τιc εωρακεν ει μη ο ων παρα του θεου ουτοc εωρακε τον πατερα.

DEF: **P**^{75} ουχ οτι τ̣[ ]ν̣ π̅ρ̅α̅ ε[ ] π̣[ ]ο̣υ̣ θ̣̅υ̣̅ [ ]κ̣ε̣ν̣ το[

τιc εωρακεν ει μη ο ων: ε[13] **P**^{75} (& cf. **P**^{66})
τιc εωρακεν: εωρακεν τιc **P**^{66} (& cf. **P**^{75})
εωρακε: εωρακεν **P**^{66}; [ ]κεν **P**^{75}

6:47

P[66] P[75]

47: αμην αμην λεγω υμιν ο πιστευων εις εμε εχει ζωην αιωνιον.

DEF: **P[75]**]μην λ̣[ ] ο πιστε̣[ ]ην [

αμην[1]: littera eras. inter α et μ **P[66]**
πιστευων εις εμε εχει ζωην: πιστε[9]ην **P[75]**
εις εμε: OM **P[66]**

6:48

P[66] P[75]

48: εγω ειμι ο αρτος της ζωης.

DEF: **P[75]**] ειμι ο αρτ̣[

6:49

P[66] P[75]

49: οι πατερες υμων εφαγον το μαννα εν τη ερημω και απεθανον.

DEF: **P[75]** ο̣ι π̣[ ]ν εφαγον [ ] α̣πεθανο[

6:50

P[66] P[75]

50: ουτος εστιν ο αρτος ο εκ του ουρανου καταβαινων ινα τις εξ
αυτου φαγη και μη αποθανη.

DEF: **P[75]**]ουρανου κ̣[ ]υ̣ και ου̣ [

καταβαινων ινα τις εξ αυτου φαγη: κ[21-24]υ **P[75]**
και: + ου **P[75]**

6:51

P^{66} **P**^{75}

51: εγω ειμι ο αρτος ο ζων ο εκ του ουρανου καταβας εαν τις φαγη εκ τουτου του αρτου ζησεται εις τον αιωνα και ο αρτος δε ον εγω δωσω η σαρξ μου εστιν ην εγω δωσω υπερ της του κοσμου ζωης.

DEF: **P**^{75}]τος ο ζων̣ ο εκ̣ [ ]ν τις φα[ ]η̣ εκ τ̣[ ] εις τον [ ]ω̣να̣ [ ]ω̣σω η σαρ̣[ ]ν υπ̣[ ]σμου ζω[

τις: τεις **P**^{66}
ην εγω δωσω: OM **P**^{66} **P**^{75}

6:52

P^{66} **P**^{75}

52: εμαχοντο ουν προς αλληλους οι ιουδαιοι λεγοντες πως δυναται ουτος ημιν δουναι την σαρκα φαγειν.

DEF: **P**^{75}]ντο̣ [ ]ιοι προς αλλ̣[ ]ντ̣ε̣ς̣ π̣[ ]α̣τ̣[ ]ι ου[ ] τ̣η̣ν̣ [ ]α̣γειν

προς αλληλους οι ιουδαιοι: [ ]ιοι προς αλλ[ ] **P**^{75}
ημιν δουναι: δουναι **P**^{66*}; δουναι ημιν **P**^{66*c}
σαρκα: σαρκαν αυτου **P**^{66}

6:53

P^{66} **P**^{75}

53: ειπεν ουν αυτοις ο ιησους αμην αμην λεγω υμιν εαν μη φαγητε την σαρκα του υιου του ανθρωπου και πιητε αυτου το αιμα ουκ εχετε ζωην εν εαυτοις.

DEF: **P**^{75}] ο̣ ι̅ς̅ α̣[ ]μ̣ην λε̣[ ]μ̣[ ]η̣ φα[ ] την σαρκ̣[ ]υ υι̣[ ]υ̣ [ ]υ̣ α̣̅ν̅ο̅υ̅ κ[ ]ητε αυτου τ̣ο... ζ[ ] εν εαυτοις

ο: OM **P**^{66}
φαγητε: φαγηται **P**^{66}
σαρκα: σαρκαν **P**^{66}
πιητε αυτου το αιμα: το αιμα αυτου πιητε **P**^{66}
εχετε: εχεται **P**^{66}

6:54

P^{66} **P**^{75}

54: ο τρωγων μου την σαρκα και πινων μου το αιμα εχει ζωην αιωνιον και εγω αναστησω αυτον τη εσχατη ημερα.

DEF: **P**^{75} ... μο̣υ το σ̣α̣ρ̣κ̣α̣ κ̣[ ]ι̣ [ ]γ̣ων... ε̣χει ζωην [ ]ον καγω... τη [ ]χ̣ατη ημερα

τρωγων μου την σαρκα και πινων: τρωνων **P**^{66*}; txt **P**^{66*c}
την: το **P**^{75*}; txt **P**^{75*c}
και εγω: καγω **P**^{66} **P**^{75}

6:55

P^{66} **P**^{75}

55: η γαρ σαρξ μου αληθως εστι βρωσις και το αιμα μου αληθως εστι ποσις.

DEF: **P**^{75} η γαρ σαρξ μου αληθης [ ]στιν...

αληθως[1]: αληθης **P**^{66*c} **P**^{75}; txt **P**^{66*}
εστι[1]: εστιν **P**^{66}; [ ]στιν **P**^{75}
αληθως[2]: αληθης **P**^{66*c} **P**^{75}; txt **P**^{66*}
εστι[2]: εστιν **P**^{66} **P**^{75}

6:56

P^{66} **P**^{75}

56: ο τρωγων μου την σαρκα και πινων μου το αιμα εν εμοι μενει καγω εν αυτω.

πινων: πεινων **P**^{75}

6:57

P66 P75

57: καθωϲ απεϲτειλε με ο ζων πατηρ καγω ζω δια τον πατερα και ο τρωγων με κακεινοϲ ζηϲεται δι εμε.

απεϲτειλε: απεϲτειλεν **P75**; απεϲταλκεν **P66**
πατερα: + μου **P75**
ζηϲεται: ζηϲει **P75**

6:58

P66 P75

58: ουτοϲ εϲτιν ο αρτοϲ ο εκ του ουρανου καταβαϲ ου καθωϲ εφαγον οι πατερεϲ υμων το μαννα και απεθανον ο τρωγων τουτον τον αρτον ζηϲεται ειϲ τον αιωνα.

εκ του: εξ **P75**
καταβαϲ: καταβαινων **P66***; txt **P66*c**
υμων: OM **P66 P75**
το μαννα: OM **P66 P75**
ζηϲεται: ζηϲει **P75**

6:59

P66 P75

59: ταυτα ειπεν εν ϲυναγωγη διδαϲκων εν καπερναουμ.

DEF: **P75** ... ϲυνạγω...

ϲυναγωγη: ϲυναγω **P75***; txt **P75*c**
καπερναουμ: καφαρναουμ **P66**

6:60

P66 P75

60: πολλοι ουν ακουσαντες εκ των μαθητων αυτου ειπον σκληρος εστιν ουτος ο λογος τις δυναται αυτου ακουειν.

DEF: **P75** πολλοι [ ]ν̣ α̣κ̣[ ]υ̣ς̣α̣ντες... αυ[ ]κ̣ληρος ες̣τ̣[ ]υτος ο λογος [ ]α̣τα̣[ ] αυτο̣[ ]υ̣ειν

ακουσαντες εκ των: των ακουσαντων **P66***; txt **P66*c**
αυτου[1]: OM **P66***; txt **P66*c**
ουτος ο λογος: ο λογος ουτος **P66**

6:61

P66 P75

61: ειδως δε ο ιησους εν εαυτω οτι γογγυζουσι περι τουτου οι μαθηται αυτου ειπεν αυτοις τουτο υμας σκανδαλιζει.

DEF: **P75** ... ο̣ ι̣ς̣ εν ε̣α̣υτω οτ[ ] γογγυζουσιν περι τουτο̣υ... υμα[ ] σκανδα̣[ ]ζει

γογγυζουσι: γογγυζουσιν **P66 P75**
αυτοις: + ις **P66**
σκανδαλιζει: σκαδαλιζει **P66***; txt **P66*c**

6:62

P66 P75

62: εαν ουν θεωρητε τον υιον του ανθρωπου αναβαινοντα οπου ην το προτερον.

DEF: **P75** ... υιον τ[ ] α̣νου α̣γα̣[ ]αινοντα [ ]που ην̣ το πρ[ ]τ̣ερον

θεωρητε: θεωρησηται **P66**
οπου: ου **P66**

6:63

P^{66} **P**^{75}

63: το πνευμα εcτι το ζωοποιουν η cαρξ ουκ ωφελει ουδεν τα ρηματα α εγω λαλω υμιν πνευμα εcτι και ζωη εcτιν.

DEF: **P**^{75} τ̣[ ]ν̣̅α̅ εcτ̣[ ] το ζωοποιου[ ] η cαρξ ο[ ]ε̣[ ] ο̣υ̣δ̣[ ]ν̣ τα ρηματ̣[ ] υμιν̣ [ ]α̣[ ] ζ[

εcτι^{1}: εcτιν **P**^{66}; εcτ[2] **P**^{75}
cαρξ: + δε **P**^{66*}; txt **P**^{66*c}
ρηματα α εγω λαλω: ρηματ[8-10 / 4] **P**^{75} (& cf. **P**^{66})
ρηματα: ρημα **P**^{66*}; txt **P**^{66*c}
λαλω: λελαληκα **P**^{66} (& cf. **P**^{75})
εcτι^{2}: εcτιν **P**^{66}

6:64

P^{66} **P**^{75}

64: αλλ ειcιν εξ υμων τινεc οι ου πιcτευουcιν ηδει γαρ εξ αρχηc ο ιηcουc τινεc ειcιν οι μη πιcτευοντεc και τιc εcτιν ο παραδωcων αυτον.

DEF: **P**^{75}]ι̣ν ε[ ]c οι ου πι[ ] η̣δ[ ] ο ι̅c̅ τινεc̣ [ ] κ̣αι τιc εcτ[

εξ υμων τινεc: τινεc εξ υμων **P**^{66}
ου: μη **P**^{66*}; txt **P**^{66*c}
πιcτευουcιν: πιcτευcουcι **P**^{66*}; πιcτευουcι **P**^{66*c}
εξ αρχηc: απ αρχηc **P**^{66}
τινεc ειcιν οι μη πιcτευοντεc και: OM **P**^{66*}; txt **P**^{66*c}
εcτιν ο παραδωcων αυτον: ην ο μελλων αυτον παραδιδοναι **P**^{66}

6:65

P^{66} **P**^{75}

65: και ελεγε δια τουτο ειρηκα υμιν οτι ουδειc δυναται ελθειν προc με εαν μη η δεδομενον αυτω εκ του πατροc μου.

DEF: **P**^{75}] ε̣λεγεν δι[ ]ε̣ιc δυνατα̣[ ]ομεν[

ελεγε: ελεγεν **P**^{66} **P**^{75}
η: ην **P**^{66}

μου: OM **P**^{66}

6:66

P^{66} **P**^{75}

66: εκ τουτου πολλοι απηλθον των μαθητων αυτου εις τα οπισω και ουκετι μετ αυτου περιεπατουν.

DEF: **P**^{75}] τ̣ο̣[ ]τ̣ου πολλο̣[ ]ν αυτ̣[ ]υ απηλ[ ] κ̣[ ]κε[ ] μ̣ετ αυτο[ ]ουν

τουτου: + ουν **P**^{66}
απηλθον των μαθητων αυτου: εκ των μαθητων αυτου απηλθον **P**^{66}; [11-12]ν αυτ[ ]υ απηλ[ ] **P**^{75}

6:67

P^{66} **P**^{75}

67: ειπεν ουν ο ιηcουc τοιc δωδεκα μη και υμειc θελετε υπαγειν.

DEF: **P**^{75}]ν ο ι̅c̅ τοιc ι̣̅[ ] υμει[ ]π̣αγειν

6:68

P^{66} **P**^{75}

68: απεκριθη ουν αυτω cιμων πετροc κυριε προc τινα απελευcομεθα ρηματα ζωηc αιωνιου εχειc.

DEF: **P**^{75} απ[ ] α̣υτω [ ]τ̣ροc κ̅ε̅ π[ ]ατ̣α̣ ζω̣[ ]ων[

απεκριθη ουν: απ[1 / 5] **P**^{75}
ουν: OM **P**^{66} (& cf. **P**^{75})
πετροc: littera eras. inter ε et τ **P**^{66}

6:69

P^{66} **P**^{75}

69: και ημειc πεπιcτευκαμεν και εγνωκαμεν οτι cυ ει ο χριcτοc ο υιοc του θεου του ζωντοc.

DEF: **P**^{75}]c πεπιcτ̣[ ]μ̣εν κ[ ]μ̣[ ]τι cυ ει ο α̣[ ] του θ̅υ̣̅

ο χριcτοc ο υιοc: ο α[3-4] **P**^{75}
υιοc: αγιοc **P**^{66}
του ζωντοc: OM **P**^{66} **P**^{75}

6:70

P^{66} **P**^{75}

70: απεκριθη αυτοιc ο ιηcουc ουκ εγω υμαc τουc δωδεκα εξελεξαμην και εξ υμων ειc διαβολοc εcτιν.

DEF: **P**^{75} α̣π̣[ ]ρ̣ιθη̣ [ ]τοιc ο ι̅c̅ [ ] ε̣γω...

ο: OM **P**^{66}
τουc: του **P**^{66*}; txt **P**^{66*c}
διαβολοc: διαβοc: **P**^{66*}; txt **P**^{66*c}

6:71

P^{66} **P**^{75}

71: ελεγε δε τον ιουδαν cιμωνοc ιcκαριωτην ουτοc γαρ ημελλεν αυτον παραδιδοναι ειc ων εκ των δωδεκα.

DEF: **P**^{75} ελεγεν δε τ[ ] ιουδαν cιμωνοc ι̣c̣κ̣αριωτ̣ου
[ ]υτο̣[ ]α̣ρ εμ̣[ ]ν̣ παραδιδοναι αυτον̣ ειc [ ] των [

ελεγε: ελεγεν **P**^{66} **P**^{75}
ιcκαριωτην: ιcκαριωτου **P**^{66} **P**^{75}
ημελλεν: εμ[ ]ν **P**^{75}
αυτον παραδιδοναι: παραδιδοναι αυτον **P**^{75}

CHAPTER SEVEN

P^{66} **P**^{75}

7:1

P^{66} **P**^{75}

1: και περιεπατει ο ιησους μετα ταυτα εν τη γαλιλαια ου γαρ ηθελεν εν τη ιουδαια περιπατειν οτι εζητουν αυτον οι ιουδαιοι αποκτειναι.

DEF: **P**^{75} και μετ̣α ταυτα [ ]επα[ ]ε̣ι ο ι̅c̅ εν [ ]λ̣α̣ια ο̣υ̣ γαρ ηθελε̅ εν τ[ ]ο̣υ̣δ̣α̣ι̣[ ]ρ̣ιπ̣ατειν [ ]τ̣ι̣ εζητου̅ αυτ̣[ ]ν̣ οι ιουδαιοι αποκτεινα̣[

και: OM **P**^{66}
περιεπατει ο ιησους μετα ταυτα: μετα ταυτα περιεπατει ο ι̅c̅ **P**^{66};
μετα ταυτα [ ]επα[ ]ει ο ι̅c̅ **P**^{75}
τη γαλιλαια: [4]λαια **P**^{75}

7:2

P^{66} **P**^{75}

2: ην δε εγγυς η εορτη των ιουδαιων η σκηνοπηγια.

DEF: **P**^{75} ... εγγυ[ ] εορτη των ιουδαιω̣ν̣ η̣ σκηνοπη̣[ ]α̣

7:3

P^{66} P^{75}

3: ειπον ουν προς αυτον οι αδελφοι αυτου μεταβηθι εντευθεν και υπαγε εις την ιουδαιαν ινα και οι μαθηται σου θεωρησωσι τα εργα σου α ποιεις.

DEF: **P^{75}** ειπον ουν π[ ]υ̣[ ]ον οι αδελφοι α̣υ̣[ ]ου̣
μ̣ε̣τ̣αβη̣θ̣[ ]θ̣ε̣ν̣ και υ̣π̣α̣γε̣ ε̣ις την [ ]υδαιαν [ ]ι μαθηται̣
[ ]υ θεωρηϲ̣ο̣υϲιν ϲοι τ[ ] π̣οιειϲ

ειπον: ειπαν **P^{66}**
προς αυτον οι αδελφοι αυτου: οι αδελφοι αυτου προς αυτον **P^{66}**
θεωρησωσι: θεορησωσι **P^{66}**; θεωρησουσιν **P^{75}**
τα εργα σου: σου τα εργα **P^{66}**; σοι τ[5-6] **P^{75*}**; σου τ[5-6] **P^{75c}**

7:4

P^{66} P^{75}

4: ουδεις γαρ εν κρυπτω τι ποιει και ζητει αυτος εν παρρησια ειναι ει ταυτα ποιεις φανερωσον σεαυτον τω κοσμω.

DEF: **P^{75}** ου[ ]ειϲ γαρ τι ε̣[ ] κ̣ρυπτ̣[ ]ι ζητει [ ]οϲ εν π̣[ ]υ̣τ̣α̣
π̣[ ]ι̣ειϲ [ ]ϲμω

εν κρυπτω τι: τι ε[ ] κρυπτ[ ] **P^{75}**
αυτος: αυτο **P^{66*}**; txt **P^{66*c}**
ειναι: εινα **P^{66*}**; txt **P^{66*c}**

7:5

P^{66} P^{75}

5: ουδε γαρ οι αδελφοι αυτου επιστευον εις αυτον.

DEF: **P^{75}** ου[ ]ε̣ [ ]τευον ε[

7:6

P^{66} P^{75}

6: λεγει ουν αυτοιϲ ο ιηϲουϲ ο καιροϲ ο εμοϲ ουπω παρεϲτιν ο δε καιροϲ ο υμετεροϲ παντοτε εϲτιν ετοιμοϲ.

DEF: **P^{75}**] ο̣υν̣ αυ[ ] κ̣α̣ι̣ροϲ [ ]μ̣οϲ [ ]αρεϲτιν [ ]ϲ ο υ[ ]τ̣ερο[ ]οτε εϲτιν [ ]μ̣οϲ

7:7

P^{66} P^{75}

7: ου δυναται ο κοϲμοϲ μιϲειν υμαϲ εμε δε μιϲει οτι εγω μαρτυρω περι αυτου οτι τα εργα αυτου πονηρα εϲτιν.

DEF: **P^{75}** ... ο κ̣[ ]ο̣ϲ μειϲειν υμ̣αϲ̣ ε̣με δε μειϲει οτι̣ [ ] μαρτυρω π[ ]ρι αυτ̣ου οτι τα εργα αυ[ ]υ πονηρα εϲτ̣ιν

μιϲειν: μειϲειν **P^{75}**
μιϲει: μειϲει **P^{66} P^{75}**

7:8

P^{66} P^{75}

8: υμειϲ αναβητε ειϲ την εορτην ταυτην εγω ουπω αναβαινω ειϲ την εορτην ταυτην οτι ο καιροϲ ο εμοϲ ουπω πεπληρωται.

DEF: **P^{75}** υ̣μειϲ αναβη̣τε ει[ ]η̣ν εορτην εγω ουπ̣ω αναβαι[ ]ι̣ϲ τ̣[ ]ν̣ εορτην ταυτ̣η[ ] οτι ο εμοϲ [ ]ϲ ουπ̣ω πεπληρωτα[

αναβητε: αναβαται **P^{66*}**; αναβηται **P^{66*c}**
ταυτην^{1}: OM **P^{66} P^{75}**
ο καιροϲ ο εμοϲ: ο εμοϲ καιροϲ **P^{66}**; ο εμοϲ [ ]ϲ **P^{75}**
ουπω^{2}: ουδεπω **P^{66}**

7:9

P^{66} **P**^{75}

9: ταυτα δε ειπων αυτοις εμεινεν εν τη γαλιλαια.

DEF: **P**^{75}]υτα δε [ ]π̣ω̣[ ] αυτοις εμεινε̣ν̣ εν̣ [ ]α̣λιλαια

ταυτα: ταυ **P**^{66*}; txt **P**^{66*c}
αυτοις: αυτος **P**^{66}
εν: OM **P**^{66*}; txt **P**^{66*c}

7:10

P^{66} **P**^{75}

10: ως δε ανεβησαν οι αδελφοι αυτου τοτε και αυτος ανεβη εις την εορτην ου φανερως αλλ ως εν κρυπτω.

DEF: **P**^{75}]ς̣ δε αν̣εβη̣σαν οι αδελ[ ] τ̣η̄ [ ]ρτην̣ τ̣[ ]τ̣ε και
αυτος̣ [ ]ε̣[ ]c αλλ[ ] ω̣[ ] εν κρυπτω

τοτε και αυτος ανεβη εις την εορτην: εις την εορτην τοτε και αυτος ανεβη **P**^{66}; [ ] την [2]ρτην τ[ ]τε και αυτος **P**^{75}
αλλ: αλλα **P**^{66}; αλλ[1] **P**^{75}

7:11

P^{66} **P**^{75}

11: οι ουν ιουδαιοι εζητουν αυτον εν τη εορτη και ελεγον που εστιν εκεινος.

DEF: **P**^{75} οι ο[ ]ι ε̣ζη̣τ̣ο̣υ̣ν̣ α̣υτον εν τη̣ εορτη και ελεγ̣ον
π[ ]υ [ ]τιν̣ εκ̣εινος

7:12

P^{66} **P**^{75}

12: και γογγυσμος πολυς περι αυτου ην εν τοις οχλοις οι μεν ελεγον οτι αγαθος εστιν αλλοι δε ελεγον ου αλλα πλανα τον οχλον.

DEF: $\mathbf{P}^{75}$ ... π̣ερι αυ̣[ ]ου... το̣[ ]c̣ οχλο̣ιc οι με̅ ελεγον [ ] ε̣cτιν̣
[ ]λ̣ο̣ι̣ δε ελεγ[ ]ν ουκ αλλα [ ]ν̣α τον οχλ̣[

πολυc περι αυτου ην: ην περι αυτου $\mathbf{P}^{66*}$; ην περι αυτου πολυc $\mathbf{P}^{66*c}$; περι αυ[ ]ου ην πολυc $\mathbf{P}^{75}$
τοιc οχλοιc: τω οχλω $\mathbf{P}^{66}$
δε: OM $\mathbf{P}^{66}$
ου: ουκ $\mathbf{P}^{75}$

7:13

$\mathbf{P}^{66}$ $\mathbf{P}^{75}$

13: ουδειc μεντοι παρρηcια ελαλει περι αυτου δια τον φοβον των ιουδαιων.

DEF: $\mathbf{P}^{75}$ ο̣υδειc μ̣ε̣ντ̣οι παρηc[ ] ε̣λαλει υπ [ ]του δια το̣ν φοβο̣ν̣ τ̣[ ] ι̣ο̣υδαιων̣

παρρηcια: παρηc[ ] $\mathbf{P}^{75}$
ελαλει περι αυτου: περι αυτου ελει $\mathbf{P}^{66*}$; περι αυτου ελαλει $\mathbf{P}^{66*c}$
περι: υπ $\mathbf{P}^{75}$

7:14

$\mathbf{P}^{66}$ $\mathbf{P}^{75}$

14: ηδη δε τηc εορτηc μεcουcηc ανεβη ο ιηcουc ειc το ιερον και εδιδαcκε.

DEF: $\mathbf{P}^{75}$]η δε τ̣ηc εορτηc με̣[ ]η̣c ανεβ̣η ι̅c̅ ειc τ̣ο ι̣ερο̅ κ̣αι εδιδα̣[

μεcουcηc: μεcαζουcηc $\mathbf{P}^{66}$ (αζ partim eras.)
ανεβη: αναβη $\mathbf{P}^{66*}$; αναιβη $\mathbf{P}^{66*c}$
ο: OM $\mathbf{P}^{66}$ $\mathbf{P}^{75}$
εδιδαcκε: εδιδαcκεν $\mathbf{P}^{66}$

7:15

P^{66} **P**^{75}

15: και εθαυμαζον οι ιουδαιοι λεγοντες πωc ουτοc γραμματα οιδε μη μεμαθηκωc.

DEF: **P**^{75} ε̣θ̣αυ[ ]αζον... ιου[ ]α̣ιοι λ̣ε̣γ̣[ ]c πωc̣ [ ]το̣c γραμματα [ ]δ̣εν [ ]μ̣αθηκ̣[

και εθαυμαζον: εθαυμαζον ουν **P**^{66}; εθαυ[ ]αζον ουν **P**^{75}
οιδε: οιδεν **P**^{66}; [ ]δεν **P**^{75}

7:16

P^{66} **P**^{75}

16: απεκριθη αυτοιc ο ιηcουc και ειπεν η εμη διδαχη ουκ εcτιν εμη αλλα του πεμψαντοc με.

DEF: **P**^{75}]ρ̣[ ]η̣ [ ]ν αυ̣τ̣[ ] και ει[ ] εμη διδαχ̣η̣ ουκ εcτ̣[ ]μ̣η αλ̣[ ] πεμψαντοc με

απεκριθη: + ουν **P**^{66}; [ ]ρ[ ]η [2]ν **P**^{75}
αυτοιc ο ιηcουc: αυτ[5] **P**^{75}

7:17

P^{66} **P**^{75}

17: εαν τιc θελη το θελημα αυτου ποιειν γνωcεται περι τηc διδαχηc ποτερον εκ του θεου εcτιν η εγω απ εμαυτου λαλω.

DEF: **P**^{75} εαν [ ] θελη̣ [ ]ε̣λημα... πε̣[ ] τη[ ]χ̣η̣c ποτερον̣... εcτιν̣ [ ] απ [ ]α̣υτ̣ο̣υ λαλω

ποιειν: OM **P**^{75}
του: OM **P**^{66}

7:18

P^{66} **P**^{75}

18: ο αφ εαυτου λαλων την δοξαν την ιδιαν ζητει ο δε ζητων την δοξαν του πεμψαντος αυτον ουτος αληθης εστι και αδικια εν αυτω ουκ εστιν.

DEF: **P**^{75} ο αφ εαυτ̣[ ]λ̣ων τ[ ] ι̣διαν̣... δ̣ε̣ ζητ̣[ ]η̣ν δοξα[ ] του πεμψα̣[ ]τος αυτ[ ] α̣λ̣[ ] εστιν κ̣αι... ες[ ]ν

την δοξαν την ιδιαν: τ[2] ιδιαν **P**^{75}
πεμψαντος: μψαντος **P**^{66*}; txt **P**^{66*c}
αυτον: με **P**^{66*}; txt **P**^{66*c}
εστι: εστιν **P**^{66} **P**^{75}

7:19

P^{66} **P**^{75}

19: ου μωσης δεδωκεν υμιν τον νομον και ουδεις εξ υμων ποιει τον νομον τι με ζητειτε αποκτειναι.

DEF: **P**^{75} ου μω̣υ̣ς̣ης... τ[ ] ν̣ομον και ου̣[ ]ε̣[ ] υμω̣ν ποιε[ ]ν [ ]ομον τ̣[ ]τειτ̣ε α̣π̣ο̣κ̣τ̣[ ]α̣ι

μωσης: μωυσης **P**^{66} **P**^{75}
ποιει: πιει **P**^{66}
αποκτειναι: αποκτιναι **P**^{66*}; txt **P**^{66*c}

7:20

P^{66} **P**^{75}

20: απεκριθη ο οχλος και ειπε δαιμονιον εχεις τις σε ζητει αποκτειναι.

DEF: **P**^{75} απεκριθ[ ] δαιμονι[ ] εχε̣ις̣ τ̣ις σε ζητ[ ]τειναι

απεκριθη ο οχλος και ειπε: απεκριθ[5-7] **P**^{75} (& cf. **P**^{66})
οχλος: οχος **P**^{66*}; txt **P**^{66*c}
και ειπε: OM **P**^{66} (& cf. **P**^{75})

7:21

P^{66} **P**^{75}

21: απεκριθη ο ιηϲουϲ και ειπεν αυτοιϲ εν εργον εποιηϲα και παντεϲ θαυμαζετε.

DEF: **P**^{75} ... ειπ̣[ ]ϲ εν εργο̣ν̣ εποιηϲα κ[ ]ι̣ π̣αντ̣[ ]ζ[

ο: OM **P**^{66} **P**^{75}

7:22

P^{66} **P**^{75}

22: δια τουτο μωϲηϲ δεδωκεν υμιν την περιτομην ουχ οτι εκ του μωϲεωϲ εϲτιν αλλ εκ των πατερων και εν ϲαββατω περιτεμνετε ανθρωπον.

DEF: **P**^{75}]ι̣α τουτο μ̣ωυϲηϲ δ̣[ ]ε̣ρι̣[ ]μ̣ην ουχ [ ]λ εκ [ ]ων και [ ]ρ̣ι̣τ̣ε̣[ ] α̅ν̅ο̅ν̅

μωϲηϲ: μωυϲηϲ **P**^{66} **P**^{75}
υμιν: υμειν **P**^{66}
μωϲεωϲ: μωυϲεωϲ **P**^{66}

7:23

P^{66} **P**^{75}

23: ει περιτομην λαμβανει ανθρωποϲ εν ϲαββατω ινα μη λυθη ο νομοϲ μωϲεωϲ εμοι χολατε οτι ολον ανθρωπον υγιη εποιηϲα εν ϲαββατω.

DEF: **P**^{75} ει [ ] λαμβανε̣[ ]ϲ̅ εν ϲαββα̣[ ]α μη̣ λυθη ο νομο̣ϲ̣ μ̣ωυϲεωϲ ε̣[ ]λ̣ατε οτι α̅ν̅ο̅ν̅ [ ]λον υγιη εποιηϲα [ ]β̣βατω

νομοϲ: + ο **P**^{66}
μωϲεωϲ: μωυϲεωϲ **P**^{66} **P**^{75}
χολατε: χολαται **P**^{66}
ολον ανθρωπον: α̅ν̅ο̅ν̅ [ ]λον **P**^{75}

7:24

P66 P75

24: μη κρινετε κατ οψιν αλλα την δικαιαν κρισιν κρινατε.

DEF: **P75** μη κρινε[ ]ε κατ οψιν αλλα τ̣[ ] δ̣ικαιαν κρισιν̣...

κρινετε: κρινε **P66**
κρινατε: κρινετε **P66 P75**

7:25

P66 P75

25: ελεγον ουν τινες εκ των ιεροcολυμιτων ουχ ουτος εστιν ον ζητουσιν αποκτειναι.

DEF: **P75** ελεγον [ ]ν̣ τινες εκ των ι̣[ ]ροcολυμειτων [ ]χ ουτο̣[ ] εστιν [ ] ζητουσιν αποκτ̣εινα[

ιεροcολυμιτων: ιεροcολυμειτων **P66**; ι[ ]ροcολυμειτων **P75**
αποκτειναι: αποκτιναι **P66***; txt **P66*c**

7:26

P66 P75

26: και ιδε παρρησια λαλει και ουδεν αυτω λεγουσι μηποτε αληθως εγνωσαν οι αρχοντες οτι ουτος εστιν αληθως ο χριστος.

DEF: **P75**] ιδε π̣[ ]ια λα̣λ̣ει... αυτ̣[ ]χ̣[ ]υ̣[ ]τε αληθως ε̣γνωσαν [ ]τ̣ι ουτος εστ̣ιν [ ] χ̅c̅

λεγουσι: λεγουσιν **P66**
μηποτε: μηπο **P66***; txt **P66*c**
αληθως ο: [1] **P75** (& cf. **P66**)
αληθως²: OM **P66** (& cf. **P75**)

7:27

P^{66} **P**^{75}

27: αλλα τουτον οιδαμεν ποθεν εστιν ο δε χριϲτοϲ οταν ερχηται ουδειϲ γινωϲκει ποθεν εστιν.

DEF: **P**^{75} αλλ̣[ ]ι̣δα̣μεν ποθεν [ ]ν ο δ[ ] χ̅ϲ̅ ο̣ταν ερχ̣ηται
ουδειϲ γειν̣ω̣ϲκε̣[ ] ποθεν εϲ̣τιν

δε χριϲτοϲ: χ̅ϲ̅ δε **P**^{66}
ερχηται: ελθη **P**^{66}
γινωϲκει: γεινωϲκε[ ] **P**^{75}

7:28

P^{66} **P**^{75}

28: εκραξεν ουν εν τω ιερω διδαϲκων ο ιηϲουϲ και λεγων καμε οιδατε και οιδατε ποθεν ειμι και απ εμαυτου ουκ εληλυθα αλλ εστιν αληθινοϲ ο πεμψαϲ με ον υμειϲ ουκ οιδατε.

DEF: **P**^{75} εκραξεν ουν̣ [ ]ν τ̣ω ιερω διδα̣ϲκων ι̅ϲ̅ και λεγω[ ]
κα̣με οιδατε κα[ ] ο̣ιδατε ποθεν̣ ε̣ι̣μ̣[ ] και απ εμα̣υτου
ου[ ]η̣λυθα αλ̣[ ] α̣ληθινοϲ ο πεμψα[ ] ον υμειϲ ο̣[ ]δατε

ουν: δε **P**^{66}
ο^{1}: OM **P**^{75}
καμε: εμε **P**^{66*}; txt **P**^{66*c}
οιδατε^{1}: οιδαται **P**^{66}
οιδατε^{2}: οιδαται **P**^{66} (οι partim eras.)
αληθινοϲ: αληθηϲ **P**^{66}
οιδατε^{3}: οιδαται **P**^{66}

7:29

P^{66} **P**^{75}

29: εγω δε οιδα αυτον οτι παρ αυτου ειμι κακεινοϲ με απεϲτειλεν.

DEF: **P**^{75} εγω̣ ο̣ιδα α̣[ ]ν οτι παρ α[ ]υ ειμι κακε̣ινο̣ϲ με
απ̣εϲτειλεν̣

δε: OM **P**^{75}

απεcτειλεν: απεcταλκεν οιδε **P^{66*}**; απεcταλκεν **P^{66*c}**

7:30

P^{66} P^{75}

30: εζητουν ουν αυτον πιαcαι και ουδειc επεβαλεν επ αυτον την χειρα οτι ουπω εληλυθει η ωρα αυτου.

DEF: **P^{75}**]η̣τουν̣ ουν αυ̣το̣ν πιαcαι̣ κα̣ι ο̣υ̣δ̣[ ]εβαλεν επ
αυτον τη̣[ ]ειρα οτ̣[ ]πω εληλυθ̣ε̣ι̣ η ω̣[ ]ου

ουν: OM **P^{66*}**; txt **P^{66*c}**
επεβαλεν: επεβαλλεν **P^{66}**
ουπω: ουδεπω **P^{66}**

7:31

P^{66} P^{75}

31: πολλοι δε εκ του οχλου επιcτευcαν ειc αυτον και ελεγον οτι ο χριcτοc οταν ελθη μητι πλειονα cημεια τουτων ποιηcει ων ουτοc εποιηcεν.

DEF: **P^{75}** εκ τ̣[ ]λ̣[ ] δε πο̣λ̣λ̣οι επ̣ιc̣[ ] ειc αυτ̣[ ] ο χ̅c̅ οταν
[ ] μη π̣[ ] c̣η̣μει[ ] ποιηcει ω̣[ ]τοc ε[ ]η̣cεν

πολλοι δε εκ του οχλου: εκ τ[ ]λ[ ] δε πολλοι **P^{75}**
δε: δει **P^{66*}**; txt **P^{66c}**
εκ του οχλου επιcτευcαν: επιcτευcαν εκ του οχλου **P^{66}**
αυτον και ελεγον οτι: αυτ[7-12] **P^{75}** (& cf. **P^{66}**)
οτι: OM **P^{66}** (& cf. **P^{75}**)
μητι: μη **P^{66} P^{75}**
cημεια τουτων: cημει[1] **P^{75}** (& cf. **P^{66}**)
τουτων: OM **P^{66}** (& cf. **P^{75}**)

7:32

P^{66} **P**^{75}

32: ηκουcαν οι φαριcαιοι του οχλου γογγυζοντοc περι αυτου ταυτα και απεcτειλαν οι φαριcαιοι και οι αρχιερειc υπηρεταc ινα πιαcωcιν αυτcν.

DEF: **P**^{75} ηκ[ ]cαν οι φαρ̣[ ]ι̣ του ο̣[ ]λ̣ου γογγυζοντοc περ̣ι̣ [ ] τ̣α̣[ ]α̣ και... αρχ[ ]ε̣ρειc... ινα [ ]αcωcιν αυτον

ηκουcαν: + δε **P**^{66}
περι αυτου ταυτα: ταυτα περι αυτου **P**^{66}
απεcτειλαν: απεcτιλαν **P**^{66}
οι φαριcαιοι και οι αρχιερειc υπηρεταc: υπηρεταc οι αρχιερειc και οι φαριcαιοι **P**^{66}
οι φαριcαιοι και οι αρχιερειc: οι αρχ[ ]ερειc και οι φαριcαιοι **P**^{75}

7:33

P^{66} **P**^{75}

33: ειπεν ουν αυτοιc ο ιηcουc ετι μικρον χρονον μεθ υμων ειμι και υπαγω προc τον πεμψαντα με.

DEF: **P**^{75} ... ετι χ[ ]ν̣ον μικρον... ε̣ι̣μι κ̣αι υπαγ[ ] προc...

αυτοιc: OM **P**^{66} **P**^{75}
ο: OM **P**^{75}
μικρον χρονον: χρονον μικρον **P**^{66}; χ[ ]νον μικρον **P**^{75}
πεμψαντα: μεψψντα **P**^{66*}; txt **P**^{66*c}; πεμψοντα **P**^{75}
με: ε partim eras. **P**^{66}

7:34

P^{66} **P**^{75}

34: ζητηcετε με και ουχ ευρηcετε και οπου ειμι εγω υμειc ου δυναcθε ελθειν.

DEF: **P**^{75}]η̣τηcατ[ ] με και ουχ ευρηcετε με [ ] οπου ειμι̣ ε̣γω υμειc ου δυναcθε [ ]λ̣θ̣ειν

ζητηcετε: ζητηcεται **P**^{66*}; txt **P**^{66*c}; [ ]ητηcατ[ ] **P**^{75}
ευρηcετε: ευρηcεται **P**^{66}; + με **P**^{75}

7:35

P[66] **P**[75]

35: ειπον ουν οι ιουδαιοι προς εαυτους που ουτος μελλει πορευεσθαι οτι ημεις ουχ ευρησομεν αυτον μη εις την διασποραν των ελληνων μελλει πορευεσθαι και διδασκειν τους ελληνας.

DEF: **P**[75] ẹιπον ουν οι ịδαιοι προς ε[ ]ụτους... ọτι [ ]ις ουχ ευρη[ ]ομεν αυτον μη εις τ̣[ ]ω̣ν ελληνων μελλ̣ει π[ ]δ̣ασκει τους ελλ̣ηνας̣

ειπον: ειπαν **P**[66]
ιουδαιοι: ιδαιοι **P**[75] (cf. 2:6)
ουτος μελλει: μελλει ουτος **P**[66]
διδασκειν: [ ]δασκει **P**[75]

7:36

P[66] **P**[75]

36: τις εστιν ουτος ο λογος ον ειπε ζητησετε με και ουχ ευρησετε και οπου ειμι εγω υμεις ου δυνασθε ελθειν.

DEF: **P**[75] τ̣[ ]υτος ον ε[ ]πεν ζητησẹτε με κα̣[ ]υ̣[ ] με κ̣αị ọπου... ου̣ δ̣[ ]σθε ελθειν

ουτος ο λογος: ο λογος ουτος **P**[66]; [ ]υτος **P**[75]
ειπε: ειπεν οτι **P**[66]; ε[ ]πεν **P**[75]
ζητησετε: ζητησεται **P**[66]
ευρησετε: ευρησεται **P**[66]; + [ ] με **P**[75]
υμεις: OM **P**[66]
ελθειν: ελθῑ **P**[66]

7:37

P66 P75

37: εν δε τη εσχατη ημερα τη μεγαλη της εορτης ειστηκει ο ιησους και εκραξε λεγων εαν τις διψα ερχεσθω προς με και πινετω.

DEF: **P75** ... ημερα [ ]ῃ μεγαλη... ις [ ]ạι... π̣ρος...

τη μεγαλη της εορτης: της μεγαλης εορτης **P66***; txt **P66*c**
ειστηκει: ιστηκει **P66**
εκραξε: εκραξεν **P66**
προς με: OM **P66***; txt **P66*c**
με: εμε **P75**
πινετω: πεινετω **P75**

7:38

P66 P75

38: ο πιστευων εις εμε καθως ειπεν η γραφη ποταμοι εκ της κοιλιας αυτου ρευσουσιν υδατος ζωντος.

DEF: **P75** ο πιστευωṿ [ ]ς̣ εμε καθως [ ]πεṿ [ ] γραφη
ποτα[ ]ι εκ της κοιλ[ ]ς αυṭ[ ] ρευσουσιν υδα[ ]ω̣ντο̣[

7:39

P66 P75

39: τουτο δε ειπε περι του πνευματος ου εμελλον λαμβανειν οι πιστευοντες εις αυτον ουπω γαρ ην πνευμα αγιον οτι ο ιησους ουδεπω εδοξασθη.

DEF: **P75**]ụτο δ[ ]π̣εν περι του [ ] ο̣ εμελλον... πιστευ[ ]τες...
πνα [ ]ṭι ις...

ειπε: ελεγεν **P66**; [ ]π̣εν **P75**
ου: ο **P75**
πιστευοντες: πιστευσαντες **P66**; πιστευ[3]τες **P75**
αγιον: OM **P66*c** **P75**; txt **P66***
ο: OM **P66** **P75**

7:40

P^{66} P^{75}

40: πολλοι ουν εκ του οχλου ακουcαντες τον λογον ελεγον ουτοc εcτιν αληθωc ο προφητηc.

DEF: **P^{75}** ... οχλου [ ]ν ακουcαντεc... τọυτων ẹλεγον... προφητ̣ηc

πολλοι: OM **P^{66*c} P^{75}**; txt **P^{66*}**
ουν εκ του οχλου: εκ του οχλου ου **P^{66*}**; εκ του οχλου ουν **P^{66*c}**; εκ του οχλου [2]ν **P^{75}**
ακουcαντεc: + αυτου **P^{66*}**; txt **P^{66*c}**
τον λογον: των λογων τουτων **P^{66} P^{75}**

7:41

P^{66} P^{75}

41: αλλοι ελεγον ουτοc εcτιν ο χριcτοc αλλοι δε ελεγον μη γαρ εκ τηc γαλιλαιαc ο χριcτοc ερχεται.

DEF: **P^{75}** ... ουτ[ ]cτιν... δ̣ε ελ̣ẹγον μ̣[ ]ρ̣ [ ]c γαλιλαιαc ο χ̅c̅ ẹρχεται

αλλοι δε ελεγον: οι δε ελεγον supra ras. **P^{66*}**; ελε super lineam (partim eras.) **P^{66*c}**; οι δε ελεγον **P^{75}**

7:42

P^{66} **P**^{75}

42: ουχι η γραφη ειπεν οτι εκ του cπερματοc δαβιδ και απο βηθλεεμ τηc κωμηc οπου ην δαβιδ ο χριcτοc ερχεται.

DEF: **P**^{75} ουχ̣ η̣ [ ]ραφ[ ]εν οτι...

ουχι: ουχ **P**^{66} **P**^{75}
του OM **P**^{66}
δαβιδ^{1}: δαυειδ **P**^{66} **P**^{75}
ην: OM **P**^{66*}; txt **P**^{66c}
δαβιδ^{2}: δαυειδ **P**^{66} **P**^{75}
ο χριcτοc ερχεται: ερχεται ο χριcτοc **P**^{75}

7:43

P^{66} **P**^{75}

43: cχιcμα ουν εν τω οχλω εγενετο δι αυτον.

DEF: **P**^{75} ... ο̣υν...

cχιcμα: cχιμα **P**^{75*}; txt **P**^{75*c}
εν τω οχλω εγενετο: εγενετο εν τω οχλω **P**^{66} **P**^{75}

7:44

P^{66} **P**^{75}

44: τινεc δε ηθελον εξ αυτων πιαcαι αυτον αλλ ουδειc επεβαλεν επ αυτον ταc χειραc.

DEF: **P**^{75} τ̣ινεc... πιαcαι α[ ]ν αλλ... αυτο̣[ ] χειραc

επεβαλεν: επεβαλλεν **P**^{66*}; εβαλεν **P**^{75}; txt **P**^{66*c}
αυτον: αυτω **P**^{66*}; txt **P**^{66*c}

7:45

P^{66} P^{75}

45: ηλθον ουν οι υπηρεται προc τουc αρχιερειc και φαριcαιουc και ειπον αυτοιc εκεινοι διατι ουκ ηγαγετε αυτον.

DEF: **P^{75}** ... υπηρεται [ ]ο̣υc αρχ̣[ ] κ̣α̣ι φαριcαιουc̣ κ[ ]ν αυτ̣[ ]νοι διατι ου[ ]αγετε α̣[

ηλθον: ηλθαν **P^{66}**
ειπον: λεγουcιν **P^{66}**
εκεινοι: εκινοι **P^{66}**
ηγαγετε: ηγαγεται **P^{66}**

7:46

P^{66} P^{75}

46: απεκριθηcαν οι υπηρεται ουδεποτε ουτωc ελαληcεν ανθρωποc ωc ουτοc ο ανθρωποc.

DEF: **P^{75}** απεκριθηcαν ο̣[ ]πηρετ̣[ ]πωτε ελαληcεν̣ [ ]υτωc α̅ν̣̅[

ουδεποτε: [ ]πωτε **P^{75}**
ουτωc ελαληcεν ανθρωποc: ουτωc α̅ν̅ο̅c̅ ελαληcεν **P^{66*}**; ελαληcεν ουτωc α̅ν̅ο̅c̅ **P^{66*c}**; ελαληcεν [ ]υτωc α̅ν̅[ ] **P^{75}**
ωc ουτοc ο ανθρωποc: ωc ουτοc λαλει ο ανθρωποc **P^{66*}**; OM **P^{66*c} P^{75}**

7:47

P^{66} P^{75}

47: απεκριθηcαν ουν αυτοιc οι φαριcαιοι μη και υμειc πεπλανηcθε.

DEF: **P^{75}**]κριθηcαν ουν αυ[ ]ι̣c οι φαρ̣[ ] μη και υμειc π̣[ ]νη̣cθε

πεπλανηcθε: πεπλανηcθαι **P^{66}**

7:48

P^{66} **P**^{75}

48: μη τις εκ των αρχοντων επιστευσεν εις αυτον η εκ των φαρισαιων.

DEF: **P**^{75} μ̣[ ] των αρχοντων ε̣[ ]τον η εκ των φ[ ]ν

7:49

P^{66} **P**^{75}

49: αλλ ο οχλος ουτος ο μη γινωσκων τον νομον επικαταρατοι εισι.

DEF: **P**^{75} α[ ] ουτος ο μη γεινω[ ]ω̣ν τον ν[ ] απ̣αρατοι εισιν

αλλ: αλλα **P**^{66}
γινωσκων: γεινω[ ]ων **P**^{75}
επικαταρατοι: επαρατοι **P**^{66}; απαρατοι **P**^{75}
εισι: εισιν **P**^{66} **P**^{75}

7:50

P^{66} **P**^{75}

50: λεγει νικοδημος προς αυτους ο ελθων νυκτος προς αυτον εις ων εξ αυτων.

DEF: **P**^{75} λεγει νεικ̣[ ]δ̣ημος πρ̣ος... π̣ρ̣[ ] α̣υτον... αυτ[ ]ν

λεγει: ειπεν δε **P**^{66}
νικοδημος: νεικ[ ]δημος **P**^{75}
νυκτος: OM **P**^{66} **P**^{75}
αυτον: + το προτερον **P**^{66} **P**^{75}

7:51

P^{66} **P**^{75}

51: μη ο νομος ημων κρινει τον ανθρωπον εαν μη ακουση παρ αυτου προτερον και γνω τι ποιει.

DEF: **P**^{75} ... κρινει τ[ ]ν̣ α̣̅ν̅ο̅ν̅... πρωτο̣ν̣ π̣αρ αυτο̣υ̣... τι π[ ]ε̣ι

παρ αυτου προτερον: πρωτον παρ αυτου **P**^{66} **P**^{75}

7:52

P^{66} **P**^{75}

52: απεκριθησαν και ειπον αυτω μη και συ εκ της γαλιλαιας ει ερευνησον και ιδε οτι προφητης εκ της γαλιλαιας ουκ εγηγερται.

DEF: **P**^{75} απ̣εκριθησαν... ε̣κ... ερ̣αυνησον και ι̣δ̣ε̣ ο̣τι εκ της γαλιλα[ ]φ[ ]τη̣[ ]κ̣ εγειρεται

ειπον: ειπαν **P**^{66} **P**^{75}
ερευνησον: εραυνησον **P**^{75}
προφητης εκ της γαλιλαιας: εκ της γαλιλα[6]φ[ ]τη[ ] **P**^{75}; εκ της γαλιλαιας ο προφητης **P**^{66*}; txt **P**^{66*c}
εγηγερται: εγιρεται **P**^{66}; εγειρεται **P**^{75}

7:53

P^{66} **P**^{75}

53: και επορευθη εκαστος εις τον οικον αυτου.

OM totum versum **P**^{66} **P**^{75} (& cf 8:1-11)

CHAPTER EIGHT

P[39] P[66] P[75]

7:53-8:11

53: και επορευθη εκαστος εις τον οικον αυτου.
8:1: ιησους δε επορευθη εις το ορος των ελαιων.
2: ορθρου δε παλιν παρεγενετο εις το ιερον και πας ο λαος
ηρχετο προς αυτον και καθισας εδιδασκεν αυτους.
3: αγουσι δε οι γραμματεις και οι φαρισαιοι προς αυτον γυναικα
εν μοιχεια κατειλημμενην και στησαντες αυτην εν μεσω.
4: λεγουσιν αυτω διδασκαλε αυτη η γυνη κατεληφθη
επαυτοφωρω μοιχευομενη.
5: εν δε τω νομω μωσης ημιν ενετειλατο τας τοιαυτας
λιθοβολεισθαι συ ουν τι λεγεις.
6: τουτο δε ελεγον πειραζοντες αυτον ινα εχωσι κατηγορειν
αυτου ο δε ιησους κατω κυψας τω δακτυλω εγραφεν εις την
γην.
7: ως δε επεμενον ερωτωντες αυτον ανακυψας ειπε προς αυτους
ο αναμαρτητος υμων πρωτος τον λιθον επ αυτη βαλετω.
8: και παλιν κατω κυψας εγραφεν εις την γην.
9: οι δε ακουσαντες και υπο της συνειδησεως ελεγχομενοι
εξηρχοντο εις καθεις αρξαμενοι απο των πρεσβυτερων εως των
εσχατων και κατελειφθη μονος ο ιησους και η γυνη εν μεσω
εστωσα.
10: ανακυψας δε ο ιησους και μηδενα θεασαμενος πλην της
γυναικος ειπεν αυτη η γυνη που εισιν εκεινοι οι κατηγοροι σου
ουδεις σε κατεκρινεν.
11: η δε ειπεν ουδεις κυριε ειπε δε αυτη ο ιησους ουδε εγω σε
κατακρινω πορευου και μηκετι αμαρτανε.

OM hanc pericopem **P[66] P[75]**

8:12

P^{66} **P**^{75}

12: παλιν ουν ο ιηcουc αυτοιc ελαληcε λεγων εγω ειμι το φωc του κοcμου ο ακολουθων εμοι ου μη περιπατηcει εν τη cκοτια αλλ εξει το φωc τηc ζωηc.

DEF: **P**^{75} πα[ ]αληcεν ι̅c̅ λεγων ε[ ]ου [ ]c̣μ̣[ ]υ̣ [ ]υ̣[ ]ο̣ι̣ ο̣υ̣ μ̣η̣ πε[ ]c̣η εν̣... τ̣ο φωc...

ο ιηcουc αυτοιc ελαληcε: αυτοιc ελαληcεν ο ι̅c̅ **P**^{66}; [ ]αληcεν ι̅c̅ **P**^{75}
περιπατηcει: περιπατηcη **P**^{66}; πε[ ]cη **P**^{75}
cκοτια: κοτια **P**^{66*}; txt **P**^{66*c}

8:13

P^{66} **P**^{75}

13: ειπον ουν αυτω οι φαριcαιοι cυ περι cεαυτου μαρτυρειc η μαρτυρια cου ουκ εcτιν αληθηc.

DEF: **P**^{75} ... αλη[ ]ηc

μαρτυρειc: μαρτυριc **P**^{66}

8:14

$\mathbf{P}^{39}$ $\mathbf{P}^{66}$ $\mathbf{P}^{75}$

14: απεκριθη ιηcουc και ειπεν αυτοιc καν εγω μαρτυρω περι εμαυτου αληθηc εcτιν η μαρτυρια μου οτι οιδα ποθεν ηλθον και που υπαγω υμειc δε ουκ οιδατε ποθεν ερχομαι και που υπαγω.

DEF: $\mathbf{P}^{39}$] αυτοιc [ ]αρτυρω [ ]ου η μαρ[ ] αληθηc [ ]ιδα
πο[ ]ν και που [ ]μειc δε [ ]ε ποθεν [ ]ι που υπα[
$\mathbf{P}^{75}$ ... αυτοιc [ ]α̣ν εγω μαρ̣[ ]υρ̣ω... μαρτυρια μ[ ] α̣λη̣θ̣[ ]c
εcτιν... ποθεν [ ]θον κ̣α̣ι... δε ου[ ]ιδατ̣[ ] π̣[ ]θ̣εν ε[ ]μαι και...

απεκριθη: ras. sub κριθη $\mathbf{P}^{66}$
εγω: γω $\mathbf{P}^{66*}$; txt $\mathbf{P}^{66*c}$
αληθηc εcτιν η μαρτυρια μου οτι οιδα: η μαρ[ ] αληθηc [ ]ιδα $\mathbf{P}^{39}$
; η μαρτυρια μ[ ] αληθ[ ]c εcτιν οτι οιδα $\mathbf{P}^{75}$
υμειc: υμιc $\mathbf{P}^{66}$
οιδατε: οιδαται $\mathbf{P}^{66}$
και^{3}: η $\mathbf{P}^{66}$ $\mathbf{P}^{75*}$; txt $\mathbf{P}^{75*c}$

8:15

$\mathbf{P}^{39}$ $\mathbf{P}^{66}$ $\mathbf{P}^{75}$

15: υμειc κατα την cαρκα κρινετε εγω ου κρινω ουδενα.

DEF: $\mathbf{P}^{39}$] κατα τη̄ [ ]νετε εγω [ ]ω ουδενα
$\mathbf{P}^{75}$ υ̣μειc κατ̣[ ] την... ου κριν̣[ ] ο̣υδενα

κρινετε: κρινεται $\mathbf{P}^{66}$
εγω: + δε $\mathbf{P}^{75}$

8:16

P^{39} **P**^{66} **P**^{75}

16: και εαν κρινω δε εγω η κριcιc η εμη αληθηc εcτιν οτι μονοc ουκ ειμι αλλ εγω και ο πεμψαc με πατηρ.

DEF: **P**^{39}]ρινω δε [ ]ιcιc η εμη [ ]cτιν ο[ ] ουκ ει[ ]ω και ο [ ] με πηρ
P^{75} ... κρ̣ι̣cιc... αλ̣λ...

αληθηc: αληθινη **P**^{75}
ειμι: ιμι **P**^{66}

8:17

P^{39} **P**^{66} **P**^{75}

17: και εν τω νομω δε τω υμετερω γεγραπται οτι δυο ανθρωπων η μαρτυρια αληθηc εcτιν.

DEF: **P**^{39}] νομω [ ]ετερω [ ]αι οτι δυ[ ] μαρτυρι[ ] εcτιν
P^{75} και εν τ̣[ ]ο̣μ̣ω δε... γεγραπ̣[ ]τ̣[ ] α̣νων η̣... εcτ[ ] α̣λ̣[ ]ηc

αληθηc: αλληθηc **P**^{66*}; λ^{2} postea eras.
αληθηc εcτιν: εcτ[ ] αλ[ ]ηc **P**^{75}

8:18

P^{39} **P**^{66} **P**^{75}

18: εγω ειμι ο μαρτυρων περι εμαυτου και μαρτυρει περι εμου ο πεμψαc με πατηρ.

DEF: **P**^{39} ε[ ] μαρτυρ[ ] εμαυτου και μ[ ] εμου [ ] πηρ
P^{75} εγω... πε̣ρι εμαυτου...

και: + περι εμου **P**^{75*}; txt **P**^{75c}
μαρτυρει: μαρτυρι **P**^{66}

8:19

$\mathbf{P}^{39}$ $\mathbf{P}^{66}$ $\mathbf{P}^{75}$

19: ελεγον ουν αυτω που εστιν ο πατηρ cου απεκριθη ο ιηcουc ουτε εμε οιδατε ουτε τον πατερα μου ει εμε ηδειτε και τον πατερα μου ηδειτε αν.

DEF: $\mathbf{P}^{39}$ ε[ ] αυτω [ ] π̅η̅ρ̅ cο[ ] ι̅η̅c̅ ου[ ]τε ουτ[ ] ει εμε [ ]
τον π̅ρ̅[ ]δειτε
$\mathbf{P}^{75}$ ε̣λεγον ουν̣... ε̣cτιν... cο̣υ απεκρι̣θη̣... τον [ ] μου... ηδειτ̣ε̣
κ̣[ ] τον πα̣[ ] μ̣ου...

ο²: OM $\mathbf{P}^{66}$ $\mathbf{P}^{75}$
ουτε¹: ουδε $\mathbf{P}^{75c}$; txt $\mathbf{P}^{75*}$
οιδατε: οιδαται $\mathbf{P}^{66}$
ηδειτε¹: ηδιται $\mathbf{P}^{66}$
ηδειτε αν: αν ηδιται $\mathbf{P}^{66}$; αν ηδειτε $\mathbf{P}^{75}$
πατερα μου ηδειτε αν: π̅ρ̅[5-10]δειτε $\mathbf{P}^{39}$

8:20

$\mathbf{P}^{39}$ $\mathbf{P}^{66}$ $\mathbf{P}^{75}$

20: ταυτα τα ρηματα ελαληcεν ο ιηcουc εν τω γαζοφυλακιω διδαcκων εν τω ιερω και ουδειc επιαcεν αυτον οτι ουπω εληλυθει η ωρα αυτου.

DEF: $\mathbf{P}^{39}$ τ[ ]ματα ελ[ ] τω γαζο[ ] διδαcκω[ ] ιερω
κα[ ] επιαc[ ]τι ουπ[ ] η ωρα α[
$\mathbf{P}^{75}$]ηματα̣ [ ]η̣cεν εν τω [ ]λακιω [ ]c̣κων εν τω [ ]α̣ι ουδειc
[ ]αcεν αυτον ο[ ] εληλυ[ ] η ωρα αυτου

ρηματα: ρητα $\mathbf{P}^{66}$
ελαληcεν ο ιηcουc εν: ελ[5-9] / $\mathbf{P}^{39}$ (& cf. $\mathbf{P}^{66}$ $\mathbf{P}^{75}$)
ο ιηcουc: OM $\mathbf{P}^{66}$ $\mathbf{P}^{75}$ (& cf. $\mathbf{P}^{39}$)

8:21

$\mathbf{P}^{39}$ $\mathbf{P}^{66}$ $\mathbf{P}^{75}$

21: ειπεν ουν παλιν αυτοιc ο ιηcουc εγω υπαγω και ζητηcετε με και εν τη αμαρτια υμων αποθανειcθε οπου εγω υπαγω υμειc ου δυναcθε ελθειν.

DEF: **P**^{39}] ουν πα[ ] εγω υπ[ ]τηcετε μ[ ]η αμαρτ[ ]
αποθαν[ ]που εγω [ ]μειc ου [ ] ελθε[ ]ν
P^{75} ει[ ]ν̣ παλιν [ ]τ̣οιc εγω υπαγω [ ]τηcετε μ̣[ ] κ̣αι εν τη
αμαρτια̅ [ ] απ̣[ ]α̣ν̣[ ]ε̣ οπου ε̣γω υπα[ ]c̣θ̣ε̣ ελθειν

παλιν αυτοιc ο ιηcουc: πα[6-10] / **P**^{39} (& cf. **P**^{66*} **P**^{75})
ο ιηcουc: OM **P**^{66*} **P**^{75} (& cf. **P**^{39}); txt **P**^{66*c}
αμαρτια: αμαρτια̅ **P**^{75}
αποθανειcθε: αποθανιcθαι **P**^{66}

8:22

P^{39} **P**^{66} **P**^{75}

22: ελεγον ουν οι ιουδαιοι μητι αποκτενει εαυτον οτι λεγει οπου εγω υπαγω υμειc ου δυναcθε ελθειν.

DEF: **P**^{39} ε[
P^{75} ελε[ ]ν οι [ ]ιοι μητι... υπαγ̣[ ] υμειc...

εγω: OM **P**^{75}
δυναcθε: δυναcθαι **P**^{66}

8:23

P^{66} **P**^{75}

23: και ειπεν αυτοιc υμειc εκ των κατω εcτε εγω εκ των ανω ειμι υμειc εκ του κοcμου τουτου εcτε εγω ουκ ειμι εκ του κοcμου τουτου.

DEF: **P**^{75} και ελεγεν̣ [ ]υ̣τοιc... εcτε ε[ ]ω̣ εκ... τουτου̣ [ ]ο̣υ
κοcμου εcτε... κο̣cμου τουτου

και ειπεν: ελεγεν ουν **P**^{66}; και ελεγεν **P**^{75}
του κοcμου τουτου[1]: τουτου του κοcμου **P**^{66}; τουτου [ ]ου κοcμου **P**^{75}

8:24

$\mathbf{P}^{66}$ $\mathbf{P}^{75}$

24: ειπον ουν υμιν οτι αποθανειcθε εν ταιc αμαρτιαιc υμων εαν γαρ μη πιcτευcητε οτι εγω ειμι αποθανειcθε εν ταιc αμαρτιαιc υμων.

DEF: $\mathbf{P}^{75}$ ... οτι απ̣οθανειcθε...

ουν: OM $\mathbf{P}^{66}$
υμιν: υμειν $\mathbf{P}^{66}$
αποθανειcθε^{1}: αποθανιcθαι $\mathbf{P}^{66}$
πιcτευcητε: πιcτευcηται $\mathbf{P}^{66}$; πιcτευητε $\mathbf{P}^{75}$
αποθανειcθε^{2}: αποθανιcθαι $\mathbf{P}^{66}$

8:25

$\mathbf{P}^{66}$ $\mathbf{P}^{75}$

25: ελεγον ουν αυτω cυ τιc ει και ειπεν αυτοιc ο ιηcουc την αρχην ο τι και λαλω υμιν.

DEF: $\mathbf{P}^{75}$ ... ι̅c̅ [ ]ην αρχην...

ελεγον ουν: και ελεγον $\mathbf{P}^{66}$
και^{1}: OM $\mathbf{P}^{66}$ $\mathbf{P}^{75}$
ο^{1}: OM $\mathbf{P}^{66*}$ $\mathbf{P}^{75}$; txt $\mathbf{P}^{66*c}$
ιηcουc: + ειπον υ̣μιν $\mathbf{P}^{66*c}$; txt $\mathbf{P}^{66*}$

8:26

$\mathbf{P}^{66}$ $\mathbf{P}^{75}$

26: πολλα εχω περι υμων λαλειν και κρινειν αλλ ο πεμψαc με αληθηc εcτι καγω α ηκουcα παρ αυτου ταυτα λεγω ειc τον κοcμον.

DEF: $\mathbf{P}^{75}$ πολλα ε[ ]ω περι... κρινειν [ ]λ̣λ̣ [ ] πεμψαc... η̣κουcα...

εχω: εχων **P**[66]
εστι: εστιν **P**[66] **P**[75]
λεγω: λαλω **P**[66] **P**[75]

8:27

P[66] **P**[75]

27: ουκ εγνωσαν οτι τον πατερα αυτοις ελεγεν.

DEF: **P**[75] ... α̣υτοις...

8:28

P[66] **P**[75]

28: ειπεν ουν αυτοις ο ιησους οταν υψωσητε τον υιον του ανθρωπου τοτε γνωσεσθε οτι εγω ειμι και απ εμαυτου ποιω ουδεν αλλα καθως εδιδαξε με ο πατηρ μου ταυτα λαλω.

αυτοις: OM **P**[66*]; txt **P**[66*c]
ιησους: + οτι **P**[66] **P**[75]
οταν: οτανε **P**[66*] (ε postea eras.)
υψωσητε: υψωσηται **P**[66]
ουδεν: ουδε εν **P**[66]
εδιδαξε: εδειδαξεν **P**[66]; εδιδαξεν **P**[75]
με: μοι **P**[66*]; txt **P**[66*c]
μου: OM **P**[66] **P**[75]

8:29

P[66] **P**[75]

29: και ο πεμψας με μετ εμου εστιν ουκ αφηκε με μονον ο πατηρ οτι εγω τα αρεστα αυτω ποιω παντοτε.

αφηκε: αφηκεν **P**[66] **P**[75]
ο πατηρ: OM **P**[66] **P**[75]

8:30

$\mathbf{P}^{66}$ $\mathbf{P}^{75}$

30: ταυτα αυτου λαλουντος πολλοι επιστευσαν εις αυτον.

DEF: $\mathbf{P}^{75}$ ... π̣ολλοι...

8:31

$\mathbf{P}^{66}$ $\mathbf{P}^{75}$

31: ελεγεν ουν ο ιησους προς τους πεπιστευκοτας αυτω ιουδαιους εαν υμεις μεινητε εν τω λογω τω εμω αληθως μαθηται μου εστε.

DEF: $\mathbf{P}^{75}$ ελεγεν [ ]υ̣ν... αυτ̣ω... εν τ̣ω... μ̣ου...

μεινητε: μεινηται $\mathbf{P}^{66}$; μενητε $\mathbf{P}^{75}$

8:32

$\mathbf{P}^{66}$ $\mathbf{P}^{75}$

32: και γνωσεσθε την αληθειαν και η αληθεια ελευθερωσει υμας.

DEF: $\mathbf{P}^{75}$ ... αλη[ ]ειαν... υμ̣ας

αληθεια: αληθια $\mathbf{P}^{66}$

8:33

$\mathbf{P}^{66}$ $\mathbf{P}^{75}$

33: απεκριθησαν αυτω σπερμα αβρααμ εσμεν και ουδενι δεδουλευκαμεν πωποτε πως συ λεγεις οτι ελευθεροι γενησεσθε.

αυτω: προς αυτον $\mathbf{P}^{66}$ $\mathbf{P}^{75}$
δεδουλευκαμεν: + ουδενι $\mathbf{P}^{66*}$; txt $\mathbf{P}^{66*c}$
πωποτε: + και $\mathbf{P}^{66}$
συ: σοι $\mathbf{P}^{75}$

8:34

P^{66} **P**^{75}

34: απεκριθη αυτοις ο ιηcουc αμην αμην λεγω υμιν οτι παc ο ποιων την αμαρτιαν δουλοc εcτι τηc αμαρτιαc.

αυτοιc: αυτω **P**^{66*}; OM **P**^{75}; txt **P**^{66*c}
ο^{1}: OM **P**^{66} **P**^{75}
δουλοc: υ eras. **P**^{66}
εcτι: εcτιν **P**^{66} **P**^{75}

8:35

P^{66} **P**^{75}

35: ο δε δουλοc ου μενει εν τη οικια ειc τον αιωνα ο υιοc μενει ειc τον αιωνα.

ο^{2}: + δε **P**^{66}

8:36

P^{66} **P**^{75}

36: εαν ουν ο υιοc υμαc ελευθερωcη οντωc ελευθεροι εcεcθε.

ουν: OM **P**^{75}
οντωc: οτωc **P**^{66*}; txt **P**^{66*c}
εcεcθε: εcτε **P**^{66}

8:37

P^{66} **P**^{75}

37: οιδα οτι cπερμα αβρααμ εcτε αλλα ζητειτε με αποκτειναι οτι ο λογοc ο εμοc ου χωρει εν υμιν.

εcτε: εcται **P**^{66}
ζητειτε: τιτε **P**^{66*}; txt **P**^{66*c}
χωρει: χωρι **P**^{66}

8:38

P^{66} P^{75}

38: εγω ο εωρακα παρα τω πατρι μου λαλω και υμειc ουν ο εωρακατε παρα τω πατρι υμων ποιειτε.

DEF: **P^{75}** ... παρα του πατροc λαλ̣[ ]ε̣

εγω ο: α εγω **P^{66} P^{75}**
εωρακα: ερακα **P^{66*}**; εορακα **P^{75}**; txt **P^{66*c}**
μου: OM **P^{66} P^{75}**
ο^{2}: α **P^{66} P^{75}**
εωρακατε: ηκουcατε **P^{75}**
τω πατρι: του πατροc **P^{66} P^{75}**
υμων: OM **P^{66} P^{75}**
ποιειτε: λαλ[3]ε **P^{75}**

8:39

P^{66} P^{75}

39: απεκριθηcαν και ειπον αυτω ο πατηρ ημων αβρααμ εcτι λεγει αυτοιc ο ιηcουc ει τεκνα του αβρααμ ητε τα εργα του αβρααμ εποιειτε αν.

DEF: **P^{75}** α̣πεκριθηcαν... ο π[ ]η̣ρ... αυτ̣[ ]c... τα [ ]ρ̣γα του̣ αβρααμ...

ειπον: ειπαν **P^{66} P^{75}**
εcτι: εcτιν **P^{66} P^{75}**
λεγει: + ουν **P^{66}**
ητε: εcτε **P^{66} P^{75}**
εποιειτε: ποιειται **P^{66}**
αν: OM **P^{66} P^{75}**

8:40

P^{66} P^{75}

40: νυν δε ζητειτε με αποκτειναι ανθρωπον οc την αληθειαν υμιν λελαληκα ην ηκουcα παρα του θεου τουτο αβρααμ ουκ εποιηcεν.

DEF: **P^{75}** ... ζη̣τειτε... ανθρωπο̄ [ ] την...

αποκτειναι: αποκτιναι **P[66]**
αληθειαν: αληθιαν **P[66]**
λελαληκα: λελαληκεν **P[66]***; txt **P[66]*c**

8:41

P[66] P[75]

41: υμεις ποιειτε τα εργα του πατρος υμων ειπον ουν αυτω ημεις εκ πορνειας ου γεγεννημεθα ενα πατερα εχομεν τον θεον.

DEF: **P[75]** ... γεγεννημεθα [ ]ν̣α̣ πατερα...

ειπον: ειπαν **P[66]**
πορνειας: πορνιας **P[66]**
ου γεγεννημεθα: ουκ εγεγεννημεθα **P[75]***; txt **P[75]c**
γεγεννημεθα: γεγενημεθα **P[66]**

8:42

P[66] P[75]

42: ειπεν ουν αυτοις ο ιηcουc ει ο θεος πατηρ υμων ην ηγαπατε αν εμε εγω γαρ εκ του θεου εξηλθον και ηκω ουδε γαρ απ εμαυτου εληλυθα αλλ εκεινος με απεστειλε.

DEF: **P[75]** ειπεν αυτ̣[ ]c ο... εḥλυθα αλλ εκεινος̣...

ουν: OM **P[66] P[75]**
ο[1]: OM **P[66]**
ο[2]: + υ postea eras. **P[66]**
εγω γαρ εκ: εκ γαρ **P[66]**
εξηλθον: εξεληλυθα **P[66]**
ουδε: ου **P[66]**
εληλυθα: littera eras. post ε **P[66]**
απεστειλε: απεσταλκεν **P[66]** (c supra ras.); απεστειλεν **P[75]**

8:43

$\mathbf{P}^{66}$ $\mathbf{P}^{75}$

43: διατι την λαλιαν την εμην ου γινωσκετε οτι ου δυνασθε ακουειν τον λογον τον εμον.

γινωσκετε: γινωσκεται $\mathbf{P}^{66}$; γεινωσκετε $\mathbf{P}^{75}$
δυνασθε: δυνασθαι $\mathbf{P}^{66}$

8:44

$\mathbf{P}^{66}$ $\mathbf{P}^{75}$

44: υμεις εκ πατρος του διαβολου εστε και τας επιθυμιας του πατρος υμων θελετε ποιειν εκεινος ανθρωποκτονος ην απ αρχης και εν τη αληθεια ουχ εστηκεν οτι ουκ εστιν αληθεια εν αυτω οταν λαλη το ψευδος εκ των ιδιων λαλει οτι ψευστης εστι και ο πατηρ αυτου.

εκ^{1}: + του $\mathbf{P}^{66}$ $\mathbf{P}^{75}$
επιθυμιας: επιθυμειας $\mathbf{P}^{66}$
θελετε: θελεται $\mathbf{P}^{66}$
απ αρχης: littera eras. post α prior $\mathbf{P}^{66}$
αληθεια: αληθια $\mathbf{P}^{66}$
ουχ: ουκ $\mathbf{P}^{66}$
ουκ εστιν αληθεια: αληθια ουκ εστιν $\mathbf{P}^{66}$
ψευδος: δευδος $\mathbf{P}^{66*}$; txt $\mathbf{P}^{66*c}$
εστι: εστιν $\mathbf{P}^{66}$ $\mathbf{P}^{75}$

8:45

$\mathbf{P}^{66}$ $\mathbf{P}^{75}$

45: εγω δε οτι την αληθειαν λεγω ου πιστευετε μοι.

αληθειαν: αληθιαν $\mathbf{P}^{66}$

8:46

$\mathbf{P}^{66}$ $\mathbf{P}^{75}$

46: τις εξ υμων ελεγχει με περι αμαρτιας ει δε αληθειαν λεγω διατι υμεις ου πιστευετε μοι.

ελεγχει: ελεγξει **P^{75}**
αμαρτιας: αμαρτειας **P^{75*}**; txt **P^{75c}**
δε: OM **P^{66} P^{75}**
μοι: OM **P^{66*}**; txt **P^{66*c}**

8:47

P^{66} P^{75}

47: ο ων εκ του θεου τα ρηματα του θεου ακουει δια τουτο υμειc ουκ ακουετε οτι εκ του θεου ουκ εcτε.

ακουετε: ακουεται **P^{66}**

8:48

P^{66} P^{75}

48: απεκριθηcαν ουν οι ιουδαιοι και ειπον αυτω ου καλωc λεγομεν ημειc οτι cαμαρειτηc ει cυ και δαιμονιον εχειc.

ουν: OM **P^{66} P^{75}**
ειπον: ειπαν **P^{75}**
λεγομεν ημειc: ημειc ελεγομεν **P^{66*}**; ημειc λεγομεν **P^{66*c}**
cαμαρειτηc: cαμαριτηc **P^{66}**

8:49

P^{66} P^{75}

49: απεκριθη ιηcουc εγω δαιμονιον ουκ εχω αλλα τιμω τον πατερα μου και υμειc ατιμαζετε με.

δαιμονιον: δαιμονι **P^{66*}**; txt **P^{66*c}**
ουκ: χ coepit, postea κ scripsit **P^{66}**
τιμω: τειμω **P^{75}**
ατιμαζετε: ατειμαζετε **P^{75}**

8:50

P^{66} **P**^{75}

50: εγω δε ου ζητω την δοξαν μου εστιν ο ζητων και κρινων.

και: OM **P**^{66*}; txt **P**^{66*c}
κρινων: κρεινων **P**^{75c}; txt **P**^{75*}

8:51

P^{66} **P**^{75}

51: αμην αμην λεγω υμιν εαν τις τον λογον τον εμον τηρηση θανατον ου μη θεωρηση εις τον αιωνα.

DEF: **P**^{66} ... εις τον [ ]ιωνα
P^{75} ... ου̣...

λεγω: λε **P**^{66*}; txt **P**^{66*c}
τον λογον τον εμον: τον εμον λογον **P**^{75}
θεωρηση: ιδη **P**^{66}

8:52

P^{66} **P**^{75}

52: ειπον ουν αυτω οι ιουδαιοι νυν εγνωκαμεν οτι δαιμονιον εχεις αβρααμ απεθανε και οι προφηται και συ λεγεις εαν τις τον λογον μου τηρηση ου μη γευσεται θανατου εις τον αιωνα.

DEF: **P**^{75} ... οτι̣... α̣π̣ε̣θ̣α̣ν̣εν... λογον̣ μ̣ου... εις το̣ν αιωνα

ουν: OM **P**^{66}
απεθανε: απεθανεν **P**^{66} **P**^{75}
λεγεις: + οτι **P**^{75}
τον λογον μου: μου τον λογον **P**^{66}
γευσεται: γευσηται **P**^{66} **P**^{75}

8:53

P^{66} P^{75}

53: μη cυ μειζων ει του πατροc ημων αβρααμ οcτιc απεθανε και οι προφηται απεθανον τινα cεαυτον cυ ποιειc.

DEF: **P^{75}** ... α̣β̣ρ̣ααμ... προφη̣ται...

μειζων: μιζων **P^{66}**
πατροc: πτροc **P^{66*}**; txt **P^{66*c}**
οcτιc: οτι **P^{66*}**; txt **P^{66*c}**
απεθανε: απεθανεν **P^{66} P^{75}**
cυ^{2}: OM **P^{66} P^{75}**

8:54

P^{66} P^{75}

54: απεκριθη ιηcουc εαν εγω δοξαζω εμαυτον η δοξα μου ουδεν εcτιν εcτιν ο πατηρ μου ο δοξαζων με ον υμειc λεγετε οτι θεοc υμων εcτι.

DEF: **P^{66}**]πεκριθη...

δοξαζω: δοξαcω **P^{66*c} P^{75}**; txt **P^{66*}**
λεγετε: λεγεται **P^{66}**
θεοc: ο θεοc **P^{66}**
υμων: ημων **P^{66*c} P^{75}**; txt **P^{66*}**
εcτι: εcτιν **P^{66} P^{75}**

8:55

P^{66} P^{75}

55: και ουκ εγνωκατε αυτον εγω δε οιδα αυτον και εαν ειπω οτι ουκ οιδα αυτον εσομαι ομοιος υμων ψευστης αλλ οιδα αυτον και τον λογον αυτου τηρω.

DEF: **P^{66}** ... ειπω [ ]τι...
P^{75} ... λογο̣̄...

ουκ εγνωκατε: ου γεγνωκατε **P^{66*}**; txt **P^{66*c}**
και εαν: καν **P^{75}**
ειπω: + υμιν **P^{75}**
ομοιος υμων: υμων ομοιος **P^{66}**
υμων: υμιν **P^{75}**
αλλ: αλλα **P^{66}**

8:56

P^{66} P^{75}

56: αβρααμ ο πατηρ υμων ηγαλλιασατο ινα ιδη την ημεραν την εμην και ειδε και εχαρη.

P^{75} ... και ιδη̣...

αβρααμ: αβραμ **P^{66*}**; txt **P^{66*c}**
ειδε: ειδεν **P^{66}**; ιδη **P^{75*}**; ιδεν **P^{75c}**

8:57

P^{66} P^{75}

57: ειπον ουν οι ιουδαιοι προς αυτον πεντηκοντα ετη ουπω εχεις και αβρααμ εωρακας.

εωρακας: εορακας **P^{66}**; εορακεν σε **P^{75}**

8:58

P^{66} **P**^{75}

58: ειπεν αυτοις ο ιηcουc αμην αμην λεγω υμιν πριν αβρααμ γενεcθαι εγω ειμι.

DEF: **P**^{66}]πεν... αμην λε[ ] υμιν... γενεcθαι [ ] ειμι

ο: OM **P**^{75}

8:59

P^{66} **P**^{75}

59: ηραν ουν λιθουc ινα βαλωcιν επ αυτον ιηcουc δε εκρυβη και εξηλθεν εκ του ιερου διελθων δια μεcου αυτων και παρηγεν ουτωc.

DEF: **P**^{66} ... βαλω̣[ ] επ... εξη[ ] εκ...

διελθων δια μεcου αυτων και παρηγεν ουτωc: OM **P**^{66} **P**^{75}

CHAPTER NINE

P^{44B} **P**^{66} **P**^{75}

9:1

P^{66} **P**^{75}

1: και παραγων ειδεν ανθρωπον τυφλον εκ γενετης.

DEF: **P**^{66} ... ειδ[ ] ανθρωπον τυφλον εκ γενε[

9:2

P^{66} **P**^{75}

2: και ηρωτησαν αυτον οι μαθηται αυτου λεγοντες ραββι τις ημαρτεν ουτος η οι γονεις αυτου ινα τυφλος γεννηθη.

DEF: **P**^{66} ... μαθη[ ] αυτου... τις η[ ]τεν... αυτου ι[ ] τυφλος...

ραββι: ραββει **P**^{66} **P**^{75}

9:3

P^{44B} **P**^{66} **P**^{75}

3: απεκριθη ο ιησους ουτε ουτος ημαρτεν ουτε οι γονεις αυτου αλλ ινα φανερωθη τα εργα του θεου εν αυτω.

DEF: **P**^{44B}] ουτε οι γ[ ]θη τα εργ[
P^{66} απεκριθ[ ] ουτε... ουτε ο[ ]νεις... φανερωθ[ ] εργα... (teste ed. pr.)

απεκριθη ο ιησους: απεκριθ[2-3 /] **P**^{66} (& cf. **P**^{75})
ο: OM **P**^{75} (& cf. **P**^{66})

9:4

P44B P66 P75

4: εμε δει εργαζεσθαι τα εργα του πεμψαντος με εως ημερα εστιν ερχεται νυξ οτε ουδεις δυναται εργαζεσθαι.

DEF: **P44B**]ζεσθαι τ[ ]υ π[ ]ως ημ[ ]ρχ[ ] δυνατ[
P66 ημας δ[ ] εργαζεσθαι... πεμ[ ]τος... εστιν [ ]χεται...
δυνη[ ]ται...

εμε: ημας **P66 P75**
με: ημας **P66 P75**
δυναται: δυνη[2-3 /]ται **P66**
εργαζεσθαι: εργαζεσθε **P66**

9:5

P66 P75

5: οταν εν τω κοσμω ω φως ειμι του κοσμου.

DEF: **P66** ... κο[ ]ω φως...

κοσμω ω: κο[2-3 /]ω **P66**

9:6

P66 P75

6: ταυτα ειπων επτυσε χαμαι και εποιησε πηλον εκ του πτυσματος και επεχρισε τον πηλον επι τους οφθαλμους του τυφλου.

DEF: **P66** ταυτ[ ]πων... και ε[ ]ησεν... πτυσμ[ ] και...

επτυσε: επτυσεν **P66 P75**
εποιησε: εποιησεν **P75**; ε[ ]ησεν **P66**
επεχρισε: επεχρεισεν αυτον **P75***; επεχρεισεν αυτου **P75C**; επεχρισεν αυτου **P66**
του τυφλου: OM **P66 P75**

9:7

P^{66} P^{75}

7: και ειπεν αυτω υπαγε νιψαι εις την κολυμβηθραν του σιλωαμ ο ερμηνευεται απεσταλμενος απηλθεν ουν και ενιψατο και ηλθε βλεπων.

σιλωαμ: σιωαμ **P^{66*}**; σειλωαμ **P^{75}**; txt **P^{66*c}**
ηλθε: ηλθεν **P^{66} P^{75}**

9:8

P^{66} P^{75}

8: οι ουν γειτονες και οι θεωρουντες αυτον το προτερον οτι τυφλος ην ελεγον ουχ ουτος εστιν ο καθημενος και προσαιτων.

γειτονες: + αυτου **P^{66*}**; txt **P^{66c}**
τυφλος: προσετης **P^{66}**; προσαιτης **P^{75}**
εστιν: OM **P^{75}**

9:9

P^{66} P^{75}

9: αλλοι ελεγον οτι ουτος εστιν αλλοι δε οτι ομοιος αυτω εστιν εκεινος ελεγεν οτι εγω ειμι.

DEF: **P^{75}** ... αυ̣τω... εγω ε̣[ ]μ̣ι

οτι^{1}: OM **P^{66}**
δε οτι: ελεγον ουχι αλλα **P^{66}**; ελεγον ουχι αλλ **P^{75}**
εκεινος: + δε **P^{66}**
οτι^{3}: OM **P^{66}**

9:10

P^{66} P^{75}

10: ελεγον ουν αυτω πως ανεωχθησαν σου οι οφθαλμοι.

DEF: **P^{75}** ... ηνεωχθη[ ]αν...

ελεγον: ειπαν **P^{66}**

ανεωχθηcαν cου: cου ηνεωχθηcαν **P66***; ουν ηνεωχθηcαν cου **P66*c**
ανεωχθηcαν: ηνεωχθη[ ]αν **P75**
οφθαλμοι: οφαλμοι **P66***; txt **P66*c**

9:11

P66 P75

11: απεκριθη εκεινοc και ειπεν ανθρωποc λεγομενοc ιηcουc πηλον εποιηcε και επεχριcε μου τουc οφθαλμουc και ειπε μοι υπαγε ειc την κολυμβηθραν του cιλωαμ και νιψαι απελθων δε και νιψαμενοc ανεβλεψα.

εκεινοc: εκινοc **P66**
και ειπεν: OM **P66 P75**
ανθρωποc: ο ανθρωποc ο **P66**; + ο **P75**
εποιηcε: εποιηcεν **P66 P75**
επεχριcε: επεχριcεν **P66**; επεχρειcε **P75**
ειπε: ειπεν **P66 P75**
μοι: + οτι **P66**
την κολυμβηθραν του: τον **P66 P75**
cιλωαμ: cειλωαμ **P75**
δε: ουν **P66 P75**

9:12

P66 P75

12: ειπον ουν αυτω που εcτιν εκεινοc λεγει ουκ οιδα.

DEF: **P66**]παν... εκει[ ] λεγει...
P75 ... ẹκεινοc...

ειπον ουν: και ειπον **P75**
ειπον: [ ]παν **P66**

9:13

P66 P75

13: αγουcιν αυτον προc τουc φαριcαιουc τον ποτε τυφλον.

DEF: **P66** ... αυτον π[ ] τουc... τυφ[

9:14

P^{66} **P**^{75}

14: ην δε cαββατον οτε τον πηλον εποιηcεν ο ιηcουc και ανεωξεν αυτου τουc οφθαλμουc.

DEF: **P**^{66} ην δε cαββατον εν η ημερα τ[ ] πηλον...

οτε: εν η ημερα **P**^{66} **P**^{75}

9:15

P^{66} **P**^{75}

15: παλιν ουν ηρωτων αυτον και οι φαριcαιοι πωc ανεβλεψεν ο δε ειπεν αυτοιc πηλον επεθηκεν επι τουc οφθαλμουc μου και ενιψαμην και βλεπω.

DEF: **P**^{66} πα[ ] ουν... φαριc[ ] πωc... ειπεν α[ ] πηλον... τουc [ ]φθαλμουc... ενιψαμην και [ ]πω

ηρωτων: ηρωτουν **P**^{66}
και^{1}: OM **P**^{66*}; txt **P**^{66*c}
επι τουc οφθαλμουc μου: μοι επι τουc οφθαλμουc **P**^{66*}; μου επι τουc οφθαλμουc **P**^{66*c} **P**^{75}

9:16

P^{66} **P**^{75}

16: ελεγον ουν εκ των φαριcαιων τινεc ουτοc ο ανθρωποc ουκ εcτι παρα του θεου οτι το cαββατον ου τηρει αλλοι ελεγον πωc δυναται ανθρωποc αμαρτωλοc τοιαυτα cημεια ποιειν και cχιcμα ην εν αυτοιc.

DEF: **P**^{66} ... φαριc[ ] τινεc... θ̅[ ] α̅ν̅ο̅c̅... τη[ ] αλλοι... δυνατα[ ] αμαρτωλοc... cημεια π[ ]ειν... (teste ed. pr.)

ουτοc ο ανθρωποc ουκ εcτι παρα του θεου: ουκ εcτιν ουτοc παρα θεου ο ανθρωποc **P**^{75*}; ο punctis del. **P**^{75c}; ουκ εcτιν ουτοc παρα θ̅[ ] ανθρωποc **P**^{66}
ανθρωποc^{2}: OM **P**^{66}
cχιcμα: cχιμα **P**^{66}

9:17

P^{66} P^{75}

17: λεγουcι τω τυφλω παλιν cυ τι λεγειc περι αυτου οτι ηνοιξε cου τουc οφθαλμουc ο δε ειπεν οτι προφητηc εcτιν.

DEF: **P^{66}**]ουcιν... παλιν [ ] λεγειc... (teste ed. pr.)
P^{75} ... ẹcτιν

λεγουcι: λεγουcιν ουν **P^{75}**; [ ]ουcιν ουν **P^{66}**
αυτου: cεαυτου **P^{66*} P^{75}**; txt **P^{66c}**
ηνοιξε: ηνοιξεν **P^{66}**; ηνεωξεν **P^{75}**

9:18

P^{66} P^{75}

18: ουκ επιcτευcαν ουν οι ιουδαιοι περι αυτου οτι τυφλοc ην και ανεβλεψεν εωc οτου εφωνηcαν τουc γονειc αυτου του αναβλεψαντοc.

τυφλοc ην: ην τυφλοc **P^{66} P^{75}**
οτου: ου **P^{66*}**; txt **P^{66c}**
του αναβλεψαντοc: OM **P^{66*}**; txt **P^{66*c}**

9:19

P^{66} P^{75}

19: και ηρωτηcαν αυτουc λεγοντεc ουτοc εcτιν ο υιοc υμων ον υμειc λεγετε οτι τυφλοc εγεννηθη πωc ουν αρτι βλεπει.

DEF: **P^{66}** κα[ ] επηρωτηcαν... λεγοντε[ ] ουτοc... ον υμ[ ] λεγετε...

ηρωτηcαν: επηρωτηcαν **P^{66}**
αυτουc: αυτουυc **P^{66*}**; υ^{2} postea eras.
αρτι βλεπει: βλεπει αρτι **P^{75}**

9:20

P66 P75

20: απεκριθηcαν αυτοιc οι γονειc αυτου και ειπον οιδαμεν οτι ουτοc εcτιν ο υιοc ημων και οτι τυφλοc εγεννηθη.

απεκριθηcαν: + ουν **P66 P75**
αυτοιc: OM **P66 P75**
ειπον: ειπαν **P66 P75**

9:21

P66 P75

21: πωc δε νυν βλεπει ουκ οιδαμεν η τιc ηνοιξεν αυτου τουc οφθαλμουc ημειc ουκ οιδαμεν αυτοc ηλικιαν εχει αυτον ερωτηcατε αυτοc περι αυτου λαληcει.

DEF: **P66** ... οφθα[ ]μουc... αυτον [ ]ρωτηcατε... αυτοc...

αυτοc ηλικιαν εχει αυτον ερωτηcατε: αυτον [ ]ρωτηcατε ηλικιαν εχει **P66**
αυτον ερωτηcατε: OM **P75**
αυτου²: εαυτου **P66 P75**

9:22

P66 P75

22: ταυτα ειπον οι γονειc αυτου οτι εφοβουντο τουc ιουδαιουc ηδη γαρ cυνετεθειντο οι ιουδαιοι ινα εαν τιc αυτον ομολογηcη χριcτον αποcυναγωγοc γενηται.

DEF: **P66** ταυτα ειπ[ ] οι... cυνετεθε[ ]το οι... ομο[ ]γηcη...
αποcυναγωγοc [ ]νηται
P75 ... cυνετεθειν[ ]υδαιοι...

γονειc: γονιc **P66**
γαρ: γα **P66***; txt **P66*c**
εαν: αν **P75**
αυτον ομολογηcη: ομολογηcη αυτον **P75**; ομο[ ]γηcη αυτον **P66**

9:23

P66 P75

23: δια τουτο οι γονεις αυτου ειπον οτι ηλικιαν εχει αυτον ερωτησατε.

DEF: **P66** ... αυτο[ ] ειπον... αυτο[ ] επερωτησαται
P75 ... γονεις...

ειπον: ειπαν **P75**
ηλικιαν: ηλικειαν **P75**
εχει: + και **P66**
ερωτησατε: επερωτησατε **P75**; επερωτησαται **P66**

9:24

P66 P75

24: εφωνησαν ουν εκ δευτερου τον ανθρωπον ος ην τυφλος και ειπον αυτω δος δοξαν τω θεω ημεις οιδαμεν οτι ο ανθρωπος ουτος αμαρτωλος εστιν.

DEF: **P66** ... τυφ[ ] και... τω θ̄[ ] ημεις...

εκ δευτερου τον ανθρωπον: τον ανθρωπον εκ τερου **P66*** (littera eras. inter ε et κ); τον ανθρωπον εκ δευτερου **P66*c P75**
ειπον: ειπαν **P66 P75**
ο ανθρωπος ουτος: ουτος ο ανθρωπος **P66 P75**

9:25

P66 P75

25: απεκριθη ουν εκεινος και ειπεν ει αμαρτωλος εστιν ουκ οιδα εν οιδα οτι τυφλος ων αρτι βλεπω.

DEF: **P66** απ[ ]κριθη... αμαρτωλ[ ] εστιν... τυφλος [ ] αρτι βλεπω

και ειπεν: OM **P66 P75**
ουκ οιδα: ου δα **P66***; txt **P66*c**

9:26

P66 P75

26: ειπον δε αυτω παλιν τι εποιηςε σοι πως ηνοιξε σου τους οφθαλμους.

DEF: **P66** ... αυτω π[ ]λιν... ηνε[ ]εν... (teste ed. pr.)

δε: ουν **P66 P75**
παλιν: OM **P75**
εποιηςε: εποιηςεν **P66 P75**
ηνοιξε: ηνεωξεν **P75**; ηνε[ ]εν **P66***; ηνεω[ ]εν **P66*c** (teste ed. pr.)
οφθαλμους: οφθαλμου **P66***; txt **P66*c**

9:27

P66 P75

27: απεκριθη αυτοις ειπον υμιν ηδη και ουκ ηκουςατε τι παλιν θελετε ακουειν μη και υμεις θελετε αυτου μαθηται γενεςθαι.

DEF: **P66** απεκρ[ ]η αυτοις... ηδη [ ]κουςαται... παλιν [ ]ουειν... θελεται [ ]ηται...

αυτοις: littera eras. inter ι et ς **P66**
ηκουςατε: [ ]κουςαται **P66**
τι: + ουν **P75**
παλιν θελετε: θελετε παλιν **P66**
θελετε²: θελεται **P66**
αυτου μαθηται: [ ]ηται αυτου **P66**

9:28

P66 P75

28: ελοιδορηςαν ουν αυτον και ειπον συ ει μαθητης εκεινου ημεις δε του μωςεως εςμεν μαθηται.

DEF: **P66** ελοιδọ[ ]ςαν...

ελοιδορηςαν ουν: και ελοιδορηςαν **P75**; ελοιδο[ ]ςαν **P66**
ειπον: ειπαν **P66**
ει μαθητης εκεινου: μαθητης εκεινου ει **P66**; μαθητης ει εκεινου **P75**

δε: γαρ **P^{66}**
του μωcεωc: μωεωc **P^{66*}**; μωυcεωc **P^{66*c}**; του μωυcεωc **P^{75}**

9:29

P^{66} P^{75}

29: ημειc οιδαμεν οτι μωcη λελαληκεν ο θεοc τουτον δε ουκ οιδαμεν ποθεν εcτιν.

ημειc: + δε **P^{66}**
μωcη: μωυcει **P^{66} P^{75}**

9:30

P^{66} P^{75}

30: απεκριθη ο ανθρωποc και ειπεν αυτοιc εν γαρ τουτω θαυμαcτον εcτιν οτι υμειc ουκ οιδατε ποθεν εcτι και ανεωξε μου τουc οφθαλμουc.

DEF: **P^{75}** ... και ηνο̣ι̣ξεν μου...

απεκριθη: + δ **P^{75*}**; txt **P^{75c}**
ο ανθρωποc και ειπεν αυτοιc: και ειπεν ο α̅ν̅ο̅c̅ **P^{66*}**; txt **P^{66*c}**
εν γαρ τουτω: εν τουτω γαρ **P^{75}**; τουτο γαρ **P^{66}**
θαυμαcτον: το θαυμαcτον **P^{66} P^{75}**
οιδατε: οιδαται **P^{66}**
εcτι: εcτιν **P^{66} P^{75}**
ανεωξε: ηνοιξεν **P^{66} P^{75}**

9:31

P^{66} P^{75}

31: οιδαμεν δε οτι αμαρτωλων ο θεοc ουκ ακουει αλλ εαν τιc θεοcεβηc η και το θελημα αυτου ποιη τουτου ακουει.

DEF: **P^{75}** ... τι̣c...

δε: OM **P^{66} P^{75}**
η: ην **P^{66}**

9:32

P^{66} P^{75}

32: εκ του αιωνος ουκ ηκουcθη οτι ηνοιξε τιc οφθαλμουc τυφλου γεγεννημενου.

ηνοιξε: ηνοιξεν **P^{66}**; ανεωξεν **P^{75}**

9:33

P^{66} P^{75}

33: ει μη ην ουτοc παρα θεου ουκ ηδυνατο ποιειν ουδεν.

DEF: **P^{75}** ... ο̣υτοc... ουδ[ ]‾

θεου: + ο ανθρωποc **P^{66}**

9:34

P^{66} P^{75}

34: απεκριθηcαν και ειπον αυτω εν αμαρτιαιc cυ εγεννηθηc ολοc και cυ διδαcκειc ημαc και εξεβαλον αυτον εξω.

DEF: **P^{75}** ... αμαρ̣τιαιc...διδαcκειc̣...

ειπον: ειπαν **P^{66} P^{75}**
αμαρτιαιc: αμαρτια **P^{66}**
εγεννηθηc: εγενηθηc **P^{75}**
ολοc: ο λογοc **P^{66*}**; txt **P^{66c}**
εξεβαλον: εξεβαλαν **P^{66}**

9:35

P^{66} P^{75}

35: ηκουcεν ο ιηcουc οτι εξεβαλον αυτον εξω και ευρων αυτον ειπεν αυτω cυ πιcτευειc ειc τον υιον του θεου.

ο: OM **P^{75}**
εξεβαλον: εξεβαλαν **P^{66}**
αυτω: OM **P^{75}**
θεου: ανθρωπου **P^{66} P^{75}**

9:36

P^{66} **P**^{75}

36: απεκριθη εκεινος και ειπε τις εστι κυριε ινα πιστευσω εις αυτον.

απεκριθη εκεινος και ειπε τις εστι: και τις εστιν εφη **P**^{75}; απεκριθη εκεινος και τις εστιν εφη **P**^{66*}; απεκριθη εκεινος και τις εστιν **P**^{66*c}

9:37

P^{66} **P**^{75}

37: ειπε δε αυτω ο ιησους και εωρακας αυτον και ο λαλων μετα σου εκεινος εστιν.

ειπε: ειπεν **P**^{66} **P**^{75}
δε: OM **P**^{66} **P**^{75}
ο^{1}: OM **P**^{66}
εωρακας: εορακας **P**^{66} **P**^{75}
εκεινος: αυτος **P**^{66}

9:38

P^{66} **P**^{75}

38: ο δε εφη πιστευω κυριε και προσεκυνησεν αυτω.

OM totum versum **P**^{75}

9:39

P^{66} P^{75}

39: και ειπεν ο ιηcουc ειc κριμα εγω ειc τον κοcμον τουτον ηλθον ινα οι μη βλεποντεc βλεπωcι και οι βλεποντεc τυφλοι γενωνται.

και ειπεν ο ιηcουc: OM **P^{75}**
ειc τον κοcμον τουτον ηλθον: ηλθον ειc τον κοcμον **P^{66*}**; + τουτον post κοcμον **P^{66*c}**
ηλθον: εληλυθα **P^{75}**
βλεπωcι: βλεπωcιν **P^{66*c} P^{75}**; πωcιν **P^{66*}**
οι^{2}: + μη **P^{66*}**; txt **P^{66*c}**

9:40

P^{66} P^{75}

40: και ηκουcαν εκ των φαριcαιων ταυτα οι οντεc μετ αυτου και ειπον αυτω μη και ημειc τυφλοι εcμεν.

DEF: **P^{75}** ... τυφλο̣[ ] εcμεν

και^{1}: OM **P^{66} P^{75}**
οντεc μετ αυτου: μετ αυτου οντεc **P^{66} P^{75}**
ημειc: υμειc **P^{66}**

9:41

P^{66} P^{75}

41: ειπεν αυτοιc ο ιηcουc ει τυφλοι ητε ουκ αν ειχετε αμαρτιαν νυν δε λεγετε οτι βλεπομεν η ουν αμαρτια υμων μενει.

ο: OM **P^{66} P^{75}**
ειχετε: ειχεται **P^{66}**
λεγετε: λεγεται **P^{66}**
η ουν αμαρτια: η αμαρτια **P^{66}** (α eras. inter η et α, δ eras. sub ρ); και η αμαρτια **P^{75}**

CHAPTER TEN

$\mathbf{P}^{6}$ $\mathbf{P}^{44A}$ $\mathbf{P}^{45}$ $\mathbf{P}^{66}$ $\mathbf{P}^{75}$

10:1

$\mathbf{P}^{6}$ $\mathbf{P}^{66}$ $\mathbf{P}^{75}$

1: αμην αμην λεγω υμιν ο μη εισερχομενος δια της θυρας εις την αυλην των προβατων αλλα αναβαινων αλλαχοθεν εκεινος κλεπτης εστι και ληστης.

DEF: $\mathbf{P}^{6}$]ν αμην λεγω [ ]χομενος δια [ ]ν αυλην τω[ ]α αναβ[ ]ος κλε[
$\mathbf{P}^{75}$ ... καῑ ληστης

υμιν: υμειν $\mathbf{P}^{66}$
εστι: εστιν $\mathbf{P}^{66}$ $\mathbf{P}^{75}$

10:2

$\mathbf{P}^{6}$ $\mathbf{P}^{66}$ $\mathbf{P}^{75}$

2: ο δε εισερχομενος δια της θυρας ποιμην εστι των προβατων.

DEF: $\mathbf{P}^{6}$]ε ε[

εισερχομενος: ερχομενος $\mathbf{P}^{75}$
εστι: εστιν $\mathbf{P}^{66}$ $\mathbf{P}^{75}$

10:3

$\mathbf{P}^{66}$ $\mathbf{P}^{75}$

3: τουτω ο θυρωρος ανοιγει και τα προβατα της φωνης αυτου ακουει και τα ιδια προβατα καλει κατ ονομα και εξαγει αυτα.

θυρωρος: θυρουρος $\mathbf{P}^{66}$
προβατα^{2}: προβατια $\mathbf{P}^{66}$
καλει: φωνει $\mathbf{P}^{75}$; φωνι $\mathbf{P}^{66}$

10:4

P^{6} P^{66} P^{75}

4: και οταν τα ιδια προβατα εκβαλη εμπροcθεν αυτων πορευεται και τα προβατα αυτω ακολουθει οτι οιδαcι την φωνην αυτου.

DEF: **P^{6}**] π[ ] ακ[ ] αυτου

και^{1}: OM **P^{66} P^{75}**
προβατα εκβαλη: εκβαλη παντα **P^{66*}**; παντα εκβαλη **P^{66*c} P^{75}**
την φωνην αυτου: αυτου την φωνην **P^{66}**

10:5

P^{6} P^{66} P^{75}

5: αλλοτριω δε ου μη ακολουθηcωcιν αλλα φευξονται απ αυτου οτι ουκ οιδαcι των αλλοτριων την φωνην.

DEF: **P^{6}** α[ ]ρ[ ]ω δ[ ]cωcιν α[ ] φε[ ] οτι ουκ οι[ ]cι τ[ ]τριων

απ αυτου: τ aut ι eras. inter π et α **P^{66}**
των αλλοτριων την φωνην: τ[ ] / τριων **P^{6}**

10:6

P^{6} P^{66} P^{75}

6: ταυτην την παροιμιαν ειπεν αυτοιc ο ιηcουc εκεινοι δε ουκ εγνωcαν τινα ην α ελαλει αυτοιc.

DEF: **P^{6}** τα[ ]ην [ ] αυτοιc ο $\overline{\text{ιc}}$ [ ]κ[ ] τι ην α [

εγνωcαν: εγνω **P^{66*}**; txt **P^{66*c}**
τινα: τι **P^{6} P^{66*}**; txt **P^{66*c}**
ην α: OM **P^{66*}**; txt **P^{66*c}**

10:7

P6 P45 P66 P75

7: ειπεν ουν παλιν αυτοις ο ιηcουc αμην αμην λεγω υμιν οτι εγω ειμι η θυρα των προβατων.

DEF: **P6**]λιν ο ιc̄ [ ] ε[ ]μ[
P45]ε[ ] αυτοιc ο ιη̄ αμ[ ]ω υμιν [ ] ε[ ] ε[ ] προβατων

ειπεν ουν παλιν: [ ]ε[4] **P45**; ειπεν **P66***; ειπεν ουν **P66*c**
αυτοιc: OM **P6 P75**
οτι: OM **P75**
η θυρα: ο ποιμην **P75**

10:8

P44A P45 P66 P75

8: παντεc οcοι προ εμου ηλθον κλεπται ειcι και ληcται αλλ ουκ ηκουcαν αυτων τα προβατα.

DEF: **P44A**] προ[
P45 παντεc οcοι [ ]αι... ληcται α[ ]κουcεν...

προ εμου ηλθον κλεπται: [10]αι **P45**
προ εμου ηλθον: ηλθον προ εμου **P66**
προ εμου: OM **P75**
κλεπται: κλεπτε **P66**
ειcι: ειcιν **P45 P66 P75**
ηκουcαν: [ ]κουcεν **P45**

10:9

$\mathbf{P}^{6}$ $\mathbf{P}^{44A}$ $\mathbf{P}^{45}$ $\mathbf{P}^{66}$ $\mathbf{P}^{75}$

9: εγω ειμι η θυρα δι εμου εαν τιc ειcελθη cωθηcεται και ειcελευcεται και εξελευcεται και νομην ευρηcει.

DEF: $\mathbf{P}^{6}$]η [ ] εξελ[
$\mathbf{P}^{44A}$]υ εα[ ] κ[
$\mathbf{P}^{45}$]υ[ ]α δι... ειc[ ]cεται και ειcελευcεται και
εξ[ ]λ[ ]υcεται...
$\mathbf{P}^{75}$ ... ειcελευ[ ]εται και εξελευcεται... ευρ̣ηcει

εαν: αν $\mathbf{P}^{75}$
εξελευcεται: εξελευcετε $\mathbf{P}^{66}$

10:10

$\mathbf{P}^{6}$ $\mathbf{P}^{44A}$ $\mathbf{P}^{45}$ $\mathbf{P}^{66}$ $\mathbf{P}^{75}$

10: ο κλεπτηc ουκ ερχεται ει μη ινα κλεψη και θυcη και απολεcη εγω ηλθον ινα ζωην εχωcι και περιccον εχωcιν.

DEF: $\mathbf{P}^{6}$]ε κλ[ ]εψη[
$\mathbf{P}^{44A}$]λθ[ ]ν ινα [ ]αι περιccοτερον ε[
$\mathbf{P}^{45}$] ουκ... εγω δ[ ] ινα...
$\mathbf{P}^{75}$ ... ι̣να...

ο: [ ]ε $\mathbf{P}^{6}$
κλεπτηc: κλεπηc $\mathbf{P}^{66*}$; txt $\mathbf{P}^{66*c}$
ει: τ sub ε $\mathbf{P}^{75}$
ινα: εινα $\mathbf{P}^{66}$
κλεψη: κεψη $\mathbf{P}^{66*}$; txt $\mathbf{P}^{66*c}$
εγω: + δ[ ] $\mathbf{P}^{45}$
εχωcι: εχωcιν $\mathbf{P}^{66}$ $\mathbf{P}^{75}$
και περιccον εχωcιν: OM $\mathbf{P}^{66*}$; txt $\mathbf{P}^{66*c}$
περιccον: περιccοτερον $\mathbf{P}^{44A}$ $\mathbf{P}^{75}$

10:11

$\mathbf{P}^{44A}$ $\mathbf{P}^{45}$ $\mathbf{P}^{66}$ $\mathbf{P}^{75}$

11: εγω ειμι ο ποιμην ο καλοc ο ποιμην ο καλοc την ψυχην αυτου τιθηcιν υπερ των προβατων.

DEF: **P**[44A]]ιμι ο π[ ] καλως [ ]ερ τω[
P[45] ... καλος ποι[ ] ο καλος ποιμην... προβ[

ποιμην ο καλος[1]: καλος ποι[ ] **P**[45]
ποιμην ο καλος[2]: καλος ποιμην **P**[45]
καλος[2]: καλως **P**[44A]
τιθησιν: διδωσιν **P**[45]

10:12

P[44A] **P**[45] **P**[66] **P**[75]

12: ο μισθωτος δε και ουκ ων ποιμην ου ουκ εισι τα προβατα ιδια θεωρει τον λυκον ερχομενον και αφιησι τα προβατα και φευγει και ο λυκος αρπαζει αυτα και σκορπιζει τα προβατα.

DEF: **P**[44A]] αρπα[ ]α [
P[45]] μισθωτος... προβατα θ[ ] τον... φευγει κα[ ] αρ[ ]αζει...

μισθωτος δε: δε μισθωτος **P**[66]
δε: OM **P**[45] **P**[75]
εισι: εστιν **P**[45] **P**[66] **P**[75]
τα προβατα ιδια: ιδια τα προβατα **P**[45]; τα προβατα τα ιδια **P**[75]
αφιησι: αφειησιν **P**[45]; αφιησιν **P**[66] **P**[75]
τα προβατα[3]: OM **P**[45] **P**[66] **P**[75] (& cf. **P**[44A])
(12-13) και σκορπιζει τα προβατα ο δε μισθωτος φευγει οτι: [15] **P**[44A] (& cf. **P**[45] **P**[66] **P**[75])

10:13

P[44A] **P**[45] **P**[66] **P**[75]

13: ο δε μισθωτος φευγει οτι μισθωτος εστι και ου μελει αυτω περι των προβατων.

DEF: **P**[44A]] μισθω[ ] και [ ]των
P[45] ... μελε[ ] περι...

ο δε μισθωτος φευγει: OM **P**[45] **P**[66] **P**[75] (& cf. **P**[44A] supra)
εστι: εστιν **P**[45] **P**[66] **P**[75]
μελει: μελι **P**[66]

10:14

P^{44A} **P**^{45} **P**^{66} **P**^{75}

14: εγω ειμι ο ποιμην ο καλος και γινωσκω τα εμα και γινωσκομαι υπο των εμων.

DEF: **P**^{44A} εγω ε[ ]ι γινωσκω [
P^{45} ... καλος και γειν[ ] εμα και...
P^{75}... και γει[ ] τ̣α εμα... γεινωσκουcι μ̣[ ]μα

γινωσκω: γειν[ ] **P**^{45}; γει[ ] **P**^{75}
γινωσκομαι υπο των εμων: γεινωσκουcι με τα εμα **P**^{45*}; γεινωσκει με τα εμα **P**^{45*c}; γινωσκουcι με τα εμα **P**^{66}; γεινωσκουcι μ[ ]μα **P**^{75}

10:15

P^{45} **P**^{66} **P**^{75}

15: καθως γινωσκει με ο πατηρ καγω γινωσκω τον πατερα και την ψυχην μου τιθημι υπερ των προβατων.

DEF: **P**^{45} ... γεινωσκει [ ] καγω... υπε[ ] προβατων
P^{75}]θως γεινωσκει με ο [ ] γ̣ειν[ ]ο̣ν π̣α̣τερα κ̣[ ]ι υπερ των π̣[

καθως: και καθως **P**^{45}
γινωσκει: γεινωσκει **P**^{45} **P**^{66} **P**^{75}
γινωσκω: γεινωσκω **P**^{45}; γειν[ ] **P**^{75}
τιθημι: διδωμι **P**^{45} **P**^{66}
των προβατων: ι eras. inter ν et π **P**^{66}

10:16

P^{45} **P**^{66} **P**^{75}

16: και αλλα προβατα εχω α ουκ εστιν εκ της αυλης ταυτης κακεινα με δει αγαγειν και της φωνης μου ακουσουσι και γενησεται μια ποιμνη εις ποιμην.

DEF: **P**^{45} ... εκ της [ ] ταυτης... μου α[ ]cιν...
P^{75}] π̣ρ̣οβατα... ου[ ] ταυτης κ̣ακειν̣α δει μ̣[ ] φωνης μ̣ου ακ̣ο̣υcουc[ ]ται μια π̣ο̣ιμνη εις ποι̣[

αλλα: + δε **P^{66}**
α: απερ **P^{45}**
αυληc: αυχηc **P^{66*}**; txt **P^{66*c}**
με δει: δει με **P^{45}** **P^{66}**; δει μ[ ] **P^{75}**
αγαγειν: cυναγαγειν **P^{66}**
ακουcουcι: α[ ]cιν **P^{45}**; ακουcουcιν **P^{66}**
γενηcεται: γενηcονται **P^{45}**

10:17

P^{45} **P^{66}** **P^{75}**

17: δια τουτο ο πατηρ με αγαπα οτι εγω τιθημι την ψυχην μου ινα παλιν λαβω αυτην.

DEF: **P^{45}** δια [ ] αγαπα... τη[ ] ψυχην... παλι[
P^{75}] με ο πατηρ [ ]π̣α οτι̣ [ ]χ̣η̣ν ινα̣ π̣[ ]λιν λα[

ο πατηρ με: με ο πατηρ **P^{66}** **P^{75}**
μου: OM **P^{75}**

10:18

P^{45} **P^{66}** **P^{75}**

18: ουδειc αιρει αυτην απ εμου αλλ εγω τιθημι αυτην απ εμαυτου εξουcιαν εχω θειναι αυτην και εξουcιαν εχω παλιν λαβειν αυτην ταυτην την εντολην ελαβον παρα του πατροc μου.

DEF: **P^{45}** ... απ εμ[ ] αλλα... αυ[ ] εξουcιαν εχω θειναι
αυ[ ]ην... εξου[ ]την ταυτην ελαβον [ ]ντολην... του [
P^{75}] αυτην̣ απ εμου α[ ]την απ... εχω̣ [ ] αυτην και...
λαβει̣[ ] την τα̣υτην τ[ ]ν̣ εντολην ελαβον παρ̣[ ] του π̣[

αιρει: ηρεν **P^{45}**; ερι **P^{66}**
αλλ: αλλα **P^{45}**
θειναι: θιναι **P^{66}**
εξουcιαν εχω παλιν: παλιν εξου[ ] **P^{45}**
λαβειν: λαβιν **P^{66}**
την εντολην ελαβον: ελαβον [1]ντολην **P^{45}**

10:19

P45 P66 P75

19: σχισμα ουν παλιν εγενετο εν τοις ιουδαιοις δια τους λογους τουτους.

DEF: **P45**]ενετο... λογους του[
P75... εγεν[ ]τọ εν̣ [ ]ọυ̣δαι̣[ ]ς δια τọυ̣ς λογους τ[ ]του[

ουν: OM **P75**

10:20

P45 P66 P75

20: ελεγον δε πολλοι εξ αυτων δαιμονιον εχει και μαινεται τι αυτου ακουετε.

DEF: **P45**]ι εξ... δαιμον[ ]ν εχει και μαινε[
P75]γον δε π̣[ ]λλοι εξ αυτων̣ [ ]μονιο[ ]χ̣ει και μα̣[ ]ται τ̣ι̣ α̣υτ[

αυτων: + οτι **P45**
μαινεται: μενεται **P66**
αυτου: ατου **P66***; txt **P66*c**
ακουετε: ακουεται **P66**

10:21

P45 P66 P75

21: αλλοι ελεγον ταυτα τα ρηματα ουκ εστι δαιμονιζομενου μη δαιμονιον δυναται τυφλων οφθαλμους ανοιγειν.

DEF: **P45**]λοι... ρη[ ]ατα ουκ εστιν δα[ ]ιμονιον... τυ[ ]λων οφθαλμους [
P66 ... δαιμονιον [ ]υναται
P75]λ̣λọι ελεχ[ ] δαιμον̣[ ]μεν[ ]υ̣ [ ]ται τυφλ̣[ ]ν οφθαλ̣[

αλλοι: + δε **P66**
εστι: εστιν **P45 P66**
δυναται: [ ]υναται **P66***; txt **P66*c**
ανοιγειν: ανοιξαι **P66**

10:22

P45 P66 P75

22: εγενετο δε τα εγκαινια εν τοις ιεροσολυμοις και χειμων ην.

DEF: **P45**] ενκαινια εν ιεροσ[ ]οις χειμων δε [
P75]τ̣ο̣ τοτε τα̣ [ ]γκαι̣ν̣[ ]μ̣οις χειμων̣ ην

δε: τοτε **P66*c P75**; txt **P66***
εγκαινια: ενκαινια **P45 P66**
τοις: OM **P45**
και χειμων: χειμων δε **P45**; χειμων **P66 P75**

10:23

P45 P66 P75

23: και περιεπατει ο ιησους εν τω ιερω εν τη στοα του σολομωντος.

DEF: **P45**]ν τωι... στ[ ]ολομωνος
P75 κα̣[ ] περιε̣π̣α̣τ̣ε̣ι̣ [ ]ω̣ ιερω εν τ̣η... σολομω[

τω ιερω: τωι ιερωι **P45**
τη:τηι **P45**
σολομωντος: σολομωνος **P66**; [ ]ολομωνος **P45**

10:24

P45 P66 P75

24: εκυκλωσαν ουν αυτον οι ιουδαιοι και ελεγον αυτω εως ποτε την ψυχην ημων αιρεις ει συ ει ο χριστος ειπε ημιν παρρησια.

DEF: **P45** εκ[ ] ιουδαιοι και αυτ[ ] εως ποτε τη[ ] συ ει [
P75 ε̣κυκλωσαν... ιουδαι[ ]ι ε[ ]ε̣γο̣ν αυ[ ] ε̣ως πο̣τ̣ε την ψυχη̣[ ] η̣μ[ ] α̣ιρεις [ ] π̣αρη̣[ ]α̣

ελεγον αυτω: αυτ[ ] **P45**
ημιν: ημειν **P66**
παρρησια: παρη[ ]α **P75**

10:25

P^{45} P^{66} P^{75}

25: απεκριθη αυτοις ο ιηϲουϲ ειπον υμιν και ου πιϲτευετε τα εργα α εγω ποιω εν τω ονοματι του πατροϲ μου ταυτα μαρτυρει περι εμου.

DEF: **P^{45}**]αι απε[
P^{75} απ̣εκρ̣[ ] α̣υ̣[ ]οιϲ ο... υ̣μιν... πιϲτ̣[ ]υετε̣... ονο̣ματι... μ̣ου...

απεκριθη: [ ]αι απε[ ] **P^{45}**
αυτοιϲ: OM **P^{66}**
υμιν: υμειν **P^{66}**
πιϲτευετε: πιϲτευεται **P^{66}**

10:26

P^{66} P^{75}

26: αλλ υμειϲ ου πιϲτευετε ου γαρ εϲτε εκ των προβατων των εμων καθωϲ ειπον υμιν.

DEF: **P^{75}** αλλα υ̣[ ]ϲ̣ ου... εϲτε [ ]κ̣ τ̣ω̣[ ]ρ̣ο̣βατω̣ν των εμων

αλλ: αλλα **P^{66} P^{75}**
πιϲτευετε: πιϲτευεται **P^{66}**
ου γαρ: οτι ουκ **P^{66} P^{75}**
καθωϲ ειπον υμιν: καθωϲ ειπον υμειν οτι **P^{66*}**; OM **P^{66*c} P^{75}**

10:27

P^{66} P^{75}

27: τα προβατα τα εμα τηϲ φωνηϲ μου ακουει καγω γινωϲκω αυτα και ακολουθουϲι μοι.

DEF: **P^{75}** τα π̣ροβ̣ατα... φω[ ]ηϲ μου α[ ]ο̣υει καγω
γεινω̣ϲ̣κ̣[ ]τ̣α και α[ ]υ̣θ̣ο̣υϲ̣ι̣ν̣ [

ακουει: ακουουϲιν **P^{66}**
γινωϲκω: γεινωϲκ[ ] **P^{75}**
ακολουθουϲι: ακολουθουϲιν **P^{66}**; α[ ]υθουϲιν **P^{75}**

10:28

P^{66} P^{75}

28: καγω ζωην αιωνιον διδωμι αυτοις και ου μη απολωνται εις τον αιωνα και ουχ αρπασει τις αυτα εκ της χειρος μου.

DEF: **P^{75}** κ̣α̣[ ]ω̣μ̣ι̣ αυ[ ]ω̣ην α[ ]νιον [ ] μ̣η απο[ ]ν̣τ̣α̣ι̣ εις
τ̣ον αιωνα [ ]υχ αρπα[ ] τ̣ις αυτα εκ τ̣η̣ς χειρ[ ]υ

ζωην αιωνιον διδωμι αυτοις: διδωμι αυτοις ζωην αιωνιον **P^{66*c}**;
[ ]ωμι αυ[ ]ωην α[ ]νιον **P^{75}**; txt **P^{66*}**
αρπασει: αρπαση **P^{66}**

10:29

P^{45} P^{66} P^{75}

29: ο πατηρ μου ος δεδωκε μοι μειζων παντων εστι και ουδεις δυναται αρπαζειν εκ της χειρος του πατρος μου.

DEF: **P^{45}**]ε[ ]υ π̅ρ̅ς̅ μο[
P^{75} ο πατηρ [ ]ι ος εδωκε̣[ ]τ̣ων μει[ ]ν εστιν και̣ [ ]α̣τ̣α̣ι̣
α̣ρ̣[ ]α̣[ ] ε̣κ... πατρ[

μου: [2]ι **P^{75}**
δεδωκε μοι μειζων παντων: εδωκεν μιζων παντων **P^{66*}**; εδωκεν μοι μιζων παντων **P^{66*c}**; εδωκε[7-10]των μει[2]ν **P^{75}**
εστι: εστιν **P^{66} P^{75}**
πατρος μου: πατρ[ ] **P^{75}** (& cf. **P^{66}**)
μου^2: OM **P^{66}** (& cf. **P^{75}**)

10:30

P^{45} P^{66} P^{75}

30: εγω και ο πατηρ εν εσμεν.

DEF: **P^{45}**]εν
P^{75} ε̣γω [ ]η̣ρ εν εσμεν

10:31

P^{45} **P**^{66} **P**^{75}

31: εβαστασαν ουν παλιν λιθους οι ιουδαιοι ινα λιθασωσιν αυτον.

DEF: **P**^{45} ... λιθ[ ]αιοι ινα λιθασωσ[
P^{75} εβ̣αστ̣[ ]α̣ν [ ]ι ιουδαιοι ιν̣α̣ λ̣[

ουν παλιν λιθους οι: / [12]ι **P**^{75}
ουν παλιν: OM **P**^{45}
λιθασωσιν αυτον: αυτον λιθασωσιν **P**^{66}
31-32 λιθασωσιν αυτον απεκριθη: λιθασωσ[11]πεκριθη **P**^{45}

10:32

P^{45} **P**^{66} **P**^{75}

32: απεκριθη αυτοις ο ιησους πολλα καλα εργα εδειξα υμιν εκ του πατρος μου δια ποιον αυτων εργον λιθαζετε με.

DEF: **P**^{45}]πεκριθη αυτοις [ ] ι̅η̅ [ ]αλα... εκ τ[ ] ποιον αυτων εργον εμε [ ]ζετε
P^{75}]ιθη αυτο̣ι̣ς̣ ο̣ [ ]μ̣ι̣ν̣ εργα καλα εκ του [ ]α π̣ο̣ι̣ον̣ α̣υ̣τ̣[ ]ν̣ εργ[ ]ν [

απεκριθη: cf. v. 31
ιησους πολλα καλα εργα εδειξα υμιν: [2 / 11-12]μιν εργα καλα **P**^{75}
καλα εργα: [ ]αλα **P**^{45}
εδειξα: εδιξα **P**^{66}
του πατρος μου δια: τ[8] **P**^{45}
ποιον: + ουν **P**^{66}
λιθαζετε με: εμε [ ]ζετε **P**^{45}
λιθαζετε: λιθαζεται **P**^{66}

10:33

P^{45} **P**^{66} **P**^{75}

33: απεκριθησαν αυτω οι ιουδαιοι λεγοντες περι καλου εργου ου λιθαζομεν σε αλλα περι βλασφημιας και οτι συ ανθρωπος ων ποιεις σεαυτον θεον.

DEF: **P**^{45} ... αυτ[ ]ουδαιοι... ου λ[ ]μεν... ων [ ]ις σεαυτον θ̅ν̅
P^{75} απε̣κ̣ρ̣ι̣θ̣η̣ς̣[ ] αυ̣τ̣ω̣ [ ] καλου̣ ε̣ρ̣γο̣υ̣ ο̣υ λι̣θ̣α̣[ ]α
περ[ ]φημει[ ]ρ̣ωπος ων πο̣ιεις σε̣[ ]ν̅

οι ιουδαιοι λεγοντες περι: [11-14] **P**^{75} (& cf. **P**^{45} **P**^{66})
λεγοντες: OM **P**^{45} **P**^{66} (& cf. **P**^{75})
βλασφημιας: βλασφημειας **P**^{66*}; [ ]φημει[ ] **P**^{75}; txt **P**^{66*c}
σεαυτον: + τον **P**^{66*}; txt **P**^{66*c}

10:34

P^{45} **P**^{66} **P**^{75}

34: απεκριθη αυτοις ο ιησους ουκ εστι γεγραμμενον εν τω νομω υμων εγω ειπα θεοι εστε.

DEF: **P**^{45} ... γεγραμμενον [ ]ι γραφηι...
P^{75} απ̣εκριθη... ου̣κ̣ [ ]ι̣ν̣ γεγραμμενον̣... οτι̣ εγω ει̣π̣α θ̣εοι ε̣ς̣τ̣ε̣

αυτοις ο ιησους: ι̅ς̅ και ειπεν αυτοις **P**^{66}
ο: OM **P**^{45}
εστι: εστιν **P**^{45} **P**^{66}; [ ]ιν **P**^{75}
γεγραμμενον: + [/ 4]ι γραφηι **P**^{45}
εν: εκ **P**^{66*}; txt **P**^{66*c}
τω νομω: τωι νομωι **P**^{45}
υμων: OM **P**^{45}; + οτι **P**^{45} **P**^{66} **P**^{75}

10:35

P^{45} **P**^{66} **P**^{75}

35: ει εκεινους ειπε θεους προς ους ο λογος του θεου εγενετο και ου δυναται λυθηναι η γραφη.

DEF: **P**^{45} ει εκεινους ε[ ] θεους...
P^{75} ε̣ι εκεινους ε[ ]πε θεο[ ] λογος... εγενε̣[ ]ο̣ και̣ ο̣υ̣ [ ]τ̣αι
[ ]θηναι η γραφ[

ειπε: ειπεν **P**^{66}
προς ους ο λογος του θεου εγενετο: OM **P**^{45}
η γραφη: OM **P**^{45}

10:36

P^{45} **P**^{66} **P**^{75}

36: ον ο πατηρ ηγιαϲε και απεϲτειλεν ειϲ τον κοϲμον υμειϲ λεγετε οτι βλαϲφημειϲ οτι ειπον υιοϲ του θεου ειμι.

DEF: **P**^{45} ... απεϲτει[ ]ϲ τον... υ̅ϲ̅ [ ] ειμι
P^{66} ... απεϲτειλ̣εν... λεγεται [ ]τι... ε̣ιμι
P^{75} ον ο πα[ ]ι[ ] και απεϲτ[ ]λ̣εν ειϲ τ[ ]μ̣ον [ ]φημειϲ [ ]ϲ̣ τ̣ο̣[ ]υ̅ ειμι

ηγιαϲε: ηγιαϲεν **P**^{45} **P**^{66}
λεγετε: λεγεται **P**^{66}
υιοϲ: ο υιοϲ **P**^{45}
του: OM **P**^{66*}; txt **P**^{66*c}

10:37

P^{45} **P**^{66} **P**^{75}

37: ει ου ποιω τα εργα του πατροϲ μου μη πιϲτευετε μοι.

DEF: **P**^{75} ει [ ]ρ̣γα του π̣[ ]τροϲ μου μ̣[ ] μ̣οι

ου: ουν **P**^{66*}; ν postea eras.
μη: μημ **P**^{66*}; μ^2 postea eras.
πιϲτευετε: πιϲτευεται **P**^{66}

10:38

P^{45} **P**^{66} **P**^{75}

38: ει δε ποιω καν εμοι μη πιϲτευητε τοιϲ εργοιϲ πιϲτευϲατε ινα γνωτε και πιϲτευϲητε οτι εν εμοι ο πατηρ καγω εν αυτω.

DEF: **P**^{45} ει δε [ ] καν... γνωτε [ ]ενωϲκητε...
P^{75} ε[ ] δ̣ε ποιω κα̣[ ] ε̣μ̣ο̣ι̣ μη π̣ιϲτε̣υ̣ητε το̣ιϲ εργ[ ]
π̣ι̣ϲτευετε... γειν̣[ ]ϲκητε... πατη̣ρ καγ[ ] εν τω π̣[ ]τρι

πιϲτευητε: πιϲτευϲηται **P**^{66*}; πιϲτευηται **P**^{66*c}
πιϲτευϲατε: πιϲτευϲαται **P**^{66}; πιϲτευετε **P**^{75}
πιϲτευϲητε: [ ]ενωϲκητε **P**^{45}; γινωϲκηται **P**^{66}; γειν[ ]ϲκητε **P**^{75}

εν αυτω: τω π[ ]τρι **P^{75}**; εν [2]τω π̅ρ̅ι̅ **P^{66}** (duae litterae post εν postea eras.)
αυτω: αυτωι **P^{45}**

10:39

P^{45} P^{66} P^{75}

39: εζητουν ουν παλιν αυτον πιασαι και εξηλθεν εκ της χειρος αυτων.

DEF: **P^{45}** ... αυτον [ ] και...
P^{75} ε[ ]ο̣υν αυτ̣[ ]ν [ ]λθεν ε[ ] τ̣η[ ] χειρος α̣υ̣[

ουν: δε **P^{45}**; OM **P^{75}**
παλιν: OM **P^{45} P^{75}**
αυτον πιασαι και εξηλθεν: αυτ[ ]ν [/ 12-14]λθεν **P^{75}**

10:40

P^{45} P^{66} P^{75}

40: και απηλθε παλιν περαν του ιορδανου εις τον τοπον οπου ην ιωαννης το πρωτον βαπτιζων και εμεινεν εκει.

DEF: **P^{45}** ... παλιν πε[ ]υ ιορδανου... βα[ ]ων...
P^{66} ... και [ ]μεινεν εκει
P^{75}]α̣ι̣ απ[ ]λ[ ]λ̣ι̣ν περαν τ̣[ ]υ̣ ιορ[ ]ανου εις τ[ ]ν̣ τοπο̣̅ οπου...

απηλθε: απηλθεν **P^{45} P^{66}**
παλιν: OM **P^{66}**
οπου: ου **P^{66}**
ιωαννης: ιωανης **P^{75*}**; txt **P^{75*c}**
πρωτον: προτερον **P^{45}**

10:41

P[45] P[66] P[75]

41: και πολλοι ηλθον προς αυτον και ελεγον οτι ιωαννης μεν σημειον εποιησεν ουδεν παντα δε οσα ειπεν ιωαννης περι τουτου αληθη ην.

DEF: **P[45]** ... ελε[ ] ιωαννης... οσα [ ]ης...
P[66] ... ηλθον [ ]ρος... ιω[ ]ννης... εποιησεν [ ]υδεν... ιω[ ]ννης...
P[75] ... ελεγο̣ν οτι ιωαν̣νης μ̣εν σημει̣ο̣ν̣ [ ]ησεν... ε̣ι̣π̣εν
ιωανν[ ]ϲ̣ περι τουτου αληθ̣η̣ ην

ουδεν: ουδε εν **P[45]**
ειπεν ιωαννης: [ ]ης ειπεν **P[45]**
ην: ειν **P[66*]**; txt **P[66*c]**

10:42

P[45] P[66] P[75]

42: και επιστευσαν πολλοι εκει εις αυτον.

DEF: **P[45]** ... ει[ς
P[66]]αι...
P[75] και π̣[ ]ϲ̣[ ]ε̣υ̣ϲ̣α̣ν̣ εις αυτον̣ εκε̣[

επιστευσαν πολλοι: πολλοι επιστευσαν **P[45] P[66]**; π[8]ς[ ]ευσαν **P[75]**
εκει εις αυτον: εις αυτον εκει **P[66]**; εις αυτον εκε[ ] **P[75]**
εκει: OM **P[45]**

CHAPTER ELEVEN

P^{6} **P**^{45} **P**^{59} **P**^{66} **P**^{75}

11:1

P^{6} **P**^{45} **P**^{66} **P**^{75}

1: ην δε τις ασθενων λαζαρος απο βηθανιας εκ της κωμης μαριας και μαρθας της αδελφης αυτης.

DEF: **P**^{6}]ν δε τις εκε[ ]cθ[ ] απο βηθανια[ ] εκ τ[ ] και μαρθ[ ] της αδε[
P^{45}] δε τις [ ]cθενων... κωμη[ ] και...
P^{75} ην δε̣ τ̣[ ]ν̣ω̣ν̣ [ ]ζαροc̣ [ ]η̣θανειᾳ[ ] τ̣ης κωμ̣[ ]c μαρια[ ]
μαρθ̣ᾳ[ ]c̣ αδελφηc̣ ᾳυ̣τη̣c

τιc: + εκε[ ] **P**^{6}
βηθανιαc: βηθανιαμ **P**^{45}; [ ]ηθανεια[ ] **P**^{75}
μαρθαc: μαριαc **P**^{66*}; txt **P**^{66*c}
αυτηc: αυτου **P**^{66*}; txt **P**^{66*c}

11:2

P^{6} **P**^{45} **P**^{66} **P**^{75}

2: ην δε μαρια η αλειψαcα τον κυριον μυρω και εκμαξαcα τουc ποδαc αυτου ταιc θριξιν αυτηc ηc ο αδελφοc λαζαροc ηcθενει.

DEF: **P**^{6}] δε μαριϩα[ ] η αλε[ ] μυρωι κα[ ] εκμ[ ] αυτου ταιc θριξι[ ]φοc λαζαροc [ ]cθενει
P^{45} ... μαρ[ ]ν κ̅ν̅... εκμ[ ]α τουc... θρι[ ] ο... η[ ]νει
P^{75} η̣[ ] μαρια [ ]λ̣[ ]ψ[ ] τ̣ο̣ν κ̅ν̅ μυρ[ ] και εκμ[ ] π̣ο̣δαc αυτου τ̣[ ] θριξιν α[ ] α̣δελφοc λαζα[ ]cθενει

δε: + αυτη η **P**^{45}
μαρια: μαριϩα[ ] **P**^{6}
αλειψαcα: αλιψαcα **P**^{66}
μυρω: μυρωι **P**^{6} **P**^{45}
ο αδελφοc λαζαροc ηcθενει: και αδελφοc ην λαζαροc αcθενων **P**^{66*}; txt **P**^{66*c}
λαζαροc: λαζαρ **P**^{45}

11:3

P^{6} **P**^{45} **P**^{66} **P**^{75}

3: απεcτειλαν ουν αι αδελφαι προc αυτον λεγουcαι κυριε ιδε ον φιλειc αcθενει.

DEF: **P**^{6}]λαν ουν αι αδελφαι πρ[ ] λεγουcαι κ̅ε̅ ιδε [ ]ν φιλε[ ]θενει
P^{45} απεcτειλαν [ ]υν αι αδε[ ]ουcαι... φ[ ]λειc...
P^{75} α[ ]cτειλαν... αδελ̣[ ]ον λεγου̣cαι κ̅ε̅ ιδε ο̣ν φ[ ]ε̣ι απεcτειλαν ουν αι αδελφ[ ]ο̣ν

απεcτειλαν ουν αι αδελφαι προc αυτον λεγουcαι: απεcτιλεν ουν μαρια προc αυτον λεγουcα **P**^{66*}; απεcτιλαν ουν αι αδελφαι προc αυτον λεγουcαι **P**^{66*c}
αcθενει: + απεcτειλαν ουν αι αδελφ[9]ον **P**^{75*}; txt **P**^{75c}

11:4

P^{6} **P**^{45} **P**^{66} **P**^{75}

4: ακουcαc δε ο ιηcουc ειπεν αυτη η αcθενεια ουκ εcτι προc

θανατον αλλ υπερ της δοξης του θεου ινα δοξαcθη ο υιος του θεου δι αυτηc.

DEF: P[6]]υcαc δε [ ] ιc ειπ[ ]τη η α[ ]ενεια [ ] εc[ ] θ[ ]ν αλλ [ ]υ ινα δ[ ]η ο υ[ ]ι αυτη[
P[45] ... δε [ ] ̣ [ ] αcθενεια ουκ εc[ ]ιν... αλλ [ ]υ θυ ινα δοξαcθη [ ] υc...
P[75] ακουcαc̣ δ̣ε... α̣υ̣[ ]ενεια ουκ ε[ ]ν προc θ[ ]ν̣ατο̣[ ]π̣ερ τηc... ινα δ̣[ ]ξαcθη̣ ο̣ υc [ ] θ̣υ δι...

αcθενεια: αcθενια P[66]
εcτι: εcτιν P[45] P[66]; ε[3]ν P[75]
του θεου[2]: αυτου P[45]; OM P[66]

11:5

P[6] P[45] P[66] P[75]

5: ηγαπα δε ο ιηcουc την μαρθαν και την αδελφην αυτηc και τον λαζαρον.

DEF: P[6]]α δε [ ] μαρ[ ]ν μ[ ]λφην αυ[ ] τον [
P[45] ηγαπα [ ] και την αδελφη[ ] αυτηc...
P[75] ηγαπ̣α δε ο [ ] τ̣ην μαρ[ ] α̣δελφηc... λα̣ζα[ ]ν̣

μαρθαν και: μαρ[8]ν μ[5] P[6] (aut μαρ[θαν και τη]ν μ[αριαμ] aut μαρ[ιαμ και τη]ν μ[αρθαν])
αδελφην: αδελφηc P[75]
αυτηc: OM P[66*]; txt P[66*c]

11:6

P[6] P[45] P[66] P[75]

6: ωc ουν ηκουcεν οτι αcθενει τοτε μεν εμεινεν εν ω ην τοπω δυο ημεραc.

DEF: P[6]]ν ηκουcε[ ]ν εμει[ ]εραc
P[45] ω[ ] αcθενει τοτε με[ ] εμεινεν... τοπ[
P[75] ω̣c̣ ο̣υ̣[ ]υ̣cεν ο̣τι... με [ ]εινεν εν [ ]πω δυο...

εν ω ην: επι τωι P[45]
εν: OM P[66*]; txt P[66*c]

11:7

P6 P45 P66 P75

7: επειτα μετα τουτο λεγει τοις μαθηταις αγωμεν εις την ιουδαιαν παλιν.

DEF: **P6**] μαθ[ ]αιαν [
P45] μετα τουτο λεγε[ ]ωμεν εις την ιουδαι[
P66 ... ιου[ ]αιαν...
P75 ε[ ]τα μετα ṭ[ ]γει τοις μαθηταις [ ]ω̣μεν εις ṭ[ ]α̣ν παλιν

επειτα: ειτα **P66**
λεγει τοις μαθηταις αγωμεν: λεγε[3]ωμεν **P45**
τοις μαθηταις: αυτοις **P66***; txt **P66*c**

11:8

P6 P45 P66 P75

8: λεγουσιν αυτω οι μαθηται ραββι νυν εζητουν σε λιθασαι οι ιουδαιοι και παλιν υπαγεις εκει.

DEF: **P6**]η[
P45]υτωι οι μαθητα[ ]βει... σε λ[ ]αλιν υπαγεις [
P66 ... αυτω [ ] μαθηται... εζητου̅ [ ]ε λιθασαι... πα[ ]ιν...
P75 λεγου[ ]ιν [ ]τω οι μαθ[ ]ε̣ι νυν εζητο[ ] λ̣ιθασαι οι ι[ ] παλιν υπαγ[ ]ι̣

αυτω: [ ]υτωι **P45**
ραββι: [ ]βει **P45**; ραββει **P66**; [ ]ει **P75**

11:9

P45 P66 P75

9: απεκριθη ο ιησους ουχι δωδεκα εισιν ωραι της ημερας εαν τις περιπατη εν τη ημερα ου προσκοπτει οτι το φως του κοσμου τουτου βλεπει.

DEF: **P45**]πεκριθη... δω[ ] ημερας εαν [ ] ημερα περιπατη [ ]ως του κ[ ]ς[
P66 ... ι̅ς̅ [ ]υχι... της η[ ]ερας... τη [ ]ερα... το [ ]ως... βλε[ ]ει

P[75] απεκριθη ις ουχ[ ]ωδεκα [ ]μερας... πε[ ]πατη ε[ ]υ
προσκοπτει οτι... του κ[ ]ου τουτου βλεπει

ο[1]: OM **P**[66] **P**[75]
εισιν ωραι: ωραι εισιν **P**[66]
περιπατη εν τη ημερα: [ ] ημερα περιπατη **P**[45]

11:10

P[45] **P**[66] **P**[75]

10: εαν δε τις περιπατη εν τη νυκτι προσκοπτει οτι το φως ουκ εστιν εν αυτω.

DEF: **P**[45]]ις περιπ[
P[66] ... τη [ ]υκτι... φως [ ]υκ...
P[75] ... περιπα[ ] εν τη νυκτι... φως [ ]κ εστιν εν αυτω

11:11

P[45] **P**[66] **P**[75]

11: ταυτα ειπε και μετα τουτο λεγει αυτοις λαζαρος ο φιλος ημων κεκοιμηται αλλα πορευομαι ινα εξυπνισω αυτον.

DEF: **P**[45] τα]υ[
P[66] ταυτα ει[ ]εν και... λεγει αυ[ ]οις... ημων [ ]εκοιμηται...
πορευομαι [ ]να...
P[75] ... με[ ] τουτο λε[ ]ει αυτοις [ ]ς η φιλος [ ]ων
κ[ ]οιμητα[ ]ορευομαι [ ] εξυπ[ ]ω αυτον

ειπε: ειπεν **P**[75]; ει[ ]εν **P**[66]
ο: η **P**[75]

11:12

P66 P75

12: ειπον ουν οι μαθηται αυτου κυριε ει κεκοιμηται cωθηcεται.

DEF: **P75** ειπον ọụν οι μạθηṭαι αυτω κ̣̅[ ] ει... εγερθηcεται

ειπον: ειπαν **P66**
αυτου: αυτω **P66 P75**
cωθηcεται: εγερθηcεται **P75**

11:13

P66 P75

13: ειρηκει δε ο ιηcουc περι του θανατου αυτου εκεινοι δε εδοξαν οτι περι τηc κοιμηcεωc του υπνου λεγει.

DEF: **P75** ειρηκε[ ] ι̅c̅... ẹδοξαν περι τηc̣ κοιμηcεωc...

του θανατου: τηc κοιμηcεωc **P66***; txt **P66*c**
του[1]: OM **P75**
οτι: OM **P75**

11:14

P66 P75

14: τοτε ουν ειπεν αυτοιc ο ιηcουc παρρηcια λαζαροc απεθανε.

DEF: **P75** τοṭ[ ]υν ειπεν... παρρηcια [ ]ρ̣οc απεθανεν

ο: OM **P66**
απεθανε: απεθανεν **P66 P75**

11:15

P66 P75

15: και χαιρω δι υμαc ινα πιcτευcητε οτι ουκ ημην εκει αλλ αγωμεν προc αυτον.

DEF: **P**^{66} ... ουκ ημη̣[ ] εκει...
P^{75} ... υμας [ ]cτευ[ ]η̣[ ]ε̣ οτι ουκ ημην ε̣[ ]ω̣μεν πρ̣[

πιcτευcητε: πιcτευcηται **P**^{66}
αλλ: αλλα **P**^{66}

11:16

P^{66} **P**^{75}

16: ειπεν ουν θωμας ο λεγομενος διδυμος τοιc cυμμαθηταιc αγωμεν και ημειc ινα αποθανωμεν μετ αυτου.

DEF: **P**^{75} ... λ̣εγομ̣[ ]υ̣μος τοιc cυμμαθηται[ ] κ̣αι... απ̣ο̣θα[

cυμμαθηταιc: cυνμαθηταιc **P**^{66}

11:17

P^{45} **P**^{66} **P**^{75}

17: ελθων ουν ο ιηcουc ευρεν αυτον τεccαραc ημεραc ηδη εχοντα εν τω μνημειω.

DEF: **P**^{45}] ημ[
P^{66} ... τεccαρα̣[ ] ημεραc... εχ̣[ ]τα
P^{75} ε̣λθ̣ω̣[ ]υ̣ν̣ ο̣ [ ]c̣̄ ε[ ]ν̣ τεcc̣αρα̣c ηδη ημε̣ραc ε[ ] τ̣ω μνημειω̣

ευρεν: ευρον **P**^{66*}; txt **P**^{66*c}
τεccαραc ημεραc ηδη: ηδη τεccαρα[ ] ημεραc **P**^{66}; τεccαραc ηδη ημεραc **P**^{75}
εχοντα εν τω μνημειω: εν τω μνημειω εχ[ ]τα **P**^{66}

11:18

$\mathbf{P}^{45}$ $\mathbf{P}^{66}$ $\mathbf{P}^{75}$

18: ην δε η βηθανια εγγυc των ιεροcολυμων ωc απο cταδιων δεκαπεντε.

DEF: $\mathbf{P}^{45}$] των ιε[ ]εκαπεντε
$\mathbf{P}^{75}$]ν̣ δε [ ]ηθα̣[ ]γυc των ιεροcολυμων [ ]διων δε̣καπεντε

η: OM $\mathbf{P}^{75}$ (nisi linea in marginem proiecta fuit)

11:19

$\mathbf{P}^{45}$ $\mathbf{P}^{66}$ $\mathbf{P}^{75}$

19: και πολλοι εκ των ιουδαιων εληλυθειcαν προc ταc περι μαρθαν και μαριαν ινα παραμυθηcωνται αυταc περι του αδελφου αυτων.

DEF: $\mathbf{P}^{45}$ πο[ ] εκ... εληλυθ[ ]ερι μαρθαν και μ[ ] ινα... αυ[ ] περι...
$\mathbf{P}^{66}$ πολλοι δ̣[ ] εκ... εληλυθειc[ ]c την... πα[ ]μυθηcωνται... του α[ ]λ̣φου
$\mathbf{P}^{75}$ πολλ̣οι δ̣[ ]ω̣ν ι[ ]υ̣δ̣α̣ι̣ω̣ν εληλυθ̣ειc̣α̣ν̣ [ ]ν̣ μ̣[ ]ν και μαριαμ [ ]α̣ παραμυθηcωντ̣[ ]ταc πε[ ]υ̣ αδελφου

και πολλοι: πο[ ] $\mathbf{P}^{45}$; πολλοι δ[ ] $\mathbf{P}^{66}$ $\mathbf{P}^{75}$
προc ταc περι: [ ]c την $\mathbf{P}^{66}$; [6]ν $\mathbf{P}^{75}$
μαριαν: μαριαμ $\mathbf{P}^{75}$
αυτων: OM $\mathbf{P}^{45}$ $\mathbf{P}^{66}$ $\mathbf{P}^{75}$

11:20

$\mathbf{P}^{45}$ $\mathbf{P}^{66}$ $\mathbf{P}^{75}$

20: η ουν μαρθα ωc ηκουcεν οτι ο ιηcουc ερχεται υπηντηcεν αυτω μαρια δε εν τω οικω εκαθεζετο.

DEF: $\mathbf{P}^{45}$ ... ωc [ ]κουcεν... υπη[ ]τηcεν... οικω [
$\mathbf{P}^{66}$ ...ηκουcεν ο[ ] ι̣c... μα[ ] δε... εκαθε[ ]ο
$\mathbf{P}^{75}$ η ουν μ̣[ ]ρθα ωc η[ ] ο̣τι... υπηντη̣[ ]ω̣ μαρια δε εν [ ] ο̣ικω ε[ ]ζετ̣[

οτι ο: ο[2] **P**^{66} (& cf. **P**^{45} **P**^{75})
ο: OM **P**^{45} **P**^{75} (& cf. **P**^{66})
αυτω: αυτωι **P**^{45}
τω οικω: τωι οικωι **P**^{45}
οικω: + εαυτης **P**^{66}

11:21

P^{45} **P**^{66} **P**^{75}

21: ειπεν ουν η μαρθα προς τον ιηcουν κυριε ει ηc ωδε ο αδελφοc μου ουκ αν ετεθνηκει.

DEF: **P**^{45} ... μαρθ[ ] προc... α[ ]φοc...
P^{66} ... τον κ̅ν̅ [ ] ει... ουκ α̅[ ]εθανεν
P^{75} ειπεν ουῃ[ ] ῃ... προc τ̣[ ]ν̣ ι̅ν̅ κ̣[ ] ει̣ η̣c̣ ω̣δ̣ε ο̣υ̣κ... ο̣ [ ]ελφο̣c
μ̣ου

η: OM **P**^{45}
ιηcουν: κ̅ν̅ **P**^{66*}; txt **P**^{66*c}
ει ηc: littera (forsan c) eras. inter ι et η **P**^{66}
ο αδελφοc μου ουκ αν ετεθνηκει: ουκ αν απεθανεν ο [ ]ελφοc μου **P**^{75}
ετεθνηκει: απεθανεν **P**^{45}; [ ]εθανεν **P**^{66}

11:22

P^{45} **P**^{66} **P**^{75}

22: αλλα και νυν οιδα οτι οcα αν αιτηcη τον θεον δωcει coι ο θεοc.

DEF: **P**^{45} αλλ[ ]ι νυν οιδα οτι οc[ ] αν...
P^{66} ... οτι [ ] αν...
P^{75} και ν̣υν̣ οιδα οτ̣ι ο̣cα εαν αιτη̣c̣η̣ το̣ν θ̅ν̅ δ̣[ ]c̣ε̣ι̣ c̣[ ] ο̣ θ̅c̅

αλλα: OM **P**^{75}
αν: εαν **P**^{75}
αιτηcη: αιτηcηc **P**^{45} **P**^{66}
δωcει: δωcι **P**^{66}

11:23

P^{45} **P**^{66} **P**^{75}

23: λεγει αυτη ο ιηcουc αναcτηcεται ο αδελφοc cου.

DEF: **P**^{45} λ[ ]γει α[ ]αcτηcε[ ]αι ο αδελφ[ ] cου
P^{66}]γει... ο α[ ]λφο̣c̣ cου
P^{75} λεγει̣ αυτη̣ ο ι̅c̅ αν̣[ ] ο...

11:24

P^{45} **P**^{66} **P**^{75}

24: λεγει αυτω μαρθα οιδα οτι αναcτηcεται εν τη αναcταcει εν τη εcχατη ημερα.

DEF: **P**^{45} ... οιδα [ ]εται εν τ[ ]cει...
P^{66} ... οι[ ] οτι... αναcταcει [ ] τη...
P^{75} λ[ ]γ̣ε̣[ ]ω̣ μαρθα οιδα ο̣τι αναcτη[ ]ν̣ τη... εν τη̣ [ ]μερα

αυτω: αυτωι **P**^{45}; + η **P**^{66}
τη εcχατη: τηι εcχατηι **P**^{45}

11:25

P^{45} **P**^{66} **P**^{75}

25: ειπεν αυτη ο ιηcουc εγω ειμι η αναcταcιc και η ζωη ο πιcτευων ειc εμε καν αποθανη ζηcεται.

DEF: **P**^{45} ειπ[ ]η̅ εγω ειμ[ ]cιc... καν α[ ]cει
P^{66} ... αυτη [ ]γω... ζω[ ] πιcτευων... αποθα[ ] ζηcεται
P^{75}]ι̣πεν ουν αυ[ ] ειμι η α[ ]α̣cταcιc και η [ ]τευων [ ] ε̣μ̣[ ]
κ̣αν [ ]η̣cεται

ειπεν: + ουν **P**^{75}
ο ιηcουc εγω: [2-3]γω **P**^{66}
και η ζωη: OM **P**^{45}
ζηcεται: [ ]cει **P**^{45}

11:26

P^{45} **P**^{66} **P**^{75}

26: και πας ο ζων και πιστευων εις εμε ου μη αποθανη εις τον αιωνα πιστευεις τουτο.

DEF: **P^{45}** κα[ ] και... απ[ ] τουτο
P^{66} ... πις[ ]υων... αποθανη [ ]ον...
P^{75} και [ ] ζων κα̣[ ]στευων̣... απ̣οθαν̣η̣ ε̣ις... π[ ]τ̣ε̣[ ]εις του̣το

εις τον: [2-3]ον **P^{66}**

11:27

P^{45} P^{66} P^{75}

27: λεγει αυτω ναι κυριε εγω πεπιστευκα οτι συ ει ο χριστος ο υιος του θεου ο εις τον κοσμον ερχομενος.

DEF: **P^{45}** ... εγω π[ ] θ̅υ̅... ερ[ ]ομενο[
P^{75} ... να̣ι̣... πεπι̣στε̣υκα... κοσμο[ ] ερχομενος

λεγει: λεγι **P^{66}**
αυτω: αυτωι **P^{45}**
κυριε: + πιστευω **P^{66}**

11:28

P^{45} P^{66} P^{75}

28: και ταυτα ειπουσα απηλθε και εφωνησε μαριαν την αδελφην αυτης λαθρα ειπουσα ο διδασκαλος παρεστι και φωνει σε.

DEF: **P^{45}**] εφωνησεν... αδελφ[ ]δ[ ]σκαλος...
P^{66} ... κα[ ] εφωνησεν... φωνι σ[_
P^{75} και̣ τ̣ο̣υ̣τ̣ο ειπου[ ]α απηλθε̄ και ε̣φ[ ]ε̣ν μαριαμ̣ την αδε[ ]φην α̣υ̣τ̣ης λα̣θρα ειπ[ ] δ̣ιδ[ ]σκαλ[ ]ς παρεσ̣τιν κα̣[ ] φωνει σε̣

ταυτα: τουτο **P^{75}**
απηλθε: απηλθεν **P^{66} P^{75}**
εφωνησε: εφωνησεν **P^{45} P^{66}**; εφ[ ]εν **P^{75}**
μαριαν: μαριαμ **P^{75}**
ειπουσα: ειπασα οτι **P^{66}**
παρεστι: παρεστιν **P^{45} P^{66} P^{75}**
φωνει: φωνι **P^{66}**

11:29

P^{45} **P**^{66} **P**^{75}

29: εκεινη ωϲ ηκουϲεν εγειρεται ταχυ και ερχεται προϲ αυτον.

DEF: **P**^{45}]ειρεται... προϲ α[ ]τον
P^{66} ... εγειρετα[ ] ταχυ...
P^{75} ... ηκου[ ]ε̣ν ηγερθη ταχ̣υ̣ και η̣ρχετ[ ] π̣ροϲ αυτον

εκεινη: εκεινηϲ **P**^{66*}; εκεινη δε **P**^{66*c} **P**^{75}
εγειρεται: ηγερθη **P**^{75}
ερχεται: ηρχετ[ ] **P**^{75}

11:30

P^{45} **P**^{66} **P**^{75}

30: ουπω δε εληλυθει ο ιηϲουϲ ειϲ την κωμην αλλ ην εν τω τοπω οπου υπηντηϲεν αυτω η μαρθα.

DEF: **P**^{45} ο[ ]η̅ ειϲ τ[ ] κωμην... τω[ ] τοπωι [ ]τωι μ[ ]θα
P^{75} ουπ[ ] δε... κωμην [ ]λ̣ ην... οπο̣υ υπη[ ]εν αυτω...

εληλυθει ο ιηϲουϲ: ι̅ϲ̅ εληλυθει **P**^{66}
αλλ: αλλα **P**^{66}; aut [2]λ aut [3]α **P**^{75}
ην: + ετι **P**^{66} **P**^{75}
εν: επι **P**^{45} **P**^{66}
τω τοπω: τω[ ] τοπωι **P**^{45}
αυτω: [ ]τωι **P**^{45}
η: OM **P**^{45}

11:31

P^{45} **P**^{66} **P**^{75}

31: οι ουν ιουδαιοι οι οντες μετ αυτης εν τη οικια και παραμυθουμενοι αυτην ιδοντες την μαριαν οτι ταχεως ανεστη και εξηλθεν ηκολουθηcαν αυτη λεγοντες οτι υπαγει ειc το μνημειον ινα κλαυcη εκει.

DEF: **P**^{45} ... οντ[ ] μετ α[ ] παραμ[ ]θουμενοι αυτην ιδοντ[ ]ην μ[ ]τη κα[ ]ξηλθεν ηκολουθηc[ ]τεc [ ]τ[ ]ημειο[ ]παγει... εκε[
P^{75} ... ιουδ[ ]τεc μετ... κα̣ι̣ παρα̣μ̣υ̣θ̣ο̣υμενοι αυτην ιδ̣ο̣̅τεc... οτι [ ]τ̣η̣ και... ηκο̣[ ]τ̣η δοξ[ ]ζοντεc ο̣τι υπ[ ]ν̣ημε̣[ ]ν ινα̣ [ ]αυcη̣ [

μαριαν: μαριαμ **P**^{75}
ταχεωc ανεστη: ανεστη ταχεωc **P**^{66}
εξηλθεν: + και **P**^{75}
λεγοντεc: δοξ[1]ζοντεc **P**^{75}
υπαγει ειc το μνημειον: [ ]ημειο[ ]παγει **P**^{45}

11:32

P^{45} **P**^{66} **P**^{75}

32: η ουν μαρια ωc ηλθεν οπου ην ο ιηcουc ιδουcα αυτον επεcεν ειc τουc ποδαc αυτου λεγουcα αυτω κυριε ει ηc ωδε ουκ αν απεθανε μου ο αδελφοc.

DEF: **P**^{45}]ια ωc η[ ] ην ο ι̅η̅ [ ]ι ιδουcα... επεc[ ]υc ποδ[ ]c λ[ ]ε̅ ει... αν απ[ ]φοc
P^{75}] μ̣αριαμ ω̣c η̣λθεν οπου [ ] αυτον̣... αυτου [ ]οδαc λεγουcα... ε̣ι̣ ηc [ ]κ̣ αν μου απεθανεν̣ ο αδελφ[

μαρια: μαριαμ **P**^{66*c} **P**^{75}; txt **P**^{66*}
ο^{1}: OM **P**^{66}
ην ο ιηcουc ιδουcα: [9-10] **P**^{75}
ιδουcα: [2]ι ιδουcα **P**^{45}; και ιδουcα **P**^{66}
επεcεν ειc τουc ποδαc αυτου: επεcεν αυτου ειc τουc ποδαc **P**^{66}; επεc[8-10]υc ποδ[ ]c **P**^{45}; επεcεν αυτου [9-10]οδαc **P**^{75}
αυτω: OM **P**^{66}
απεθανε μου: μου απεθανεν **P**^{66} **P**^{75}

11:33

P[45] P[66] P[75]

33: ιηcουc ουν ωc ειδεν αυτην κλαιουcαν και τουc cυνελθονταc αυτη ιουδαιουc κλαιονταc ενεβριμηcατο τω πνευματι και εταραξεν εαυτον.

DEF: **P[45]** ι̅[ ]την κλαιουcαν κα[ ]νταc τ[ ]θοταc αυτηι εταραχ[ ]ουμενο[
P[75]] ιδεν αυτην [ ]υcαν [ ]ϲ̣ cυν̣ελθονταc αυ[ ]υδ[ ]λ̣α̣ι[ ]α̣c εβρειμ̣ηcατο̣ τ[ ]ρ̣α̣ξε̣[ ]υ̣τον

ειδεν: ιδεν **P[75]**
και τουc cυνελθονταc αυτη ιουδαιουc κλαιονταc: κα[15-19]νταc τ[11]θοταc αυτηι **P[45]**
cυνελθονταc: cυνεληλυθοταc cυν **P[66]**
αυτη: αυτηι **P[45]**
ενεβριμηcατο τω πνευματι και εταραξεν εαυτον: εταραχ[15-19] ουμενο[ ] **P[45]**; εβρειμηcατο τω π̅ν̅ι̅ και εταραξεν εαυτον **P[66*]**; εταραχθη τω π̅ν̅ι̅ ωc εμβριμωμενοc **P[66*c]**
ενεβριμηcατο: εβρειμηcατο **P[75]**

11:34

P[45] P[66] P[75]

34: και ειπε που τεθεικατε αυτον λεγουcιν αυτω κυριε ερχου και ιδε.

DEF: **P[45]**]ου τεθεικατε αυ[
P[75] και ειπεν π[ ]ε̣ αυτ[ ]γουcιν αυ̣τω κ̣̅[

ειπε: ειπεν **P[66] P[75]**
τεθεικατε: τεθικαται **P[66]**
κυριε: OM **P[66*]**; txt **P[66*c]**
και[2]: OM **P[66*]**; txt **P[66*c]**
ιδε: ειδε **P[66]**

11:35

P[45] P[66] P[75]

35: εδακρυcεν ο ιηcουc.

DEF: **P**^{45}] ι̅η̅
P^{75}]δα[ ]ρ̣[

εδακρυσεν: εδρακυσεν **P**^{66}
ο: OM **P**^{66*}; txt **P**^{66*c}

11:36

P^{45} **P**^{66} **P**^{75}

36: ελεγον ουν οι ιουδαιοι ιδε πως εφιλει αυτον.

DEF: **P**^{45} ελεγον ου[
P^{75}]δ̣ε π̣ως ε̣[

ιδε: ειδε **P**^{66}

11:37

P^{45} **P**^{66} **P**^{75}

37: τινες δε εξ αυτων ειπον ουκ ηδυνατο ουτος ο ανοιξας τους οφθαλμους του τυφλου ποιησαι ινα και ουτος μη αποθανη.

DEF: **P**^{45}]υτ[
P^{75}] αυτ̣ω̣ [ ]ποṿ [ ]ο̣ιξας τ̣ους ο̣[ ] π̣οιησ[ ]ṿα κ[

εξ αυτων ειπον: ειπον εξ αυτων **P**^{66}
ηδυνατο: εδυνατο **P**^{66}
αποθανη: littera eras. post θ **P**^{66}

11:38

P^{66} **P**^{75}

38: ιησους ουν παλιν εμβριμωμενος εν εαυτω ερχεται εις το μνημειον ην δε σπηλαιον και λιθος επεκειτο επ αυτω.

DEF: **P**^{75}]σ̅ ουν πα[ ]μ̣βρει[ ]ω ερχεται [ ]λ̣αιον και [

εμβριμωμενος: [ ]μβρει[ ] **P**^{75}
εαυτω: εαυαυτω **P**^{66}

11:39

P[66] **P**[75]

39: λεγει ο ιηϲουϲ αρατε τον λιθον λεγει αυτω η αδελφη του τεθνηκοτοϲ μαρθα κυριε ηδη οζει τεταρταιοϲ γαρ εϲτι.

DEF: **P**[75]]ε̣[ ]ει ο ι̅ϲ̅ αρα[ ]τω η α̣δελφη τ̣ο̣υ̣ [ ] μ̣αρθα κ̅ε̅ η̣δη οζ[τετα]ρ̣[

αρατε: αραται **P**[66]
τεθνηκοτοϲ: τετελευκοτοϲ **P**[66*]; τετελευτηκοτοϲ **P**[66*c]
κυριε: OM **P**[66]
εϲτι: εϲτιν **P**[66]

11:40

P[59] **P**[66] **P**[75]

40: λεγει αυτη ο ιηϲουϲ ουκ ειπον ϲοι οτι εαν πιϲτευϲηϲ οψει την δοξαν του θεου.

DEF: **P**[59] λεγει αυ[ ]ι οτι εαν [ ]η την δ[
P[75] λ̣εγει [ ] ι̣ϲ̣ [ ] ειπον ϲοι ο̣τ̣[ ]τευϲηϲ [ ]η̣ν̣ [ ]ξαν του θ̅υ̅

λεγει: λεγι **P**[66*]; txt **P**[66*c]
ο: OM **P**[66]
οτι: OM **P**[66]
οψει: [ ]η **P**[59]; οψη **P**[66]

11:41

P[59] **P**[66] **P**[75]

41: ηραν ουν τον λιθον ου ην ο τεθνηκωϲ κειμενοϲ ο δε ιηϲουϲ ηρε τουϲ οφθαλμουϲ ανω και ειπε πατερ ευχαριϲτω ϲοι οτι ηκουϲαϲ μου.

DEF: **P**[59]]αν [ ]ν τ[ ] ο ι̅[ ] του[ ] και ε[ ] ϲοι οτ[
P[75] ηρα̣[ ]ν̣ τον λιθο[ ] δε ι̅ϲ̅ [ ]ε̣ν τουϲ οφθ[ ]μουϲ ανω κα̣[ ]πεν [ ] ευχαρ̣ι̣ϲ̣τ̣ω̣ ϲοι ο̣τ̣ι ηκ̣ο̣υ̣[ ]ϲ̣ μου

τον λιθον ου ην ο τεθνηκωϲ κειμενοϲ ο δε ιηϲουϲ ηρε τουϲ: τ[12-19] ο ι̅[1-4] του[ ] **P**[59] (& cf. **P**[66] **P**[75])

λιθον ου ην ο τεθνηκωϲ κειμενοϲ ο δε: λιθο[2] δε $\mathbf{P}^{75}$ (& cf. $\mathbf{P}^{59}$ $\mathbf{P}^{66}$)
ου ην ο τεθνηκωϲ κειμενοϲ: OM $\mathbf{P}^{66}$ (& cf. $\mathbf{P}^{59}$ $\mathbf{P}^{75}$)
ηρε: ηρεν $\mathbf{P}^{66}$; [ ]εν $\mathbf{P}^{75}$
οφθαλμουϲ: + αυτου $\mathbf{P}^{66*c}$; txt $\mathbf{P}^{66*}$
ειπε: ειπεν $\mathbf{P}^{66}$; [ ]πεν $\mathbf{P}^{75}$

11:42

$\mathbf{P}^{45}$ $\mathbf{P}^{59}$ $\mathbf{P}^{66}$ $\mathbf{P}^{75}$

42: εγω δε ηδειν οτι παντοτε μου ακουειϲ αλλα δια τον οχλον τον περιεϲτωτα ειπον ινα πιϲτευϲωϲιν οτι ϲυ με απεϲτειλαϲ.

DEF: $\mathbf{P}^{45}$]ν[ ]τειλαϲ
$\mathbf{P}^{59}$ εγω [ ]ε ηδι[ ]τοτε μου ακ[ ] τον οχλον το[ ]τα ειπον ινα [ ]ϲιν οτ[ ] ϲυ με [
$\mathbf{P}^{75}$] π̣αντ̣οτε μο̣υ ακουειϲ [ ]ν̣ περιεϲτωτα [ ]ν̣ ο[ ]υ με α̣π̣ε[

ηδειν: ηδι[ ] $\mathbf{P}^{59}$
παντοτε: παντοται $\mathbf{P}^{66}$

11:43

$\mathbf{P}^{45}$ $\mathbf{P}^{59}$ $\mathbf{P}^{66}$ $\mathbf{P}^{75}$

43: και ταυτα ειπων φωνη μεγαλη εκραυγαϲε λαζαρε δευρο εξω.

DEF: $\mathbf{P}^{45}$ κ[ ] ταυτα [ ]νηι μεγα[ ]ϲεν [ ]αρ[ ] δευρο εξω
$\mathbf{P}^{59}$ και ταυτα [ ]γαϲεν λαζαρ[
$\mathbf{P}^{75}$]π̣ω̣[ ]ω̣νη μεγα̣[ ]α̣ζαρε δε̣[ ]ο̣ εξω

ειπων φωνη μεγαλη εκραυγαϲε: [7-15]γαϲεν $\mathbf{P}^{59}$
φωνη: [ ]νηι $\mathbf{P}^{45}$
εκραυγαϲε: [ ]ϲεν $\mathbf{P}^{45}$; εκραυγαϲεν $\mathbf{P}^{66}$

11:44

P^{45} P^{59} P^{66} P^{75}

44: και εξηλθεν ο τεθνηκως δεδεμενος τους ποδας και τας χειρας κειριαις και η οψις αυτου σουδαριω περιεδεδετο λεγει αυτοις ο ιησους λυσατε αυτον και αφετε υπαγειν.

DEF: **P^{45}** εξηλ[ ]νηκως δεδεμεν[ ]ς [ ]υς π[ ]ας και τας χειρας κηριαις και [ ]ψις... εδεδετο λ[ ]γει... κ[ ]ι [ ]φετε...
P^{59} εξ[ ]κως δε[ ] ποδας κα[ ]αις [ ]δαρ[ ]ι [ ] και [ ]αγιν
P^{75} ε[ ]ς δεδεμεν[ ]ς̣ του̣[ ]ς κηριαις... α̣υ̣[ ]α̣ρ̣ιω π̣ε̣ριεδεδετο...
αυ[ ] λ̣υσατε... αφετε αυτον [ ]γ̣ειν

και[1]: OM **P^{45} P^{59} P^{66} P^{75}**
κειριαις: κηριαις **P^{45} P^{66} P^{75}**
σουδαριω: σουδαριωι **P^{45}**
περιεδεδετο λεγει: [18]ι **P^{59}**
περιεδεδετο: εδεδετο **P^{45}**
αυτοις ο ιησους λυσατε αυτον και: [13-19] και **P^{59}**
αυτοις ο ιησους: ιησους αυ[ ] **P^{75}**
λυσατε: λυσαται **P^{66}**
αφετε υπαγειν: [12-18]αγιν **P^{59}** (& cf. **P^{45} P^{66} P^{75}**)
αφετε: αφεται **P^{66}**; + αυτον **P^{45} P^{66} P^{75}** (& cf. **P^{59}**)

11:45

P^{6} P^{45} P^{59} P^{66} P^{75}

45: πολλοι ουν εκ των ιουδαιων οι ελθοντες προς την μαριαν και θεασαμενοι α εποιησεν ο ιησους επιστευσαν εις αυτον.

DEF: **P^{6}** πολλοι... μαριαμ: κα[ ] θεασαμενοι... επις[
P^{45} πολ[ ]οι εκ [ ]ων ιουδαιων... προς [ ]ην μ[ ]ριαν εωρακοτε[ ] α [ ]ποιησεν...
P^{59}]ν εκ τ[ ] ιου[ ]λθοντες προς [ ]μ και θεασα[ ]ποιησεν επι[ ]υτον
P^{75} πο[ ]λοι... ιου̣δαι[ ] μ̣α̣ρ̣[ ]μ̣ [

ουν: OM **P^{45}**
προς: OM **P^{66*}**; txt **P^{66*c}**
μαριαν: μαριαμ **P^{6}**; μαρ[ ]μ **P^{75}**; [ ]μ **P^{59}**
και θεασαμενοι: εωρακοτε[1] **P^{45}**; εωρακοτες **P^{66}**
α: οσα **P^{66*c}**; txt **P^{66*}**

ο ιηcουc: OM **P**[6] **P**[45] **P**[59] **P**[66]

11:46

P[6] **P**[45] **P**[59] **P**[66]

46: τινεc δε εξ αυτων απηλθον προc τουc φαριcαιουc και ειπον αυτοιc α εποιηcεν ο ιηcουc.

DEF: **P**[6]]εc δε εξ αυ[ ]ουc φαριcαιουc [ ] εποιηcεν ι̅c̅
P[45] τι[ ]εc δε ε[ ]των απη[ ] προc [ ]ουc φαρειcαιουc... αυ[ ]
ε[ ]οιηcεν [
P[59] τι[ ]ων απηλ[ ] του[ ] φαριcαι[ ]ν [ ]υτοιc [ ] ο [

απηλθον: απηλθαν **P**[66]
φαριcαιουc: φαρειcαιουc **P**[45]
ειπον: ειπαν **P**[66]
ο: OM **P**[6] **P**[66]

11:47

P[6] **P**[45] **P**[59] **P**[66]

47: cυνηγαγον ουν οι αρχιερειc και οι φαριcαιοι cυνεδριον και ελεγον τι ποιουμεν οτι ουτοc ο ανθρωποc πολλα cημεια ποιει.

DEF: **P**[6]]χιερειc [ ]ν και ελε[ ]c ο ανθρ[
P[45]]αγον [ ]υν οι... φαρειcαι[ ]δριον και [ ]οιηcομεν... πολ[ ]
cημεια
P[59] cυν[ ]ριc κ[ ]δριο[ ]ου[ ] π[

αρχιερειc: [ ]ριc **P**[59]
φαριcαιοι: φαρειcαι[ ] **P**[45]
ποιουμεν: ποιηcομεν **P**[45*]; txt **P**[45*c]
οτι: OM **P**[45]
cημεια ποιει: [ ] cημεια **P**[45]; ποιει cημεια **P**[66]

11:48

$\mathbf{P}^{6}$ $\mathbf{P}^{45}$ $\mathbf{P}^{59}$ $\mathbf{P}^{66}$ $\mathbf{P}^{75}$

48: εαν αφωμεν αυτον ουτω παντες πιcτευcουcιν ειc αυτον και ελευcονται οι ρωμαιοι και αρουcιν ημων και τον τοπον και το εθνοc.

DEF: $\mathbf{P}^{6}$ εαν [ ]c παντεc [ ] και ελευ[ ]cιν ημων [ ]c
$\mathbf{P}^{45}$]μεν... πιcτευ[ ] αυτ[ ]αι οι... ημων [
$\mathbf{P}^{59}$] αφ[ ] πα[ ] ειc [ ]τε [ ] και ερ[ ] ημ[ ]ν το[ ] και τ[
$\mathbf{P}^{75}$] . [

ουτω: [ ]c $\mathbf{P}^{6}$; ουτωc $\mathbf{P}^{45}$ $\mathbf{P}^{66}$
πιcτευcουcιν: πιcτευcωcιν $\mathbf{P}^{66}$
ελευcονται: [ ]τε $\mathbf{P}^{59}$
αρουcιν: ερ[ ] $\mathbf{P}^{59}$
τον: το $\mathbf{P}^{66*}$; txt $\mathbf{P}^{66*c}$

11:49

$\mathbf{P}^{6}$ $\mathbf{P}^{45}$ $\mathbf{P}^{59}$ $\mathbf{P}^{66}$ $\mathbf{P}^{75}$

49: ειc δε τιc εξ αυτων καιαφαc αρχιερευc ων του ενιαυτου εκεινου ειπεν αυτοιc υμειc ουκ οιδατε ουδεν.

DEF: $\mathbf{P}^{6}$]φαc [ ]υ εκειν[ ]με[ ] οιδατ[
$\mathbf{P}^{45}$ ... αρχιε[ ]ου ειπεν... οιδατε αυ[
$\mathbf{P}^{59}$] καιαφαc [ ] ενιαυτου [ ]τ[ ]ιc υ[ ]δεν
$\mathbf{P}^{75}$]ε̣ τιc... κ̣αιφ[ ]c ων του ενιαυτου ε̣[ ]υ̣τοιc υ̣μειc ουκ̣ ο̣[

τιc: OM $\mathbf{P}^{66}$
καιαφαc: καιφαc $\mathbf{P}^{45}$; καιφ[ ] $\mathbf{P}^{75}$
οιδατε: οιδαται $\mathbf{P}^{66}$
(49-50): οιδατε ουδεν ουδε διαλογιζεcθε οτι: ο[22-27] $\mathbf{P}^{75}$ (& cf. $\mathbf{P}^{6}$ $\mathbf{P}^{45}$ $\mathbf{P}^{59}$ $\mathbf{P}^{66}$)
(49-50): ουδεν ουδε διαλογιζεcθε οτι cυμφερει: αυ[/ 21-22]φερει $\mathbf{P}^{45*}$; ου[/ 21-22]φερει $\mathbf{P}^{45*c}$ (& cf. $\mathbf{P}^{6}$ $\mathbf{P}^{59}$ $\mathbf{P}^{66}$ $\mathbf{P}^{75}$)
(49-50): ουδεν ουδε διαλογιζεcθε: [11]χιζε[ ] $\mathbf{P}^{6}$ (& cf. $\mathbf{P}^{45}$ $\mathbf{P}^{59}$ $\mathbf{P}^{66}$ $\mathbf{P}^{75}$)

11:50

P^{6} P^{45} P^{59} P^{66} P^{75}

50: ουδε διαλογιζεcθε οτι cυμφερει ημιν ινα ειc ανθρωποc αποθανη υπερ του λαου και μη ολον το εθνοc αποληται.

DEF: **P^{6}**]γιζε[ ]τι cυμ[ ]ν[ ]θρω[ ] υ[ ]υ [ ] ε[ ]ν[ ]τα[
P^{45}]φερει... απο[ ]ον...
P^{59}] οτι [ ]να ειc [ ]ρ του [ ] και μ[ ]νοc [ ]λητ[
P^{75}] c̣[ ]μ[ ]ποθαν[ ]ν το εθν̣ο̣[

ουδε διαλογιζεcθε: [13-15] **P^{59}** (& cf. **P^{6} P^{45} P^{66} P^{75}**)
διαλογιζεcθε: λογιζεcθαι **P^{66}** (& cf. **P^{6} P^{45} P^{59} P^{75}**)
ημιν: υμιν **P^{45} P^{66}**
ινα: OM **P^{66*}**; txt **P^{66*c}**

11:51

P^{6} P^{45} P^{59} P^{66} P^{75}

51: τουτο δε αφ εαυτου ουκ ειπεν αλλα αρχιερευc ων του ενιαυτου εκεινου προεφητευcεν οτι εμελλεν ο ιηcουc αποθνηcκειν υπερ του εθνουc.

DEF: **P^{6}**] ουκ ε[ ] αλλα [ ] του ε[ ]υτου εκ[ ]μελλε[ ]υ εθ[
P^{45} ... αφ ε[ ]υτου [ ]ερευ[ ]ν επροφητευcεν οτι ημελ[ ]εν ι̅η̅
[ ] του ε[ ]ουc
P^{59}]φ εαυ[ ]χιερευc [ ] εκινου [ ] οτι με[ ] ι̅c̅ [ ]περ του [
P^{75}]φ εαυτου̣ [ ]υ̣c ω̅ του εν[ ]η̣τευcεν̣ [ ]cκειν υ[ ]ρ̣ [ ]υ̣ [

αλλα: αλλ **P^{66*}**; txt **P^{66*c}**
του ενιαυτου εκεινου: OM **P^{45}**
εκεινου: OM **P^{66}**; εκινου **P^{59}**
προεφητευcεν: επροφητευcεν **P^{45} P^{66}**
εμελλεν ο ιηcουc: με[4] ι̅c̅ **P^{59}** (& cf. **P^{45} P^{66}** (OM ο))
εμελλεν: ημελ[ ]εν **P^{45}**; ημελλεν **P^{66}**
ο: OM **P^{45} P^{66}** (& cf. **P^{59}**)

11:52

P^{6} **P**^{45} **P**^{59} **P**^{66} **P**^{75}

52: και ουχ υπερ του εθνουc μονον αλλ ινα και τα τεκνα του θεου τα διεcκορπιcμενα cυναγαγη ειc εν.

DEF: **P**^{6}]να του [ ]υ [ ] cυναγαγη ειc εν
P^{45} ... εθνο[ ]ονο[ ]α του [ ] τα εcκορπιcμενα c͟υναγα[ ]ιc εν
P^{59}]περ του ε[ ]ν αλλ ινα και [ ] τεκνα του θ̅υ̅ τα
δ[ ]κορπιcμενα cυναγαγη ειc ε[
P^{75}] του εθνουc μο[ ] τεκνα του θ̅υ̅ τ̣[ ] c̣υ̣ν̣α̣[ ]γη ειc εν̣

ουχ: υ sub ο **P**^{45}
διεcκορπιcμενα: εcκορπιcμενα **P**^{45} **P**^{66}

11:53

P^{45} **P**^{66} **P**^{75}

53: απ εκεινηc ουν τηc ημεραc cυνεβουλευcαντο ινα αποκτεινωcιν αυτον.

DEF: **P**^{45}] τηc η[ ]εραc... ιν[ ] αποκτ[
P^{75}] τ̣[ ]ρ̣α̣c εβ[ ]τ̣ο̣ ινα̣ απ̣[ ]κ[ ]νωcι̣ν α̣υ̣[

εκεινηc: εκινηc **P**^{66}
cυνεβουλευcαντο: εβουλευcαντο **P**^{45} **P**^{66}; εβ[ ]το **P**^{75}
αποκτεινωcιν: αποκτινωcιν **P**^{66}

11:54

P^{45} **P**^{66} **P**^{75}

54: ιηcουc ουν ουκ ετι παρρηcια περιεπατει εν τοιc ιουδαιοιc αλλα απηλθεν εκειθεν ειc την χωραν εγγυc τηc ερημου ειc εφραιμ λεγομενην πολιν κακει διετριβε μετα των μαθητων αυτου.

DEF: **P**^{45}]ν [ ] παρηcια περιεπατει [ ]οιc ϊου[ ]α απη[ ]ν
χωραν εγγυc τηc ε[ ]φ[ ] λεγομε[ ] κακει... με[ ]ων
P^{75} ο̣... ουκ ετι̣ [ ]α̣ρρηcια περ̣[ ]π̣ατει εν τοιc ιο[ ]ο̣ιc̣ αλ̣λα
απ̣η̣λθεν εκε̣ι̣θ̣ε̣ν̣ ειc̣ [ ]ν χωρα̣ν εγ[ ]ρ̣[ ] ειc ε̣φραιμ λ̣[ ]κει
εμ̣ε̣ι̣νεν̣ [

ιηcουc ουν: ο ουν ιηcουc **P^{75}**; ο δε ιηcουc **P^{66}**
παρρηcια: παρηcια **P^{45}**
απηλθεν εκειθεν ειc την: απη[8-9]ν **P^{45}**
ειc^{2}: OM **P^{66}**
λεγομενην: λεγουμενην **P^{66*}**; txt **P^{66*c}**
πολιν: OM **P^{66*}**; txt **P^{66*c}**
κακει: και εκει **P^{66}**
διετριβε: διετρειβεν **P^{45}**; διετριβεν **P^{66*c}**; εμεινεν **P^{75}**; εμινεν **P^{66*}**
μετα των μαθητων αυτου: [14] **P^{75}**
αυτου: OM **P^{45}** **P^{66}** (& cf. **P^{75}**)

11:55

P^{45} P^{66} P^{75}

55: ην δε εγγυc το παcχα των ιουδαιων και ανεβηcαν πολλοι ειc ιεροcολυμα εκ τηc χωραc προ του παcχα ινα αγνιcωcιν εαυτουc.

DEF: **P^{45}** η[ ]α των... και α[ ]λοι ειc [ ]ωραc... ιν[ ]cιν εαυτ[
P^{75} ην δε̣ [ ]ων κα̣[ ]ε̣β̣ηcα[ ]υ̣μα [ ]κ̣ τη̣[ ] χωρα̣[ ] ι̣να
α[ ]γ̣ιcωcιν εαυ[

11:56

P^{45} P^{66} P^{75}

56: εζητουν ουν τον ιηcουν και ελεγον μετ αλληλων εν τω ιερω εcτηκοτεc τι δοκει υμιν οτι ου μη ελθη ειc την εορτην.

DEF: **P^{45}**]η̅ και ελεγον μετ [ ]μιν... ελθ[
P^{75}] ουν... ελεγ[ ] εν... εcτηκοτεc̣ [ ] υμιν... ελθ̣η ειc την
ε̣[ ]τ̣[ ]ν

δοκει: δοκι **P^{66}**
υμιν: υμειν **P^{66}**
56-57: ειc την εορτην δεδωκειcαν δε και οι αρχιερειc: [34-5] **P^{45}**

11:57

P^{45} **P**^{66} **P**^{75}

57: δεδωκειcαν δε και οι αρχιερειc και οι φαριcαιοι εντολην ινα εαν τιc γνω που εcτι μηνυcη οπωc πιαcωcιν αυτον.

DEF: **P**^{45}] και οι πρεc[ ]cη [
P^{75} δεδωκειcαν̣ [ ]ε οι αρχιε[ ] . [ ] .....

δεδωκειcαν δε και οι αρχιερειc: vid. v. 56
και[1]: OM **P**^{66} **P**^{75}
φαριcαιοι: πρεc[ ] **P**^{45}
εcτι: εcτιν **P**^{66}

CHAPTER TWELVE

P^{2} **P**^{44B} **P**^{59} **P**^{66} **P**^{75}

12:1

P^{66}

1: ο ουν ιηcουc προ εξ ημερων του παcχα ηλθεν ειc βηθανιαν οπου ην λαζαροc ο τεθνηκωc ον ηγειρεν εκ νεκρων.

εξ: πεντε **P**^{66*}; txt **P**^{66*c}
νεκρων: + ι̅c̅ **P**^{66}

12:2

P^{66}

2: εποιηcαν ουν αυτω δειπνον εκει και η μαρθα διηκονει ο δε λαζαροc ειc ην των cυνανακειμενων αυτω.

εποιηcαν: εποιηcεν **P**^{66}
ουν: OM **P**^{66*}; txt **P**^{66*c}
η: OM **P**^{66}
ην: OM **P**^{66*}; txt **P**^{66*c}
των cυνανακειμενων: εκ των ανακειμενων cυν **P**^{66}

12:3

$\mathbf{P}^{66}$ $\mathbf{P}^{75}$

3: η ουν μαρια λαβουcα λιτραν μυρου ναρδου πιcτικηc πολυτιμου ηλειψε τουc ποδαc του ιηcου και εξεμαξε ταιc θριξιν αυτηc τουc ποδαc αυτου η δε οικια επληρωθη εκ τηc οcμηc του μυρου.

DEF: $\mathbf{P}^{75}$]κ̣ια επ̣[ ]κ̣ τηc οcμηc του μ̣[ ]ρ̣ου

λιτραν: λειτραν $\mathbf{P}^{66}$
ναρδου: OM $\mathbf{P}^{66*}$; txt $\mathbf{P}^{66*c}$
ηλειψε: ηλειψεν $\mathbf{P}^{66}$
εξεμαξε: εξεμαξεν $\mathbf{P}^{66}$
επληρωθη: επληρουτο $\mathbf{P}^{66*}$; txt $\mathbf{P}^{66*c}$

12:4

$\mathbf{P}^{66}$ $\mathbf{P}^{75}$

4: λεγει ουν ειc εκ των μαθητων αυτου ιουδαc cιμωνοc ιcκαριωτηc ο μελλων αυτον παραδιδοναι.

DEF: $\mathbf{P}^{75}$ λ[ ]υ̣δ̣α̣c̣ [ ] ι̣c̣κ̣α̣ρ̣ι̣ω̣τη̣c [ ]ʽ[ ] τωṿ [ ]θητων αυṭου ọ μελλων αυṭọṿ [ ]ρ̣αδιδοναι

λεγει ουν ειc εκ των μαθητων αυτου ιουδαc cιμωνοc ιcκαριωτηc:
λ[5-6]υδαc [1] ιcκαριωτηc [1]ʽ[1] των [2]θητων αυτου $\mathbf{P}^{75}$
ουν ειc εκ των μαθητων αυτου ιουδαc cιμωνοc ιcκαριωτηc: δε ιουδαc ο ιcκαριωτηc ειc των μαθητων αυτου $\mathbf{P}^{66}$

12:5

$\mathbf{P}^{66}$ $\mathbf{P}^{75}$

5: διατι τουτο το μυρον ουκ επραθη τριακοcιων δηναριων και εδοθη πτωχοιc.

DEF: $\mathbf{P}^{75}$ ... μυρον [ ]αθη... δηναριων [ ]θη πτωχοιc̣

τουτο: ουτο $\mathbf{P}^{66*}$; txt $\mathbf{P}^{66*c}$

12:6

P^{66} P^{75}

6: ειπε δε τουτο ουχ οτι περι των πτωχων εμελεν αυτω αλλ οτι κλεπτηϲ ην και το γλωϲϲοκομον ειχε και τα βαλλομενα εβαϲταζεν.

DEF: **P^{75}** ε̣[ ]π̣ε... ουχ [ ]ω̣ν πτ[ ] εμελεν αυτω [ ]λ̣ οτι κλ̣[ ]π̣τηϲ̣ η̣[ ] τ̣ο γλωϲϲοκο[ ]ο̣ν εχων̣ [ ]α βαλλομεν̣[ ]β̣αϲ̣ταζεν

ειπε: ειπεν **P^{66}**
ειχε: ειχεν **P^{66}**; εχων **P^{75}**
και²: OM **P^{75}**

12:7

P^{66} P^{75}

7: ειπεν ουν ο ιηϲουϲ αφεϲ αυτην ειϲ την ημεραν του ενταφιαϲμου μου τετηρηκεν αυτο.

DEF: **P^{75}**]πεν ουν [ ] ι̅ϲ̅ αφεϲ αυτη̣ν ινα ε̣ι̣ϲ̣ τη̅ [ ]μεραν... μου [ ]η̣ αυ̣το

αυτην: + ινα **P^{66} P^{75}**
τετηρηκεν: τηρηϲη **P^{66}**; [5]η **P^{75}**

12:8

P^{66} P^{75}

8: τουϲ πτωχουϲ γαρ παντοτε εχετε μεθ εαυτων εμε δε ου παντοτε εχετε.

DEF: **P^{75}** τουϲ πτωχουϲ γα̣[ ] παντο̣τ̣ε [ ]χετε

πτωχουϲ γαρ: πτω **P^{66*}**; txt **P^{66*c}**
εχετε¹: εχεται **P^{66}**
μεθ εαυτων εμε δε ου παντοτε εχετε: OM **P^{75}**
παντοτε²: παντοται **P^{66}**
εχετε²: εχεται **P^{66}**

12:9

P^{66} **P**^{75}

9: εγνω ουν οχλος πολυς εκ των ιουδαιων οτι εκει εστι και ηλθον ου δια τον ιηcουν μονον αλλ ινα και τον λαζαρον ιδωcιν ον ηγειρεν εκ νεκρων.

DEF: **P**^{75} ... των [ ]αιων... δι[ ] τ̣ον... λαζα[ ] ι̣δ̣ωc[ ]ν̣ ηγειρε̣ν̣ ε̣κ ν̣εκρων

οχλος: ο οχλος ο **P**^{66*c}; txt **P**^{66*}
εκ^{1}: OM **P**^{66}
εcτι: εcτιν **P**^{66} **P**^{75}
λαζαρον: λαον **P**^{66*}; txt **P**^{66*c}
ηγειρεν: ηγιρεν **P**^{66}

12:10

P^{66} **P**^{75}

10: εβουλευcαντο δε οι αρχιερειc ινα και τον λαζαρον αποκτεινωcιν.

DEF: **P**^{75} ε[ ]λ̣ε̣υ̣[ ]χιερειc ινα̣ [ ] τον [ ]ζαρον αποκτ̣[ ]νω[ ]ι̣ν̣

12:11

P^{66} **P**^{75}

11: οτι πολλοι δι αυτον υπηγον των ιουδαιων και επιcτευον ειc τον ιηcουν.

DEF: **P**^{75}] δι [ ]τον υπηγον̣ των̣ [ ]ι[ ]τευον ε̣ιc τον ι̅ν̣̅

υπηγον: OM **P**^{66}
και: OM **P**^{66}
επιcτευον: επιcτευcαν **P**^{66}

12:12

P^{2} **P**^{44B} **P**^{66} **P**^{75}

12: τη επαυριον οχλος πολυς ο ελθων εις την εορτην ακουσαντες οτι ερχεται ο ιησους εις ιεροσολυμα

DEF: **P**^{2} τη... οχλος π[ ] εορτην ακουσαντ[ ] εις ιερου[ ]ημ
P^{44B}] ερ[
P^{75} τη [ ]π̣αυριο̣ν̣ [ ]ο̣λυς ο ελθω̣[ ] ε̣ι̣ς̣ τ̣η̣ν̣ [ ]ορτην [ ]ν̣τες οτι ερχεται ο ι̅ς̅ [ ]ς ιερος[

οχλος: ο οχλος **P**^{66*}; ο οχλος ο **P**^{66*c}
ιεροσολυμα: ιερου[ ]ημ **P**^{2}

12:13

P^{2} **P**^{44B} **P**^{66} **P**^{75}

13: ελαβον τα βαια των φοινικων και εξηλθον εις υπαντησιν αυτω και εκραζον ωσαννα ευλογημενος ο ερχομενος εν ονοματι κυριου ο βασιλευς του ισραηλ.

DEF: **P**^{2} ε[ ] φοινικων κ[ ]ι εκραυ[ ] ερχομε[ ]ου ι̅η̅λ̅
P^{44B}]αια [
P^{75}]ο̣ν τα... φοι[ ]ν̣ και εξη̣λ̣θ̣[ ]ν εις... αυ[ ]αι εκραυγαζον... ευλογημ[ ]νος ο ερχομενος... κα̣[ ] βασιλευς του ι̣η̅λ̅

ελαβον: ελαβαν **P**^{66}
βαια: βαλια **P**^{66*}; βαια **P**^{66*c}
εκραζον: εκραυγαζον **P**^{75}; εκραυ[ ] **P**^{2}; εκραυγασαν λεγοντες **P**^{66}
κυριου: + κα[1] **P**^{75}

12:14

P^{2} **P**^{66} **P**^{75}

14: ευρων δε ο ιησους οναριον εκαθισεν επ αυτο καθως εστι γεγραμμενον.

DEF: **P**^{2} ε[ ]π αυτ[
P^{75} ... ι̅ς̣̅ ο̣[ ]ιον εκα[ ]ν̣ επ αυτο καθως̣ [ ]ε̣γραμμε[

εστι: εστιν **P**^{66}

12:15

P^{2} P^{66} P^{75}

15: μη φοβου θυγατερ cιων ιδου ο βαcιλευc cου ερχεται καθημενοc επι πωλον ονου.

DEF: **P^{2}**] φ̣[
P^{75} μ̣η... θ̣[ ] c̣ειων ιδου [ ]λευc... κ[ ]μ̣ε̣[ ] π̣ωλον ονου

φοβου: + η **P^{75}**
θυγατερ: θυγατηρ **P^{66}**; η θ[ ] **P^{75}**
cιων: cειων **P^{66} P^{75}**
πωλον: πωλου **P^{66*}**; txt **P^{66*c}**

12:16

P^{44B} P^{66} P^{75}

16: ταυτα δε ουκ εγνωcαν οι μαθηται αυτου το πρωτον αλλ οτε εδοξαcθη ο ιηcουc τοτε εμνηcθηcαν οτι ταυτα ην επ αυτω γεγραμμενα και ταυτα εποιηcαν αυτω.

DEF: **P^{44B}**]ε[ ]α και [
P^{75} ταυτα [ ]υ̣του ο̣ι μαθηται τ̣[ ]τ̣[ ] αλλ οτε εδ̣ο̣[ ]cθη ι̅c̅
τοτε εμνηc̣θ̣[ ]cαν οτι ταυ[ ] ην επ αυτω γεγραμμ[ ]ν̣α και
ταυτ̣[ ]π̣οιηcα̣ν αυτω

δε: OM **P^{66}**
οι μαθηται αυτου: [ ]υτου οι μαθηται **P^{75}**
ο: OM **P^{66*} P^{75}**; txt **P^{66*c}**
τοτε: OM **P^{66*}**; txt **P^{66*c}**
ην: η **P^{66*}**; txt **P^{66*c}**
επ: εν **P^{66*}**; txt **P^{66*c}**

12:17

P^{44B} **P**^{66} **P**^{75}

17: εμαρτυρει ουν ο οχλος ο ων μετ αυτου οτε τον λαζαρον εφωνησεν εκ του μνημειου και ηγειρεν αυτον εκ νεκρων.

DEF: **P**^{44B}] ουν ο οχλο[ ] οτε [ ]ν εφων[ ]ειο[ ]εν αυτον [
P^{75} εμαρ̣τυρει... με[ ] α̣υτου οτ[ ] τον... εκ̣ τ̣ο̣υ μνη̣[ ]ι̣ου...

οτε: οτι **P**^{66}

12:18

P^{44B} **P**^{66} **P**^{75}

18: δια τουτο και υπηντησεν αυτω ο οχλος οτι ηκουσε τουτο αυτον πεποιηκεναι το σημειον.

DEF: **P**^{44B}]ησεν α[
P^{75} δια̣ τ̣[ ]υ̣τ̣[ ] υ̣πηντη̣σεν... ηκου̣[ ] τουτ̣[ ]υτον
π̣[ ]ποιηκ̣εναι το̣ [ ]ειον

και: OM **P**^{66*} **P**^{75}; txt **P**^{66*c}
ο: OM **P**^{75*}; txt **P**^{75c}
ηκουσε: ηκουσαν **P**^{66}; ηκου[3] **P**^{75}
τουτο αυτον: αυτον τουτο **P**^{66}
σημειον: σημιον **P**^{66}

12:19

P^{66} **P**^{75}

19: οι ουν φαρισαιοι ειπον προς εαυτους θεωρειτε οτι ουκ ωφελειτε ουδεν ιδε ο κοσμος οπισω αυτου απηλθεν.

DEF: **P**^{75}] φαρισαοι ει[ ]τ̣ε̣ οτι ουκ [ ]φελειτε ουδεν ιδε̣
[ ]σ̣ω α̣υτ̣ο̣υ α̣π̣η̣λ̣θ̣εν

ειπον: ειπαν **P**^{66}
εαυτους: αυτους **P**^{66*}; txt **P**^{66*c}
θεωρειτε: θεωριτε **P**^{66}
ωφελειτε: ωφελιται **P**^{66}

12:20

P^{66} P^{75}

20: ηcαν δε τινεc ελληνεc εκ των αναβαινοντων ινα προcκυνηcωcιν εν τη εορτη.

DEF: **P^{75}** η̣cαν δε ελ̣λ̣η̣[ ]ε̣c... α̣ναβαινοντωγ̣ [ ]α
προcκυνηcωcιν εν τη εορ̣τ[

τινεc ελληνεc: ελληνεc τινεc **P^{66}**; ελλη[ ]εc τινεc **P^{75}**

12:21

P^{66} P^{75}

21: ουτοι ουν προcηλθον φιλιππω τω απο βηθcαιδα τηc γαλιλαιαc και ηρωτων αυτον λεγοντεc κυριε θελομεν τον ιηcουν ιδειν.

DEF: **P^{75}**]τοι ουν προcη̣λ̣θο̣ν φιλιππω [ ] απο βηθcαιδ[ ]
γαλιλαιαc̣ [ ]των αυ̣τ̣ον [ ] κ̅ε̅ θ[ ]μ̣ε̣ν̣ τον ι̅ν̣̅ ι̣δ̣ε̣ι̣[

βηθcαιδα: βηδcαιδα **P^{66}**

12:22

P^{66} P^{75}

22: ερχεται φιλιπποc και λεγει τω ανδρεα και παλιν ανδρεαc και φιλιπποc λεγουcι τω ιηcου.

DEF: **P^{75}** ε̣[ ]χεται ο φι̣[ ]πποc και λ̣ε̣γ̣ε̣ι̣ [ ]ω̣ ανδρεα ερχετ̣αι
αν̣δρεαc [ ] φιλιπποc κα̣ι̣ λ̣εγουcιν̣ τω ι̅η̅υ̅

ερχεται: + ο **P^{66} P^{75}**
και παλιν ανδρεαc και φιλιπποc: ερχεται ανδρεαc [3] φιλιπποc και **P^{75}**
και παλιν ανδρεαc: και παλιν ο ανδρεαc δε **P^{66*}**; ανδρεαc δε **P^{66*c}**
φιλιπποc: ο φιλιπποc **P^{66*}**; txt **P^{66c}**
λεγουcι: λεγουcιν **P^{66} P^{75}**

12:23

P66 P75

23: ο δε ιηcουc απεκρινατο αυτοιc λεγων εληλυθεν η ωρα ινα δοξαcθη ο υιοc του ανθρωπου.

DEF: **P75**] δε ῑc̄ αποκ[ ]νεται αυτοιc λεγων εληλυθεν...
δοξαcθη [ ] ῡc̄ του ανου

απεκρινατο: αποκρινεται **P66**; αποκ[ ]νεται **P75**
εληλυθεν: εληλευθεν **P66***; txt **P66*c**

12:24

P66 P75

24: αμην αμην λεγω υμιν εαν μη ο κοκκοc του cιτου πεcων ειc την γην αποθανη αυτοc μονοc μενει εαν δε αποθανη πολυν καρπον φερει.

DEF: **P75**] αμην... αν... γην αποθανη αυτοc μον[ ]ενει εαν
δ[ ]ποθανη πο[ ]υ[ ] φ[ ]ρ[ ]ι

εαν[1]: αν **P75** (aut εαν, si linea in marginem proiecta fuit)
υμιν: υμειν **P66**

12:25

P59 P66 P75

25: ο φιλων την ψυχην αυτου απολεcει αυτην και ο μιcων την ψυχην αυτου εν τω κοcμω τουτω ειc ζωην αιωνιον φυλαξει αυτην.

DEF: **P59**] ζωην αιων[
P75 ο φ[ ]υχην αυτου απολλυε[ ]ν κα[ ]ειcω[ ] την ψυχην [ ]
εν τω κ[ ]cμω τ[ ]υτω [ ]ιc ζω[ ]νιον φυ[ ]ξει αυτ[ ]ν

απολεcει: απολλυει **P66**; απολλυε[ ] **P75**
μιcων: [ ]ειcω[ ] **P75**

12:26

P^{66} **P**^{75}

26: εαν εμοι διακονη τις εμοι ακολουθειτω και οπου ειμι εγω εκει και ο διακονος ο εμος εσται και εαν τις εμοι διακονη τιμησει αυτον ο πατηρ.

DEF: **P**^{75} εαν εμοι̣ τ̣[ ] δ̣ι̣α̣κ̣[ ]η εμοι ακ̣ολουθειτω και οπου [ ]γω εκει και ο διακονο̣[ ] ο εμος εστα̣[ ] εαν τις εμο̣ι δι̣ακονη τιμησει αυτ̣ον ο πατηρ

διακονη τις: τις διακονη εμοι τις διακονη **P**^{66*}; τις διακονη **P**^{66*c}; τ[ ] διακ[ ]η **P**^{75}
ακολουθειτω: ακολουθιτω **P**^{66}
ειμι εγω: εγω ειμι **P**^{66}
εσται: εστιν **P**^{66*}; εστε **P**^{66*c}
και εαν: εαν **P**^{66*} **P**^{75}; εαν δε **P**^{66*c}
πατηρ: + μου **P**^{66*c}; txt **P**^{66*}

12:27

P^{66} **P**^{75}

27: νυν η ψυχη μου τεταρακται και τι ειπω πατερ σωσον με εκ της ωρας ταυτης αλλα δια τουτο ηλθον εις την ωραν ταυτην.

DEF: **P**^{75} ... τετα̣[ ]ται και... με̣ [ ]η̣ς ωρας ταυτης α[ ]α̣ δ̣ι̣α τουτο η̣[ ] την ωραν τα[

αλλα: α[1] α **P**^{75}

12:28

P^{66} **P**^{75}

28: πατερ δοξασον σου το ονομα ηλθεν ουν φωνη εκ του ουρανου και εδοξασα και παλιν δοξασω.

DEF: **P**^{75}] δοξασον... ονομ̣[ ] φωνη... ουραν[ ]δ̣ο̣ξα̣ς̣α̣...

12:29

P^{59} **P**^{66} **P**^{75}

29: ο ουν οχλος ο εστως και ακουσας ελεγε βροντην γεγονεναι αλλοι ελεγον αγγελος αυτω λελαληκεν.

DEF: **P**^{59}]ηκωc κ[ ]εγεν βροντη̅

P^{75} ο [ ]χ̣λοc ο εcτω[ ] και ακου[ ] ε̣λεγε̣[ ]ροντην... αλ̣[ ]ι̣

ελεγον αγγε̣λοc α̣υ̣τ̣ω λ̣ε̣λαληκ̣ε̣ν̣

εcτωc: [ ]ηκωc **P**^{59}

ελεγε: [ ]εγεν **P**^{59}; ελεγε[ ] **P**^{75}; ελεγον **P**^{66}

γεγονεναι: γεγοναιναι **P**^{66*}; txt **P**^{66*c}

λελαληκεν: ελαληcεν **P**^{66}

12:30

P^{66} **P**^{75}

30: απεκριθη ο ιηcουc και ειπεν ου δι εμε αυτη η φωνη γεγονεν αλλα δι υμαc.

DEF: **P**^{75} απεκριθη [ ]αι ειπεν [ ]c̣̄ ου δ̣ι̣... γεχο̣νεν αλλα δ̣ι...

ο ιηcουc και ειπεν: [1]αι ειπεν [2]c̄ **P**^{75}

ο: OM **P**^{66}

αυτη η φωνη: η φωνη αυτη **P**^{66} **P**^{75}

γεγονεν: ηλθεν **P**^{66}

12:31

P^{59} **P**^{66} **P**^{75}

31: νυν κριcιc εcτι του κοcμου τουτου νυν ο αρχων του κοcμου τουτου εκβληθηcεται εξω.

DEF: **P**^{59}] εcτιν του [

P^{75} ... αρχω̣ν του κο[ ]μ̣ου τ̣ο̣υ̣[ ]ο̣υ ε̣κ̣β̣λ̣η̣θηcεται εξω̣

εcτι: εcτιν **P**^{59} **P**^{66} **P**^{75}

τουτου^{1}: OM **P**^{66*}; txt **P**^{66*c}

εκβληθηcεται: βληθηcεται **P**^{66}

12:32

P^{66} **P**^{75}

32: καγω εαν υψωθω εκ τηc γηc παντac ελκυcω προc εμαυτον.

DEF: **P**^{59}]ω εαν [ ]θ̣ω... παντα̣[ ]c̣ω π̣[ ]α̣υ̣το̣ν

πανταc: παντα **P**^{66}

12:33

P^{66} P^{75}

33: τουτο δε ελεγε cημαινων ποιω θανατω ημελλεν αποθνηcκειν.

DEF: **P^{59}** ... δε ε̣[ ]ω ημελλεν αποθνη̣[

ελεγε: ελεγεν **P^{66}**
αποθνηcκειν: αποθνηc[ ]ειν (una littera eras. post c) **P^{66*}**; txt **P^{66*c}**

12:34

P^{66} P^{75}

34: απεκριθη αυτω ο οχλοc ημειc ηκουcαμεν εκ του νομου οτι ο
χριcτοc μενει ειc τον αιωνα και πωc cυ λεγειc οτι δει υψωθηναι
τον υιον του ανθρωπου τιc εcτιν ουτοc ο υιοc του ανθρωπου.

DEF: **P^{75}**]ρ̣ι̣[ ]υν αυτω... ημ̣ε̣ιc ηκουcαμεν [ ]υ̣ νομου... αι[ ]α̣ι
πωc λεγειc [ ]υ̣ δει υψωθηναι [ ]ιον του α̣ν̣[ ]που

απεκριθη: + ουν **P^{66}**; [ ]ρι[3]υν **P^{75}**
ημειc: ημιc **P^{66}**
cυ λεγειc: λεγειc [ ]υ **P^{75}**
οτι^{2}: OM **P^{75}**
δει: δι **P^{66}**
τιc εcτιν ουτοc ο υιοc του ανθρωπου: OM **P^{75}**

12:35

P^{59} P^{66} P^{75}

35: ειπεν ουν αυτοιc ο ιηcουc ετι μικρον χρονον το φωc μεθ
υμων εcτι περιπατειτε εωc το φωc εχετε ινα μη cκοτια υμαc
καταλαβη και ο περιπατων εν τη cκοτια ουκ οιδε που υπαγει.

DEF: **P^{59}** ειπεν ουν [ ]κρο[
P^{75} ... ουν [ ]οιc... μει[ ]ν̣ χρονον το φωc [ ]ν̣ υμιν εcτιν̣
[ ]ατ[ ]τ̣ε̣ ωc το φωc ε̣χετε ινα μη c̣[ ]μαc̣ κ̣α̣τ̣α̣λ̣αβη κ̣αι ο
περιπατων̣ [ ]κοτια [ ]υ̣[ ] οιδεν π̣ου υπαγει̣

αυτοιc: ουτοιc **P^{66*}**; txt **P^{66c}**
μικρον: μει[ ]ν **P^{75}**
μεθ υμων: εν υμιν **P^{66}**; [ ]ν υμιν **P^{75}**

εστι: εστιν **P**^{66} **P**^{75}
εως: ως **P**^{75}
εχετε: εχεται **P**^{66}
οιδε: οιδεν **P**^{66} **P**^{75}

12:36

P^{66} **P**^{75}

36: εως το φως εχετε πιστευετε εις το φως ινα υιοι φωτος γενησθε ταυτα ελαλησεν ο ιησους και απελθων εκρυβη απ αυτων.

DEF: **P**^{75} ως τ̣ο φ[ ] ε̣χετε̣ πιστευε[ ]ε ει̣ς το φως̣... γενη[ ]θ̣ε̣ ταυτ̣α ε̣λαλη̣σεν... απελθων [ ]κ̣ρ̣υβη̣ [ ]π̣ α̣υ̣[ ]ω̣ν

εως: ως **P**^{75}
εχετε: εχεται **P**^{66}
πιστευετε: πιστευεται **P**^{66}
υιοι: ιοι **P**^{66*}; txt **P**^{66*c}
γενησθε: γενησθαι **P**^{66}
ο: OM **P**^{66}

12:37

P^{66} **P**^{75}

37: τοσαυτα δε αυτου σημεια πεποιηκοτος εμπροσθεν αυτων ουκ επιστευον εις αυτον.

DEF: **P**^{75} τοσ[ ]υ̣τα δε... σημ̣εια π̣[ ]π̣ροσθεν... ο̣υκ επιστ̣[

τοσαυτα: ταυτα **P**^{66*}; txt **P**^{66*c}
επιστευον: επιστευσαν **P**^{66}

12:38

P^{66} P^{75}

38: ινα ο λογος ηcαιου του προφητου πληρωθη ον ειπε κυριε τιc επιcτευcε τη ακοη ημων και ο βραχιων κυριου τινι απεκαλυφθη.

DEF: **P^{75}** ... προφη̣[ ]θη κ̅ε̅ τιc επιc̣τευcεν τη̣ [ ]κοη η̣μων
κ̣α̣ι̣... κ̅υ̅ τινι απεκ̣αλυφθη

ον ειπε: OM **P^{75}**
ειπε: ειπεν **P^{66}**
επιcτευcε: επιcτευcεν **P^{66} P^{75}**
βραχιων: βραχειων **P^{66}**

12:39

P^{66} P^{75}

39: δια τουτο ουκ ηδυναντο πιcτευειν οτι παλιν ειπεν ηcαιαc.

DEF: **P^{75}** δι̣α̣ του̣το ουκ ηδ̣υναντο πιcτ[ ]υ̣ειν... η̣cαιαc

ουκ: ου / κυ **P^{66*}**; txt **P^{66*c}**
ηδυναντο: εδυναντο **P^{66}**

12:40

P^{66} P^{75}

40: τετυφλωκεν αυτων τουc οφθαλμουc και πεπωρωκεν αυτων την καρδιαν ινα μη ιδωcι τοιc οφθαλμοιc και νοηcωcι τη καρδια και επιcτραφωcι και ιαcωμαι αυτουc.

DEF: **P^{75}** τετυφλ̣ωκεν... τουc ο[ ]μ̣ουc και επηρωc̣εν αυτων
τη̅ [ ]ν ινα μ[ ] ιδωcι[ ] τ̣οιc οφ[ ] νοηcω[ ]η καρδια
κ̣[ ]τ̣ραφω̣[ ]ι̣[ ] ι̣αcομαι...

πεπωρωκεν: επηρωcεν **P^{66} P^{75}**
ιδωcι: ιδωcι[ ] **P^{75}**
και^{2}: + μη **P^{66*}**; txt **P^{66*c}**
και επιcτραφωcι: και cτραφωcι **P^{66}**; κ[3]τραφω[ ]ι[ ] / **P^{75}**
ιαcωμαι: ιαcομαι **P^{75}**; ειαcομαι **P^{66}**

12:41

P^{66} **P**^{75}

41: ταυτα ειπεν ηϲαιαϲ οτε ειδε την δοξαν αυτου και ελαληϲε περι αυτου.

DEF: **P**^{75} ταυ̣τ̣α ειπεν ηϲαι[ ] οτι... και ε[ ]η̣ϲ̣εν...

οτε: οτι **P**^{66} **P**^{75}
ειδε: ειδεν **P**^{66} **P**^{75}
ελαληϲε: ελαληϲεν **P**^{66}; ε[ ]ηϲεν **P**^{75}

12:42

P^{66} **P**^{75}

42: ομωϲ μεντοι και εκ των αρχοντων πολλοι επιϲτευϲαν ειϲ αυτον αλλα δια τουϲ φαριϲαιουϲ ουχ ωμολογουν ινα μη αποϲυναγωγοι γενωνται.

DEF: **P**^{75} ... και [ ]ω̣ν αρχοντων πολλο̣ι επιϲτευϲ̣αν ε̣[ ]
α̣υτον... ουχ ω̣μολογουν ινα μη απ̣ο̣ϲυναγωγοι...

αποϲυναγωγοι: αποϲυναγωγου̣ **P**^{66*}; txt **P**^{66*c}

12:43

P^{66} **P**^{75}

43: ηγαπηϲαν γαρ την δοξαν των ανθρωπων μαλλον ηπερ την δοξαν του θεου.

DEF: **P**^{75} ... τω[ ] α̣νθρωπων... δοξαν̣...

ηπερ: υπερ **P**^{66*c}; txt **P**^{66*}

12:44

$\mathbf{P}^{66}$ $\mathbf{P}^{75}$

44: ιηcουc δε εκραξε και ειπεν ο πιcτευων ειc εμε ου πιcτευει ειc εμε αλλ ειc τον πεμψαντα με.

DEF: $\mathbf{P}^{75}$ ... πιcτε[ ]ων... πιcṭευει...

εκραξε: εκραξεν $\mathbf{P}^{66}$ $\mathbf{P}^{75}$
αλλ: αλλα $\mathbf{P}^{75}$

12:45

$\mathbf{P}^{66}$ $\mathbf{P}^{75}$

45: και ο θεωρων εμε θεωρει τον πεμψαντα με.

θεωρει: + και $\mathbf{P}^{66*}$; txt $\mathbf{P}^{66*c}$

12:46

$\mathbf{P}^{66}$ $\mathbf{P}^{75}$

46: εγω φωc ειc τον κοcμον εληλυθα ινα παc ο πιcτευων ειc εμε εν τη cκοτια μη μεινη.

DEF: $\mathbf{P}^{75}$ εγω φωc ε̣[ ]c̣ τον... πι̣cτευων... τη [ ]κ̣οτια μ̣[

παc: OM $\mathbf{P}^{66*}$; txt $\mathbf{P}^{66*c}$

12:47

$\mathbf{P}^{66}$ $\mathbf{P}^{75}$

47: και εαν τιc μου ακουcη των ρηματων και μη πιcτευcη εγω ου κρινω αυτον ου γαρ ηλθον ινα κρινω τον κοcμον αλλ ινα cωcω τον κοcμον.

DEF: $\mathbf{P}^{75}$ ... ακο̣υcη [ ]η̣μ̣[ ] και... ου̣ [ ]ι̣νω α̣υ̣τ̣ο̣ν̣... ινα κ̣[ ]
τ̣ον κο̣cμ̣[ ] α̣λ̣[ ]ν̣ κοcμον (teste ed. pr.)

μη: OM $\mathbf{P}^{66*c}$; txt $\mathbf{P}^{66*}$
πιcτευcη: φυλαξη $\mathbf{P}^{75}$; φυλαξη αυτα $\mathbf{P}^{66}$
ινα²: εινα $\mathbf{P}^{66}$

12:48

P^{66} **P**^{75}

48: ο αθετων εμε και μη λαμβανων τα ρηματα μου εχει τον κρινοντα αυτον ο λογος ον ελαληcα εκεινος κρινει αυτον εν τη εcχατη ημερα.

DEF: **P**^{75} ... λαμβ̣α̣νων τα ρηματ̣α̣ μου εχ[ ] τον... λογος [ ]λ̣ηc[ ]οc [ ]ι̣νει αυτον εν τ̣[ ]τ̣[ ]με̣[(teste ed. pr.)

εμε: με **P**^{75}
εχει τον κρινοντα: εκρινοντα **P**^{66*}; txt **P**^{66*c}
εν: OM **P**^{66}

12:49

P^{66} **P**^{75}

49: οτι εγω εξ εμαυτου ουκ ελαληcα αλλ ο πεμψαc με πατηρ αυτοc μοι εντολην εδωκε τι ειπω και τι λαληcω.

DEF: **P**^{75}] ε̣ξ ε̣μ̣α̣υ̣τ̣ο̣[ ]ε̣ π̣α̣τ̣η̣ρ αυτ̣[ ]π̣ω κ̣αι̣ τι λ[(teste ed. pr.)

εδωκε: δεδωκεν **P**^{66}

12:50

P^{66} **P**^{75}

50: και οιδα οτι η εντολη αυτου ζωη αιωνιοc εcτιν α ουν λαλω εγω καθωc ειρηκε μοι ο πατηρ ουτω λαλω.

DEF: **P**^{75}]η̣ [ ]υ̣του̣ ζωη [ ]αλω καθω̣c̣ [ ]τ̣ωc λαλ̣ω (teste ed. pr.)

λαλω εγω: εγω λαλω **P**^{66}; [ ]αλω **P**^{75}
ειρηκε: ειρηκεν **P**^{66}
ουτω: [ ]τωc **P**^{75}

CHAPTER THIRTEEN

P^{66} P^{75} P^{93}

13:1

P^{66} P^{75}

1: προ δε της εορτης του πασχα ειδως ο ιησους οτι εληλυθεν αυτου η ωρα ινα μεταβη εκ του κοσμου τουτου προς τον πατερα αγαπησας τους ιδιους τους εν τω κοσμω εις τελος ηγαπησεν αυτους.

DEF: **P^{75}**]χα ει̣[ ]ω[ ]α̣ ινα̣ [ ] π̣[(teste ed. pr.)

ο ιησους οτι εληλυθεν αυτου η ωρα: [19]α **P^{75}**
εληλυθεν: ηκει **P^{66}**
του κοσμου τουτου: τουτου του κοσμου **P^{66}**
προς τον: προν **P^{66*}**; txt **P^{66*c}**

13:2

P^{66}

2: και δειπνου γενομενου του διαβολου ηδη βεβληκοτος εις την καρδιαν ιουδα σιμωνος ισκαριωτου ινα αυτον παραδω.

δειπνου: διπνου **P^{66}**
γενομενου: γεναμενου **P^{66}**
του: + τε **P^{66}**
ιουδα σιμωνος ισκαριωτου ινα αυτον παραδω: ινα παραδω αυτον ιουδας σιμωννος ισκαριωτης **P^{66}**

13:3

P^{66}

3: ειδως ο ιησους οτι παντα δεδωκεν αυτω ο πατηρ εις τας χειρας και οτι απο θεου εξηλθε και προς τον θεον υπαγει.

ο ιηcουc: OM **P^{66}**
εξηλθε: εξηλθεν **P^{66}**

13:4

P^{66}

4: εγειρεται εκ του δειπνου και τιθηcι τα ιματια και λαβων λεντιον διεζωcεν εαυτον.

εγειρεται: εγειρετε **P^{66}**
δειπνου: διπνου **P^{66}**
τιθηcι: τιθηcιν **P^{66}**

13:5

P^{66}

5: ειτα βαλλει υδωρ ειc τον νιπτηρα και ηρξατο νιπτειν τουc ποδαc των μαθητων και εκμαccειν τω λεντιω ω ην διεζωcμενοc.

νιπτηρα: ποδονι>πτηρα **P^{66}**

13:6

P^{66}

6: ερχεται ουν προc cιμωνα πετρον και λεγει αυτω εκεινοc κυριε cυ μου νιπτειc τουc ποδαc.

και: OM **P^{66}**
εκεινοc: OM **P^{66}**

13:7

P^{66}

7: απεκριθη ιηcουc και ειπεν αυτω ο εγω ποιω cυ ουκ οιδαc αρτι γνωcη δε μετα ταυτα.

αρτι: αρ super rasuram **P^{66*}**; γαρ τι **P^{66*c}**; γ postea del.

13:8

P^{66} **P**^{75}

8: λεγει αυτω πετρος ου μη νιψης τους ποδας μου εις τον αιωνα απεκριθη αυτω ο ιηςους εαν μη νιψω cε ουκ εχεις μερος μετ εμου.

DEF: **P**^{75}]ς̣ τον αιωνα̣ [ ]ρ̣ι̣[ ] μ̣η̣ [ ]χ̣ε̣[(teste ed. pr.)

τους ποδας μου: μου τας ποδας **P**^{66}
ο: OM **P**^{66}

13:9

P^{66} **P**^{75}

9: λεγει αυτω cιμων πετρος κυριε μη τους ποδας μου μονον αλλα και τας χειρας και την κεφαλην.

DEF: **P**^{75} λ̣εγει α̣[ ]μω̣[ ]ο̣δ̣[ ]ν̣[ ]ν [ ]ς̣ κα[(teste ed. pr.)

λεγει: λεγι **P**^{66}
μου: OM **P**^{66}
χειρας: χει **P**^{66*}; txt **P**^{66*c}

13:10

P^{66}

10: λεγει αυτω ο ιηcους ο λελουμενος ου χρειαν εχει η τους ποδας νιψαcθαι αλλ εcτι καθαρος ολος και υμεις καθαροι εcτε αλλ ουχι παντες.

λελουμενος: λειλουμενος **P**^{66*}; ι postea eras.
ου χρειαν εχει: ουκ εχει χρειαν **P**^{66}
η: ει μη **P**^{66}
ποδας: ποδας μονον **P**^{66*}; postea α eras., et littera supra lineam scripta; haec etiam postea eras.
εcτι: εcτιν **P**^{66}
ολος: ολος supra ras. **P**^{66*c}; forsan πιcτος **P**^{66*}

13:11

P[66]

11: ηδει γαρ τον παραδιδοντα αυτον δια τουτο ειπεν ουχι παντες καθαροι εστε.

ειπεν: + οτι **P**[66]

13:12

P[66]

12: οτε ουν ενιψε τους ποδας αυτων και ελαβε τα ιματια αυτου αναπεσων παλιν ειπεν αυτοις γινωσκετε τι πεποιηκα υμιν.

ενιψε: ενιψεν **P**[66]
και: OM **P**[66]
ελαβε: ελαβεν **P**[66]
αυτου: + και **P**[66]
υμιν: υμειν **P**[66]

13:13

P[66]

13: υμεις φωνειτε με ο διδασκαλος και ο κυριος και καλως λεγετε ειμι γαρ.

φωνειτε: φωνιται **P**[66]
λεγετε: λεγεται **P**[66]

13:14

P[66]

14: ει ουν εγω ενιψα υμων τους ποδας ο κυριος και ο διδασκαλος και υμεις οφειλετε αλληλων νιπτειν τους ποδας.

υμεις: υμις **P**[66]
οφειλετε: οφειλεται **P**[66] (ι eras. inter φ et ε)

13:15

$\mathbf{P}^{66}$ $\mathbf{P}^{93}$

15: υποδειγμα γαρ εδωκα υμιν ινα καθως εγω εποιηcα υμιν και υμειc ποιητε.

DEF: $\mathbf{P}^{93}$] και [

υποδειγμα γαρ εδωκα υμιν: υποδιγμα δεδωκα υμειν $\mathbf{P}^{66*}$; υποδιγμα γαρ δεδωκα υμειν $\mathbf{P}^{66*c}$
ποιητε: ποιηται $\mathbf{P}^{66}$

13:16

$\mathbf{P}^{66}$ $\mathbf{P}^{93}$

16: αμην αμην λεγω υμιν ουκ εcτι δουλοc μειζων του κυριου αυτου ουδε αποcτολοc μειζων του πεμψαντοc αυτον.

DEF: $\mathbf{P}^{93}$] λεγω ιμ[ ] του κυρ[ ] μιζων [

υμιν: ιμ[ ] $\mathbf{P}^{93}$
εcτι: εcτιν $\mathbf{P}^{66}$
μειζων²: OM $\mathbf{P}^{66*}$; μιζον $\mathbf{P}^{66*c}$; μιζων $\mathbf{P}^{93}$

13:17

$\mathbf{P}^{66}$ $\mathbf{P}^{93}$

17: ει ταυτα οιδατε μακαριοι εcτε εαν ποιητε αυτα.

DEF: $\mathbf{P}^{93}$ ι ταυτα [ ] πιιτε [

ει: ι $\mathbf{P}^{93}$
οιδατε: οιδαται $\mathbf{P}^{66}$
ποιητε: ποιηται $\mathbf{P}^{66}$; πιιτε $\mathbf{P}^{93}$

13:18

$\mathbf{P}^{66}$

18: ου περι παντων υμων λεγω εγω οιδα ουc εξελεξαμην αλλ ινα η γραφη πληρωθη ο τρωγων μετ εμου τον αρτον επηρεν επ εμε την πτερναν αυτου.

επ: OM $\mathbf{P}^{66*}$; txt $\mathbf{P}^{66*c}$

13:19

$\mathbf{P}^{66}$

19: απ αρτι λεγω υμιν προ του γενεcθαι ινα οταν γενηται πιcτευcητε οτι εγω ειμι.

απ αρτι λεγω υμιν προ: OM $\mathbf{P}^{66*}$; txt $\mathbf{P}^{66c}$
οταν γενηται πιcτευcητε: πιcτευcηται οταν γενηται $\mathbf{P}^{66}$
οτι: οcτι $\mathbf{P}^{66*}$; txt $\mathbf{P}^{66*c}$
ειμι: μι $\mathbf{P}^{66}$

13:20

$\mathbf{P}^{66}$

20: αμην αμην λεγω υμιν ο λαμβανων εαν τινα πεμψω εμε λαμβανει ο δε εμε λαμβανων λαμβανει τον πεμψαντα με.

υμιν: υμειν $\mathbf{P}^{66}$
εαν: αν $\mathbf{P}^{66*}$; txt $\mathbf{P}^{66*c}$
λαμβανει^{2}: + και $\mathbf{P}^{66*}$; txt $\mathbf{P}^{66*c}$
πεμψαντα: μεψαντα $\mathbf{P}^{66*}$; txt $\mathbf{P}^{66*c}$

13:21

$\mathbf{P}^{66}$

21: ταυτα ειπων ο ιηcουc εταραχθη τω πνευματι και εμαρτυρηcε και ειπεν αμην αμην λεγω υμιν οτι ειc εξ υμων παραδωcει με.

ο: OM $\mathbf{P}^{66*}$; txt $\mathbf{P}^{66*c}$
πνευματι: $\overline{\text{πνα}}$ $\mathbf{P}^{66*}$; txt $\mathbf{P}^{66*c}$
εμαρτυρηcε: εμαρτυρηcεν $\mathbf{P}^{66}$
λεγω: λεγων $\mathbf{P}^{66*}$; txt $\mathbf{P}^{66*c}$

13:22

P66

22: εβλεπον ουν εις αλληλους οι μαθηται απορουμενοι περι τινος λεγει.

μαθηται: + αυτου **P66**

13:23

P66

23: ην δε ανακειμενος εις των μαθητων αυτου εν τω κολπω του ιηςου ον ηγαπα ο ιηςους.

εις: + εκ **P66**
κολπω: κοπω **P66***; txt **P66*c**
ο: OM **P66***; txt **P66*c**

13:24

P66

24: νευει ουν τουτω ςιμων πετρος πυθεςθαι τις αν ειη περι ου λεγει.

πυθεςθαι τις αν ειη: forsan ϗ λεγει αυτω εςτιν **P66***; txt **P66*c**
λεγει: ειπεν **P66*c**; txt **P66***

13:25

P66

25: επιπεςων δε εκεινος επι το ςτηθος του ιηςου λεγει αυτω κυριε τις εςτιν.

επιπεςων: αναπεςων **P66***; txt **P66*c**
δε: ουν **P66**
εκεινος: + ουτως **P66**

13:26

P[66]

26: αποκρινεται ο ιηϲουϲ εκεινοϲ εϲτιν ω εγω βαψαϲ το ψωμιον επιδωϲω και εμβαψαϲ το ψωμιον διδωϲιν ιουδα ϲιμωνοϲ ιϲκαριωτη.

ο: OM **P**[66]
εμβαψαϲ: ψαϲ **P**[66*]; txt **P**[66*c]

13:27

P[66]

27: και μετα το ψωμιον τοτε ειϲηλθεν ειϲ εκεινον ο ϲαταναϲ λεγει ουν αυτω ο ιηϲουϲ ο ποιειϲ ποιηϲον ταχιον.

ταχιον: ταχειον **P**[66]

13:28

P[66]

28: τουτο δε ουδειϲ εγνω των ανακειμενων προϲ τι ειπεν αυτω.

13:29

P[66]

29: τινεϲ γαρ εδοκουν επει το γλωϲϲοκομον ειχεν ο ιουδαϲ οτι λεγει αυτω ο ιηϲουϲ αγοραϲον ων χρειαν εχομεν ειϲ την εορτην η τοιϲ πτωχοιϲ ινα τι δω.

γαρ: δε **P**[66]
επει: επι **P**[66]

13:30

P^{66}

30: λαβων ουν το ψωμιον εκεινος ευθεως εξηλθεν ην δε νυξ.

ευθεως εξηλθεν: εξηλθεν ευθυς **P^{66}**

13:31

P^{66}

31: οτε ουν εξηλθε λεγει ο ιηcουc νυν εδοξαcθη ο υιοc του ανθρωπου και ο θεοc εδοξαcθη εν αυτω.

εξηλθε: εξηλθεν **P^{66}**
ο^{1}: OM **P^{66}**
31-32 και ο θεοc εδοξαcθη εν αυτω ει ο θεοc εδοξαcθη εν αυτω και: και ο θεοc εδοξαcθη εν αυτω κς **P^{66*}**; και ο θεοc εδοξαcθη εν αυτω **P^{66*c}**

13:32

P^{66}

32: ει ο θεοc εδοξαcθη εν αυτω και ο θεοc δοξαcει αυτον εν εαυτω και ευθυc δοξαcει αυτον.

ει ο θεοc εδοξαcθη εν αυτω και: vid. v. 31
εαυτω: αυτω **P^{66}**

13:33

P^{66}

33: τεκνια ετι μικρον μεθ υμων ειμι ζητηcετε με και καθωc ειπον τοιc ιουδαιοιc οτι οπου υπαγω εγω υμειc ου δυναcθε ελθειν και υμιν λεγω αρτι.

ζητηcετε: ζητηcεται **P^{66}**
οτι: OM **P^{66}**
εγω: OM **P^{66}**
υμειc: υμιc **P^{66}**
δυναcθε: δυναcθαι **P^{66}**
υμιν: υμειν **P^{66}**

λεγω: + πλην **P66**

13:34

P66

34: εντολην καινην διδωμι υμιν ινα αγαπατε αλληλους καθως ηγαπηςα υμας ινα και υμεις αγαπατε αλληλους.

καθως: + εγω **P66**
αγαπατε αλληλους: αλληλους αγαπαται **P66**

13:35

P66

35: εν τουτω γνωςονται παντες οτι εμοι μαθηται εςτε εαν αγαπην εχητε εν αλληλοις.

εμοι: εμου **P66**
μαθηται εςτε: εςται αθηται **P66***; εςται μαθηται **P66*c**
εχητε: εχηται **P66**

13:36

P66

36: λεγει αυτω ςιμων πετρος κυριε που υπαγεις απεκριθη αυτω ο ιηςους οπου υπαγω ου δυναςαι μοι νυν ακολουθηςαι υςτερον δε ακολουθηςεις μοι.

ο: OM **P66**
υςτερον δε ακολουθηςεις: ακολουθηςις δε υςτερον **P66**
μοι: OM **P66**

13:37

P66

37: λεγει αυτω ο πετρος κυριε διατι ου δυναμαι σοι ακολουθησαι αρτι την ψυχην μου υπερ σου θησω.

δυναμαι: δυναμε **P66**
ακολουθησαι: ακολουθησε **P66**
την ψυχην μου υπερ σου: υπερ σου την ψυχην μου **P66**

13:38

P66

38: απεκριθη αυτω ο ιησους την ψυχην σου υπερ εμου θησεις αμην αμην λεγω σοι ου μη αλεκτωρ φωνησει εως ου απαρνηση με τρις.

απεκριθη: αποκρινεται **P66**
αυτω: OM **P66**
ο: OM **P66**
φωνησει: φωνηση **P66**
απαρνηση: αρνηση **P66**

CHAPTER FOURTEEN

P[66] **P**[75]

14:1

P[66]

1: μη ταραccεcθω υμων η καρδια πιcτευετε εις τον θεον και εις εμε πιcτευετε.

πιcτευετε[1]: πιcτευεται **P**[66]
πιcτευετε[2]: πιcτευεται **P**[66]

14:2

P[66]

2: εν τη οικια του πατροc μου μοναι πολλαι ειcιν ει δε μη ειπον αν υμιν πορευομαι ετοιμαcαι τοπον υμιν.

ειπον αν: αν ειπον **P**[66*]; txt **P**[66*c]
υμιν: υμειν **P**[66*]; + οτι **P**[66*c]
πορευομαι: πορευομε **P**[66]
τοπον υμιν: υμειν τοπον **P**[66]

14:3

P[66]

3: και εαν πορευθω και ετοιμαcω υμιν τοπον παλιν ερχομαι και παραληψομαι υμαc προc εμαυτον ινα οπου ειμι εγω και υμειc ητε.

υμιν: υμειν **P**[66]
παλιν ερχομαι: bis **P**[66*]; txt **P**[66c]
παραληψομαι: παραλημψομαι **P**[66]
ειμι: ιμι **P**[66]
ητε: ηται **P**[66]

14:4

P[66]

4: και οπου εγω υπαγω οιδατε και την οδον οιδατε.

εγω: OM **P[66]**
οιδατε[1]: οιδαται **P[66]**
και την οδον οιδατε: και την οδον οιδαται **P[66*]**; την οδον **P[66*c]**

14:5

P[66]

5: λεγει αυτω θωμας κυριε ουκ οιδαμεν που υπαγεις και πως δυναμεθα την οδον ειδεναι.

και: OM **P[66]**

14:6

P[66]

6: λεγει αυτω ο ιηcουc εγω ειμι η οδοc και η αληθεια και η ζωη ουδειc ερχεται προc τον πατερα ει μη δι εμου.

ο: OM **P[66]**
αληθεια: αληθια **P[66]**

14:7

P[66]

7: ει εγνωκειτε με και τον πατερα μου εγνωκειτε αν και απ αρτι γινωcκετε αυτον και εωρακατε αυτον.

εγνωκειτε[1]: εγνωκαται **P[66]**
εγνωκειτε[2]: γνωcεcθε **P[66]**
αν: OM **P[66]**
γινωcκετε: γιωνcκεται **P[66]**
εωρακατε: εωρακαται **P[66]**

14:8

P^{66} P^{75}

8: λεγει αυτω φιλιππος κυριε δειξον ημιν τον πατερα και αρκει ημιν.

DEF: **P^{75}**]μ̣ιν

ημιν^{1}: ημειν **P^{66}**
ημιν^{2}: ημειν **P^{66}**

14:9

P^{66} P^{75}

9: λεγει αυτω ο ιηcουc τοcουτον χρονον μεθ υμων ειμι και ουκ εγνωκαc με φιλιππε ο εωρακωc εμε εωρακε τον πατερα και πωc cυ λεγειc δειξον ημιν τον πατερα.

DEF: **P^{75}** ... ο̣ ι̣̅[ ] ειμι και ουκ εγνωκαc μ̣[ ] εμε... πατ̣[ ]ξον...

λεγει: λεγι **P^{66}**
ο^{1}: OM **P^{66}**
εγνωκαc: ενωκαc **P^{66*}**; txt **P^{66*c}**
εμε: εμαι **P^{66}**
εωρακε: εωρακεν και **P^{75}**
και^{2}: OM **P^{66}**

14:10

P^{66} P^{75}

10: ου πιϲτευειϲ οτι εγω εν τω πατρι και ο πατηρ εν εμοι εϲτι τα ρηματα α εγω λαλω υμιν απ εμαυτου ου λαλω ο δε πατηρ ο εν εμοι μενων αυτοϲ ποιει τα εργα.

DEF: **P^{75}** ου [ ] εν... ο πατ̣[ ] ε̣μοι εϲτιν τ[ ] ρ̣ηματα... υμ̣[ ]π̣ εμαυτου ου λαλω̣... εμοι μ̣[ ] π̣οιει...

εϲτι: εϲτιν **P^{66} P^{75}**
λαλω^{1}: λεγω **P^{75}**
υμιν: υμειν **P^{66}**
ου^{2}: OM **P^{66*}**; txt **P^{66*c}**
ο^{3}: OM **P^{66} P^{75}**
εμοι^{2}: papyrus asper inter ε et μ **P^{66}**
αυτοϲ ποιει τα εργα: ποιει τα εργα αυτου **P^{66}**; ποιει τα εργα αυτοϲ **P^{75}**

14:11

P^{66} P^{75}

11: πιϲτευετε μοι οτι εγω εν τω πατρι και ο πατηρ εν εμοι ει δε μη δια τα εργα αυτα πιϲτευετε μοι.

DEF: **P^{75}** ... οτι [ ]ω π̅ρ̅ι̅... δε μη δια τα [ ]ου... (teste ed. pr.)

πιϲτευετε^{1}: πιϲτευεται **P^{66}**
εν^{2}: ο **P^{66*}**; txt **P^{66c}**
αυτα: αυτου **P^{66*}**; txt **P^{66*c}**; [ ]ου **P^{75}**
πιϲτευετε^{2}: πιϲτευεται **P^{66}**
μοι^{2}: OM **P^{66} P^{75}**

14:12

P^{66} P^{75}

12: αμην αμην λεγω υμιν ο πιϲτευων ειϲ εμε τα εργα α εγω ποιω κακεινοϲ ποιηϲει και μειζονα τουτων ποιηϲει οτι εγω προϲ τον πατερα μου πορευομαι.

DEF: **P^{75}** ... υμ[ ]ν̣ ο πι[ ]τευων...κακειν̣[ ]ϲ ποιηϲει... ποι̣η̣ϲει οτ[ ]γω προϲ...

αμην αμην: αμην αμη **P**^{66*}; αμην **P**^{66*c1}; txt **P**^{66*c2}
υμιν: υμειν **P**^{66}
ο: OM **P**^{66*}; txt **P**^{66*c}
πιστευων: ειστευων **P**^{66*}; πειστευων **P**^{66*c}
ποιησει: ποιησι **P**^{66}
και μειζονα τουτων: κακει μιζονα **P**^{66*}; και μιζονα τουτων **P**^{66*c}
μου: OM **P**^{66} **P**^{75}
πορευομαι: πορευσομαι **P**^{75}

14:13

P^{66} **P**^{75}

13: και ο τι αν αιτησητε εν τω ονοματι μου τουτο ποιησω ινα δοξασθη ο πατηρ εν τω υιω.

DEF: **P**^{75} και ο [ ]ι αν αιτ̣[ ] ε̣ν... ποι[ ]σ̣ω ινα̣ [ ]η̣ρ̣...

τι: OM **P**^{66}
αν: εαν **P**^{66}
αιτησητε: αιτησηται **P**^{66}; αιτ[3] **P**^{75}
ο²: OM **P**^{66}

14:14

P^{66} **P**^{75}

14: εαν τι αιτησητε εν τω ονοματι μου εγω ποιησω.

DEF: **P**^{75} ... αιτ[ ]ε̣ [ ]ν̣οματι... ποιησ[

αιτησητε: αιτησηται μαι **P**^{66}
εν τω ονοματι: [7]ν̣οματι **P**^{75}
μου: + τουτο **P**^{66*c} **P**^{75}; txt **P**^{66*}
εγω: OM **P**^{75}

14:15

P^{66} P^{75}

15: εαν αγαπατε με ταc εντολαc ταc εμαc τηρηcατε.

DEF: **P^{75}**]μ̣ε... τηρη̣[ ]τ̣ε̣

αγαπατε: αγαπηται **P^{66*}**; αγαπαται **P^{66*c}**
τηρηcατε: τηρηcηται **P^{66}**

14:16

P^{66} P^{75}

16: και εγω ερωτηcω τον πατερα και αλλον παρακλητον δωcει υμιν ινα μενη μεθ υμων ειc τον αιωνα.

DEF: **P^{75}** κ̣[ ] ερωτηcω... παρακλη̣τ̣ο̣ν δωcει υ̣μιν... υμων̣ ε̣ιc...

και εγω: καγω **P^{66}**; κ[3] **P^{75}**
αλλον: αλλα **P^{66*}**; txt **P^{66*c}**
υμιν: υμειν **P^{66}**
μενη μεθ υμων ειc τον αιωνα: μεθ υμων ειc τον αιωνα η **P^{75}**

14:17

P^{66} P^{75}

17: το πνευμα τηc αληθειαc ο ο κοcμοc ου δυναται λαβειν οτι ου θεωρει αυτο ουδε γινωcκει αυτο υμειc δε γινωcκετε αυτο οτι παρ υμιν μενει και εν υμιν εcται.

DEF: **P^{75}** ... κοcμ̣ο̣c ου δυ[ ]αται... θεωρε̣ι αυτ̣ο ο̣[ ]δε γεινω̣cκει υμειc γε̣ι̣ν̣ωcκετε αυτο οτι̣... κα̣[ ]α̣ι̣ (teste ed. pr.)

αληθειαc: αληθιαc **P^{66}**
αυτο^{1}: αυτον **P^{66*}**; txt **P^{66*c}**
γινωcκει: γεινωcκει **P^{66} P^{75}**
αυτο^{2}: OM **P^{66*} P^{75}**; txt **P^{66*c}**
δε: OM **P^{66} P^{75}**
γινωcκετε: γεινωcκεται **P^{66}**; γεινωcκετε **P^{75}**
αυτο^{3}: αυτον **P^{66*}**; txt **P^{66*c}**
υμιν^{1}: υμειν **P^{66}**
εcται: εcτι̅ **P^{66*}**; txt **P^{66*c}**

14:18

P^{66} P^{75}

18: ουκ αφηϲω υμαϲ ορφανουϲ ερχομαι προϲ υμαϲ.

DEF: **P^{66}** ... ορφανουϲ ε[ ]χομαι...
P^{75}]η̣[ ] υμ̣α̣ϲ ορφανου̣[ ]α̣ι̣ π̣ροϲ υμ̣[(teste ed. pr.)

14:19

P^{66} P^{75}

19: ετι μικρον και ο κοϲμοϲ με ουκ ετι θεωρει υμειϲ δε θεωρειτε με οτι εγω ζω και υμειϲ ζηϲεϲθε.

DEF: **P^{66}** ετι μικρον κ̣[ ] ο... ζω̣...
P^{75} ε̣τι μεικρον̣ [ ]α̣ι ο κοϲμοϲ με [ ]υκ ετι θεωρει υ̣μειϲ... με̣... υμε̣[ ] ζηϲετε

μικρον: μεικρον **P^{75}**
δε: OM **P^{66}**
θεωρειτε: θεωριται **P^{66}**
εγω ζω: ζω εγω **P^{75}**
ζηϲεϲθε: ζηϲετε **P^{75}**

14:20

P^{66} P^{75}

20: εν εκεινη τη ημερα γνωϲεϲθε υμειϲ οτι εγω εν τω πατρι μου και υμειϲ εν εμοι καγω εν υμιν.

DEF: **P^{66}** εν εκει[ ] τη... υμειϲ̣ [ ] εγω... και υμ[ ] εν εμοι...
P^{75} ... ημε̣ρα υμειϲ γνωϲ̣ε̣ϲθε...

γνωϲεϲθε υμειϲ: υμειϲ γνωϲεϲθε **P^{75}**

14:21

$\mathbf{P^{66}}$ $\mathbf{P^{75}}$

21: ο εχων τας εντολας μου και τηρων αυτας εκεινος εστιν ο αγαπων με ο δε αγαπων με αγαπηθησεται υπο του πατρος μου και εγω αγαπησω αυτον και εμφανισω αυτω εμαυτον.

DEF: $\mathbf{P^{66}}$ ο [ ]χων... και [ ]ρων... εστιν ο αγ[ ]πων με...
$\mathbf{P^{75}}$ ... τ̣ηρων... εστι̣ν̣... με [ ]ε αγαπων με τηρηθης̣[ ]τ̣[ ] υ̣πο...
αγαπησω αυ[ ] ε̣ν̣φανισω αυτω ε̣μαυτον

αγαπηθησεται: τηρηθης[ ]τ[ ] $\mathbf{P^{75}}$
και εγω: καγω $\mathbf{P^{66}}$ $\mathbf{P^{75}}$
εμφανιζω: ενφανιζω $\mathbf{P^{75}}$

14:22

$\mathbf{P^{66}}$ $\mathbf{P^{75}}$

22: λεγει αυτω ιουδας ουχ ο ισκαριωτης κυριε τι γεγονεν οτι ημιν μελλεις εμφανιζειν σεαυτον και ουχι τω κοσμω.

DEF: $\mathbf{P^{66}}$ ... σεαυ[ ]ον και...
$\mathbf{P^{75}}$ λεγει αυ[ ]δας ουχ... γεγονεν [ ]μ̣ι̣ν μελλεις...

λεγει: λεγι $\mathbf{P^{66}}$
αυτω: προς αυτον $\mathbf{P^{66}}$
ο: OM $\mathbf{P^{75}}$
κυριε: + ϛ $\mathbf{P^{66c}}$; txt $\mathbf{P^{66*}}$
ημιν: ημειν $\mathbf{P^{66}}$
εμφανιζειν: ενφανιζειν $\mathbf{P^{75}}$

14:23

$\mathbf{P^{66}}$ $\mathbf{P^{75}}$

23: απεκριθη ο ιησους και ειπεν αυτω εαν τις αγαπα με τον λογον μου τηρησει και ο πατηρ μου αγαπησει αυτον και προς αυτον ελευσομεθα και μονην παρ αυτω ποιησομεν.

DEF: $\mathbf{P^{66}}$ απε[ ]ριθη... τις [ ]γαπα... τηρη[ ] και ο... αγαπησει
αυτο̄ [ ] παρ αυτον εισελευσομεθα [ ] μονην... ποιησο[ ]θ̣α
$\mathbf{P^{75}}$ ... α̣υτω... κ̣αι π̣[ ]ο̣ς α̣υτον... κ̣α̣ι̣ μονην παρ̣ [ ]ο̣ιησομ̣ε̣θα

ο^{1}: OM **P**^{66} **P**^{75}
προc: παρ **P**^{66*}; txt **P**^{66*c}
ελευcομεθα: ειcελευcομεθα **P**^{66*}; txt **P**^{66*c}
ποιηcομεν: ποιηcο[ ]α **P**^{66}; [ ]οιηcομεθα **P**^{75}

14:24

P^{66} **P**^{75}

24: ο μη αγαπων με τουc λογουc μου ου τηρει και ο λογοc ον ακουετε ουκ εcτιν εμοc αλλα του πεμψαντοc με πατροc.

DEF: **P**^{66} ... λογουc [ ]υ̣ ου... ακου[ ]α̣ι ουκ... του [ ]εμψαντοc...
P^{75} ... με τ̣[ ]γου̣[ ] ο̣υ τηρει... ακουε̣τε ουκ ε̣[ ]ν εμοc...
πεμψ[ ]ν̣τοc με πα̣[ ]οc

τουc: του **P**^{66*}; txt **P**^{66*c}
ακουετε: ακου[ ]αι **P**^{66}

14:25

P^{66} **P**^{75}

25: ταυτα λελαληκα υμιν παρ υμιν μενων.

DEF: **P**^{75} ... παρ υμιν [ ]ω̣ν

υμιν^{1}: υμειν **P**^{66}
υμιν^{2}: υμειν **P**^{66}

14:26

P^{66} **P**^{75}

26: ο δε παρακλητοc το πνευμα το αγιον ο πεμψει ο πατηρ εν τω ονοματι μου εκεινοc υμαc διδαξει παντα και υπομνηcει υμαc παντα α ειπον υμιν.

DEF: **P**^{66} ... ειπον υ[
P^{75} ο δε παρακλητοc [ ]η̣ρ̣ [ ]ν τω [ ] υ̣μ̣αc διδαξει πα̣[ ] υ̣μαc
παντα α̣ [(teste ed. pr.)

πεμψει: + υμιν **P**^{66*c}; txt **P**^{66*}

14:27

P^{75}

27: ειρηνην αφιημι υμιν, ειρηνην την εμην διδωμι υμιν ου καθως ο κοcμοc διδωcιν εγω διδωμι υμιν μη ταραccεcθω υμων η καρδια μηδε δειλιατω.

DEF: **P**^{75} αφιη]μ̣[ ]μ̣η̣ν δι̣[ ] ο̣υ̣ [ ] διδωcιν̣ [ ]cθω υμω[(teste ed. pr.)

14:28

P^{75}

28: ηκουcατε οτι εγω ειπον υμιν υπαγω και ερχομαι προc υμαc ει ηγαπατε με εχαρητε αν οτι ειπον πορευομαι προc τον πατερα οτι ο πατηρ μου μειζων μου εcτι.

DEF: **P**^{75}]κουcατ̣[ ] ερχομα̣[ ] π̣[ ] α̣ν̣ ο̣[ ] π̣α̣τ̣[(teste ed. pr.)

οτι ειπον πορευομαι προc τον πατερα οτι ο: ο[27] **P**^{75}

14:29

P^{66} **P**^{75}

29: και νυν ειρηκα υμιν πριν γενεcθαι ινα οταν γενηται πιcτευcητε.

DEF: **P**^{66}]μ̣ειν πριν [ ]ν γενηται πιcτευ[
P^{75}]α̣ [ ]μ[ ]τ̣[(teste ed. pr.)

υμιν:]μειν **P**^{66}

14:30

P^{66}

30: ουκ ετι πολλα λαληcω μεθ υμων ερχεται γαρ ο του κοcμου τουτου αρχων και εν εμοι ουκ εχει ουδεν.

DEF: **P**^{66}] πολλα λαληcω . [ ]χεται γαρ ο του [

14:31

31: αλλ ινα γνω ο κοcμοc οτι αγαπω τον πατερα και καθωc
ενετειλατο μοι ο πατηρ ουτω ποιω εγειρεcθε αγωμεν εντευθεν.

CHAPTER FIFTEEN

P^{22} **P**^{66} **P**^{75}

15:1

1: εγω ειμι η αμπελος η αληθινη και ο πατηρ μου ο γεωργος εστι.

15:2

P^{66}

2: παν κλημα εν εμοι μη φερον καρπον αιρει αυτο και παν το καρπον φερον καθαιρει αυτο ινα πλειονα καρπον φερη.

DEF: **P**^{66}]ν̣α̣ [

15:3

P^{66}

3: ηδη υμεις καθαροι εστε δια τον λογον ον λελαληκα υμιν.

DEF: **P**^{66}] ε̣στε δια τον̣ [ ]κα εν υμειν

λελαληκα: + εν **P**^{66*}; txt **P**^{66*c}
υμιν: υμειν **P**^{66}

15:4

P^{66}

4: μεινατε εν εμοι καγω εν υμιν καθως το κλημα ου δυναται καρπον φερειν αφ εαυτου εαν μη μεινη εν τη αμπελω ουτως ουδε υμεις εαν μη εν εμοι μεινητε.

DEF: **P**^{66} μ[ ]μοι καγω εν υμ̣[ ] το κημα ου δυν̣[ ]ερειν αφ εαυτ[ ]αν μη μει[ ]η εν τη αμπελ[ ] ο̣υ̣τως κα[ ]ν εμοι μενων

κλημα: κημα **P**^{66*}; txt **P**^{66*c}
ουδε υμεις εαν μη εν: κα[1 / 1-2]ν **P**^{66}

μεινητε: μενων **P**[66]

15:5

P[66]

5: εγω ειμι η αμπελος υμεις τα κληματα ο μενων εν εμοι καγω εν αυτω ουτος φερει καρπον πολυν οτι χωρις εμου ου δυνασθε ποιειν ουδεν.

DEF: **P**[66] ... η [ ]μπελος... κληματ[ ]ενων εν ε[ ]οι καγω
ε[ ]ω ουτος φ[ ]ει καρπον πολυν [ ]ις εμου ου δυνασθε
π[ ]εν

15:6

P[66]

6: εαν μη τις μεινη εν εμοι εβληθη εξω ως το κλημα και εξηρανθη και συναγουσιν αυτα και εις πυρ βαλλουσι και καιεται.

DEF: **P**[66] ... εν [ ]θη... κλημα [ ]ρανθη και συναγουσιν
[ ]ι ει[ ] πυρ βαλλουσιν [ ]τα και κα[ ]αι

εαν: ε **P**[66*]; txt **P**[66*c]
μεινη: μενη **P**[66]
εις πυρ: ει[3] πυρ **P**[66]
βαλλουσι: βαλλουσιν [ ]τα **P**[66]

15:7

P[66] **P**[75]

7: εαν μεινητε εν εμοι και τα ρηματα μου εν υμιν μεινη ο εαν θελητε αιτησεσθε και γενησεται υμιν.

DEF: **P**[66] εα[ ] εμοι και τα ρηματ[ ]εινη ο εαν
θελ̣η̣τ̣α̣[ ]σθαι και γ[ ]σεται
P[75]] μ̣ε̣ινη̣[ ] ρ̣η̣[ ]μ̣[ ]ν̣ [ ]η̣τ̣[γ]ε̣[

μεινη: [ ]εινει **P**[66*c]; [ ]εινη **P**[66*]
θελητε: θελητα[ ] **P**[66]
αιτησεσθε: [ ]σθαι **P**[66]
υμιν²: OM **P**[66]

15:8

P^{66} **P**^{75}

8: εν τουτω εδοξαcθη ο πατηρ μου ινα καρπον πολυν φερητε και γενηcεcθε εμοι μαθηται.

DEF: **P**^{66} ... εδοξαcθ[ ]π̅ρ̅ μου ινα κα[ ]ον πλιονα φερηται και γεν[ ]θαι μου μαθηται
P^{75}]υ̣[ ]η̣ ο̣ π̣[ ]ο̣υ [ ]π̣[

πολυν φερητε: πλιονα φερηται **P**^{66}
γενηcεcθε: γεν[ ]θαι **P**^{66}
εμοι: μου **P**^{66}

15:9

P^{66}

9: καθωc ηγαπηcε με ο πατηρ καγω ηγαπηcα υμαc μεινατε εν τη αγαπη τη εμη.

DEF: **P**^{66} καθω[ ] η[ ]ηcεν με... υμαc [ ]ιναται εν τ[ ]γαπη τη εμη

ηγαπηcε: η[ ]ηcεν **P**^{66}
μεινατε: [ ]ιναται **P**^{66}

15:10

P^{66}

10: εαν ταc εντολαc μου τηρηcητε μενειτε εν τη αγαπη μου καθωc εγω ταc εντολαc του πατροc μου τετηρηκα και μενω αυτου εν τη αγαπη.

DEF: **P**^{66} τηρηcηται μεν[ ]αι εν τη αγαπη καθ[ ] τ̣ου π̅ρ̅c̅ ταc εντολα[ ]α και μενω αυτου [

εαν ταc εντολαc μου: OM **P**^{66*}; εαν τα̣c εντολαc μο[ ] **P**^{66*c}
τηρηcετε: τηρηcηται **P**^{66}
μενειτε: μεν[ ]αι **P**^{66}
μου²: OM **P**^{66*}; txt **P**^{66*c}
ταc εντολαc του πατροc μου: του π̅ρ̅c̅ ταc εντολα[ ] **P**^{66}

15:11

P[66]

11: ταυτα λελαληκα υμιν ινα η χαρα η εμη εν υμιν μεινη και η χαρα υμων πληρωθη.

DEF: **P**[66]]αυτα λελαληκα [ ] η εμη [ ] υμ[ ]μω[ ]ρωθη

15:12

P[66]

12: αυτη εστιν η εντολη η εμη ινα αγαπατε αλληλους καθως ηγαπηςα υμας.

DEF: **P**[66] α[ ] η εντολη η εμη ιν[ ]λληλους ως ηγ[

καθως: ως **P**[66]

15:13

P[66]

13: μειζονα ταυτης αγαπην ουδεις εχει ινα τις την ψυχην αυτου θη υπερ των φιλων αυτου.

DEF: **P**[66]]ιζονα ταυτης [ ]γαπην ο[ ]δεις... εαυτου θ[ ] υπερ...

τις: OM **P**[66]
αυτου: την εαυτου **P**[66]

15:14

P[66]

14: υμεις φιλοι μου εστε εαν ποιητε οσα εγω εντελλομαι υμιν.

DEF: **P**[66] υμεις φηλ̣[ ] μου... εντελλ[ ]μαι υμιν

φιλοι: φηλ[ ] **P**[66]
ποιητε: ποιηται **P**[66]
οσα: α **P**[66]

15:15

P^{66}

15: ουκετι υμας λεγω δουλους οτι ο δουλος ουκ οιδε τι ποιει αυτου ο κυριος υμας δε ειρηκα φιλους οτι παντα α ηκουσα παρα του πατρος μου εγνωριcα υμιν.

DEF: **P^{66}** ... ποιει α[ ]του ο κ̅c̅ υμας δε̣ λ̣ε̣γω̣ [ ]λους οτ[ ]ντα α̣ [ ]υcα προ το[ ] μου εγ[ ]ωριcα υμιν

υμας λεγω: λεγω υμας **P^{66}**
οιδε: οιδεν **P^{66}**
ειρηκα: λεγω **P^{66}**
παρα: προ **P^{66*}**; txt **P^{66*c}**

15:16

P^{66}

16: ουχ υμεις με εξελεξαcθε αλλ εγω εξελεξαμην υμας και εθηκα υμας ινα υμεις υπαγητε και καρπον φερητε και ο καρπος υμων μενη ινα ο τι αν αιτηcητε τον πατερα εν τω ονοματι μου δω υμιν.

DEF: **P^{66}** ουχ υμιc [ ] εξελεξ[ ]cθαι αλλ εγω εξ[ ] υμας και εθηκα ιν υμε[ ]ται κα κα[ ]πον ο φερηται κ[ ] υμων μ̣[ ]νη ι̣ν̣[ ] ο τι αν α̣[ ] τον π̅ρ̅α̅ [ ] τω ον[ ]ματι μο̣[

υμεις: υμιc **P^{66}**
εξελεξαcθε: εξελεξ[ ]cθαι **P^{66}**
υμας²: OM **P^{66}**
ινα υμεις: ιν υμε[ ] **P^{66*}**; υμε[ ] ιν **P^{66*c}**
υπαγητε: [ ]ται **P^{66}**
και²: κα **P^{66*}**; txt **P^{66*c}**
καρπον: + ο **P^{66*}**; forsan puncto del. **P^{66*c}**
φερητε: φερηται **P^{66}**

15:17

P^{66}

17: ταυτα εντελλομαι υμιν ινα αγαπατε αλληλους.

DEF: **P^{66}** ταυτα ε[ ]λλομαι ... αλληλ[ ]c

ινα: OM **P66***; ιν̣[ ] **P66*c**
αγαπατε: αγαπαται **P66**

15:18

P66

18: ει ο κοϲμοϲ υμαϲ μιϲει γινωϲκετε οτι εμε πρωτον υμων μεμιϲηκεν.

DEF: **P66** ... γινω[ ]κετε... πρ[ ]ον υ̣μων μ[ ]μειϲηκεν

μιϲει: εμιϲει ϲε **P66***; εμιϲει **P66*c**
μεμιϲηκεν: μ[ ]μειϲηκεν **P66**

15:19

P66

19: ει εκ του κοϲμου ητε ο κοϲμοϲ αν το ιδιον εφιλει οτι δε εκ του κοϲμου ουκ εϲτε αλλ εγω εξελεξαμην υμαϲ εκ του κοϲμου δια τουτο μιϲει υμαϲ ο κοϲμοϲ.

DEF: **P66** ... ητ[ ] ο κοϲμοϲ... οτ[ ] δ̣ε... κοϲμου δ[ ]α̣ του[ ] υμαϲ μιϲει ο κοϲμοϲ (teste ed. pr.)

το: τον **P66**
εκ του κοϲμου ουκ: ουκ εκ του τουτου κοϲμου **P66***; ουκ εκ του κοϲμου **P66*c**
μιϲει υμαϲ: υμαϲ μιϲει **P66**

15:20

P66

20: μνημονευετε του λογου ου εγω ειπον υμιν ουκ εϲτι δουλοϲ μειζων του κυριου αυτου ει εμε εδιωξαν και υμαϲ διωξουϲιν ει τον λογον μου ετηρηϲαν και τον υμετερον τηρηϲουϲιν.

DEF: **P66** μνημ̣ο̣νευεται του... ειπον υ̣[ ]ν ουκ... αυτου [ ]ωξαν... διωξουϲι̅ [ ]ν λογον... τον υ[ ]ερον τηρη[(teste ed. pr.)

μνημονευετε: μνημονευεται **P66**
εϲτι: εϲτιν **P66**

15:21

P[66]

21: αλλα ταυτα παντα ποιηcουcιν υμιν δια το ονομα μου οτι ουκ οιδαcι τον πεμψαντα με.

DEF: **P[66]**]λα ταυ[ ]ạντα ποιουcιν ειc ụṃ[ ]c̣ δια το [ ]ου οτι ουκ οιδαc[ ] τον πεμ[ ] ṃε

ποιηcουcιν: ποιουcιν **P[66]**
υμιν: ειc υμ[ ]c **P[66]**

15:22

P[66]

22: ει μη ηλθον και ελαληcα αυτοιc αμαρτιαν ουκ ειχον νυν δε προφαcιν ουκ εχουcι περι τηc αμαρτιαc αυτων.

DEF: **P[66]** ... κ[ ]ι ελαλη[ ]c αμαρτιαν ουκ [ ]ιχοcαν [ ]ροφαc[ ]ν ουκ εχουcιν περ[ ] τ̣η̣[ ]αρτιαc̣

ειχον: [ ]ιχοcαν **P[66]**
εχουcι: εχουcιν **P[66]**
αυτων: OM **P[66*]**; [ ]ṿ **P[66*c]**

15:23

P[66]

23: ο εμε μιcων και τον πατερα μου μιcει.

DEF: **P[66]**] εμε μ[ ]ων και...

15:24

P[66]

24: ει τα εργα μη εποιηcα εν αυτοιc α ουδειc αλλοc πεποιηκεν αμαρτιαν ουκ ειχον νυν δε και εωρακαcι και μεμιcηκαcι και εμε και τον πατερα μου.

DEF: **P[66]** ει τα̣ [ ]γα μη εποιη[ ]ν αυτοιc α μηδ[ ] αλλοc εποιηc[ ]ν αμαρτιαν... εορακαcιν [ ]αι... τον [ ]ρα μου

ουδεις: μηδ[2] **P66**
πεποιηκεν: εποιης[ ]ν **P66**
ειχον: ειχοσαν **P66**
εωρακασι: εορακασιν **P66**
μεμισηκασι: μεμεισηκασιν **P66**
και[3]: OM **P66**

15:25

P22 P66

25: αλλ ινα πληρωθη ο λογος ο γεγραμμενος εν τω νομω αυτων οτι εμισησαν με δωρεαν.

DEF: **P22**] των γεγραμμ[
P66 ... τω [ ]ọμω [ ] οτι εμιση[ ]ν με [

ο γεγραμμενος εν τω νομω αυτων:] των γεγραμμ[4] **P22**; ο εν τω [ ]ομω [11] **P66***; + αυτων post [ ]ομω **P66*c**

15:26

P22 P66

26: οταν δε ελθη ο παρακλητος ον εγω πεμψω υμιν παρα του πατρος το πνευμα της αληθειας ο παρα του πατρος εκπορευεται εκεινος μαρτυρησει περι εμου.

DEF: **P22** οταν ελθη ο πα[ ]ιν παρα του π̄ρ̄σ̄ [ ] π̄ρ̄σ̄ εκπορευε[ ]μου
P66]αρạ[

δε: OM **P22**

15:27

P22

27: και υμεις δε μαρτυρειτε οτι απ αρχης μετ εμου εστε.

DEF: **P22** και υμ[ ]μου εστε

CHAPTER SIXTEEN

P[5] P[22] P[60] P[66]

16:1

P[22]

1: ταυτα λελαληκα υμιν ινα μη cκανδαλιcθητε.

DEF: **P[22]** τ[ ]αλιcθητε

16:2

P[22] P[66]

2: αποcυναγωγουc ποιηcουcιν υμαc αλλ ερχεται ωρα ινα παc ο αποκτεινας υμας δοξη λατρειαν προcφερειν τω θεω.

DEF: **P[22]**]ρχε[ ]αι ω[
P[66]]ω θ[

16:3

P[66]

3: και ταυτα ποιηcουcιν υμιν οτι ουκ εγνωcαν τον πατερα ουδε εμε.

DEF: **P[66]**]νω[

16:4

P[66]

4: αλλα ταυτα λελαληκα υμιν ινα οταν ελθη η ωρα μνημονευητε αυτων οτι εγω ειπον υμιν ταυτα δε υμιν εξ αρχηc ουκ ειπον οτι μεθ υμων ημην.

DEF: **P[66]**]α λε[ ] ωρα [ ]τι εχ[ ] αρχ[

16:5

P^{66}

5: νυν δε υπαγω προς τον πεμψαντα με και ουδεις εξ υμων ερωτα με που υπαγεις.

DEF: **P**^{66}]μων ερωτα με π[

16:6

P^{66}

6: αλλ οτι ταυτα λελαληκα υμιν η λυπη πεπληρωκεν υμων την καρδιαν.

DEF: **P**^{66}]λ οτι τ̣α̣υ̣[ ]α̣λ̣η̣κ̣α υ[

16:7

P^{66}

7: αλλ εγω την αληθειαν λεγω υμιν συμφερει υμιν ινα εγω απελθω εαν γαρ μη απελθω ο παρακλητος ουκ ελευσεται προς υμας εαν δε πορευθω πεμψω αυτον προς υμας.

DEF: **P**^{66*} (sed vid. infra)

εαν δε πορευθω πεμψω αυτον προς υμας: OM **P**^{66*} vid; in margine superiore scripsit εαν δε πορευθω πεμψω̣ [ ] υμας **P**^{66*c}

16:8

8: και ελθων εκεινος ελεγξει τον κοσμον περι αμαρτιας και περι δικαιοσυνης και περι κρισεως.

16:9

9: περι αμαρτιας μεν οτι ου πιστευουσιν εις εμε.

16:10

P^{66}

10: περι δικαιοcυνηc δε οτι προc τον πατερα μου υπαγω και ουκ ετι θεωρειτε με.

DEF: **P^{66}**]γω [ ]εω[

10-11 θεωρειτε με περι δε κριcεωc οτι ο αρχων του κοcμου τουτου κεκριται:]εω[13-17 / 10-11]ου κ[13-17 /] **P^{66}** (forsan legit θεωρειτε με οτι ο αρ / χων τουτου του κοcμου κεκριται)

16:11

P^{66}

11: περι δε κριcεωc οτι ο αρχων του κοcμου τουτου κεκριται.

DEF: **P^{66}**]ου κ[

περι δε κριcεωc: vid. v. 10
του κοcμου τουτου: vid v. 10

16:12

P^{66}

12: ετι πολλα εχω λεγειν υμιν αλλ ου δυναcθε βαcταζειν αρτι.

DEF: **P^{66}**] λεγει[ ]τι

16:13

P^{66}

13: οταν δε ελθη εκεινοc το πνευμα τηc αληθειαc οδηγηcει υμαc ειc παcαν την αληθειαν ου γαρ λαληcει αφ εαυτου αλλ οcα αν ακουcη λαληcει και τα ερχομενα αναγγελει υμιν.

DEF: **P^{66}** ο[ ] α̣ληθ[ ]υ αλλ ο[ ]χομε̣ν[

16:14

P^{5} **P**^{66}

14: εκεινος εμε δοξασει οτι εκ του εμου λημψεται και αναγγελει υμιν.

DEF: **P**^{5}]αι και ανα[
P^{66}] δο̣[ ] αναγχ[

16:15

P^{5} **P**^{66}

15: παντα οσα εχει ο πατηρ εμα εστι δια τουτο ειπον οτι εκ του εμου λημψεται και αναγγελει υμιν.

DEF: **P**^{5}]α εχει ο π̅ρ̅ ε[ ]ν οτι εκ τ[ ]γελει υμι̅

OM totum versum **P**^{66}

16:16

P^{5} **P**^{66}

16: μικρον και ου θεωρειτε με και παλιν μικρον και οψεσθε με οτι εγω υπαγω προς τον πατερα.

DEF: **P**^{5}]αι [ ]αι οψεσθε [
P^{66} μ̣ι̣κ̣[ ]ον και [ ]τι θεωριτ̣[ ]αι παλιν μικρο̣[ ] και οψεσ[ ] με

ου: [ ]τι **P**^{66}
θεωρειτε: θεωριτ[ ] **P**^{66}
οτι εγω υπαγω προς τον πατερα: OM **P**^{66}
16-17 με οτι εγω υπαγω προς τον πατερα ειπον ουν εκ των μαθητων: [2-8 / 12-17]αθητων **P**^{5}

16:17

P[5] P[66]

17: ειπον ουν εκ των μαθητων αυτου προς αλληλους τι εστι τουτο ο λεγει ημιν μικρον και ου θεωρειτε με και παλιν μικρον και οψεσθε με και οτι εγω υπαγω προς τον πατερα.

DEF: **P[5]**]αθητων αυτου [ ] εστιν τουτο ο λε[ ]εωρειτε με [ ]εσθε με και [ ]ι [ ] πρα
P[66] ... εκ ṭων... π[ ]οσ... λε[ ] ημειν... θεωριται μ[ ]αι παλιν μịḳρο και οψεσθε με κα[ ] ụπαγω προ̣[ ] τον πρα

ειπον ουν εκ των μαθητων: cf. v. 16
ειπον: ειπαν **P[66]**
εστι: εστιν **P[5] P[66]**
ημιν: ημειν **P[66]**
θεωρειτε: θεωριται **P[66]**
και οτι εγω: κα[4] **P[66]**

16:18

P[5] P[66]

18: ελεγον ουν τουτο τι εστιν ο λεγει το μικρον ουκ οιδαμεν τι λαλει.

DEF: **P[5]** ελεγον ουν [ ] μεικρον ουκ οιδα[
P[66] ελεγον ο[ ]ν [ ] εσ[ ] τουτọ μịḳ[ ]ọν ου[ ]ιδαμεν...

τουτο τι εστιν ο λεγει το: / [10-12] **P[5]**; [2] εσ[3] τουτο **P[66]**
μικρον: μεικρον **P[5]**

16:19

P[5] P[66]

19: εγνω ουν ο ιησους οτι ηθελον αυτον ερωταν και ειπεν αυτοις περι τουτου ζητειτε μετ αλληλων οτι ειπον μικρον και ου θεωρειτε με και παλιν μικρον και οψεσθε με.

DEF: **P[5]**]νω ιησ οτι η[ ]ελον [ ] και ειπεν αυτ[ ]ις [ ]ειτε μετ αλληλω[ ]ον και ου θεωρει[ ]ν και οψεσθε μ[
P[66] εγνω [ ] ηṃελλον κ[ ]θελον αυτον [ ]ταν ẹịπ̣ẹṿ α̣[ ] ṭουτου [ ]τι[ειπ]ο[

ουν ο ιηcουc οτι: [5] **P^{66}**
ουν: OM **P^{5}**
ο: OM **P^{5*}**; txt **P^{5*c}**
οτι: + ημελλον κ[ ] **P^{66}**
και^{1}: OM **P^{66*}**; + ϗ supra lineam **P^{66*c}**
ζητειτε: [ ]τι[ ] **P^{66}**

16:20

P^{5} P^{66}

20: αμην αμην λεγω υμιν οτι κλαυcετε και θρηνηcετε υμειc ο δε κοcμοc χαρηcεται υμειc δε λυπηθηcεcθε αλλ η λυπη υμων ειc χαραν γενηcεται.

DEF: **P^{5}**]ω υμειν οτ[ ]λα[ ]ετε υμειc ο δε [ ]αι υμειc λουπηθη[ ]η υμων ειc χαραν [
P^{66}]μ̣ην [ ] . [ ]θε [ ] η [ ]ηc̣ẹται

υμιν: υμειν **P^{5}**
δε^{2}: OM **P^{5}**
λυπηθηcεcθε: λουπηθη[ ] **P^{5}**

16:21

P^{5} P^{22} P^{66}

21: η γυνη οταν τικτη λυπην εχει οτι ηλθεν η ωρα αυτηc οταν δε γεννηcη το παιδιον ουκ ετι μνημονευει τηc θλιψεωc δια την χαραν οτι εγεννηθη ανθρωποc ειc τον κοcμον.

DEF: **P^{5}**]η οταν τικτη λοι[ ] η ωρα αυτηc [ ] παιδ[ ]ον ουκ ε[ ]ειψ[ ]ωc δι[ ]ηθη ανθρω[
P^{22}]υνη οταν τικτη λυ[ ]τηc οταν δε γεννη[ ]νευει τηc θλειψεω[ ]ηθη ανο̅c̅ ειc τον κ[
P^{66} η γυνη οταν [ ]υπην εχει οτι ηλθεν η ημ̣[ ]τηc οτα̅ ... παιδιο̣ν [ ]υκ ετι μνημονευ[ ] τηc... τ̣ην χαραν οτ[ ]εννηθη ανθρω[ ]c̣ ειc τον κο[ ]ον

λυπην: λοι[ ] **P^{5*}**; λυ[ ] **P^{5*c}**
ωρα αυτηc: ημ[5]τηc **P^{66}**
θλιψεωc: [ ]ειψ[ ]ωc **P^{5}**; θλειψεω[ ] **P^{22}**; θλειψεωc **P^{66}**

16:22

P5 P22 P66

22: και υμεις ουν λυπην μεν νυν εχετε παλιν δε οψομαι υμας και χαρησεται υμων η καρδια και την χαραν υμων ουδεις αιρει αφ υμων.

DEF: **P5** και [ ]μεις ουν νυν μεν [ ] οψομαι υμ[ ] η καρδια [ ]δεις αρει [ ] υ[
P22]εν λυπην εχετε π[ ]cεται υμων η καρ[ ]δεις αιρει αφ [ ]μων
P66 ... ουν [ ]ụν μεν λụπ̣[ ]ṿ εξεται παλιν... χαρη[ ]εται υμω̄ ẹ καρδια την [ ]ạραν ụμων [ ] ẹρι αφ ụ[

λυπην μεν νυν: νυν μεν [ ] **P5**; [ ]εν λυπην **P22**; [ ]υν μεν λυπ[ ]ν **P66**
εχετε: εξεται **P66**
και[3]: OM **P66***; + ϗ supra lineam **P66*c**
αιρει: αρει **P5**; ερι **P66**

16:23

P5 P22 P66

23: και εν εκεινη τη ημερα εμε ουκ ερωτησετε ουδεν αμην αμην λεγω υμιν οτι οσα αν αιτησητε τον πατερα εν τω ονοματι μου δωσει υμιν.

DEF: **P5**]τ[ ] ημερ[ ]ε [ ] ουδεν [ ]μην α[ ] αν τι αιτη[ ]ητε [ ] εν τω ον[ ]ατ[
P22]κ ερωτησετε [ ]δε[ ]τι εαν αιτηc[ ]τ[ ] υμειν
P66 . . [ ]ν εκεινη τη [ ].[ ]εν [ ] ο[

οσα αν: εαν **P22**
αν: + τι **P5**
υμιν[2]: υμειν **P22**
23-24 τον πατερα εν τω ονοματι μου δωσει υμιν εως αρτι ουκ ητησατε ουδεν εν τω ονοματι μου αιτειτε και: [9-16] / εν τω ον[ ]ατ[10-17] / **P5***; + εν τω ονοματι [ ] τ[ ] in margine inferiore **P5*c**
23-24 ονοματι μου δωσει υμιν εως αρτι ουκ ητησατε: ο[22-26]cαται **P66**

16:24

$\mathbf{P}^{5}$ $\mathbf{P}^{22}$ $\mathbf{P}^{66}$

24: εωc αρτι ουκ ητηcατε ουδεν εν τω ονοματι μου αιτειτε και ληψεcθε ινα η χαρα υμων η πεπληρωμενη.

DEF: $\mathbf{P}^{5}$] λημψεcθε ι[ ] πεπληρω[
$\mathbf{P}^{22}$ εω[ ]τι [ ]ματι μου αιτ[
$\mathbf{P}^{66}$]cαται ουδ̣[ ]τηcαcθ̣α̣ι [ ]ρα υμω̣[

εωc αρτι ουκ ητηcατε ουδεν εν τω ονοματι μου αιτειτε και: vid. v. 23
ητηcατε: [ ]cαται $\mathbf{P}^{66}$
αιτειτε: [ ]τηcαcθαι $\mathbf{P}^{66}$
ληψεcθε: λημψεcθε $\mathbf{P}^{5}$

16:25

$\mathbf{P}^{5}$ $\mathbf{P}^{22}$ $\mathbf{P}^{66}$

25: ταυτα εν παροιμιαιc λελαληκα υμιν αλλ ερχεται ωρα οτε ουκ ετι εν παροιμιαιc λαληcω υμιν αλλα παρρηcια περι του πατροc αναγγελω υμιν.

DEF: $\mathbf{P}^{5}$]μια[ ]c λελαληκα [ ] ωρα οτε ουκ ετ[ ]ληcω υμειν αλ[ ] του πρc απαγγε[
$\mathbf{P}^{22}$]ρc [ ]ω [
$\mathbf{P}^{66}$]τα εν π̣[ ]ε̣λ̣α̣λ̣η̣[ ]ρχε[ ] οτ̣ε̣ ο̣υκ ετι ε̣ν πα̣[ ] υμειν αλλ[ ] παρ[ ]c̣ια περι̣ [ ]c... [ ]μ̣ειν

λελαληκα υμιν αλλ: [ ]ελαλη[6-7] $\mathbf{P}^{66}$
υμιν²: υμειν $\mathbf{P}^{5}$ $\mathbf{P}^{66}$
πατροc: + λαληcω υμειν $\mathbf{P}^{66*}$; txt $\mathbf{P}^{66*c}$
αναγγελω: απαγγε[ ] $\mathbf{P}^{5}$; απαγγελω $\mathbf{P}^{66}$
υμιν³: [ ]μειν $\mathbf{P}^{66}$

16:26

$\mathbf{P}^{5}$ $\mathbf{P}^{22}$ $\mathbf{P}^{66}$

26: εν εκεινη τη ημερα εν τω ονοματι μου αιτηcεcθε και ου λεγω υμιν οτι εγω ερωτηcω τον πατερα περι υμων.

DEF: $\mathbf{P}^{5}$]κεινη τη ημερα [ ] μου αιτηcεcθε [ ]τι εγω ερωτηc[
$\mathbf{P}^{22}$]ω [ ]ω τον π̅ρ̅α̅ [
$\mathbf{P}^{66}$ εν [ ]ι̣ν̣η̣ τ̣η̣ η̣μερα εν τω [ ]ν̣ομα̣[ ]θαι ϗ ου λε̣[ ]
υ̣μ̣[ ]ρ̣ω̣[ ]η̣cω τον π̅ρ̅[

αιτηcεcθε: [ ]θαι $\mathbf{P}^{66}$
26-27 ερωτηcω τον πατερα περι υμων αυτοc γαρ: ερωτηc[9-16 / 1]αρ $\mathbf{P}^{5}$; [ ]ρω[ ]ηcω τον π̅ρ̅[8-13]ρ $\mathbf{P}^{66}$

16:27

$\mathbf{P}^{5}$ $\mathbf{P}^{22}$ $\mathbf{P}^{66}$

27: αυτοc γαρ ο πατηρ φιλει υμαc οτι υμειc εμε πεφιληκατε και πεπιcτευκατε οτι εγω παρα του θεου εξηλθον.

DEF: $\mathbf{P}^{5}$]αρ ο π̅ρ̅ φιλει υμ[ ] πεφιληκατε και [ ] οτι παρα θ̅υ̅
εξηλθ[
$\mathbf{P}^{22}$] π̅η̅[ ] φ[ ] υμ[ ] οτι υμ[ ]ι π[ ]κατε οτι εγ[ ]ν
$\mathbf{P}^{66}$]ρ̣ ο π̅η̅ρ̅ [ ] υμαc οτι̣ [ ]μ̣ε πε̣[ ] πεπι̣c̣τ̣[ ] ο̣τ̣ι̣ [ ]υ̅
ε̣ξηλθον

αυτοc γαρ: vid. v. 26
εγω: OM $\mathbf{P}^{5}$
του: OM $\mathbf{P}^{5}$

16:28

$\mathbf{P}^{5}$ $\mathbf{P}^{22}$ $\mathbf{P}^{66}$

28: εξηλθον παρα του πατροc και εληλυθα ειc τον κοcμον παλιν αφιημι τον κοcμον και πορευομαι προc τον πατερα.

DEF: $\mathbf{P}^{5}$] παρα του π̅ρ̅c̅ και ε[ ] κοcμον παλιν α[ ] και
πορευομαι προ[
$\mathbf{P}^{22}$ ε[ ]η[ ]ν παρα [ ]ου π̅[ ]ον [ ] παλιν α[ ] πρ[ ] τ[ ]ν [
$\mathbf{P}^{66}$] ε̣[ ]ν̣ αφι̣η̣[ ]ο̣ρευο̣[

16:29

P^{5} **P**^{22} **P**^{60} **P**^{66}

29: λεγουϲιν αυτω οι μαθηται αυτου ιδε νυν παρρηϲια λαλειϲ και παροιμιαν ουδεμιαν λεγειϲ.

DEF: **P**^{5}]γουϲιν οι μ[ ] παρρηϲια λ[ ]δεμιαν λ[
P^{22}]τ[ ]υ ιδε [ ]δεμι[ ] λ[
P^{60}]ε ν[ ]ειϲ [ ]αν [
P^{66}]α̣ι παρο[ ]μ̣ια̅ [

αυτω: OM **P**^{5*}; txt **P**^{5*c}
νυν παρρηϲια λαλειϲ: ν[9-12 / 6]ειϲ **P**^{60}

16:30

P^{5} **P**^{22} **P**^{60} **P**^{66}

30: νυν οιδαμεν οτι οιδαϲ παντα και ου χρειαν εχειϲ ινα τιϲ ϲε ερωτα εν τουτω πιϲτευομεν οτι απο θεου εξηλθεϲ.

DEF: **P**^{5}] οτι οιδαϲ πα[
P^{22}]ντα και ου χρει[ ]ουτω [ ]τευομ[
P^{60}] οιδαμεν [
P^{66}] ο̣ιδαμεν ο[ ]ν εχειϲ [ ]ϲ̣ ϲ̣[ ]τ̣α̣ ε̣ν̣ [ ] π̣ιϲτευομε[ ] οτι απ̣ο θ̅υ̅ εξ[

16:31

P^{22} **P**^{66}

31: απεκριθη αυτοιϲ ο ιηϲουϲ αρτι πιϲτευετε.

DEF: **P**^{22}]εκρι[ ] αυ̣τοιϲ ι̅η̅[ ] α[
P^{66}]ε̣κριθη αυτοιϲ ι̅ϲ̣̅ α̣ρτι πιϲτευ[

ο: OM **P**^{22} **P**^{66}
31-32 πιϲτευετε ιδου: πιϲτευ[5]δε **P**^{66} (fortasse πιϲτευεται ιδε)

16:32

P^{22} **P**^{60} **P**^{66}

32: ιδου ερχεται ωρα και νυν εληλυθεν ινα σκορπισθητε εκαστος εις τα ιδια και εμε μονον αφητε και ουκ ειμι μονος οτι ο πατηρ μετ εμου εστι.

DEF: **P**^{22}] ωρα [ ]ληλυθεν [ ]ις [ ]δια κα[ ] εμ[
P^{60}] ωρα και ελη[ ]σθη[ ] εις τα ιδια [ ] αφ[
P^{66}]δ̣ε̣ ερ[ ]ται... εληλυθεν [ ]̲η̣ται π[ ] ε̣κ̣α̣στος ει[ ] κ̣αμ̣ε̣
μον[ ] ο̣υκ ει̣[ ]ι̣ μονος [ ]τ̣ι̣ ο π̣̄[ ]τιν

και νυν εληλυθεν: [4]ληλυθεν **P**^{22} (& cf. **P**^{60} **P**^{66})
νυν: OM **P**^{60} **P**^{66} (& cf. **P**^{22})
σκορπισθητε: [ ]ηται **P**^{66}; + π[5] **P**^{66*}; txt **P**^{66*c}
και εμε μονον: [9] **P**^{60} (& cf. **P**^{66})
και εμε: καμε **P**^{66} (& cf. **P**^{60})
εστι: [ ]τιν **P**^{66}

16:33

P^{60} **P**^{66}

33: ταυτα λελαληκα υμιν ινα εν εμοι ειρηνην εχητε εν τω κοσμω θλιψιν εξετε αλλα θαρσειτε εγω νενικηκα τον κοσμον.

DEF: **P**^{60}] ε[ ]ρην[ ]ω κοσμ[ ]ται αλλα [ ] νενικηκα τ[
P^{66} τ̣αυτα δε [ ]ηκα [ ]ο̣ι ειρη[ ]η̣ν [ ]λλα̣ [ ]α̣ι εγω
νε[ ]κη̣[κ]ο[

ταυτα: + δε **P**^{66}
εχητε εν τω κοσμω θλιψιν εξετε αλλα: [6]λλα **P**^{66}
εξετε: [ ]ται **P**^{60}
θαρσειτε εγω: [7-8] **P**^{60}
θαρσειτε: [ ]αι **P**^{66}

CHAPTER SEVENTEEN

P^{59} **P**^{60} **P**^{66} **P**^{84}

17:1

P^{60} **P**^{66}

1: ταυτα ελαλησεν ο ιησους και επηρε τους οφθαλμους αυτου εις τον ουρανον και ειπε πατερ εληλυθεν η ωρα δοξασον σου τον υιον ινα και ο υιος σου δοξαση σε.

DEF: **P**^{60}] ο ι̅ς̅ κα[ ]λμους [ ]νον [ ]θεν η ωρα [ ] τον υ̅ν̅
ιν[ ]ε
P^{66}]ν [ ]παρας τους ο[ ] . τ̣[ ]ν̣ υ̅ν̅ ιν̣α̣ [

ο ιησους και επηρε: [6]παρας **P**^{66}
οφθαλμους αυτου εις τον ουρανον και ειπε πατερ εληλυθεν η ωρα δοξασον σου: ο[20-27 / 20-27] / **P**^{66}
οφθαλμους αυτου εις τον ουρανον: [ ]λμους / [10-15]νον **P**^{60}
ινα και ο υιος σου δοξαση σε: ιν[1] / [10-14]ε **P**^{60}

17:2

P^{60} **P**^{66}

2: καθως εδωκας αυτω εξουσιαν πασης σαρκος ινα παν ο δεδωκας αυτω δωση αυτοις ζωην αιωνιον.

DEF: **P**^{60} καθω[ ]ξουσιαν [ ]ς [ ]ν[ ] πα[
P^{66}]δωκας αυτ[ ]κος ινα πα[ ] αυτοις ζ[ ]ην [ ]ν̣ι̣ο̣[

17:3

P60 P66 P84

3: αυτη δε εστιν η αιωνιος ζωη ινα γινωσκωσι σε τον μονον αληθινον θεον και ον απεστειλας ιησουν χριστον.

DEF: **P60**]ε ε[ ]νον [ ] ον απ[
P66]τιν η α̣ι̣ω̣[ ] ζωη ιν̣[ ] σε τον μονο[ ]ληθινο[ ]π̣εμψας ι̅ν̅ χ̅ν̅
P84] γινωσκ[ ] c[ ] τον μ[

απεστειλας: [ ]πεμψας **P66**

17:4

P60 P66

4: εγω σε εδοξασα επι της γης το εργον ετελειωσα ο δεδωκας μοι ινα ποιησω.

DEF: **P60**]γω σε εδο[ ]ης το ε[ ] δεδω[
P66 εγω σ̣[ ]δοξ[ ]α επι της γης το εργον τ[ ]ω̣σας [ ]δωκας μο̣[ ] ι̣να ποιη[

ετελειωσα: τ[4]ωσας **P66**

17:5

P60 P66

5: και νυν δοξασον με συ πατερ παρα σεαυτω τη δοξη η ειχον προ του τον κοσμον ειναι παρα σοι.

DEF: **P60**] με σ[ ] π[ ]ρ [ ] τη δο[ ]η [ ] προ του τον [ ]αι παρα σο[
P66 και νυν δοξασ̣[ ]ε συ π̅[ ]ρ̣α σεαυτω τη δ[ ]ιχον πα[ ]α̣ σ̣οι προ το[ ]ον ειναι

προ του τον κοσμον ειναι παρα σοι: πα[ ]α σοι προ το[8]ον ειναι **P66***; + πα[ ] super lineam post ειναι **P66*c** (et παρα σοι ante προ abrogavit punctis nunc deperditis?)

17:6

P^{60} **P**^{66}

6: εφανερωϲα ϲου το ονομα τοιϲ ανθρωποιϲ ουϲ δεδωκαϲ μοι εκ του κοϲμου ϲοι ηϲαν και εμοι αυτουϲ δεδωκαϲ και τον λογον ϲου τετηρηκαϲι.

DEF: **P**^{60}]ρωϲα ϲου το [ ]ιϲ α̅ν̅ο̅ι̅ϲ̅ ουϲ δ[ ]ι εκ του κ[ ]ν καμ[
P^{66} ε[ ]ρωϲα [ ]ι ε̣[ ]υτου του κοϲμο[ ]α̣[ ] α̣υτουϲ
εδωκα[ ]ου τερ̣[

εκ: ε[2]υτου **P**^{66}
δεδωκαϲ^{2}: εδωκα[ ] **P**^{66}
και εμοι: καμ[ ] **P**^{60}
τετηρηκαϲι: τερ[ ] **P**^{66*}; + τη super lineam **P**^{66*c} (teste ed. pr; nunc vidimus τ̣[ ])

17:7

P^{66} **P**^{84}

7: νυν εγνωκαν οτι παντα οϲα δεδωκαϲ μοι παρα ϲου εϲτιν.

DEF: **P**^{66}]α οϲα̱ [
P^{84}]ρα ϲου ειϲι̅

εϲτιν: ειϲιν **P**^{84}

17:8

P^{60} P^{66} P^{84}

8: οτι τα ρηματα α δεδωκαϲ μοι δεδωκα αυτοιϲ και αυτοι ελαβον και εγνωϲαν αληθωϲ οτι παρα ϲου εξηλθον και επιϲτευϲαν οτι ϲυ με απεϲτειλαϲ.

DEF: **P^{60}**] τα ρειματ[ ]εδωκα α[ ] ελαβον κα[ ] αληθωϲ οτι π[ ]ον και επιϲτ[ ]ε απεϲτιλα[
P^{66}]ρα ϲου εξ[ ]λ̣[ ]αν οτι ϲυ με [
P^{84}]ι τα ρ[ ]α [

ρηματα: ρειματ[ ] **P^{60}**
Duo primae lineae paginae eras. **P^{66}**; [ ]ω̣κα αυτοιϲ κα[ ] supra lineam primam **P^{66*c}**
απεϲτειλαϲ: απεϲτιλα[ ] **P^{60}**
8-9 απεϲτειλαϲ εγω περι αυτων ερωτω ου περι του κοϲμου: απεϲτιλα[9-11 / 2]ϲμου **P^{60}**

17:9

P^{60} P^{66}

9: εγω περι αυτων ερωτω ου περι του κοϲμου ερωτω αλλα περι ων δεδωκαϲ μοι οτι ϲοι ειϲι.

DEF: **P^{60}**]ϲμου ερωτ[ ] δεδωκ[
P^{66}]ρι αυτων ου [ ]ω̣τω αλλα πε[ ]καϲ μ[ ]ι̣ [ ] ειϲιν

εγω περι αυτων ερωτω ου περι του κοϲμου: vid. v. 8
ερωτω^{1}: OM **P^{66}**
ειϲι: ειϲιν **P^{66}**

17:10

P^{66}

10: και τα εμα παντα ϲα εϲτι και τα ϲα εμα και δεδοξαϲμαι εν αυτοιϲ.

DEF: **P^{66}**]α παντ[ ]τ̣ιν και τα ϲα ε̣[ ] κ̣αι ε̣δ̣ο̣ξ̣α̣ϲ̣με εν αυτοιϲ

εϲτι: [ ]τιν **P^{66}**
δεδοξαϲμαι: εδοξαϲμε **P^{66*}**; δεδοξαϲμε **P^{66*c}**

17:11

P^{60} P^{66}

11: και ουκ ετι ειμι εν τω κοσμω και ουτοι εν τω κοσμω εισι και εγω προς σε ερχομαι πατερ αγιε τηρησον αυτους εν τω ονοματι σου ους δεδωκας μοι ινα ωσιν εν καθως ημεις.

DEF: **P^{60}**]ιμι εν τω [ ]ω κοσμω [ ] σε ερχομε [ ]ησον αυτους εν [ ]ατι σου ω δεδ[ ]α ωσιν εν κα[
P^{66} και [ ] ετι ειμι ε̣ν̣ τω κοσμω και [ ] τω κοσμω εισιν και [ ] προς ς̣[ ]χομα̣ι̣ [ ]ε̅ρ̅ αγιε τηρ[ ] αυ̣τ̣[ ]ς εν τω ο[ ]ατι σου ω [ ]κ̣ας μοι

ουτοι εν: [3-4] **P^{66}**
εισι: εισιν **P^{66}**
ερχομαι: ερχομε **P^{60}**
σου: μου **P^{66*}**; txt **P^{66*c}**
ους: ω **P^{60} P^{66}**
ινα ωσιν εν καθως ημεις: OM **P^{66*}**; ·/. post μοι **P^{66*c}** (et + verba omissa in margine inferiore nunc deperdita?)

17:12

P^{60} P^{66}

12: οτε ημην μετ αυτων εν τω κοσμω εγω ετηρουν αυτους εν τω ονοματι σου ους δεδωκας μοι εφυλαξα και ουδεις εξ αυτων απωλετο ει μη ο υιος της απωλειας ινα η γραφη πληρωθη.

DEF: **P^{60}**]τε ημην μ[ ] ετηρου[ ] τ[ ] ονοματι [ ]κας μοι και [ ] ουδεις εξ αυτ̣[ ]ι μη ο υ[ ]ειας ινα γ[ ]θη
P^{66} οτε [ ]τ αυτω̅ [ ]ω ε̣τη̣[ ]ω ονοματι μου και ε̣[ ]λ̣αξ[ ]υ̣δεις̣ α̣υτω[ ] α̣[ ] τ̣ης απ[

μετ αυτων εν τω κοσμω εγω: μ[7-9 / 3] **P^{60}**
εν τω κοσμω εγω: / [2]ω **P^{66}**
σου: μου **P^{66*}**; txt **P^{66*c}**
ους δεδωκας μοι: και **P^{66*}**; δ[ ] supra lineam **P^{66*c}**
μοι: + και **P^{60}**
εξ: OM **P^{66*}**; txt **P^{66*c}**
η: OM **P^{60}**

17:13

P^{60} P^{66}

13: νυν δε προc cε ερχομαι και ταυτα λαλω εν τω κοcμω ινα εχωcι την χαραν την εμην πεπληρωμενην εν αυτοιc.

DEF: **P^{60}** νυν [ ] κα[
P^{66}] cε̣ [ ]χ̣ομαι [ ] τω̣ κοcμ̣[ ] την εμην [ ]μ̣ε̣ν̣[ ]ν αυτοιc

17:14

P^{60} P^{66}

14: εγω δεδωκα αυτοιc τον λογον cου και ο κοcμοc εμιcηcεν αυτουc οτι ουκ ειcιν εκ του κοcμου καθωc εγω ουκ ειμι εκ του κοcμου.

DEF: **P^{60}**]α αυτο[ ]c τον [ ] και ο κοcμοc [ ]ουc οτι ου[ ]ιcι[ ]οcμου καθωc εγω [ ] εκ του κοcμου
P^{66} εγω̣ [ ]δωκ̣α αυτο̣[ ] λο̣γον̣ cου κ̣[ ] κοcμοc εμ̣[ ] αυτουc οτι [ ] ειcιν εκ τ̣ο̣υ̣ κ[ ]μου

καθωc εγω ουκ ειμι εκ του κοcμου: OM **P^{66*}**; καθωc εγω εκ τ[ ] in margine superiore **P^{66*c}**

17:15

P^{60} P^{66}

15: ουκ ερωτω ινα αρηc αυτουc εκ του κοcμου αλλ ινα τηρηcηc αυτουc εκ του πονηρου.

DEF: **P^{60}**]τω ινα αρηc αυ[ ]υ κοcμου [ ]λ̣[ ]ηc αυτου[
P^{66} ... αυτ[ ]κ του... τηρηcη[ ] α̣υτουc...

17:16

P^{66}

16: εκ του κοcμου ουκ ειcι καθωc εγω εκ του κοcμου ουκ ειμι.

DEF: **P^{66}** εκ [ ]ου [ ]οcμου ουκ ε[ ]cιν καθωc [ ]κ το[ ] κοc[ ]ου ου[

εκ του κοcμου ουκ ειcι καθωc: OM **P**^{66*c}; εκ [ ]ου [ ]οcμου ουκ ε[ ]cιν καθωc **P**^{66*}
εγω: OM **P**^{66}

17:17

P^{66}

17: αγιαcον αυτουc εν τη αληθεια cου ο λογοc ο coc αληθεια εcτι.

DEF: **P**^{66} ... εν [ ]ια... αληθε[ ]α ε[

cου: OM **P**^{66}

17:18

P^{60} **P**^{66}

18: καθωc εμε απεcτειλαc ειc τον κοcμον καγω απεcτειλα αυτουc ειc τον κοcμον.

DEF: **P**^{60}]ωc εμε απ[ ] τον κοcμον [ ]λα αυτουc ειc τον [
P^{66}]θω[ ]με απεc̣τιλαc [

απεcτειλαc: απεcτιλαc **P**^{66}
ειc τον κοcμον καγω απεcτειλα αυτουc ειc τον κοcμον: [12] **P**^{66}

17:19

P^{60} **P**^{66}

19: και υπερ αυτων εγω αγιαζω εμαυτον ινα και αυτοι ωcιν ηγιαcμενοι εν αληθεια.

DEF: **P**^{60} και υπερ αυτων [ ] αγιαζω εμαυτο[ ] ωcιν και αυτοι η[ ]νοι εν αληθεια
P^{66} και υπερ αυτων [ ]ον ινα ωcιν αυ[ ] ηγιαc[ ]ι εν αλ[

και αυτοι ωcιν: ωcιν αυ[ ] **P**^{66*}; ωcιν ϗ αυ[ ] **P**^{66*c}; ωcιν και αυτοι **P**^{60}

17:20

P^{60} P^{66}

20: ου περι τουτων δε ερωτω μονον αλλα και περι των πιστευσοντων δια του λογου αυτων εις εμε.

DEF: **P^{60}**]ρι του[ ]ων δε [ ] αλλα κα[
P^{66}]ντων [ ]ια του [

17:21

P^{60} P^{66}

21: ινα παντες εν ωσι καθως συ πατερ εν εμοι καγω εν σοι ινα και αυτοι εν ημιν εν ωσιν ινα ο κοσμος πιστευση οτι συ με απεστειλας.

DEF: **P^{60}**] πιστευση ο[ ]τιλας
P^{66}] παντες [ ]ν̣ κ̣[ ] εν εμοι [ ] εν σοι ι̣ν̣α κ[ ] αυτοι εν ημεῑ [ ] ι̣να ο κοσμο[ ]ιστευη οτι συ [ ] απεστιλας

ωσι: [ ]ν **P^{66}**
ημιν: ημειν **P^{66}**
πιστευση: [ ]ιστευη **P^{66}**
απεστειλας: απεστιλας **P^{66}**; [ ]τιλας **P^{60}**

17:22

P^{60} P^{66}

22: και εγω την δοξαν ην δεδωκας μοι δεδωκα αυτοις ινα ωσιν εν καθως ημεις εν εσμεν.

DEF: **P^{60}** καγω [ ] δεδωκας μοι [ ]α αυτοις ινα ωσ[ ]ν [ ] ημις εν
P^{66} καγω [ ]ν δοξαν ην [ ]δωκας... ινα [ ]ιν ... ημεις εν

και εγω: καγω **P^{60} P^{66}**
ημεις: ημις **P^{60}**
εσμεν: OM **P^{60} P^{66}**

17:23

P[60] **P**[66]

23: εγω εν αυτοις και cυ εν εμοι ινα ωcι τετελειωμενοι ειc εν και ινα γινωcκη ο κοcμοc οτι cυ με απεcτειλαc και ηγαπηcαc αυτουc καθωc εμε ηγαπηcαc.

DEF: **P**[60] εγω ε[ ]αι cυ εν εμοι ινα [ ]τελιωμενοι [ ] γινω[ ]η ο κοc[ ] απ[ ]τιλα[ ]ηcα[
P[66] εγω [ ]τοιc... και γ[ ]νωcκη ο κοcμ[ ]τι cυ με απ[ ]ιλαc και ηγαπηcα[ ]ου[ ]α[ ]ωc εμε...

τετελειωμενοι: [ ]τελιωμενοι **P**[60]
ινα[2]: OM **P**[66]
απεcτειλαc: απ[ ]τιλα[ ] **P**[60]; απ[2 / 1]ιλαc **P**[66]

17:24

P[59] **P**[60] **P**[66]

24: πατερ ουc δεδωκαc μοι θελω ινα οπου ειμι εγω κακεινοι ωcι μετ εμου ινα θεωρωcι την δοξαν την εμην ην εδωκαc μοι οτι ηγαπηcαc με προ καταβοληc κοcμου.

DEF: **P**[59]]ωcι [ ]μην [ ] οτι η[ ] προ κατα[ ]μου
P[60]]ρ ο δεδω[ ]ν[ ] οπου ειμ[ ]οι ωcιν μετ [ ] θεωρουcιν τ[ ] την εμην ην [ ] μοι οτι ηγαπ[ ] καταβοληc [
P[66] π[ ]ω[ ]αc μοι θελω ιν[ ]μι [ ]κεινοι ωcιν μ[ ] την δο[ ] την [ ]οι [ ]τι ηγα[

ουc: ο **P**[60]
εγω: OM **P**[66]
ωcι: ωcιν **P**[60] **P**[66]
θεωρωcι: θεωρουcιν **P**[60]

17:25

$\mathbf{P}^{59}$ $\mathbf{P}^{60}$ $\mathbf{P}^{66}$

25: πατερ δικαιε και ο κοσμος σε ουκ εγνω εγω δε σε εγνων και ουτοι εγνωσαν οτι συ με απεστειλας.

DEF: $\mathbf{P}^{59}$ $\overline{\text{περ}}$ δι[ ]σμος σε ουκ [ ]ω δε [ ] εγν$\overline{\text{ω}}$ [ ]εστ[ ]λας
$\mathbf{P}^{60}$]ικαι[ ] και ο [ ] ουκ [ ]νω[
$\mathbf{P}^{66}$]νω [ ]νω[ ]αν [

και ουτοι εγνωσαν οτι συ με απεστειλας: [6-10]εστ[ ]λας $\mathbf{P}^{59}$

17:26

$\mathbf{P}^{59}$ $\mathbf{P}^{66}$

26: και εγνωρισα αυτοις το ονομα σου και γνωρισω ινα η αγαπη ην ηγαπησας με εν αυτοις η καγω εν αυτοις.

DEF: $\mathbf{P}^{59}$ και [
$\mathbf{P}^{66}$]ρισα αυ[ ]νωρ[ ] εν αυ[ ] ην κ[

η^{2}: ην $\mathbf{P}^{66}$

CHAPTER EIGHTEEN

P52 P59 P60 P66 P90

18:1

P59 P60 P66

1: ταυτα ειπων ο ιηcουc εξηλθε cυν τοιc μαθηταιc αυτου περαν του χειμαρρου των κεδρων οπου ην κηποc ειc ον ειcηλθεν αυτοc και οι μαθηται αυτου.

DEF: **P59**] χει[ ] οπο[ ] ειcη[ ]θ[ ]θηται αυτ[
P60]ν ο ι̅c̅ εξηλθ[ ]ητεc αυτ[ ]ου χιμαρρου [ ]δρων οπου ην [ ]c ον ειcηλθεν [ ] μαθητε [
P66]τ̣α ει[ ] ι̅c̅ εξ[ ] μαθη[ ]τ̣ου [ ]α̣ρου τ[ ] ε̣ιc̣ ο̅ ειcηλθε̣ν̣ [ ]τ̣ο̣υ̣

μαθηταιc: [ ]ητεc **P60**
χειμαρρου: χιμαρρου **P60**; [ ]αρου **P66***; [ ]αρρου **P66*c**
μαθηται: μαθητε **P60**

18:2

P59 P60 P66

2: ηδει δε και ιουδαc ο παραδιδουc αυτον τον τοπον οτι πολλακιc cυνηχθη ο ιηcουc εκει μετα των μαθητων αυτου.

DEF: **P59**] και ιουδαc ο [ ] αυτον τον [ ] πολλακιc c[ ] εκι μετα τω[ ] α[ ]το[
P60] δε και ιου[ ]διδ[ ]c αυτο[ ]ν οτ[
P66 ηδ̣ε̣ι δ[ ] τ̣ον τ̣[ ]c cυνηχθ[ ]θητων

δε και ιουδαc ο παραδιδουc αυτον: δ[13-22 / 5] **P66**
εκει: εκι **P59**
αυτου: OM **P66***; αυτ̣[ ] **P66*c**

18:3

$\mathbf{P}^{66}$

3: ο ουν ιουδας λαβων την σπειραν και εκ των αρχιερεων και φαρισαιων υπηρετας ερχεται εκει μετα φανων και λαμπαδων και οπλων.

DEF: $\mathbf{P}^{66}$] την σπιρα[ ] κ̣α̣[ ] ερ[ ]π[ ]δ̣[

σπειραν: σπιρα[ ] $\mathbf{P}^{66}$

18:4

$\mathbf{P}^{60}$ $\mathbf{P}^{66}$

4: ιησους ουν ειδως παντα τα ερχομενα επ αυτον εξελθων ειπεν αυτοις τινα ζητειτε.

DEF: $\mathbf{P}^{60}$] ουν ειδ[ ]χ[ ]μενα [ ]θεν εξω κ[ ] τινα ζητιτε
$\mathbf{P}^{66}$]ντα τ[ ]ξ[ ]θω̣[

εξελθων: [ ]θεν εξω κ[ ] $\mathbf{P}^{60}$
ζητειτε: ζητιτε $\mathbf{P}^{60}$

18:5

$\mathbf{P}^{60}$ $\mathbf{P}^{66}$

5: απεκριθησαν αυτω ιησουν τον ναζωραιον λεγει αυτοις ο ιησους εγω ειμι ειστηκει δε και ιουδας ο παραδιδους αυτον μετ αυτων.

DEF: $\mathbf{P}^{60}$] ι̅ν̅ τον ναζωρ[ ] αυτοις εγω ε[ ] δε και ιουδας [
$\mathbf{P}^{66}$ απ[ ]ζ[ ]ρ̣[ ] ιστη̣κ̣[ ] μετ α[

ναζωραιον λεγει αυτοις ο ιησους εγω ειμι: [ ]ζ[ ]ρ[19-23] $\mathbf{P}^{66}$ (& cf. $\mathbf{P}^{60}$)
ο ιησους: OM $\mathbf{P}^{60}$ (& cf. $\mathbf{P}^{66}$)
ειστηκει: ιστηκ[ ] $\mathbf{P}^{66}$
ο παραδιδους αυτον μετ αυτων: μετ α[ ] $\mathbf{P}^{66*}$; + [ ] παραδιδ[ ] supra μετ $\mathbf{P}^{66*c}$

18:6

P66

6: ωc ουν ειπεν αυτοιc οτι εγω ειμι απηλθον ειc τα οπιcω και επεcον χαμαι.

DEF: **P66** ωc ου̣[ ]μι α[

18:7

P60 P66

7: παλιν ουν αυτουc επηρωτηcε τινα ζητειτε οι δε ειπον ιηcουν τον ναζωραιον.

DEF: **P60**]ωτηc[ ]ητιτε οι δε [ ] τον ναζωρεον
P66]ω̣τηc[ ]ι δε ειπαν [

αυτουc επηρωτηcε τινα ζητειτε: [ ]ωτηc[2-3 / 11]ητιτε **P60**
ειπον: ειπαν **P66**
ναζωραιον: ναζωρεον **P60**

18:8

P60 P66

8: απεκριθη ο ιηcουc ειπον υμιν οτι εγω ειμι ει ουν εμε ζητειτε αφετε τουτουc υπαγειν.

DEF: **P60**] ι̅c̅ ειπον υμιν [ ]μι ει ουν εμε [ ]ετε τουτουc [
P66 απ̣[ ]μειν ο̣τι ε[ ]τειται αφ[

απεκριθη ο: [7-8] **P60**
υμιν: [ ]μειν **P66**
ζητειτε: [ ]τειται **P66**

18:9

P^{60} **P**^{66}

9: ινα πληρωθη ο λογος ον ειπεν οτι ους δεδωκας μοι ουκ απωλεσα εξ αυτων ουδενα.

DEF: **P**^{60}] πληρωθη ο [ ]ν οτ[ ]υc δεδ[
P^{66}]ν̣α πληρῳ[ ] ουc εδῳκ̣αc [ ]οι ọụ[ ]πωλ̣[ ] εξ α̣[ ]ενα

δεδωκαc: εδωκαc **P**^{66}

18:10

P^{60} **P**^{66}

10: cιμων ουν πετροc εχων μαχαιραν ειλκυcεν αυτην και επαιcε τον του αρχιερεωc δουλον και απεκοψεν αυτου το ωτιον το δεξιον ην δε ονομα τω δουλω μαλχοc.

DEF: **P**^{60}]μων ουν π[ ] μαχαιραν ηλκυ[ ] και επεcεν τον [ ]ρεωc δουλον κα[ ] αυτου το ωταρ[ ]ξιον ην δε ονο[ ]ω μαλχοc
P^{66} cιμῳ[ ] ου[ ]χαιραν [ ]λκ[ ]ẹcεν τον [ ]υλ̣[ ]ν̣ τ̣[ ]ẹ[ ]c και απε[ ]ẹν το [ ] αυτου το δεξιọ[ ]ν̣ δε ο[ ] τω δουλ[ ]λχοc

ειλκυcεν: ηλκυ[ ] **P**^{60}
επαιcε: επεcεν **P**^{60}; [ ]εcεν **P**^{66}
του αρχιερεωc δουλον: [ ]υλ[ ]ν τ[ ]ε[ ]c **P**^{66}
αυτου το ωτιον: το [ ] αυτου **P**^{66}
ωτιον: ωταρ[ ] **P**^{60}

18:11

P^{60} **P**^{66}

11: ειπεν ουν ο ιηcουc τω πετρω βαλε την μαχαιραν cου ειc την θηκην το ποτηριον ο δεδωκε μοι ο πατηρ ου μη πιω αυτο.

DEF: **P**^{60} ειπ[ ]ω πετρω βα[ ]ιραν ε[ ]c την [
P^{66} ειπ[ ]ν ου[ ]c̣̄ τω πετρῳ [ ] τηṿ μαχ̣α̣ιραṿ ειc την [ ]
ποτηρịον ο δεδωκεν μ̣[ ]ου ου μη πιῳ αυτ[

ουν ο ιηcουc: ου[2]c̄ **P**^{66}
cου: OM **P**^{60} **P**^{66}

δεδωκε: δεδωκεν **P**^{66}
μοι ο πατηρ: μ[6 / 1]ου **P**^{66}

18:12

P^{60} **P**^{66}

12: η ουν cπειρα και ο χιλιαρχοc και οι υπηρεται των ιουδαιων cυνελαβον τον ιηcουν και εδηcαν αυτον.

DEF: **P**^{60}]α και ο χιλιαρχο[ ]τε των ιου[ ]νελαβον τον ι̅ν̅
[ ]αν αυτον
P^{66} η ουν c[ ]αι ο χιλι̣αρχο̣[ ] και υπηρε[ ]ο̣υδαιων
cυ̣[ ]ελαβον τ[ ] ι̅ν̅ [ ]α̣ν̣ αυτο[

οι: OM **P**^{66*}; txt **P**^{66*c}
υπηρεται: [ ]τε **P**^{60}

18:13

P^{60} **P**^{66}

13: και απηγαγον αυτον προc ανναν πρωτον ην γαρ πενθεροc του καιαφα οc ην αρχιερευc του ενιαυτου εκεινου.

DEF: **P**^{60} και α[ ] προc ανναν [ ]τον ην γαρ πενθε[ ]αιαφα οc
ην αρχ[
P^{66} και ηγαχ[ ] προ[ ]ωτο[ ] ην χα̣[ ]θερο̣[ ]φα [ ]ευc τ[ ] ε̣[κ

απηγαγον αυτον: α[7] **P**^{60}; ηγαγ[2] **P**^{66}
13-14 αρχιερευc του ενιαυτου εκεινου ην: αρχ[8] **P**^{60}

18:14

P^{60} **P**^{66}

14: ην δε καιαφαc ο cυμβουλευcαc τοιc ιουδαιοιc οτι cυμφερει ενα ανθρωπον απολεcθαι υπερ του λαου.

DEF: **P**^{60}] δε καιαφαc cυμ[ ] τοιc ιουδα[
P^{66}] κ̣α̣ι̣α̣[ ]c ιουδα[ ] ο̣[ ]ερε[ ] α̅ν̅ο̅[ ] α̣ποθ[ ]υ

ο: OM **P**^{60}
απολεcθαι: αποθ[ ] **P**^{66}

18:15

P^{60} P^{66}

15: ηκολουθει δε τω ιηcου cιμων πετρος και ο αλλος μαθητης ο δε μαθητης εκεινος ην γνωcτος τω αρχιερει και cυνειcηλθε τω ιηcου ειc την αυλην του αρχιερεωc.

DEF: **P^{60}** ηκολουθι δε [ ] πετρος και ο [ ]της ο δε μαθη[ ] ην γνωcτος τω [ ] cυνιcηλθεν τω [ ] αυλην του αρχ[
P^{66} η[ ]ο̣λουθι δ[ ]τρ[ ]ς̣ και αλλ̣ο̣ς̣ μ̣α̣[ ] cυ̣ν̣[ ]cηλθεν τω ι̅υ̅
ει̣[ ] α̣υλην̣ [ ]υ αρχιερεωc

ηκολουθει: ηκολουθι **P^{60}**; η[ ]ολουθι **P^{66}**
ο^{1}: OM **P^{66}**
ο δε μαθητης εκεινος ην γνωcτος τω αρχιερει: OM **P^{66*}**;
ο δ[11]ινο[7]τος τω αρχιερε[ ] **P^{66*c}**
cυνειcηλθε: cυνιcηλθεν **P^{60}**; cυν[ ]cηλθεν **P^{66}**

18:16

P^{59} P^{60} P^{66}

16: ο δε πετρος ειcτηκει προς τη θυρα εξω εξηλθεν ουν ο μαθητης ο αλλος ος ην γνωcτος τω αρχιερει και ειπε τη θυρωρω και ειcηγαγε τον πετρον.

DEF: **P^{59}**] και ειπ[ ]ω και ει[ ]ετρον
P^{60}] δε πετρος ι[ ]η θυρα εξω εξ[
P^{66} ο δ̣[ ]ρος ιc[ ]ει προς τη̣ θυρα εξω ε̣[ ]η̣λθεν̣ ο̣υ̣ν̣ ο μαθ̣η̣[ ]
ην γνω̣cτος τ[ ]υ αρχιερε[ ]πεν [ ]η̣ θυρω κα̣ι
ει[ ]ηγαγε̣[ ]ετρον

ειcτηκει: ι[ ] **P^{60}**; ιc[3]ει **P^{66}**
τω αρχιερει: τ[1]υ αρχιερε[ ] **P^{66}**
ειπε: [ ]πεν **P^{66}**
θυρωρω: θυρω **P^{66*}**; θυρουρω **P^{66*c}**

18:17

P^{59} **P**^{66}

17: λεγει ουν η παιδισκη η θυρωρος τω πετρω μη και συ εκ των μαθητων ει του ανθρωπου τουτου λεγει εκεινος ουκ ειμι.

DEF: **P**^{59}]τρω η [ ]υρωρ[ ]ων μ[
P^{66} λεγει̣ ο̣υν η παιδισκ[ ]υρος τω πε[ ]ω μη και συ ε[ ]ων
[ ]θητων τ̣[ ]υ̣ ανθρωπου [ ]υτο̣[ ] λεγει εκ[ ]νος ο̣υκ ειμ̣[

η παιδισκη η θυρωρος τω πετρω: [ ]τρω η[ ]υρωρ[ ] **P**^{59}
θυρωρος: [ ]υρος **P**^{66}
των μαθητων: [1]οις [2]θητοις **P**^{66*c}; [1]ων [2]θητων **P**^{66*}
ει: OM **P**^{66*}; txt **P**^{66*c}

18:18

P^{60} **P**^{66}

18: ειστηκειςαν δε οι δουλοι και οι υπηρεται ανθρακιαν πεποιηκοτες οτι ψυχος ην και εθερμαινοντο ην δε μετ αυτων ο πετρος εστως και θερμαινομενος.

DEF: **P**^{60}]ι δουλοι και ο[ ]ρακιαν πε[ ]τι ψυχος ην και [ ] ην
δε και ο [ ] αυτων εστως [ ]μενος
P^{66}]τηκ[ ]ε οι δ[ ]υλοι κ̣[ ]επ[ ] ο̣τι ψυχ[ ]ι̣ ε̣[ ] και ο
π[ ]ενος

ειστηκειςαν: [1]τηκ[ ] **P**^{66}
εθερμαινοντο ην δε μετ αυτων: ε[9-15] και **P**^{66} (probabiliter leg. μετ αυτων post πετρος; & cf. **P**^{60})
μετ αυτων ο πετρος: και ο [ ] αυτων **P**^{60} (& cf. **P**^{66})

18:19

P^{60} **P**^{66}

19: ο ουν αρχιερευς ηρωτηςε τον ιηςουν περι των μαθητων αυτου και περι της διδαχης αυτου.

DEF: **P**^{60}] ουν αρ̣χ̣ιερ[ ]ον ι̅ν̅ περ[ ] τ[ ]υτου και περ[ ]υτου
P^{66} ο ο̣[ ]εν τον ι̅ν̅ [ ]ρι [ ]ν̣ αυτου και̣ π̣ερι [

ηρωτηςε: [ ]εν **P**^{66}

18:20

P^{60} **P**^{66}

20: απεκριθη αυτω ο ιηcουc εγω παρρηcια ελαληcα τω κοcμω εγω παντοτε εδιδαξα εν τη cυναγωγη και εν τω ιερω οπου παντοτε οι ιουδαιοι cυνερχονται και εν κρυπτω ελαληcα ουδεν.

DEF: **P**^{60} απεκρι[ ]γω παρρηcια [ ]οcμω εγω π[ ]αξα εν
cυν[ ] ιερω [ ]πο[ ] cυν[
P^{66}]εκριθη αυτω ι̅[ ]αληcα τω κ̣οc̣[ ]τοται εδιδ̣[ ]α̣ι εν̣
τω̣ [ ]ουδαιο[ ]ο̣[ ]π̣τω ελ[ ]ληcα [

ο: OM **P**^{66}
τη: OM **P**^{60}
παντοτε: [ ]τοται **P**^{66}

18:21

P^{66}

21: τι με επερωταc επερωτηcον τουc ακηκοοταc τι ελαληcα αυτοιc ιδε ουτοι οιδαcιν α ειπον εγω.

DEF: **P**^{66}]αc ερω̣τ̣η̣c̣ο̣ν̣ [ ]ο̣αc̣ τ[ ]αληλcα̣ α̣υ̣τ̣ο̣ι̣[ ]ι̣
οιδ[ ] ειπο̣ν̣ εγω

επερωτηcον: ερωτηcον **P**^{66}
ακηκοοταc: [ ]οαc **P**^{66}

18:22

P^{59} **P**^{66}

22: ταυτα δε αυτου ειπουτοc ειc των υπηρετων παρεcτηκωc εδωκε ραπιcμα τω ιηcου ειπων ουτωc αποκρινη τω αρχιερει.

DEF: **P**^{59}] ειc τω [ ]περαι[ ]δωκεν ραπει[ ] ι̅υ̅ ειπων ουτωc
[ ]ινη τω αρχιερει
P^{66}]το̣c [ ]των εδ̣[ ] ειπων̣ [ ] αρχιε[

των υπηρετων παρεcτηκωc: τω [8-11]περαι[ ] **P**^{59}
υπηρετων παρεcτηκωc: [ ]των **P**^{66}
εδωκε: [ ]δωκεν **P**^{59}
ραπιcμα: ραπει[ ] **P**^{59}

18:23

P[60] **P**[66]

23: απεκριθη αυτω ο ιηcουc ει κακωc ελαληcα μαρτυρηcον περι του κακου ει δε καλωc τι με δερειc.

DEF: **P**[60]] ῑc̄ ει κακω[ ]τυρηcον πε[ ]ου ει δε καλωc [ ]c
P[66]]κ̣ωc [ ]ο̣υ̣ [ ]ερειc

18:24

P[60] **P**[66]

24: απεcτειλεν αυτον ο αννας δεδεμενον προc καιαφαν τον αρχιερεα.

DEF: **P**[60] απεcτιλεν ου[ ]δεμενον πρ[ ] τον αρχιερεα
P[66] απ̣[ ]ν̣ν̣[ ] δεδεμε[ ]ν̣ το̣ν̣ αρχιερεα

απεcτειλεν: απεcτιλεν **P**[60]
αυτον ο αννac δεδεμενον: ου[1 / 9-10]δεμενον **P**[60]
προc καιαφαν: πρ[2 / 9-10] **P**[60]

18:25

P[60] **P**[66]

25: ην δε cιμων πετροc εcτωc και θερμαινομενοc ειπον ουν αυτω μη και cυ εκ των μαθητων αυτου ει ηρνηcατο εκεινοc και ειπεν ουκ ειμι.

DEF: **P**[60]]ροc μετ αυτ[ ]ρμενομ[
P[66]]τροc εcτωc κα[ ]ι̣πα̣ν ουν αυτω [ ]α̣θητων α[ ]κ̣[ ]ο̣c και ειπ̣[

πετροc: + μετ αυτ[ ] **P**[60]
θερμαινομενοc: [ ]ρμενομ[ ] **P**[60]
ειπον: [ ]ιπαν **P**[66]

18:26

P^{60} P^{66}

26: λεγει εις εκ των δουλων του αρχιερεωc cυγγενηc ων ου απεκοψε πετροc το ωτιον ουκ εγω cε ειδον εν τω κηπω μετ αυτου.

DEF: **P^{60}** λεγει εις εκ τω[ ] του αρχιερεωc [ ] ων ου απεκοψ[ ] το ωτιον ουκ ε[ ] εν τω κηπω [
P^{66}]ει̣ [ ]c εκ τωṿ [ ]ερεω[ ] cυγγεν[ ]ε̣ν πετ̣ροc το ω̣[ ]ε ειδ[ ]ν εν τω̣ [

απεκοψε: [ ]εν **P^{66}**

18:27

P^{60} P^{66}

27: παλιν ουν ηρνηcατο ο πετροc και ευθεωc αλεκτωρ εφωνηcεν.

DEF: **P^{60}** παλιν ουν η[ ] πετρ[ ]c κα[ ]εκ[
P^{66} παλι[ ] ουν ηρ̣[ ]η̣cατ[ ]υ̣[ ]υc α̣[ ]εκ[ ] εφω[

ευθεωc: [ ]υ[ ]υc **P^{66}**

18:28

P^{60} P^{66}

28: αγουcιν ουν τον ιηcουν απο του καιαφα εις το πραιτωριον ην δε πρωια και αυτοι ουκ ειcηλθον εις το πραιτωριον ινα μη μιανθωcιν αλλ ινα φαγωcι το παcχα.

DEF: **P^{60}**]ν τον ι̅ν̅ απο το[ ]c το πραιτωριο[ ]ωι και αυτοι ουκ [ ]ν ε̣ι̣c̣ το πραιτω[ ] μη μιανθωcιν [ ]γωcι το παcχ[
P^{66}] τ̣ον ι̅ν̅ α[ ]ιτωριο[ ] ουκ ει[ ]ο̣ν ιν[ ]cιν [

πρωια: [ ]ωι **P^{60}**
φαγωcι: [ ]cιν **P^{66}**

18:29

P^{60} **P**^{66}

29: εξηλθεν ουν ο πιλατος προς αυτους και ειπε τινα κατηγοριαν φερετε κατα του ανθρωπου τουτου.

DEF: **P**^{60}]ν ουν ο πιλα[
P^{66}]λατ̣[ ] εξω κ̣[ ] φησιν τ̣ινα [ ]ατηγοριαν φερετ[ ] κ̣ατα
του̣ ανο̣[ ]το̣υ

αυτους: + εξω **P**^{66}
ειπε: φησιν **P**^{66}

18:30

P^{66}

30: απεκριθησαν και ειπον αυτω ει μη ην ουτος κακοποιος ουκ αν σοι παρεδωκαμεν αυτον.

DEF: **P**^{66} απεκριθ̣η̣σαν κ̣[ ] α̣υ̣τ̣ω̣ ει μη ην ου̣τος κα[ ]υκ αν
παρεδωκιμ̣εν σο̣[

σοι παρεδωκαμεν: παρεδωκιμεν σο[ ] **P**^{66}

18:31

P^{52} **P**^{60} **P**^{66}

31: ειπεν ουν αυτοις ο πιλατος λαβετε αυτον υμεις και κατα τον νομον υμων κρινατε αυτον ειπον ουν αυτω οι ιουδαιοι ημιν ουκ εξεστιν αποκτειναι ουδενα.

DEF: **P**^{52}] οι ιουδαι[ ]ι ημε[ ] ουδενα
P^{60} ειπεν ουν αυ[ ]τος λαβετε [ ] και κατα τον [ ] ημων
κριν[ ] ειπον ουν α[ ]δαιοι η[ ]ιν [
P^{66}]πεν ου αυτοι[ ]ε̣ι̣λατ̣[ ] ουν αυ[ ] νομον [ ]τ̣ω οι
ιο̣[ ]στ̣[ ]ν̣ αποκ̣[

πιλατος: [ ]ειλατ[ ] **P**^{66}
λαβετε: + ουν **P**^{66}
υμων κρινατε αυτον ειπον ουν αυτω: [18-21]τω **P**^{66}
υμων: ημων **P**^{60}
ημιν: ημε[ ] **P**^{52}

18:32

P^{52} **P**^{60} **P**^{66}

32: ινα ο λογος του ιηcου πληρωθη ον ειπε cημαινων ποιω θανατω ημελλεν αποθνηcκειν.

DEF: **P**^{52} ι̣ν̣α ο λ[ ]πεν cημαινω[ ]θνηcκειν
P^{60}] του ι̅υ̅ πληρωθη [ ] cημενων [ ]νατω ημελλε[ ]ηcκιν
P^{66}]ν̣α ο λ̣ογοc του ι̅υ̣̅ [ ]ι̣πεν cημαινω[ ]τ̣[ ]λλεν απο[

ειπε: [ ]πεν **P**^{52}; [ ]ιπεν **P**^{66}
cημαινων: cημενων **P**^{60}
αποθνηcκειν: [ ]ηcκιν **P**^{60}

18:33

P^{52} **P**^{60} **P**^{66}

33: ειcηλθεν ουν ειc το πραιτωριον παλιν ο πιλατοc και εφωνηcε τον ιηcουν και ειπεν αυτω cυ ει ο βαcιλευc των ιουδαιων.

DEF: **P**^{52} ιc[ ]ριον ο π[ ] και ειπ[ ]αιω[
P^{60} εξηλθεν [ ] το πραιτωρι[ ]αι ειπεν αυτ[ ]λε[ ] των ιο[
P^{66}]cηλθ[ ]ν̣ παλιν̣ [ ]ωριον ο π̣[ ]τοc ϗ [ ] τ̣ο[ ] ι̅ν̅ κ̣[ ]πεν [ ] . [

ειcηλθεν: ιc[ ] **P**^{52}; εξηλθεν **P**^{60}
ειc το πραιτωριον παλιν: [ ]ριον **P**^{52}; παλιν [ ]ωριον **P**^{66}
πραιτωριον παλιν ο πιλατοc και εφωνηcε τον ιηcουν και: πραιτωρι[2 / 6]αι **P**^{60}

18:34

P^{60} **P**^{66}

34: απεκριθη αυτω ο ιηcουc αφ εαυτου cυ τουτο λεγειc η αλλοι cοι ειπον περι εμου.

DEF: **P**^{60}]εκριθη ο [ ]του τουτο [ ]οι cοι ειπον [
P^{66} απεκρινα̣[ ]ο ι̅c̅ απ̣ο cεαυ̣[ ] τουτο λε[ ]λοι ε̣[ ]πεν cο[ ]ρι εμου

απεκριθη: απεκρινα[ ]ο **P**^{66}
αυτω: OM **P**^{60} **P**^{66}
ο: OM **P**^{66}
αφ εαυτου cυ: απο cεαυ[ ] **P**^{66*}; + [ ]υ supra lineam **P**^{66*c}
cυ: OM **P**^{60}
cοι ειπον: ε[ ]πεν cο[ ] **P**^{66}

18:35

P^{60} **P**^{66}

35: απεκριθη ο πιλατοc μητι εγω ιουδαιοc ειμι το εθνοc το cον και οι αρχιερειc παρεδωκαν cε εμοι τι εποιηcαc.

DEF: **P**^{60} απεκριθ[ ] μη[ ]ι εγω [ ] το εθν[ ]c το c[
P^{66} απεκρ̣[ ]λατοc μ̣η̣ γαρ εγω ιου[ ]ι̣ το εθνοc το cον και οι α[ ]αρεδωκα̣ν cε εμοι τ̣[ ]c

μητι: μη γαρ **P**^{66}

18:36

P^{60} **P**^{66} **P**^{90}

36: απεκριθη ο ιηcουc η βαcιλεια η εμη ουκ εcτιν εκ του κοcμου τουτου ει εκ του κοcμου τουτου ην η βαcιλεια η εμη οι υπηρεται αν οι εμοι ηγωνιζοντο ινα μη παραδοθω τοιc ιουδαιοιc νυν δε η βαcιλεια η εμη ουκ εcτιν εντευθεν.

DEF: **P**^{60}] η βαcιλει[ ]ιν εκ του [ ]του ει εκ το[ ]του ην η βα[ ]ι υπηρετε̱ [ ]νιζοντο αν [ ]αδο[ ]ω το[
P^{66} απε[ ]θη ι̅c̅ η βαcι̣[ ]οcμο̣[ ]ο̣cμου̣ η̣ν̣ η̣ [ ]η̣ρεται ο̣ι ε[ ] παραδοθω τοιc̣ [ ] δε η βαcιλι̣[ ]τευθε[
P^{90}]ιλεια η εμ[ ]ωνιζ[ ]ντο [ ] τοιc ιου[ ]ιοιc [ ] εμη ουκ [ ]cτιν [

ο: OM **P**^{66}
του κοcμου τουτου^{2}: [ ]οcμου **P**^{66}
υπηρεται: υπηρετε **P**^{60}
αν οι εμοι ηγωνιζοντο: [ ]νιζοντο αν **P**^{60}; [ ]ωνιζ[ ]ντο [ ] **P**^{90}
αν: OM **P**^{66}
βαcιλεια: βαcιλι[ ] **P**^{66}

18:37

P^{52} **P**^{60} **P**^{66} **P**^{90}

37: ειπεν ουν αυτω ο πιλατοϲ ουκουν βαϲιλευϲ ει ϲυ απεκριθη ο ιηϲουϲ ϲυ λεγειϲ οτι βαϲιλευϲ ειμι εγω εγω ειϲ τουτο γεγεννημαι και ειϲ τουτο εληλυθα ειϲ τον κοϲμον ινα μαρτυρηϲω τη αληθεια παϲ ο ων εκ τηϲ αληθειαϲ ακουει μου τηϲ φωνηϲ.

DEF: **P**^{52}]υτο γ[ ]γεννημαι [ ]ϲμον ινα μαρτυ[ ] εκ τηϲ αληθε[
P^{60}]πεκριθη ι̅[ ]λευϲ ειμ[ ]το γεγεννη[ ]το εληλυθ[ ] ινα
μ[ ]ρτ[ ]θεια π[ ]ϲ ο ω[ ]ηθει[
P^{66}]τοϲ υ[ ]υν βαϲιλ[ ]π̣εκρ̣[ ] ι̅ϲ̅ κ[ ]ι ειπ̣[ ]υϲ ε[ ]μ̣ι
[ ]ηλυθ[ ] ειϲ τ[ ] κ̣οϲ̣μον [ ]ρη̣ϲ̣ω̣ τ[ ] αληθεια̣ παϲ ο ω̣ν ε̣κ
τ̣ηϲ αληθι[ ] ακουει μου τηϲ φωνηϲ
P^{90}] ουν αυτω [ ]ε[ ]λευϲ ϲυ ει α[ ] οτι βαϲιλευϲ [ ]
γεγενν[ ] ειϲ τ[ ]ϲω [ ]η αλ[ ] αλ[ ]θει[

πιλατοϲ: [ ]ε[ ] **P**^{90}
ουκουν: υ[ ]υν **P**^{66}
ει ϲυ: ϲυ ει **P**^{90}
ο^{2}: OM **P**^{60}
ιηϲουϲ: + κ[ ]ι ειπ[ ] **P**^{66}
ειμι εγω εγω ειϲ τουτο: ειμ[10-12]το **P**^{60}; [11-17] **P**^{90}
και ειϲ τουτο εληλυθα ειϲ τον κοϲμον: [15-19]ϲμον **P**^{52}
αληθειαϲ: αληθι[ ] **P**^{66}

18:38

P^{52} **P**^{66} **P**^{90}

38: λεγει αυτω ο πιλατοϲ τι εϲτιν αληθεια και τουτο ειπων παλιν εξηλθε προϲ τουϲ ιουδαιουϲ και λεγει αυτοιϲ εγω ουδεμιαν αιτιαν ευριϲκω εν αυτω.

DEF: **P**^{52} λεγει αυτω [ ]αι τουτο [ ] τουϲ ιο[ ]εμι[
P^{66} λεγει ου̣ν... αληθι[ ] και... παλ[ ] εξηλθ̣[ ]ροϲ τουϲ̣
ιουδαιουϲ [ ]ι̣[ ] εγω ου̣δεμιαν ευ̣[ ] αι̣[ ]α̣ν̣ εν αυτω
P^{90} λεγει αυ[ ]ω ο π[ ] αληθεια και τ[ ] εξηλθεν προϲ τ[ ]αι
λεγει αυτοιϲ [ ]ιϲκω εν αυτ[

λεγει^{1}: + ουν **P**^{66}
ο: OM **P**^{66}
πιλατοϲ: πειλατοϲ **P**^{66}
αληθεια: αληθι[ ] **P**^{66}

εξηλθε: εξηλθεν **P**^{90}
εγω ουδεμιαν αιτιαν ευριcκω εν αυτω: [8-14]ιcκω εν αυτ[7+] **P**^{90}
αιτιαν ευριcκω: ευ[ ] αι[ ]αν **P**^{66}

18:39

P^{60} **P**^{66} **P**^{90}

39: εcτι δε cυνηθεια υμιν ινα ενα υμιν απολυcω εν τω παcχα βουλεcθε ουν υμιν απολυcω τον βαcιλεα των ιουδαιων.

DEF: **P**^{60}]νηθια υμ[ ]cθαι το π[ ]θαι ουν απο[ ]ν βαcιλεα [ ]ιων
P^{66} εcτ̣ῑ̣ [ ] ι̣ν̣α̣ ε̣ν̣α α[ ] παc̣χα β[ ]υ̣[ ]cω υμιν το[ ]αcιλ[ ]δαιων
P^{90}] cυνηθ[ ]ια υμ[ ]cω υμειν [ ]cθε ουν ινα [ ] βαcιλεα τ[

εcτι: εcτιν **P**^{66}
cυνηθεια: [ ]νηθια **P**^{60}
υμιν ινα ενα υμιν απολυcω εν τω παcχα: υμ[2-4 / 5-6]cθαι το π[ ] **P**^{60}
υμιν απολυcω^{1}: α[ ] **P**^{66}; [ ]cω υμειν **P**^{90}
βουλεcθε: [ ]θαι **P**^{60}
ουν: + ινα **P**^{90}
υμιν απολυcω^{2}: απο[ ] **P**^{60}; [ ]cω υμιν **P**^{66}

18:40

P^{60} **P**^{66} **P**^{90}

40: εκραυγαcαν ουν παλιν παντεc λεγοντεc μη τουτον αλλα τον βαραββαν ην δε ο βαραββαc ληcτηc.

DEF: **P**^{60} ε[ ] παλ[ ]ν λε[ ]ν αλ[
P^{66} εκ[ ]τ̣ε̣c̣ μη τουτο[ ]λλα̣ [ ]βαν ην δε β̣[ ]τ̣η̣c
P^{90}]αcαν [ ]υν π[ ] του[ ]ν α[ ] δε ο βαραββ[

παντεc: OM **P**^{60}
λεγοντεc: OM **P**^{66*}; txt **P**^{66*c}
ο: OM **P**^{66*}; txt **P**^{66*c}

CHAPTER NINETEEN

P60 P66 P90

19:1

P66 P90

1: τοτε ουν ελαβεν ο πιλατος τον ιηcουν και εμαcτιγωcε.

DEF: **P66**] ελαβεν τ[ ]ạcτ[
P90] λαβων ο πειλ[

ελαβεν ο πιλατος: [ ] ελαβεν **P66**
ελαβεν: λαβων **P90**
πιλατος: πειλ[ ] **P90**

19:2

P60 P66 P90

2: και οι cτρατιωται πλεξαντεc cτεφανον εξ ακανθων επεθηκαν αυτου τη κεφαλη και ιματιον πορφυρουν περιεβαλον αυτον.

DEF: **P60**]ι οι cτρ[ ]ξ[ ]ν[ ]c cτ[ ]κανθων [ ] αυτου τη [ ]φυρουν ιμ[ ]ριεβα[ ]ον α[
P66 ḳ[ ]ι c̣τ̣ρατιω̣[ ]αι πλεξαντẹc εξ [ ]κανθ̣ω̣ṿ c̣τ̣εφạνοṿ... κẹ[ ]αλη... πορφυροṿṿ...
P90]ρατιωται π[ ]ν εξ ακανθ[ ]ου τη [ ]φαλη κα[ ]ου[ ] περιεβα[

cτεφανον εξ ακανθων: εξ [ ]κανθων cτεφανον **P66**
ιματιον πορφυρουν: [ ]φυρουν ιμ[ ] **P60**

19:3

P60 P66 P90

3: και ελεγον χαιρε ο βαcιλευc των ιουδαιων και εδιδουν αυτω ραπιcματα.

DEF: **P**[60]]χο[
P[66] και ηρχοντο... ελεγο[ ] χαιρε βασιλευ των ιουδα[ ] και ε[ ]ιδοσαν αυτω ραπι[
P[90]]χ[ ]ντο προς αυ[ ] χαιρε ο βασιλευ[ ]αι εδ[ ]οσαν αυ[

και: + ηρχοντο προς αυτον και **P**[66]; + [ ]χ[ ]ντο προς αυ[ ] **P**[90]; [ ]χο[ ]**P**[60]
ο βασιλευς: βασιλευ **P**[66]
εδιδουν: ε[ ]ιδοσαν **P**[66]; εδ[ ]οσαν **P**[90]

19:4

P[66] **P**[90]

4: εξηλθεν ουν παλιν εξω ο πιλατος και λεγει αυτοις ιδε αγω υμιν αυτον εξω ινα γνωτε οτι εν αυτω ουδεμιαν αιτιαν ευρισκω.

DEF: **P**[66]]ηλθεν... εξω [ ]ειλα[ ]ι λεγει αυ[ ]το[ ]ξω ινα γνω[ ] εν [ ]ω ουχ ευρισκω
P[90]]ξ[ ]θεν παλιν [ ] αυτοις ιδε [ ]ω ιν[ ]νω[ ]ν [ ] ουχ ε[ ]ισ[

ουν: OM **P**[66*] **P**[90]; txt **P**[66*c]
παλιν εξω ο πιλατος και λεγει αυτοις: παλιν / [16] αυτοις **P**[90]
πιλατος: [ ]ειλα[ ] **P**[66]
εν αυτω ουδεμιαν αιτιαν: [ ] εν [ ]ω ουχ **P**[66]; [ ]ν [4] ουχ **P**[90]

19:5

P[60] **P**[66] **P**[90]

5: εξηλθεν ουν ο ιησους εξω φορων τον ακανθινον στεφανον και το πορφυρουν ιματιον και λεγει αυτοις ιδε ο ανθρωπος.

DEF: **P**[60]]ξω φο[ ]ν στεφ[ ]ρουν ιματ[ ] ιδου ο ανο[
P[66]] ου[ ]ξ[ ] εχων τ[ ]ο[ ]τεφανον και [ ]ον
P[90]]υν [ ] ις εξω φο[ ]θινον στεφανον [ ]ουν ιματιον κ[ ]δου ο ανθρωπο[

φορων: εχων **P**[66]
και λεγει αυτοις ιδε ο ανθρωπος: OM **P**[66*]; ·/· post [ ]ον (et + verba omissa add. in margine inferiore, quae nunc deperdita est?) **P**[66*c]
ιδε: ιδου **P**[60]; [ ]δου **P**[90]

19:6

P^{60} P^{66} P^{90}

6: οτε ουν ειδον αυτον οι αρχιερειϲ και οι υπηρεται εκραυγαϲαν λεγοντεϲ ϲταυρωϲον ϲταυρωϲον λεγει αυτοιϲ ο πιλατοϲ λαβετε αυτον υμειϲ και ϲταυρωϲατε εγω γαρ ουχ ευριϲκω εν αυτω αιτιαν.

DEF: **P^{60}**]ν αυτ[ ]ν [ ]τε ε[ ]τεϲ ϲτ[
P^{66} ο̣τε ουν ε[ ] οι αρ̣[ ] υπ̣ηρ̣ε̣τ̣α̣[ ]κρ[ ]ν̣̅ λεγει... λα̣β̣ε̣τ̣αι υ[ ]ν ϲ̣̅-̅ρ̅α̣̅τ̣̅ε̣̅... ευρ[ ]κ[
P^{90}]υτον ο[ ] αρχιερε[ ] εκραζαν λ[ ]υ[ ] λεγε[ ]ετε υμειϲ [ ]ατε εγω γαρ [ ]ω αιτιαν

υπηρεται: [ ]τε **P^{60}**
εκραυγαϲαν: εκραζαν **P^{90}**
ϲταυρωϲον ϲταυρωϲον: [ ]ν̅ **P^{66*}**; + ϲ̅-̅ρ̅ο̅ν̅ **P^{66*c}**; [10-11]υ[3] **P^{90}**
αυτοιϲ: OM **P^{66}**
πιλατοϲ: πειλατοϲ **P^{66}**
λαβετε: λαβεται **P^{66}**
αυτον υμειϲ: υ[ ]ν **P^{66}**; υμειϲ / [ ] **P^{90}**
και^{2}: OM **P^{66}**

19:7

P^{60} P^{66} P^{90}

7: απεκριθηϲαν αυτω οι ιουδαιοι ημειϲ νομον εχομεν και κατα τον νομον ημων οφειλει αποθανειν οτι εαυτον υιον του θεου εποιηϲεν.

DEF: **P^{60}**]κριθηϲα[ ]δα[ ]ι ημιϲ ν[ ] και κατα τ[ ]ν [ ]φιλι απ[ ] θυ ε[ ]υτον ε[
P^{66} απεκρ̣ι̣θ̣η̣ϲ̣αν ο̣[ ]ο̣υδ̣α̣ι̣[ ]μ̣ο̣ν εχομεν... τον̣ ν̣ομ̣[ ] οφιλει... θ̅υ̣̅ [ ]υτον̣ [ ]ποιηϲεν
P^{90}]αιοι ημειϲ [ ]ι κατα τον [

απεκριθηϲαν αυτω οι ιουδαιοι: / [13-17]αιοι **P^{90}** (& cf. **P^{66}**)
αυτω: OM **P^{66}** (& cf. **P^{90}**)
ημειϲ: ημιϲ **P^{60}**
νομον ημων: νομ[2-4] **P^{66}**
οφειλει: [ ]φιλι **P^{60}**; οφιλει **P^{66}**
εαυτον υιον του θεου: [ ] θυ ε[ ]υτον **P^{60}**; υιον θεου [ ]υτον **P^{66}**

19:8

P^{60} **P**^{66}

8: οτε ουν ηκουϲεν ο πιλατοϲ τουτον τον λογον μαλλον εφοβηθη.

DEF: **P**^{60}]υν ηκουϲε[ ]υτο[
P^{66} ... ηκουϲε[ ] ο πειλ̣α[ ]ο̣ϲ̣ [ ]ο̣υ̣[ ]ν̣ τ̣ο̣[ ] λογον̣ μαλλ̣[ ]ν
εφοβηθ̣[

πιλατοϲ: πειλα[ ]οϲ **P**^{66}

19:9

P^{66}

9: καιειϲηλθεν ειϲ το πραιτωριον παλιν και λεγει τω ιηϲου
ποθεν ει ϲυ ο δε ιηϲουϲ αποκριϲιν ουκ εδωκεν αυτω.

DEF: **P**^{66}]θεν ειϲ τ̲ο̲ π[ ]αιτωρ̣ι̣ον π̣αλιν [ ]ι̣ λεγει τω ι̅υ̅
[ ]ο̣θεν [ ] ει ο δε ι̅ϲ̅ α[ ]οκριϲιν ουκ εδ[ ] αυτω

ει ϲυ: [ ] ει **P**^{66}

19:10

P^{60} **P**^{66}

10: λεγει ουν αυτω ο πιλατοϲ εμοι ου λαλειϲ ουκ οιδαϲ οτι
εξουϲιαν εχω ϲταυρωϲαι ϲε και εξουϲιαν εχω απολυϲαι ϲε.

DEF: **P**^{60}] πιλατο[ ] οιδαϲ οτι [ ]ξου[ ]ολυϲε ϲαι κα[ ]
ϲταυρωϲε [
P^{66} λεγ[ ] ο̣υ̣ν... πειλ[ ]μοι ου λαλ[ ]κ οιδαϲ οτι ε[ ] εχω
ϲταυ[ ]ι̣ ϲε και ε[ ] εχω απο[ ]αι ϲ[

πιλατοϲ: πειλ[ ] **P**^{66}
ϲταυρωϲαι ϲε και εξουϲιαν εχω απολυϲαι ϲε: [ ]ολυϲε ϲαι κα[ ]
ϲταυρωϲε [ ] **P**^{60}

19:11

P60 P66

11: απεκριθη ο ιηϲουϲ ουκ ειχεϲ εξουϲιαν ουδεμιαν κατ εμου ει μη ην ϲοι δεδομενον ανωθεν δια τουτο ο παραδιδουϲ με ϲοι μειζονα αμαρτιαν εχει.

DEF: **P60**]τω ο ις [ ] εμου [ ]ε[
P66 κ̣αι απεκ[ ] ουκ ειχε[ ]ουϲιαν κατ ε̣[ ]δεμ[ ] η̣ν̣
δεδομ[ ]υτο [ ]ν̣α̣ α̣μ̣[

απεκριθη: + [ ]τω **P60**; και απεκ[ ] **P66***; απεκ[ ] **P66*c**
εξουϲιαν ουδεμιαν κατ εμου: [10-11] εμου [ ] **P60** (& cf. **P66**)
ουδεμιαν κατ εμου: κατ ε[ ]δεμ[ ] **P66** (& cf. **P60**)
ϲοι δεδομενον: δεδομ[ ] **P66**

19:12

P60 P66

12: εκ τουτου εζητει ο πιλατοϲ απολυϲαι αυτον οι δε ιουδαιοι εκραζον λεγοντεϲ εαν τουτον απολυϲηϲ ουκ ει φιλοϲ του καιϲαροϲ παϲ ο βαϲιλεα αυτον ποιων αντιλεγει τω καιϲαρι.

DEF: **P60**] ο[ ] δ[ ]κραυγ[ ] εαν τουτον α[ ] ουκ ι φιλοϲ τ[ ]
πα[ ] ο βαϲι[ ] ποιων αντ[ ]ρι
P66]ατ̣[ ]ϲ εζητει αυτο [ ] ο̣ι̣ δ̣[ ]υ̣δαιοι εκραυ[ ]ϲ̣α̣[ ]
λ̣εγοντε̣ϲ αν του̣τ̣ον απ̣ολυ̣[ ]ηϲ ουκ... καιϲ̣αρο[ ] παϲ...
α[ ]τιλε[ ]ε̣ι τω και̣[ ]αρι

εζητει ο πιλατοϲ απολυϲαι αυτον: [5]ατ[ ]ϲ εζητει αυτον [ ] **P66**
δε ιουδαιοι εκραζον: δ[2]κραυγ[ ] **P60** (& cf. **P66**)
εκραζον: εκραυ[ ]ϲα[ ] **P66** (& cf. **P60**)
εαν: αν **P66***; txt **P66*c**
ει: ι **P60**
αυτον: εαυτον **P66**

19:13

P60 P66

13: ο ουν πιλατοϲ ακουϲαϲ τουτον τον λογον ηγαγεν εξω τον ιηϲουν και εκαθιϲεν επι του βηματοϲ ειϲ τοπον λεγομενον λιθοϲτρωτον εβραιϲτι δε γαββαθα.

DEF: $\mathbf{P}^{60}$ ο ουν πιλ[ ]c των [ ]ο[ ]εν [
$\mathbf{P}^{66}$ ου̅ πειλα[ ]οc ακουcαc̣ [ ]ν ηγαγεν ε̣ξ̣[ ] και [ ]θιcεν επι
βημ[ ]οc λιτοc[ ]τον εβραιcτι δε [ ]ομενου [ ]θ̣α

ο: OM $\mathbf{P}^{66*}$; txt $\mathbf{P}^{66*c}$
πιλατοc: πειλα[ ]οc $\mathbf{P}^{66}$
τουτον τον λογον: των [ ]ο[ ] $\mathbf{P}^{60}$
του: OM $\mathbf{P}^{66}$
ειc τοπον λεγομενον: OM $\mathbf{P}^{66*}$; + ειc τοπ[ ] in margine superiore $\mathbf{P}^{66*c}$
λιθοcτρωτον: λιτοc[ ]τον $\mathbf{P}^{66}$
δε: + [ ]ομενου $\mathbf{P}^{66}$

19:14

$\mathbf{P}^{60}$ $\mathbf{P}^{66}$

14: ην δε παραcκευη του παcχα ωρα δε ωcει εκτη και λεγει τοιc ιουδαιοιc ιδε ο βαcιλευc υμων.

DEF: $\mathbf{P}^{60}$]ουδα[ ]c υμω[
$\mathbf{P}^{66}$ ην δε πα[ ]ευη του [ ] ωρα εκτη [ ] λεγε τοιc [ ]οιc ιδε̣ ο̣
β̣αc̣[ ]υc υμων

δε ωcει: OM $\mathbf{P}^{66*}$; ην ωc $\mathbf{P}^{66*c}$
λεγει: λεγε $\mathbf{P}^{66*}$; txt $\mathbf{P}^{66*c}$

19:15

$\mathbf{P}^{60}$ $\mathbf{P}^{66}$

15: οι δε εκραυγαcαν αρον αρον cταυρωcον αυτον λεγει αυτοιc ο πιλατοc τον βαcιλεα υμων cταυρωcω απεκριθηcαν οι αρχιερειc ουκ εχομεν βαcιλεα ει μη καιcαρα.

DEF: $\mathbf{P}^{60}$ οι δε [ ] λεγοντεc [ ]ταυρωc[ ]ν αυτο̅ [ ]c ο πιλατοc
[ ]α υμων cτα[ ]ρι[ ]ηcαν ο[ ]υκ εχ[
$\mathbf{P}^{66}$] ελεγον αρον c̅ρ̅[ ]ν̅ αυτον [ ] ο̣ π̣ε̣[ ] τ̣ον βα[ ]ν̣
c̅ρ̅ω̣[ ]αcιλεα ει μη καιc̣[

εκραυγαcαν: ελεγον $\mathbf{P}^{66*}$; [ ]ραυγαcαν $\mathbf{P}^{66*c}$; + λεγοντεc $\mathbf{P}^{60}$
αρον[2]: OM $\mathbf{P}^{66*}$; txt $\mathbf{P}^{66*c}$
πιλατοc: πε[ ] $\mathbf{P}^{66}$

19:16

$\mathbf{P}^{60}$ $\mathbf{P}^{66}$

16: τοτε ουν παρεδωκεν αυτον αυτοις ινα σταυρωθη παρελαβον δε τον ιησουν και απηγαγον.

DEF: $\mathbf{P}^{60}$] δε παρ[ ] απ[ ]γαγον
$\mathbf{P}^{66}$]ạρεδωκεν ạ[ ] c⳨θη ọ[ ]ρ̣αλ̣[ ] ạυτọν̣ [ ]ν

παρελαβον δε τον ιησουν και: ο[7]ραλ[7-9] αυτον $\mathbf{P}^{66}$
παρελαβον δε τον ιησουν και απηγαγον: [2] δε παρ[13-14] απ[ ]γαγον $\mathbf{P}^{60}$

19:17

$\mathbf{P}^{60}$ $\mathbf{P}^{66}$

17: και βασταζων τον σταυρον αυτου εξηλθεν εις τον λεγομενον κρανιου τοπον ος λεγεται εβραιστι γολγοθα.

DEF: $\mathbf{P}^{60}$ κ[ ] εαυτω τον c[ ]θεν εις τον [ ] κρανιου τ[ ]ται εβραιστ[
$\mathbf{P}^{66}$ εις το[ ]ον λ[ ]μεν[ ]ου ο λεγẹται εβρα[ ]cτι γο[

και βασταζων τον σταυρον αυτου εξηλθεν: OM $\mathbf{P}^{66*}$; και βασταζων εαυτω [ ]λ̣θεν in margine superiore $\mathbf{P}^{66*c}$
τον σταυρον αυτου: εαυτω τον c[ ] $\mathbf{P}^{60}$
τον λεγομενον κρανιου τοπον ος: το[ ]ον λ[ ]μεν[ ]ου ο $\mathbf{P}^{66}$

19:18

$\mathbf{P}^{60}$ $\mathbf{P}^{66}$

18: οπου αυτον εσταυρωσαν και μετ αυτου αλλους δυο εντευθεν και εντευθεν μεσον δε τον ιησουν.

DEF: $\mathbf{P}^{60}$]υτον εc[ ]τ αυ[
$\mathbf{P}^{66}$]που αυτον c⳨αν ϗ [ ] μẹ[ ]ουc δυο εντευθεν καị [ ]ụθ̣ẹν̣ [ ]εcον δε τον ιν̣

εσταυρωσαν: c⳨αν $\mathbf{P}^{66*}$; εc⳨αν $\mathbf{P}^{66*c}$

19:19

P^{66}

19: εγραψε δε και τιτλον ο πιλατος και εθηκεν επι του σταυρου ην δε γεγραμμενον ιηcουc ο ναζωραιοc ο βαcιλευc των ιουδαιων.

DEF: **P**^{66} εγ[ ] δε κα̣[ ]ι̣τλον ο πε̣[ ]το[ ]θηκεν [ ]ου c̅⳨̅ο̅υ̅
η̣[ ] δε [ν]α̣[ ]ραι̣[ ] ο βα[ ]ν

πιλατος: πε[ ]το[ ] **P**^{66}

19:20

P^{60} **P**^{66}

20: τουτον ουν τον τιτλον πολλοι ανεγνωcαν των ιουδαιων οτι εγγυc ην τηc πολεωc ο τοποc οπου εcταυρωθη ο ιηcουc και ην γεγραμμενον εβραιcτι ελληνιcτι ρωμαιcτι.

DEF: **P**^{60}] τ̲ον τιτλ[ ]γνωcαν των [ ] οτι εγγυc ην [ ] πολεωc
[ ]ρωθη ο ι̅c̅ [ ]μμενο[ ]ιcτ[
P^{66} του̣τον [ ]λοι α[ ]γν[ ] των ιουδαιων οτι [ ]γυc̣ [ ]π̣οc
τη̣c π̣ο̣λε̣[ ] εc[ ]α̣ι̣ η̣[ ]α̣μ̣[ ] ε̣β̣[ ]λ̣ηνιcτ[

τηc πολεωc ο τοποc: [9] πολεωc **P**^{60}; [ ]ποc τηc πολε[ ] **P**^{66}
εβραιcτι ελληνιcτι ρωμαιcτι: [12]ιcτ[ ] **P**^{60}

19:21

P^{66}

21: ελεγον ουν τω πιλατω οι αρχιερειc των ιουδαιων μη γραφε ο βαcιλευc των ιουδαιων αλλ οτι εκεινοc ειπε βαcιλευc ειμι των ιουδαιων.

DEF: **P**^{66}] π̣ειλατω οι αρχ[ ]α̣ι̣ων μη γραφ[ ]α̣[ ]υ̣c τω̣[ ]ν
αλλ̣ [ ]τ̣ι εκε̣[ ]ν̣οc ειπ̣[ ]ι̣λευc ειμι των ιουδαιω̣[

πιλατω: πειλατω **P**^{66}

19:22

P^{66}

22: απεκριθη ο πιλατος ο γεγραφα γεγραφα.

DEF: **P**^{66}]ριθη ο̣... γεγρ̣[ ]ρ̣αφα

πιλατος: πειλατος **P**^{66}

19:23

P^{60} **P**^{66}

23: οι ουν στρατιωται οτε εσταυρωσαν τον ιησουν ελαβον τα ιματια αυτου και εποιησαν τεσσαρα μερη εκαστω στρατιωτη μερος και τον χιτωνα ην δε ο χιτων αρραφος εκ των ανωθεν υφαντος δι ολου.

DEF: **P**^{60} ο[ ]υν [ ]cταυρωcαν [ ]βον τα ιματ[ ]ιηcα[ ]τω
cτ[ ]c και τον [ ] ο χιτ[
P^{66} οι ουν cτρατιω[ ]cταυρω̣cαν τον ι̅ν̅ ελ̣[ ]τ̣ι̣[ ] αυτου και̣
[ ]π̣οιηcα[_]ccερ̣α μερη εκ̣[ ]ω̣ cτρα[ ]τ̣η μ̣[ ]ο̣c̣ κ̣α̣[ ]τ̣ω̣[ ] δε
ο χι̣τ̣[ ]οθε̄ υ̣φαν̣[

ανωθεν: [ ]οθεν **P**^{66}

19:24

P^{60} **P**^{66}

24: ειπον ουν προς αλληλους μη cχιcωμεν αυτον αλλα λαχωμεν περι αυτου τινος εσται ινα η γραφη πληρωθη η λεγουσα διεμεριcαντο τα ιματια μου εαυτοις και επι τον ιματιcμον μου εβαλον κληρον οι μεν ουν στρατιωται ταυτα εποιησαν.

DEF: **P**^{60}]αι τ[
P^{66}]ν π̣ροc... μη̣ [ ]με̄ [ ] α̣λλα λαχω[ ]ρι αυτ̣ου τ̣ι̣[ ]τ̣αι
ιν[ ]λη[ ]ωθη [ ]α̣ν[ ]π̣ι τον... εβ[ ]ν [ ]λ̣ηρον οι μεν ουν
[ ]ρ̣ατ[ ]τ̣αι [ ]α̣υτα ε̣[ ]ο[

19:25

P60 P66

25: ειϲτηκειϲαν δε παρα τω ϲταυρω του ιηϲου η μητηρ αυτου και η αδελφη τηϲ μητροϲ αυτου μαρια η του κλωπα και μαρια η μαγδαληνη.

DEF: **P60**]ϲτηκιϲαν [ ] ϲταυρω του [ ]αι η α[ ]λ[ ]υτου [ ]νη
P66 ι̣[ ]αν δ[ ]αρα τω̣ [ ]. ρ̄ω̣ [ ] μ̣ητηρ α[ ]τ̣ου και̣ [ ]δε[ ]η̣ϲ μητροϲ̣ [ ]ο̣υ μαρι̣[ ] του̣ κ̣λωπα και μαρι̣[

ειϲτηκειϲαν: [ ]ϲτηκιϲαν **P60**; ι[ ]αν **P66**
μαρια η του κλωπα και μαρια η μαγδαληνη: [4-8 / 7-11]νη **P60**

19:26

P60 P66

26: ιηϲουϲ ουν ιδων την μητερα και τον μαθητην παρεϲτωτα ον ηγαπα λεγει τη μητρι αυτου γυναι ιδου ο υιοϲ ϲου.

DEF: **P60** ι̅ϲ̅ [ ]α̅ και [
P66 ... τη̣[ ]ν μαθητην π[ ]α λεγει τη̣ μ[ ]ιοϲ ϲου

μητρι αυτου γυναι ιδου ο υιοϲ: μ[1-5 / 11]ιοϲ **P66**

19:27

P66

27: ειτα λεγει τω μαθητη ιδου η μητηρ ϲου και απ εκεινηϲ τηϲ ωραϲ ελαβεν αυτην ο μαθητηϲ ειϲ τα ιδια.

DEF: **P66** ειτ[ ] η̣ μητηρ ϲου̣ [ ] ωραϲ ελα[ ]ην ειϲ τα ιδια

αυτην ο μαθητηϲ: [ ]ην **P66**

19:28

P^{66}

28: μετα τουτο ειδως ο ιηcουc οτι παντα ηδη τετελεcται ινα τελειωθη η γραφη λεγει διψω.

DEF: **P**^{66} μ̣[ ]ωc οτι ηδη παν[ ]χ̣ει διψω

ο ιηcουc: OM **P**^{66}
παντα ηδη τετελεcται ινα τελειωθη η γραφη λεγει: ηδη παν[0-5 / 12]γει **P**^{66*}; ·/·ινα τελειω̣θη η χ̣ρ̣αφη in margine inferiore **P**^{66*c}

19:29

P^{66}

29: cκευοc ουν εκειτο οξουc μεcτον οι δε πληcαντεc cπογγον οξουc και υccωπω περιθεντεc προcηνεγκαν αυτου τω cτοματι.

DEF: **P**^{66} cκε̣[ ]ε̣ι̣τ̣ο̣ [ ]εcτον [ ]υ̣ν μεcτ̣ο̣[ ] τ̣[ ]υ̣
οξου̣[ ]π[ ]ε̣ριθεντεc... αυτο̣υ̣ τ̣[ ]τοματι

cκευοc ουν εκειτο: cκε[2-3 / 2]ειτο **P**^{66}
οι δε πληcαντεc cπογγον οξουc και υccωπω: [4-9 / 1]υν μεcτο[ ] τ[ ]υ οξου[5-10] / π[ ] **P**^{66}

19:30

P^{66}

30: οτε ουν ελαβε το οξοc ο ιηcουc ειπε τετελεcται και κλιναc την κεφαλην παρεδωκε το πνευμα.

DEF: **P**^{66} οτε ουν ελ[ ]εν το ο̣[_] ι̣̅c̣̅ [ ] τ̣ε̣τελεc[ ]αι
κλι[ ]ε̣φ[ ]ν παρ[ ]δωκεν το π̣̅ν̣̅[

ελαβε: ελ[ ]εν **P**^{66}
παρεδωκ: παρ[ ]δωκεν **P**^{66}

19:31

P66

31: οι ουν ιουδαιοι ινα μη μεινη επι του cταυρου τα cωματα εν τω cαββατω επει παραcκευη ην ην γαρ μεγαλη η ημερα εκεινου του cαββατου ηρωτηcαν τον πιλατον ινα κατεαγωcιν αυτων τα cκελη και αρθωcιν.

DEF: **P66**] ου[ ]ọυδαιο[ ]πι παραcκευη ην̣ ι̣ν̣[ ] μ̣η μειν[ ] του cτ⳨ρου τα cωμ̣[ ]ατω ην γαρ [ ]νου του cα[ ] τον πιλατ̣[ ]ν αυτων τ̣[ ]θωcι̣ν

ινα μη μεινη επι του cταυρου τα cωματα εν τω cαββατω επει παραcκευη ην: [ ]πι παραcκευη ην ιν[ ] μη μειν[ ] του cτ⳨ρου τα cωμ[ ]ατω **P66**

19:32

P66

32: ηλθον ουν οι cτρατιωται και του μεν πρωτου κατεαξαν τα cκελη και του αλλου του cυcταυρωθεντοc αυτω.

DEF: **P66** ηλθαν [ ]ται και του μεν̣ [ ]α̣ξ̣α̣ν τα cκ̣ε̣[ ]υ̣ cυνcτ̣[

ηλθον: ηλθαν **P66**
cυcταυρωθεντοc: cυνcτ[ ] **P66**

19:33

P66

33: επι δε τον ιηcουν ελθοντεc ωc ειδον αυτον ηδη τεθνηκοτα ου κατεαξαν αυτου τα cκελη.

DEF: **P66**]π̣ι δε [ ] ελθον̣[ ]ν̣ ηδ[ ]υτον τεθνη[ ]ε̣λη

αυτον ηδη: ηδ[ ]υτον **P66**

19:34

P^{66}

34: αλλ εις των cτρατιωτων λογχη αυτου την πλευραν ενυξε και ευθυc εξηλθεν αιμα και υδωρ.

DEF: **P**^{66}]̓ [   ]ν π̣λ̣ε̣υ̣ρ̣α[ ] ενυξ[   ]α̣ι̣ ε̣ξη̣[   ]ν ευ̣θυc α[ ]μ̣α και υ[ ]ωρ

ευθυc εξηλθεν: εξη[   ]ν ευθυc **P**^{66}

19:35

P^{66}

35: και ο εωρακωc μεμαρτυρηκε και αληθινη αυτου εcτιν η μαρτυρια κακεινοc οιδεν οτι αληθη λεγει ινα υμειc πιcτευcητε.

DEF: **P**^{66} κα[   ]ω̣ρακωc [ ]εμα̣[ ]τ̣υ[   ]κεν̣ [   ]η̣θιν[   ]cτιν̣ [ ]υ̣[   ]υ̣ η μα[   ]α̣ κ̣[   ]ε̣ι̣[   ]ν οτι αλ[   ]γ̣ε̣[   ]α κα̣[   ]ειc πιcτε̣[   ]α̣ι

μεμαρτυρηκε: [ ]εμα[ ]τυ[   ]κεν **P**^{66}
αυτου εcτιν: [ ]cτιν [ ]υ[   ]υ **P**^{66}
κακεινοc: κ[4]ει[   ] **P**^{66}
ινα: + κα[ ] **P**^{66}
πιcτευcητε: πιcτε[   ]αι **P**^{66}

19:36

P^{66}

36: εγενετο γαρ ταυτα ινα η γραφη πληρωθη οcτουν ου cυντριβηcεται αυτου.

DEF: **P**^{66} εγ̣[ ]ν̣ετ[   ]υτα [   ] γραφη πλ̣[   ]c̣το̣υ̣[   ]ντρ̣ιβηcετ[

19:37

P^{66}

37: και παλιν ετερα γραφη λεγει οψονται ειc ον εξεκεντηcαν.

DEF: **P**^{66}]αι πα̣[   ]α̣ γ̣ραφη λ[ ]γ̣ε̣ι̣ [   ] ειc̣ ο̣ν [   ]εντηcα̣ν

19:38

P^{66}

38: μετα δε ταυτα ηρωτηcε τον πιλατον ο ιωcηφ ο απο αριμαθαιαc ων μαθητηc του ιηcου κεκρυμμενοc δε δια τον φοβον των ιουδαιων ινα αρη το cωμα του ιηcου και επετρεψεν ο πιλατοc ηλθεν ουν και ηρε το cωμα του ιηcου.

DEF: **P**^{66}] ταυ̣τ̣α η[ ]c̣εν το[ ]ω̣c̣[ ]φ απ[ ]θαια[ ] δια [ ] αρ[ ]
ηλθ̣[ ] η̣ρ̣εν το [ ]ωμα αυ̣το[

ηρωτηcε: η[ ]cεν **P**^{66}
ο^{2}: OM **P**^{66}
αρη το cωμα του ιηcου και επετρεψεν ο πιλατοc: αρ[10-12] **P**^{66}
ηρε: ηρεν **P**^{66}
του ιηcου^{3}: αυτο[ ] **P**^{66}

19:39

P^{66}

39: ηλθε δε και νικοδημοc ο ελθων προc τον ιηcουν νυκτοc το πρωτον φερων μιγμα cμυρνηc και αλοηc ωcει λιτραc εκατον.

DEF: **P**^{66}] κα̣ι̣ νικο̣[ ]η̣μοc ο ελ[ ]ν̣ π̣ρο̣c̣ α̣[ ] νυκ̣[ ]ο̣c
πρ[ ]τ[ ]ρ̣ων μ[ ]υ̣[ ]η̣c κα[ ]cει λ[ ] εκ[ ]ν̣

τον ιηcουν: α[ ] **P**^{66*}; α[ ]ν **P**^{66*c}
το: OM **P**^{66*}; txt **P**^{66*c}

19:40

P^{66}

40: ελαβον ουν το cωμα του ιηcου και εδηcαν αυτο οθονιοιc μετα των αρωματων καθωc εθοc εcτι τοιc ιουδαιοιc ενταφιαζειν.

DEF: **P**^{66} ε[ ] ουν̣ το c̣[ ] τ̣ου ῑ̣[ ]αι ε̣[ ]ν̣ αυτο οθ̣[ ]c μ̣[ ]α τω
[ ]μ̣ατων̣ [ ] ε̣θοc εcτ̣[ ]ν τ̣[ ]υδα̣[ ]ταφιαζε̣ιν

των: τω **P**^{66*}; txt **P**^{66*c}
εcτι: εcτ[ ]ν **P**^{66}

19:41

P[66]

41: ην δε εν τω τοπω οπου εσταυρωθη κηπος και εν τω κηπω μνημειον καινον εν ω ουδεπω ουδεις ετεθη.

DEF: **P[66]**]ε̣ εν̣ [ ] τοπ̣ω οπου [ ]υ̣ρ̣[ ]θη κ̣[ ]ι εν τω [ ]π̣ω μ̣νημ̣[ ]ον εν̣ [ ]δ̣επ[ ] ου[ ]με[

41-42 ετεθη εκει: [6-7]με[7] **P[66]**

19:42

P[66]

42: εκει ουν δια την παρασκευην των ιουδαιων οτι εγγυς ην το μνημειον εθηκαν τον ιησουν.

DEF: **P[66]**] ο̣υν δια [ ] εγγ[ ]ν το μνημειον εθ̣[ ]κα̅ [ ]ν̣ ι̅ν̅

εκει: cf. v. 41

CHAPTER TWENTY

P^{5} **P**^{66}

20:1

P^{66}

1: τη δε μια των σαββατων μαρια η μαγδαληνη ερχεται πρωι σκοτιας ετι ουσης εις το μνημειον και βλεπει τον λιθον ηρμενον εκ του μνημειου.

DEF: **P**^{66}] δε μι[ ] των σαβ[ ]ω̅ [ ]α̣χ[ ]ηνη ερχ[ ]τι ουσης ε̣[ ]επει τον [ ]υ̣ μ[ ]με[

20:2

P^{66}

2: τρεχει ουν και ερχεται προς σιμωνα πετρον και προς τον αλλον μαθητην ον εφιλει ο ιησους και λεγει αυτοις ηραν τον κυριον εκ του μνημειου και ουκ οιδαμεν που εθηκαν αυτον.

DEF: **P**^{66}]χ̣εται̣̣ π̣ρος σ[ ]αι προς τον [ ] μαθητη[ ]ν εφιλει ο ι̅σ̅ κ[ ] α̣υτοι̣ς ηρ[ ]ν̣ το̣ν κ̅ν̅ εκ του̣ [ ]ν̣η̣μ̣ειου κα[ ]υκ ο̣ιδαμεν π̣[ ]υ̣ εθη[ ]α̣ν αυτον̣

20:3

P^{66}

3: εξηλθεν ουν ο πετρος και ο αλλος μαθητης και ηρχοντο εις το μνημειον.

DEF: **P**^{66}]ηλθεν̣ [ ]υ̣ν̣ ο̣ πε[ ]ρ̣ος και ο̣ [ ]ος μαθ[ ]η̣ς και η[ ]οντο εις̣ το μνημ[

20:4

P[66]

4: ετρεχον δε οι δυο ομου και ο αλλος μαθητης προεδραμε ταχιον του πετρου και ηλθε πρωτος εις το μνημειον.

DEF: **P**[66] ε̣τ̣ρ̣ε̣[ ]ο̣ν δε οι δ̣υο ομου [ ]τ̣η̣[ ]ρ̣α̣[ ]ε̣[ ] μν[ ]ειον

μαθητης: [ ]τη[ ] **P**[66*]; [ ]θητη[ ] **P**[66*c]

20:5

P[66]

5: και παρακυψας βλεπει κειμενα τα οθονια ου μεντοι εισηλθεν.

DEF: **P**[66] και π̣αρακυψ[ ] κει̣[ ]να τα οθον[ ] ου μεν[

20:6

P[66]

6: ερχεται ουν σιμων πετρος ακολουθων αυτω και εισηλθεν εις το μνημειον και θεωρει τα οθονια κειμενα.

DEF: **P**[66]]αι ουν και [ ]μ̣ω̣ν̣ [ ] α̣[ ]ων αυτω̣ [ ]ειον και θ̣[

ουν: + και **P**[66]

20:7

P[66]

7: και το σουδαριον ο ην επι της κεφαλης αυτου ου μετα των οθονιων κειμενον αλλα χωρις εντετυλιγμενον εις ενα τοπον.

DEF: **P**[66] και τ̣ο̣ [ ]ς αυ̣[ ]υ ο̣[ ]ιμεν̣ο̣ν α̣[ ]μ̣ε̣νον εις εν̣[

20:8

P[66]

8: τοτε ουν εισηλθε και ο αλλος μαθητης ο ελθων πρωτος εις το μνημειον και ειδε και επιστευσεν.

DEF: **P**[66]] ẹιcηλθεν ḳ[ ]λ̣ο̣ς̣ μ̣α̣[ ]λ̣θων πρωτος [ ] το μνημειο[ ] και ιδεν ḳαι ẹ[ ]ς̣τευcεν

ειcηλθε: ειcηλθεν **P**[66]
ειδε: ιδεν **P**[66]

20:9

P[66]

9: ουδεπω γαρ ηδειcαν την γραφην οτι δει αυτον εκ νεκρων αναcτηναι.

DEF: **P**[66]]υδẹπ̣[ ] γ̣[ ]ρ̣ ηδειc[ ]ην γραφ[ ]τι δι αυ̣[ ] ẹκ νεḳ[ ]ν̣ αναc[ ]α̣ι

δει: δι **P**[66]

20:10

P[66]

10: απηλθον ουν παλιν προc εαυτουc οι μαθηται.

DEF: **P**[66] απ[ ]ν ουν̣ π[ ]ν προc [ ]α̣θηται

20:11

P[5] **P**[66]

11: μαρια δε ειcτηκει προc το μνημειον κλαιουcα εξω ωc ουν εκλαιε παρεκυψεν ειc το μνημειον.

DEF: **P**[5]] μνημ[ ] παρεκυ[
P[66] ... δẹ [ ] τ̣ω μν̣[ ]μ̣ẹι̣ω̣ ε[

μαρια: μαριαμ **P**[66*c]; txt **P**[66*]
το μνημειον[1]: τω μν[ ]μειω **P**[66]
κλαιουcα εξω: ε[ ] **P**[66]

20:12

P^{5} **P**^{66}

12: και θεωρει δυο αγγελουϲ εν λευκοιϲ καθεζομενουϲ ενα προϲ τη κεφαλη και ενα προϲ τοιϲ ποϲιν οπου εκειτο το ϲωμα του ιηϲου.

DEF: **P**^{5}]ρει δυο [με]ν[ουϲ ενα... προϲ] τ[
P^{66}]ε̣ι δυο̣ [ ]λ̣ουϲ εν λευ̣[ ]ομ̣[ ]ϲ ενα προϲ τ[κ]α̣[ ]ροϲ τοιϲ ποϲι [ ] του ι̅υ̅

ποϲιν: ποϲι **P**^{66}

20:13

P^{5} **P**^{66}

13: και λεγουϲιν αυτη εκεινοι γυναι τι κλαιειϲ λεγει αυτοιϲ οτι ηραν τον κυριον μου και ουκ οιδα που εθηκαν αυτον.

DEF: **P**^{5}] μου [
P^{66} και λ̣[ ]η̣ [ ] χ̣υν̣[ ] τι κ[ ]υ̣τοι[ ] οτ̣[ ]ρ̣αν [ ]ον̣ κ̅ν̣̅ [ ] ο̣υκ̣ οιδα πο[ ] ε̣θη̣κ̣α̣ν αυ̣[

20:14

P^{5} **P**^{66}

14: και ταυτα ειπουϲα εϲτραφη ειϲ τα οπιϲω και θεωρει τον ιηϲουν εϲτωτα και ουκ ηδει οτι ο ιηϲουϲ εϲτι.

DEF: **P**^{5}] ταυτα [ ]ϲω και [ ]κ ηδει [
P^{66}]α̣υτα ειπουϲα εϲ̣[ ]αφη ειϲ τα ο̣πι̣[ ]ω και θεωρει [ ]ν̣ ι̅ν̅ εϲτ[ ]τ̣α κ̣α̣ι ουκ ηδει οτι κ̣̅ϲ̅ εϲτιν

ο: OM **P**^{66}
ιηϲουϲ: κ̅ϲ̅ fortasse **P**^{66*}; txt **P**^{66*c}
εϲτι: εϲτιν **P**^{66}

20:15

P5 P66

15: λεγει αυτη ο ιηcουc γυναι τι κλαιειc τινα ζητειc εκεινη δοκουcα οτι ο κηπουροc εcτι λεγει αυτω κυριε ει cυ εβαcταcαc αυτον ειπε μοι που αυτον εθηκαc καγω αυτον αρω.

DEF: **P5**] γυναι [ ] δοκου[ ] αυτω [ ] μοι π[ ] αρω
P66 λ̣[ ]ε̣ι̣ [ ]η ι̅c̅... κλαιειc τι[ ]ε̣ιc [ ]κ̣[ ]νη δοκουcα οτ[ ]
κ̣η̣[ ]ο̣υροc [ ]εγει αυτω κ̅[ ] ει c[ ]αcτα[ ]ν̣ ε̣ι̣π̣[ ] πο̣υ [

ο¹: OM **P66**
εκεινη: [ ]κ[1]νη **P66**

20:16

P5 P66

16: λεγει αυτη ο ιηcουc μαρια cτραφειcα εκεινη λεγει αυτω ραββουνι ο λεγεται διδαcκαλε.

DEF: **P5**]β[
P66] ι̅c̅ μα̣[ ]γει αυτω̣ [ ]εγετ̣[

λεγει αυτη ο ιηcουc μαρια cτραφειcα εκεινη λεγει αυτω ραββουνι: [23-28 / 26-31] / β[ ] **P5**
ραββουνι ο λεγεται: [7-15 / 10]εγετ[ ] **P66**
16-17 ραββουνι ο λεγεται διδαcκαλε λεγει αυτη ο ιηcουc:
[ ] / β[25-30] **P5** (fortasse legit κ̅ε̅ pro διδαcκαλε)

20:17

P5 P66

17: λεγει αυτη ο ιηcουc μη μου απτου ουπω γαρ αναβεβηκα προc τον πατερα μου πορευου δε προc τουc αδελφουc μου και ειπε αυτοιc αναβαινω προc τον πατερα μου και πατερα υμων και θεον μου και θεον υμων.

DEF: **P5**] μ[ ] τ[
P66]ω γαρ αναβ[ ]α̣ π[ ]α̣ μου πορευ[ ]λ̣φουc μου
κ̣[ ]α̣βαι[ ]ω π[ ]ν̣ π̣[ ]ι̣ π̅ρ̅α̅ [ ]μ̣ων̣ και θ̅ν̅ [ ] θ̅[ ] υμων

20:18

P^{66}

18: ερχεται μαρια η μαγδαληνη απαγγελλουςα τοις μαθηταις οτι εωρακε τον κυριον και ταυτα ειπεν αυτη.

DEF: **P**^{66} ε̣[ ]χεται μαριαμ [ ]γδ[ ]η̣νη αγ[ ]λλου̣ςα τοις
μ[ ]θ̣η̣[ ]α̣ις οτι εορακα τον κ̅ν̅ κα[ ]τ̣α...

μαρια: μαριαμ **P**^{66}
απαγγελλουςα: αγ[2]λλουςα **P**^{66*}; απαγ[ ]λλουςα **P**^{66*c}
εωρακε: εορακα **P**^{66}

20:19

P^{5} **P**^{66}

19: ουςης ουν οψιας τη ημερα εκεινη τη μια των ςαββατων και των θυρων κεκλειςμενων οπου ηςαν οι μαθηται ςυνηγμενοι δια τον φοβον των ιουδαιων ηλθεν ο ιηςους και εςτη εις το μεςον και λεγει αυτοις ειρηνη υμιν.

DEF: **P**^{5}] η[λθεν]ν λεγει [
P^{66} ουςης ουν̣ [ ]ψ̣ι̣α̣ς̣... τη [ ] ςαβ[ ]ατων κ̣α̣ι̣
τ[ ]θυρω[ ]εκ̣[ ]ς̣μ̣ενω̣[ ]υ ηςαν̣ [ ] εις το μ̣[ ]ις ειρην̣[

και^{3}: OM **P**^{5*}; txt **P**^{5*c}

20:20

P^{5} **P**^{66}

20: και τουτο ειπων εδειξεν αυτοις τας χειρας και την πλευραν αυτου εχαρηςαν ουν οι μαθηται ιδοντες τον κυριον.

DEF: **P**^{5}]ουτ ειπω̅ [ ]υ[ ]αι ι[
P^{66}]ς χειρα[ ]υ εχαρη[ ]ες τ̣[

τουτο: τουτ **P**^{5}
εδειξεν αυτοις τας χειρας και την πλευραν: / [20-27]υ[ ] **P**^{5}
20-22 ιδοντες τον κυριον ειπεν ουν αυτοις ο ιηςους παλιν ειρηνη υμιν καθως απεςταλκε με ο πατηρ καγω πεμπω υμας και τουτο ειπων ενεφυςηςε και λεγει αυτοις λαβετε πνευμα αγιον: ι[66-87

/ 23-24]να̅ α[ ] **P**[5] (textus receptus 140 litteras habet)

20:21

21: ειπεν ουν αυτοις ο ιηςους παλιν ειρηνη υμιν καθως απεςταλκε με ο πατηρ καγω πεμπω υμας.

vid. v. 20

20:22

P[5] **P**[66]

22: και τουτο ειπων ενεφυςηςε και λεγει αυτοις λαβετε πνευμα αγιον.

DEF: **P**[5]]να̅ α[
P[66]] ε̣ι[ ]ε̣ι αυτ̣[ ]ι̣[

vid. v. 20

20:23

P[5] **P**[66]

23: αν τινων αφητε τας αμαρτιας αφιενται αυτοις αν τινων κρατητε κεκρατηνται.

DEF: **P**[5]]αρτιας [ ] κρατητε [
P[66]]ν τινω̣[

20:24

P[5]

24: θωμας δε εις εκ των δωδεκα ο λεγομενος διδυμος ουκ ην μετ αυτων οτε ηλθεν ο ιηςους.

DEF: **P**[5]]ν δω[ ]κ ην [ ]εν ι̅η̅ς̅

μετ αυτων οτε ηλθεν: [17-22]εν **P**[5]
ο²: OM **P**[5]

20:25

P^{5} **P**^{66}

25: ελεγον ουν αυτω οι αλλοι μαθηται εωρακαμεν τον κυριον ο δε ειπεν αυτοις εαν μη ιδω εν ταις χερσιν αυτου τον τυπον των ηλων και βαλω τον δακτυλον μου εις τον τυπον των ηλων και βαλω την χειρα μου εις την πλευραν αυτου ου μη πιστευσω.

DEF: **P**^{5}]ρακα[ ]ς εαν [ ]πον [
P^{66}] ẹịδ̣ω̣ ẹ[ ] τυπους [ ]ω̣ τον δ̣[

ελεγον ουν αυτω οι αλλοι μαθηται εωρακαμεν: [21-22]ρακα[ ] **P**^{5}
μη ιδω εν ταις χερσιν αυτου τον τυπον: [21-22]πον **P**^{5}
ιδω: ειδω **P**^{66}
τυπον^{1}: τυπους **P**^{66}

20:26

P^{66}

26: και μεθ ημερας οκτω παλιν ησαν εσω οι μαθηται αυτου και θωμας μετ αυτων ερχεται ο ιησους των θυρων κεκλεισμενων και εστη εις το μεσον και ειπεν ειρηνη υμιν.

DEF: **P**^{66}]ητ[ ]τ̣ αυτ̣[ ]ων κ[

20:27

P^{66}

27: ειτα λεγει τω θωμα φερε τον δακτυλον σου ωδε και ιδε τας χειρας μου και φερε την χειρα σου και βαλε εις την πλευραν μου και μη γινου απιστος αλλα πιστος.

DEF: **P**^{66}]ι̣ μη γινου απ[

20:28

P^{66}

28: και απεκριθη ο θωμας και ειπεν αυτω ο κυριος μου και ο θεος μου.

DEF: **P**^{66} ... θω̣[ ]υ̣τω ο κ̅c̅ μου κ̣[

και^{1}: OM **P**^{66}
ο^{1}: OM **P**^{66}

20:29

P^{66}

29: λεγει αυτω ο ιηcουc οτι εωρακαc με θωμα πεπιcτευκαc μακαριοι οι μη ιδοντεc και πιcτευcαντεc.

DEF: **P**^{66}]υ̣τω ι̅c̅ οτι ε[ ]ευκα̣c μα[ ]ρ̣ι[ ]εc και πι̣[ ]ε̣υc̣[

ο: OM **P**^{66}

20:30

P^{66}

30: πολλα μεν ουν και αλλα cημεια εποιηcεν ο ιηcουc ενωπιον των μαθητων αυτου α ουκ εcτι γεγραμμενα εν τω βιβλιω τουτω.

DEF: **P**^{66}] μ̣ε̣ν̣ ο̣υ̣ν και [ ] εποιηcεν ο ι̅c̅ ενωπ̣[ ] μαθητων αυ̣τ̣ου α ου̣[ ]γραμ̣μ̣ενα [ ]ν βιβλ[ ]τω̣

τω: OM **P**^{66*}; txt **P**^{66*c}

20:31

P^{66}

31: ταυτα δε γεγραπται ινα πιcτευcητε οτι ο ιηcουc εcτιν ο χριcτοc ο υιοc του θεου και ινα πιcτευοντεc ζωην εχητε εν τω ονοματι αυτου.

DEF: **P**^{66} ταυ̣τ̣α̣ δε γεγραπται [ ]τ̣ε̣υ̣ητ̣α̣ι̣ οτι ι̅c̅ ε̣c̣[ ] κ̣αι ι̣ν̣α̣ π̣[ ]μα[

πιcτευcητε: [ ]τευηται **P**^{66}
ο^{1}: OM **P**^{66}

CHAPTER TWENTY-ONE

P^{59} **P**^{66}

21:1

P^{66}

1: μετα ταυτα εφανερωσεν εαυτον παλιν ο ιηcουc τοιc μαθηταιc επι τηc θαλαccηc τηc τιβεριαδοc εφανερωcε δε ουτωc.

DEF: **P**^{66} μ[ ]ạ εφạν̣[ ]ρ̣ω̣[ ]εν̣ [ ]οιc μαθητα[ ] τηc τιβεριαδ[ ]υτωc

21:2

P^{66}

2: ηcαν ομου cιμων πετροc και θωμαc ο λεγομενοc διδυμοc και ναθαναηλ ο απο κανα τηc γαλιλαιαc και οι του ζεβεδαιου και αλλοι εκ των μαθητων αυτου δυο.

DEF: **P**^{66} ηcα[ ]c̣ και θωμ̣[ ] δ[ ]δυ̣μοc̣ καị [ ]ο κα[ ] γαλ[ ] οι τοụ ζεβ̣εδα[ ]ο̣υ̣ κ̣[ ] εκ των μ̣ạθητων αυ̣[

21:3

P^{66}

3: λεγει αυτοιc cιμων πετροc υπαγω αλιευειν λεγουcιν αυτω ερχομεθα και ημειc cυν coι εξηλθον και ανεβηcαν ειc το πλοιον ευθυc και εν εκεινη τη νυκτι επιαcαν ουδεν.

DEF: **P**^{66}]εγει αυ̣[ ]c cιμω̣ν π̣[ ]γω α[ ]ε̣υε[ ]ν λ̣εγο[ ]ρχο[ ]με[ ]η̣c̣[

21:4

P^{66}

4: πρωιαc δε ηδη γενομενηc εcτη ο ιηcουc ειc τον αιγιαλον ου μεντοι ηδειcαν οι μαθηται οτι ιηcουc εcτι.

DEF: **P**[66]]γιαλ[ ] εγνω[ ]ṭιν

ηδειcαν: εγνω[ ] **P**[66]
εcτι: [ ]τιν **P**[66]

21:5

P[66]

5: λεγει ουν αυτοιc ο ιηcουc παιδια μη τι προcφαγιον εχετε απεκριθηcαν αυτω ου.

DEF: **P**[66] λε[ ]ạ μ[ ]θηc̣[

21:6

P[66]

6: ο δε ειπεν αυτοιc βαλετε ειc τα δεξια μερη του πλοιου το δικτυον και ευρηcετε εβαλον ουν και ουκ ετι αυτο ελκυcαι ιcχυcαν απο του πληθουc των ιχθυων.

DEF: **P**[66]]ν αυ[ ]c β̣[ ] ṭα δεξια μẹρη τ[ ]υον και
ευρηcετạ[ ]ν και ουδẹ[ ] ελαβ̣[ ] cω [ ]νομ[

ευρηcετε: ευρηcετα[ ] **P**[66]; + [ ]ν και ουδε[ ] ελαβ[ ] cω [ ]νομ[ ] **P**[66]

21:7

P[59] **P**[66]

7: λεγει ουν ο μαθητηc εκεινοc ον ηγαπα ο ιηcουc τω πετρω ο κυριοc εcτι cιμων ουν πετροc ακουcαc οτι ο κυριοc εcτι τον επενδυτην διεζωcατο ην γαρ γυμνοc και εβαλεν εαυτον ειc την θαλαccαν.

DEF: **P**[59]]ζω[
P[66] $\overline{\text{κc}}$] εcτι[ ]ην δ[ ]το η[ ]ạ[ ]ṭοṿ [

21:8

P^{66}

8: οι δε αλλοι μαθηται τω πλοιαριω ηλθον ου γαρ ηϲαν μακραν απο τηϲ γηϲ αλλ ωϲ απο πηχων διακοϲιων ϲυροντεϲ το δικτυον των ιχθυων.

DEF: **P^{66}**] α̣λ̣λ[ ]λθο[ ]η̣[ ] γηϲ α̣λ̣λ̣ ωϲ απο̣ [ ]ϲιων ϲυροντεϲ τ[ ]ω̣ν ιχθυ̣ων

21:9

P^{66}

9: ωϲ ουν απεβηϲαν ειϲ την γην βλεπουϲιν ανθρακιαν κειμενην και οψαριον επικειμενον και αρτον.

DEF: **P^{66}** ωϲ ουν̣ [ ] την [ ]η̣ν βλεπου̣[ ]ν̣ην και [

21:10

10: λεγει αυτοιϲ ο ιηϲουϲ ενεγκατε απο των οψαριων ων επιαϲατε νυν.

21:11

11: ανεβη ϲιμων πετροϲ και ειλκυϲε το δικτυον επι τηϲ γηϲ μεϲτον ιχθυων μεγαλων εκατον πεντηκοντατριων και τοϲουτων οντων ουκ εϲχιϲθη το δικτυον.

21:12

P^{59}

12: λεγει αυτοιϲ ο ιηϲουϲ δευτε αριϲτηϲατε ουδειϲ δε ετολμα των μαθητων εξεταϲαι αυτον ϲυ τιϲ ει ειδοτεϲ οτι ο κυριοϲ εϲτιν.

DEF: **P^{59}**]ξ[ ] ειδ[

21:13

P^{59}

13: ερχεται ουν ο ιηϲουϲ και λαμβανει τον αρτον και διδωϲιν αυτοιϲ και το οψαριον ομοιωϲ.

DEF: **P^{59}** ερχ[

21:14

14: τουτο ηδη τριτον εφανερωθη ο ιηcουc τοιc μαθηταιc αυτου εγερθειc εκ νεκρων.

21:15

P59

15: οτε ουν ηριcτηcαν λεγει τω cιμωνι πετρω ο ιηcουc cιμων ιωνα αγαπαc με πλειον τουτων λεγει αυτω ναι κυριε cυ οιδαc οτι φιλω cε λεγει αυτω βοcκε τα αρνια μου.

DEF: **P59**] πλι[ ] κε cυ [

πλειον: πλι[ ] **P59**

21:16

16: λεγει αυτω παλιν δευτερον cιμων ιωνα αγαπαc με λεγει αυτω ναι κυριε cυ οιδαc οτι φιλω cε λεγει αυτω ποιμαινε τα προβατα μου.

21:17

P59

17: λεγει αυτω το τριτον cιμων ιωνα φιλειc με ελυπηθη ο πετροc οτι ειπεν αυτω το τριτον φιλειc με και ειπεν αυτω κυριε cυ παντα οιδαc cυ γινωcκειc οτι φιλω cε λεγει αυτω ο ιηcουc βοcκε τα προβατα μου.

DEF: **P59** λεγει αυτ[ ] cιμων [ ]λειc με ελ[ ]τροc οτι ε[ ] τρι[ ] πα[ ]νω[ ] cε λ[ ]c[

ιωνα φιλειc: [9-13 /]λειc **P59**
τριτον φιλειc με και ειπεν αυτω κυριε: τρι[11-14] **P59**
cυ παντα οιδαc cυ γινωcκειc: πα[12-16 /]νω[ ] **P59**

21:18

P[59]

18: αμην αμην λεγω σοι οτε ης νεωτερος εζωννυες σεαυτον και περιεπατεις οπου ηθελες οταν δε γηρασης εκτενεις τας χειρας σου και αλλος σε ζωσει και οισει οπου ου θελεις.

DEF: **P**[59]]ν λεγω σοι [ ]τερος εζω̅ [ ]ν και περι[ ] ηθελες ο[ ]τενεις [ ] αλλοι [ ] ποισου[

αλλος σε ζωσει και οισει: αλλοι [/ 14-15] ποισου[ ] **P**[59]

21:19

P[59]

19: τουτο δε ειπε σημαινων ποιω θανατω δοξασει τον θεον και τουτο ειπων λεγει αυτω ακολουθει μοι.

DEF: **P**[59]] και το[ ]τ[ ]τω ακολ[

21:20

P[59]

20: επιστραφεις δε ο πετρος βλεπει τον μαθητην ον ηγαπα ο ιησους ακολουθουντα ος και ανεπεσεν εν τω δειπνω επι το στηθος αυτου και ειπε κυριε τις εστιν ο παραδιδους σε.

DEF: **P**[59]]στραφεις δ[ ]πι τον μα[ ]γαπα ο ι̅ς̅ [ ] και α[ ]πνω [ ] ιυ κ[

βλεπει: [ ]πι **P**[59]
αυτου: ιυ **P**[59]

21:21

21: τουτον ιδων ο πετρος λεγει τω ιησου κυριε ουτος δε τι.

21:22

22: λεγει αυτω ο ιησους εαν αυτον θελω μενειν εως ερχομαι τι προς σε συ ακολουθει μοι.

21:23

P[59]

23: εξηλθεν ουν ο λογος ουτος εις τους αδελφους οτι ο μαθητης εκεινος ουκ αποθνησκει και ουκ ειπεν αυτω ο ιησους οτι ουκ αποθνησκει αλλ εαν αυτον θελω μενειν εως ερχομαι τι προς σε.

DEF: **P**[59]]ν ο λογος [ ]υς αδελ[ ] μαθητης [ ]υκ αποθνη[ ]πεν δε αυ[ ]θνη[ ] θε[ ]ρχο[

και ουκ ειπεν: [ ]πεν δε **P**[59]

21:24

24: ουτος εστιν ο μαθητης ο μαρτυρων περι τουτων και γραψας ταυτα και οιδαμεν οτι αληθης εστιν η μαρτυρια αυτου.

21:25

25: εστι δε και αλλα πολλα οσα εποιησεν ο ιησους ατινα εαν γραφηται καθ εν ουδε αυτον οιμαι τον κοσμον χωρησαι τα γραφομενα βιβλια αμην.

PLATES

LIST OF PLATES

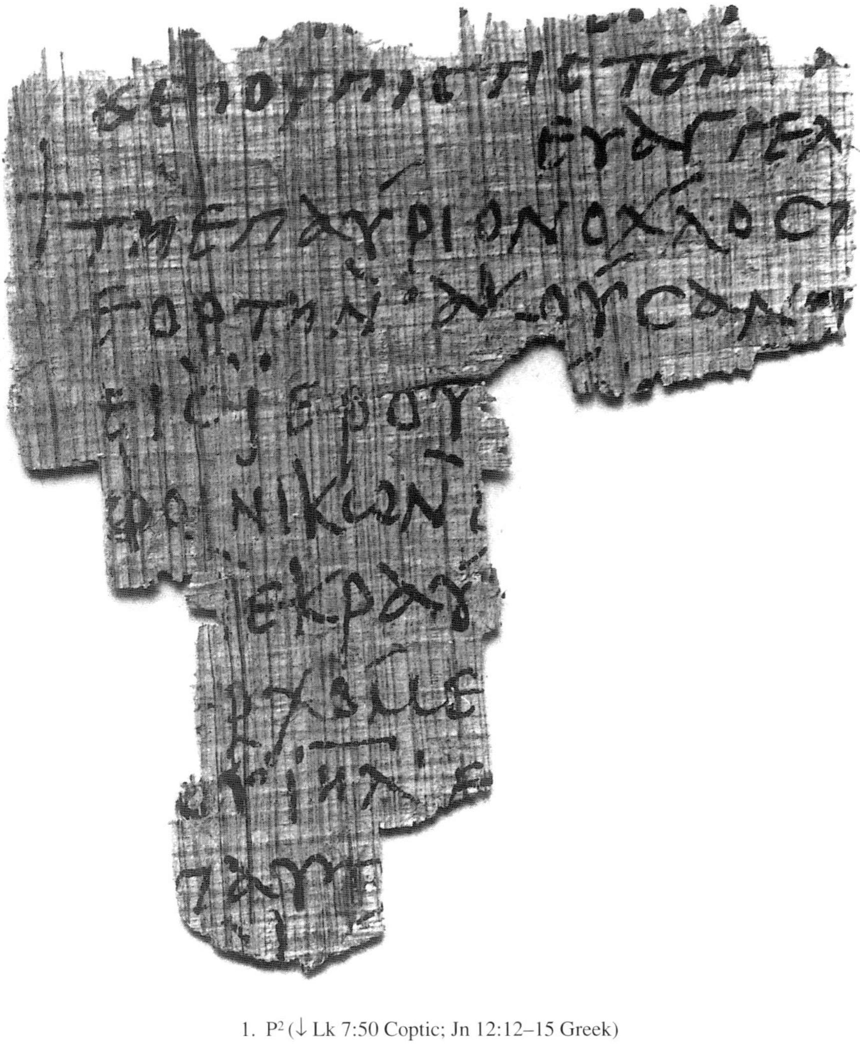

1. P2 (↓ Lk 7:50 Coptic; Jn 12:12–15 Greek)

2. P^5 first fragment ↓; first page (1:23–31) and sixth page (20:19–25)

3. P[5] first fragment →; second page (1:33–40) and fifth page (20:11–17)

4. P[5] second fragment →; third page (16:14–22)

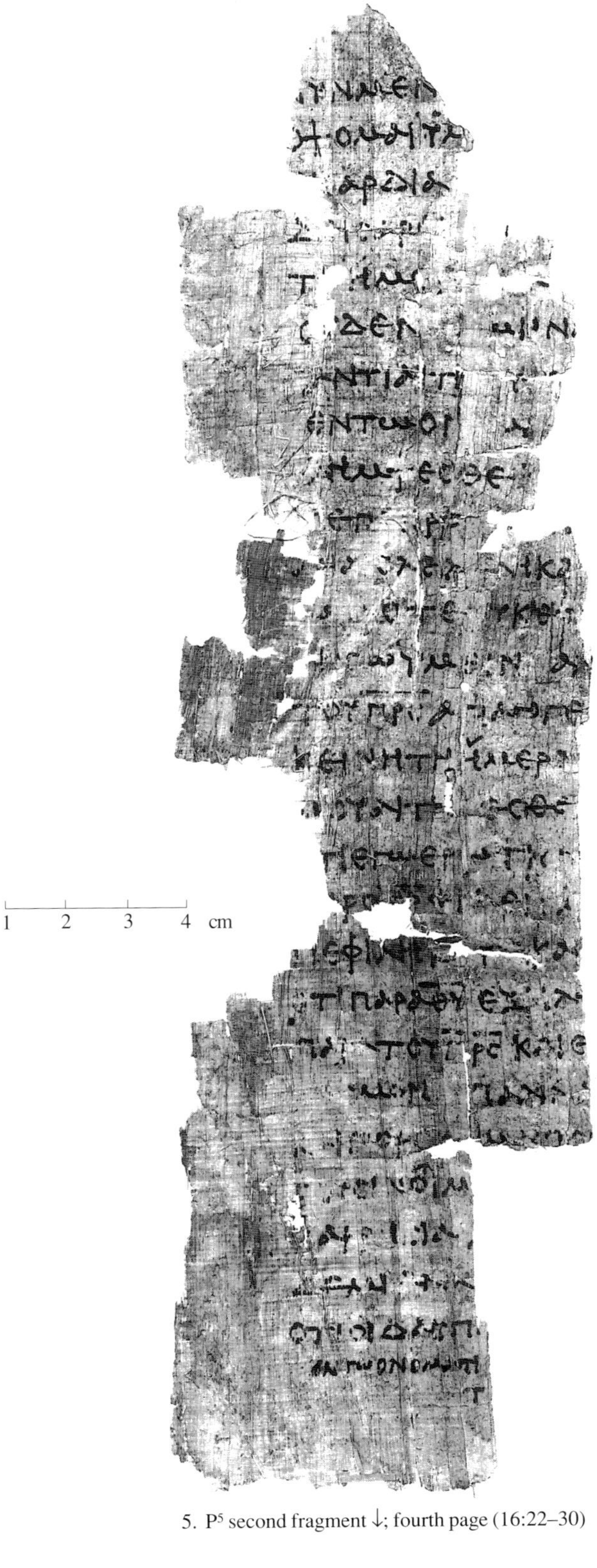

5. P[5] second fragment ↓; fourth page (16:22–30)

6. P[6] first page ↓ (10:1–2, 4–7, 9–10 Greek; 10:1 Coptic)

1 2 3 4 cm

7. P6 second page → (10:40–42 Coptic; 11:1– 8 Greek)

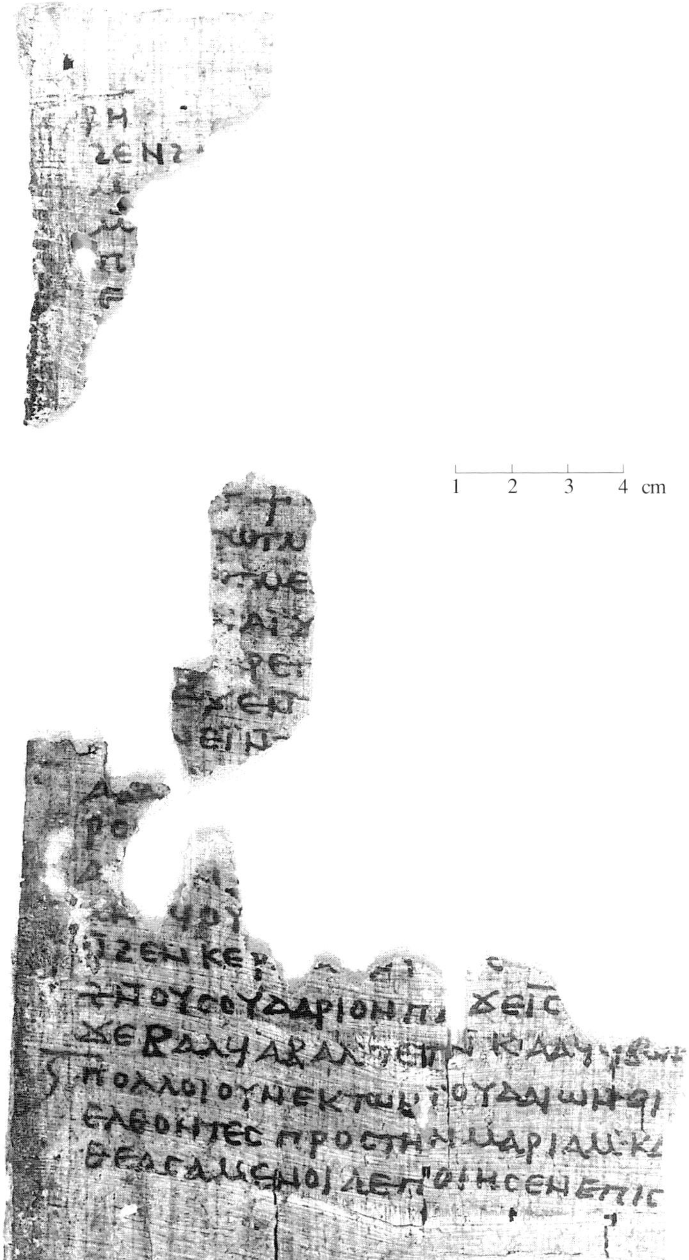

8. P6 third page → (11:37–44 Coptic; 11:45 Greek)

9. P^{6} fourth page ↓ (11:45–52 Greek; 45–47 Coptic)

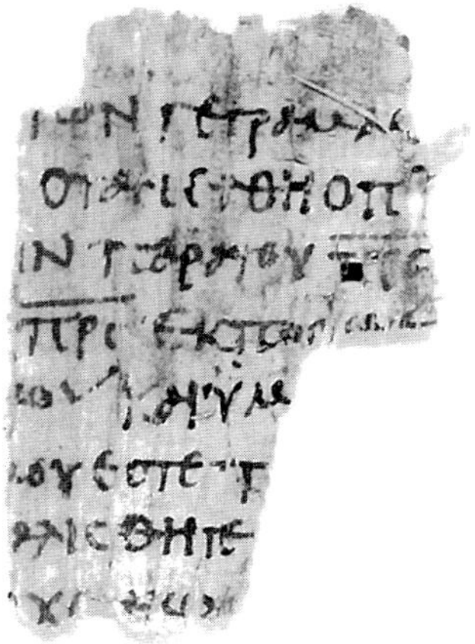

10.(a) P[22] first fragment (15:25–16:2)

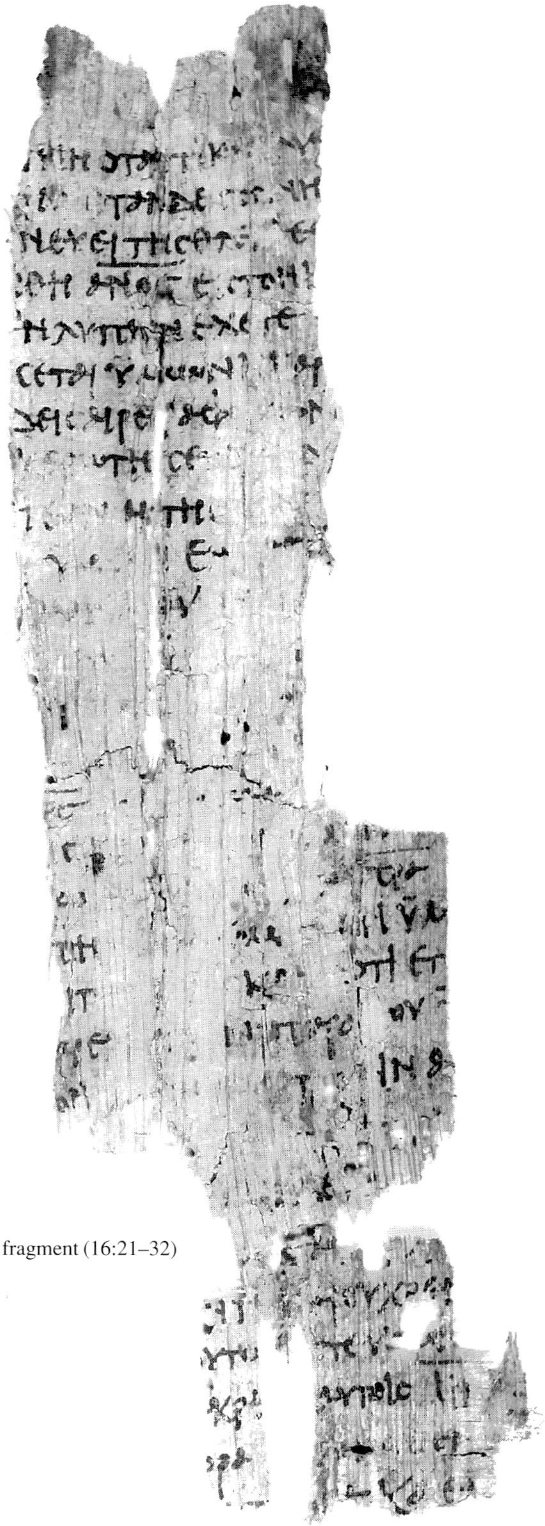

10.(b) P[22] second fragment (16:21–32)

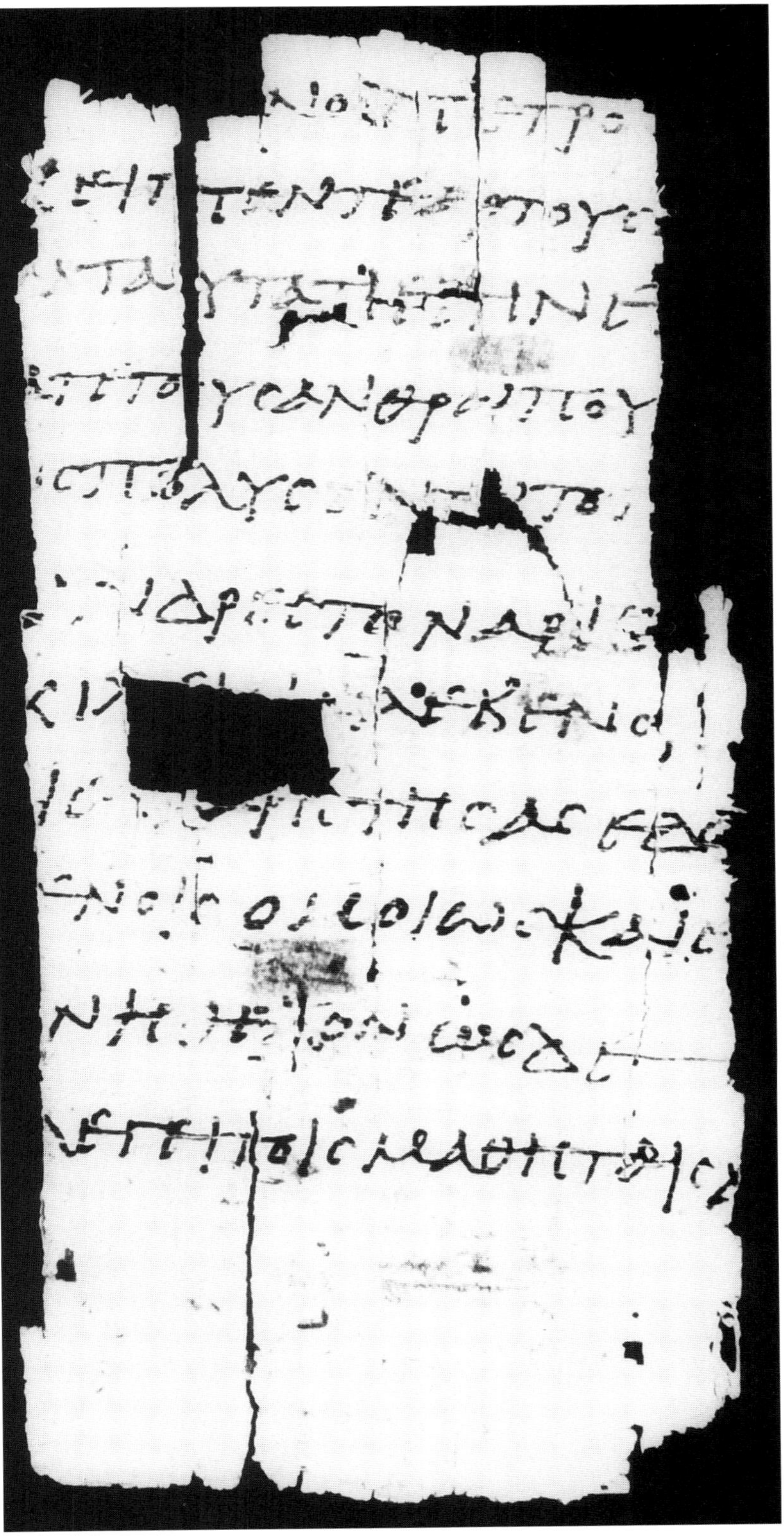

11. P28 → (6:8–12)

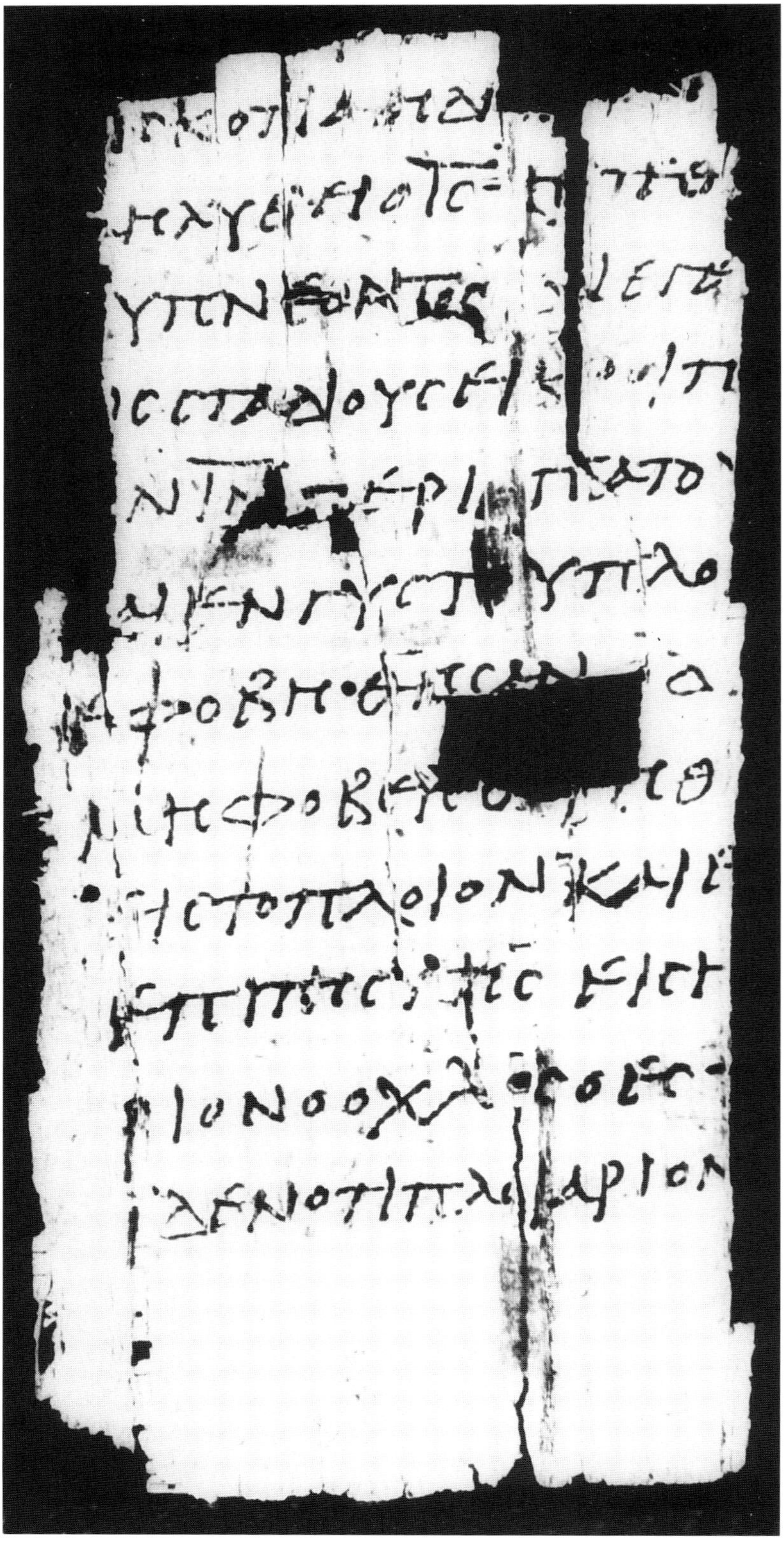

12. P^{28} ↓ (6:17–22)

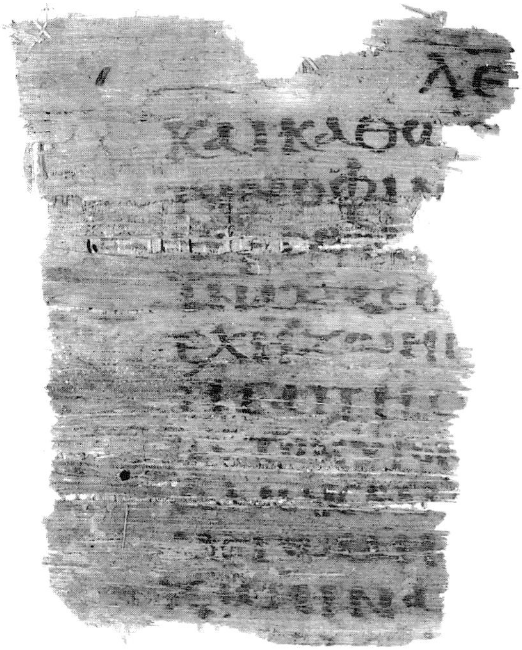

13.(a) P[36] first fragment → (3:14–16)

13.(c) P[36] second fragment ↓ (3:31–32)

13.(b) P[36] first fragment ↓ (3:17–18)

13.(d) P[36] second fragment → (3:34–36)

1 2 3 4 cm

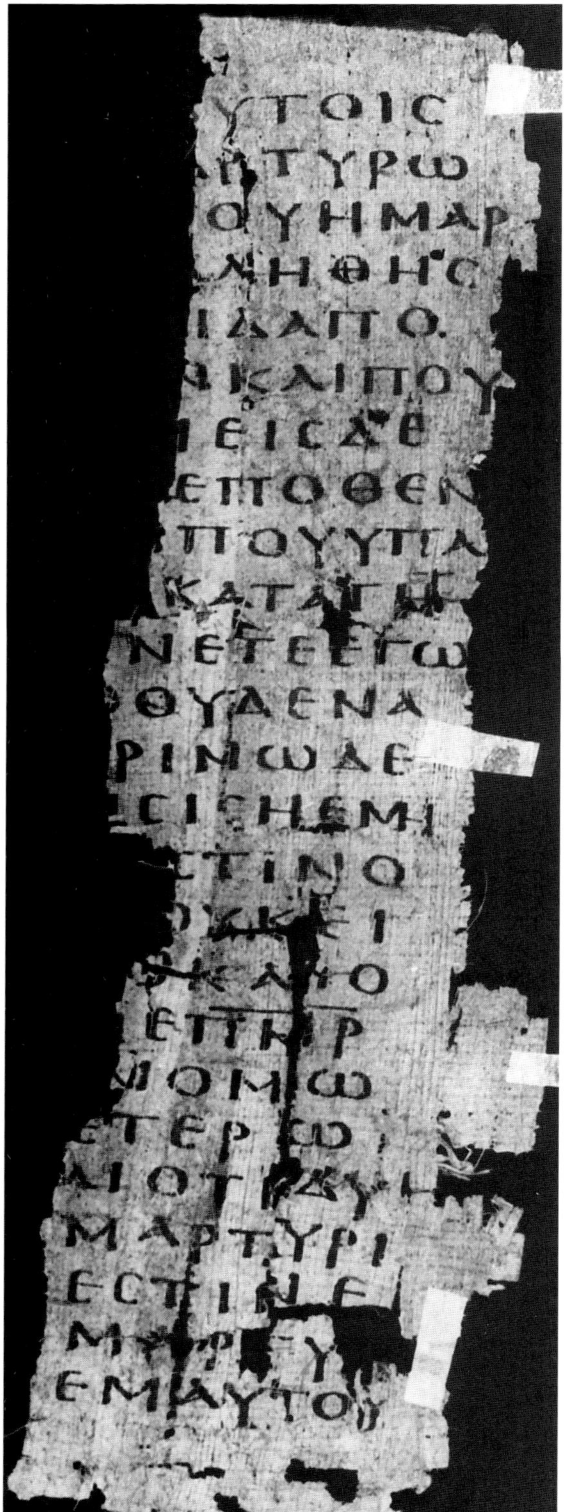

14.(a) P39 ↓ (8:14–18)

14.(b) P39 → (8:18–22)

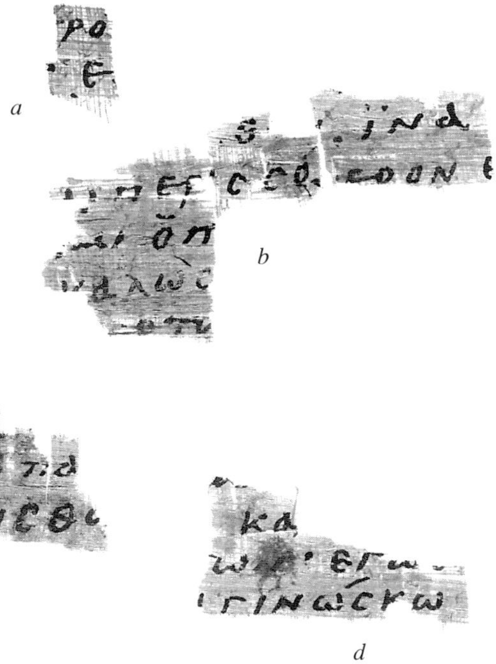

15.(a–d) P44A (→ 10:8–14)

15.(e) P44B fragment I → (9:3–4); (f) P44B fragment II → (9:4); (g) P44B fragment III ↓ (12:12–13)

15.(h) P44B fragment I ↓ (12:16–18)

15.(i) P44B fragment II ↓ (12:17)

16.(a) P^{45} fragment B → (4:51–53)

16.(b) P^{45} fragment C → (4:53–5:2)

16.(c) P^{45} fragment B ↓ (5:21–23)

16.(d) P^{45} fragment C ↓ (5:24–25)

17. P45 F16v ↓ (10:7–25)

18. P45 F16r → (10:29–11:11)

19. P45 F17r →(11:17–37)

20. P^{45} F17v ↓ (11:42–57)

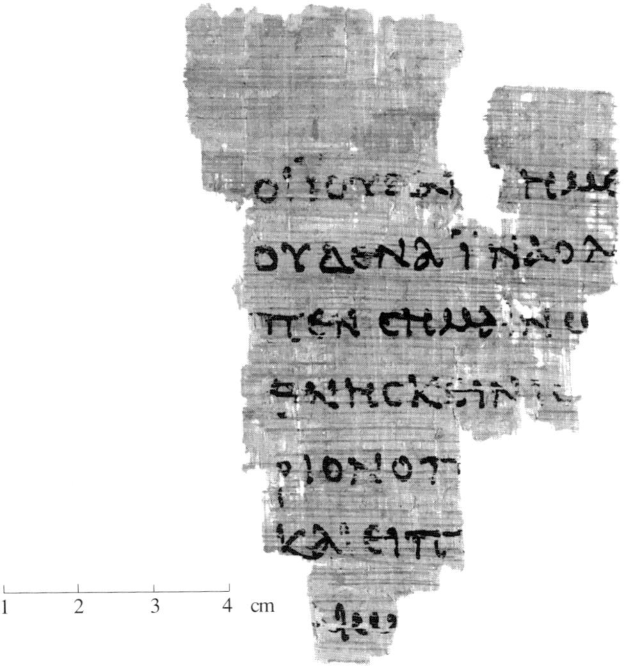

21.(a) P[52] → (18:31–33)

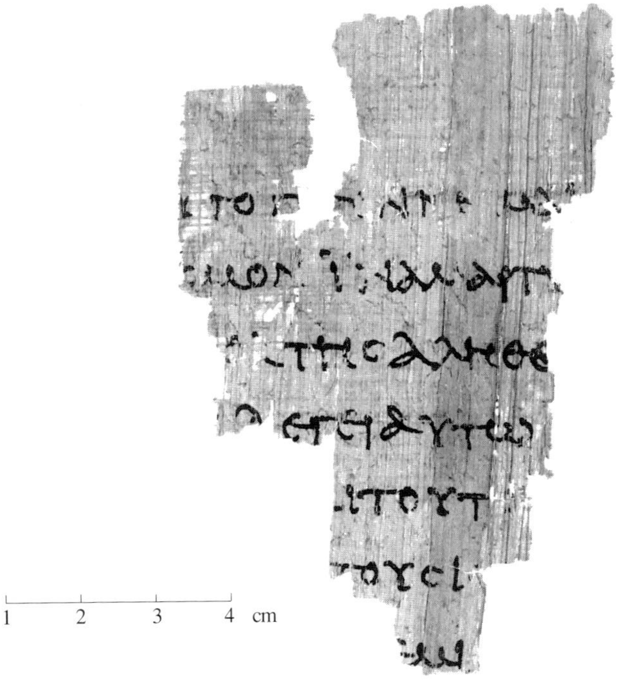

21.(b) P[52] ↓ (18:37–38)

22. P^{55} → (1:31–33)

23. P55 ↓ (1:35–38 and hermeneia heading)

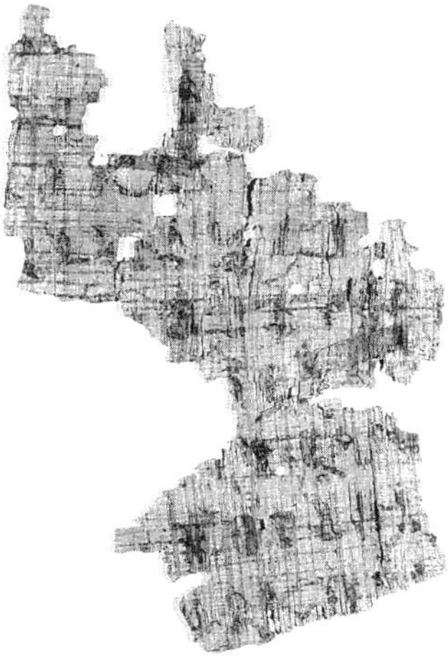

24.(a) P[59] fragment III ↓ (2:15–16)

24.(d) P[59] fragment VI → (12:31)

24.(b) P[59] fragment V ↓ (12:25)

24.(e) P[59] fragment VI ↓ (12:35)

24.(c) P[59] fragment V → (12:29)

24.(f) P[59] fragment IV (d) (ii) (11:51–52)

25. P[59] fragment IV (a) (11:40–43 and hermeneia) and IV (d) (i) (11:49–52 and hermeneia)

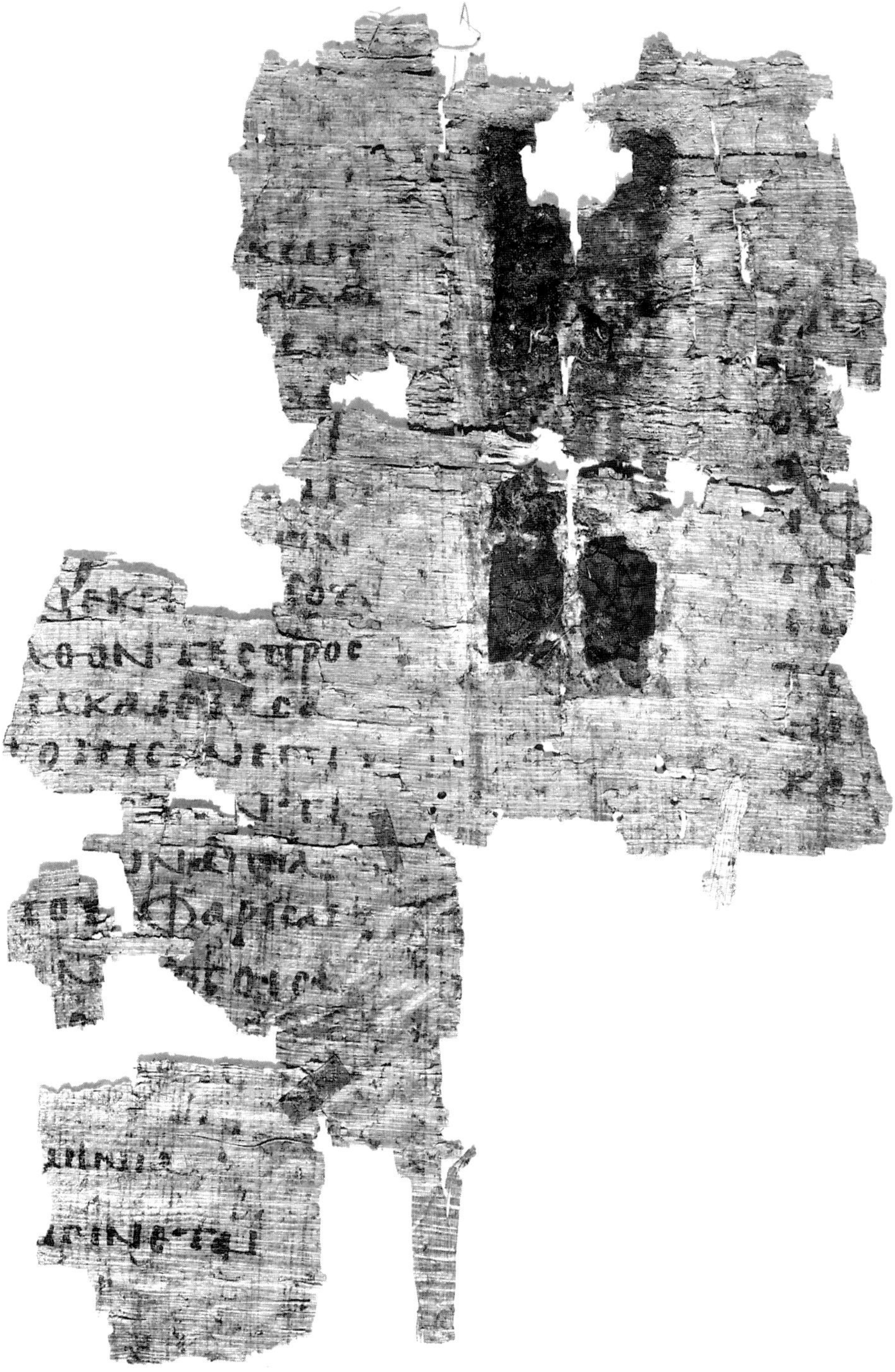

26. P[59] fragment IV (b) (11:44–46 and hermeneia) and IV (c) (11:47–48)

27.(a) P[59] fragment VII ↓ (17:24–26)

27.(b) P[59] fragment VII → (18:1–2)

28.(a) P^{59} fragment IX ↓ (18:22)

28.(b) P^{59} fragment XI ↓ (21:12–13)

28.(c) P^{59} fragment XI → (21:15)

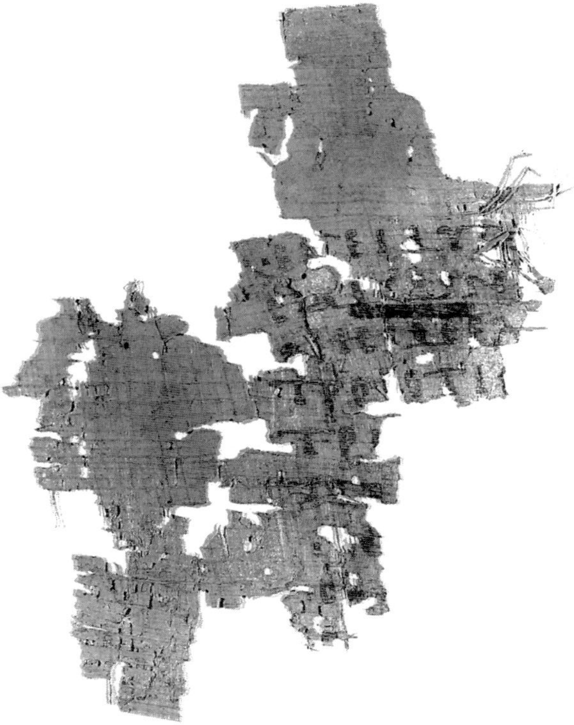

29.(a) P^{59} fragment XII → (21:17)

29.(b) P^{59} fragment XII ↓ (21:18)

30.(a) P^{59} fragment X (c) (21:19–20)

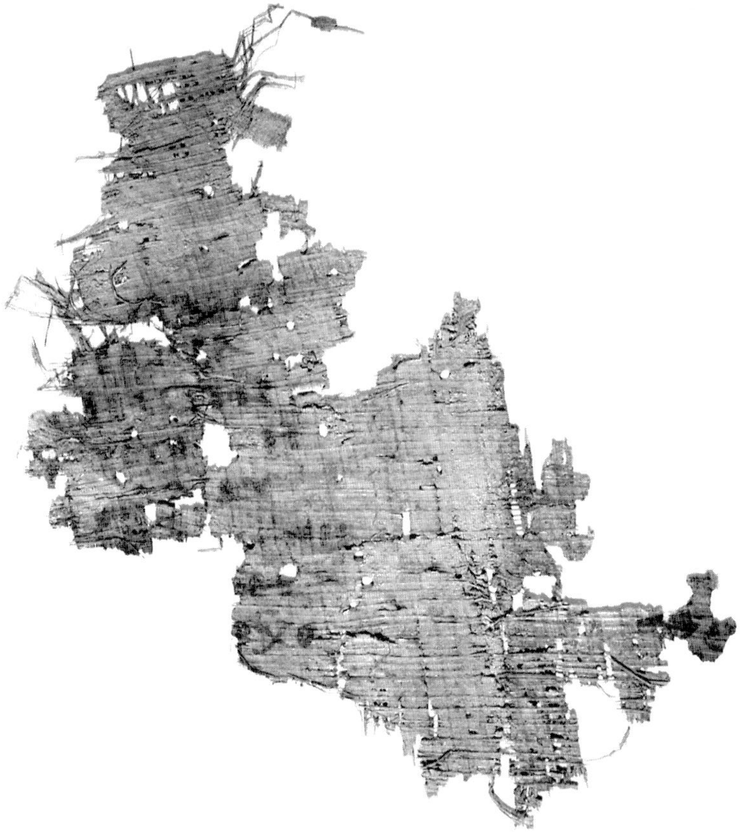

30.(b) P^{59} fragment X (d) (21:23)

31.(a) P⁶⁰ fragment I ↓ (16:30)

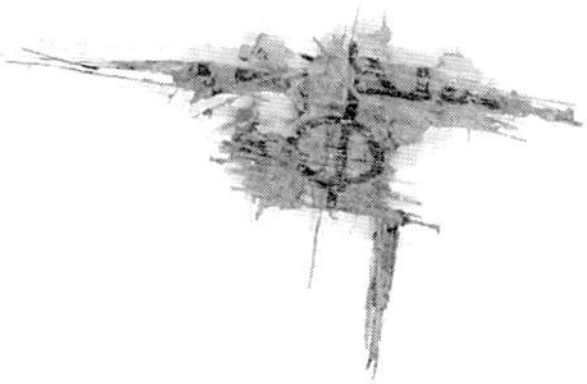

31.(b) P⁶⁰ fragment I → (16:32)

31.(c) P⁶⁰ fragment II → (16:33)

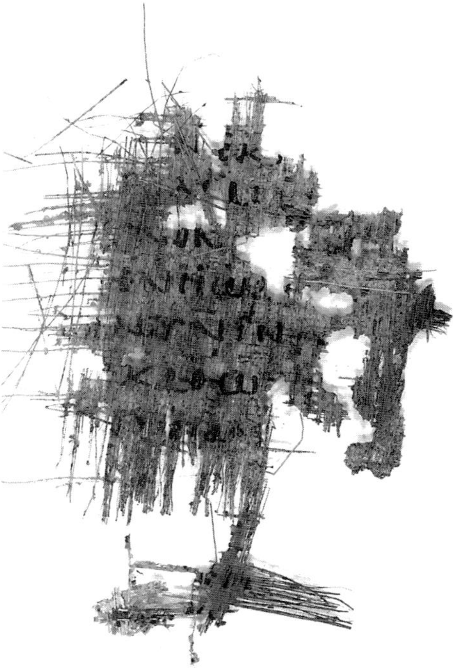

31.(d) P⁶⁰ fragment II ↓ (17:1–2)

32.(a) P⁶⁰ fragment III ↓ (17:3–4)

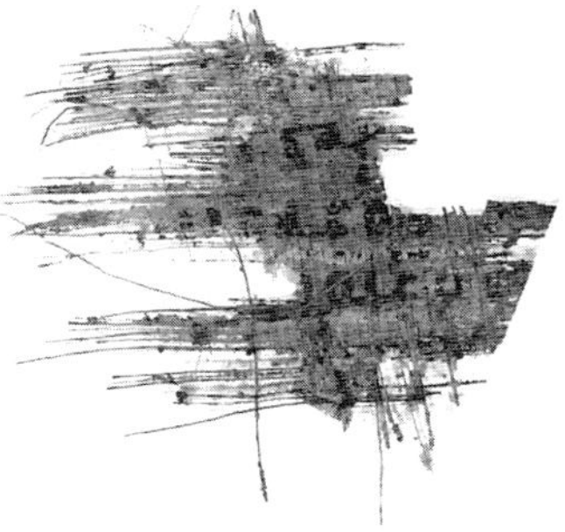

32.(b) P⁶⁰ fragment III → (17:5–6)

32.(c) P⁶⁰ fragment IV → (17:8–9)

32.(d) P⁶⁰ fragment IV ↓ (17:11)

33.(a) P[60] fragment V ↓ (17:12–13)

33.(b) P[60] fragment V → (17:14–15)

33.(c) P[60] fragment VI → (17:18–20)

33.(d) P[60] fragment VI ↓ (17:21–23)

34.(a) P⁶⁰ fragment VII ↓ (17:24–25)

34.(b) P⁶⁰ fragment VII → (18:1–2)

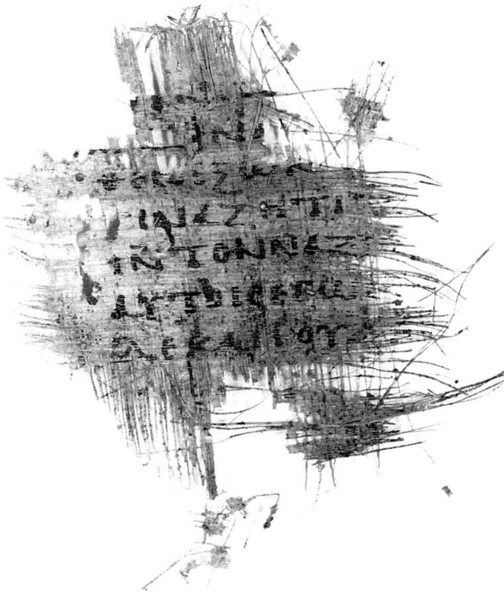

34.(c) P⁶⁰ fragment VIII → (18:4–5)

34.(d) P⁶⁰ fragment VIII ↓ (18:7–9)

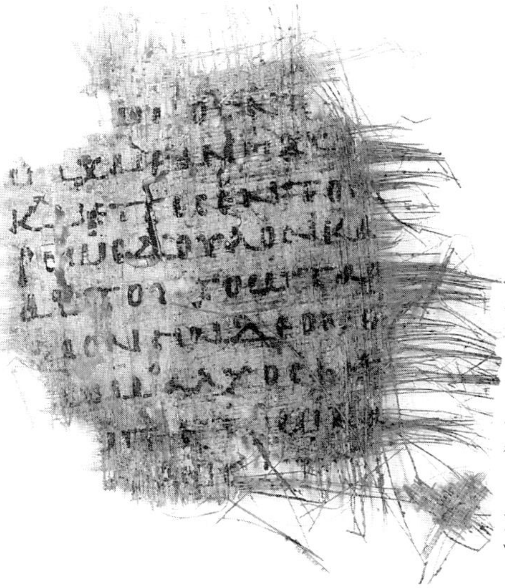

35.(a) P[60] fragment IX ↓ (18:10–11)

35.(b) P[60] fragment IX → (18:12–14)

35.(c) P[60] fragment X → (18:15–16)

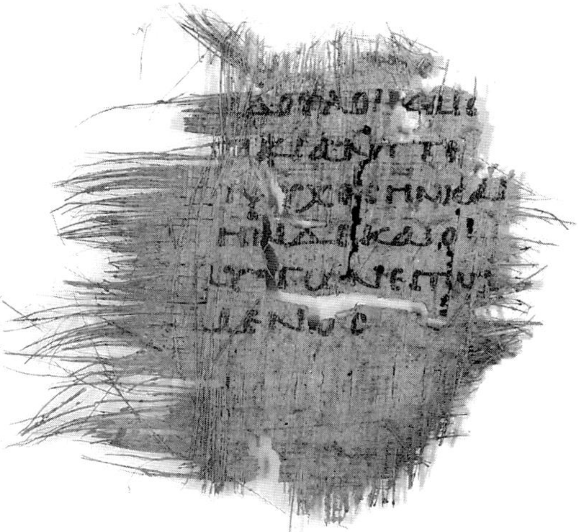

35.(d) P[60] fragment X ↓ (18:18)

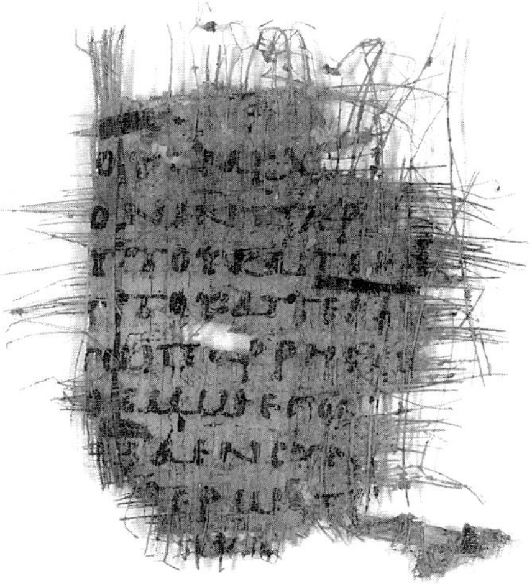

36.(a) P^{60} fragment XI ↓ (18:19–20)

36.(b) P^{60} fragment XI → (18:23–25)

36.(c) P^{60} fragment XII → (18:26–27)

36.(d) P^{60} fragment XII ↓ (18:28–29)

37.(a) P⁶⁰ fragment XIII ↓ (18:31)

37.(b) P⁶⁰ fragment XIII → (18:32–33)

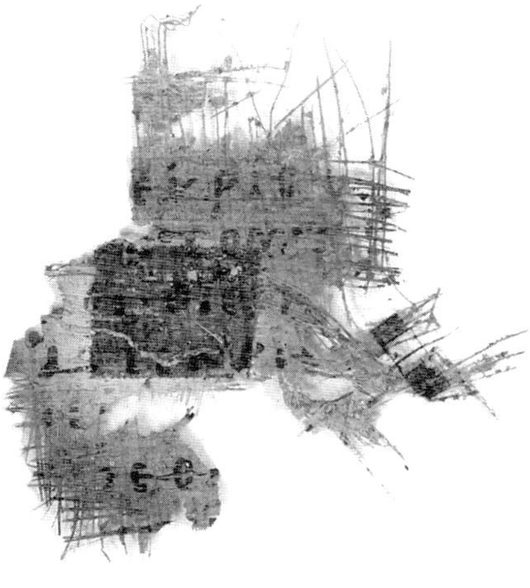

37.(c) P⁶⁰ fragment XIV → (18:34–35)

37.(d) P⁶⁰ fragment XIV ↓ (18:36)

38.(a) P[60] fragment XV ↓ (18:37)

38.(b) P[60] fragment XV → (18:39–40)

38.(c) P[60] fragment XVI → (19:2–3)

38.(d) P[60] fragment XVI ↓ (19:5–6)

39.(a) P^{60} fragment XVII ↓ (19:7–8)

39.(b) P^{60} fragment XVII → (19:10–11)

39.(c) P^{60} fragment XVIII → (19:12–13)

39.(d) P^{60} fragment XVIII ↓ (19:14–15)

40.(a) P^{60} fragment XIX ↓ (19:16–18)

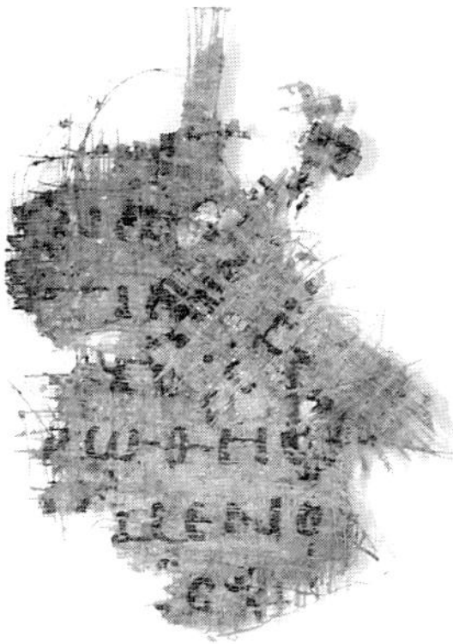

40.(b) P^{60} fragment XIX → (19:20)

40.(c) P^{60} fragment XX → (19:23)

40.(d) P^{60} fragment XX ↓ (19:24–26)

41. P63 → : first page (3:14–15 and hermeneia) and fourth page (4:10 and hermeneia)

42. P[63] ↓: second page (3:16–18 and hermeneia) and third page (4:9 and hermeneia)

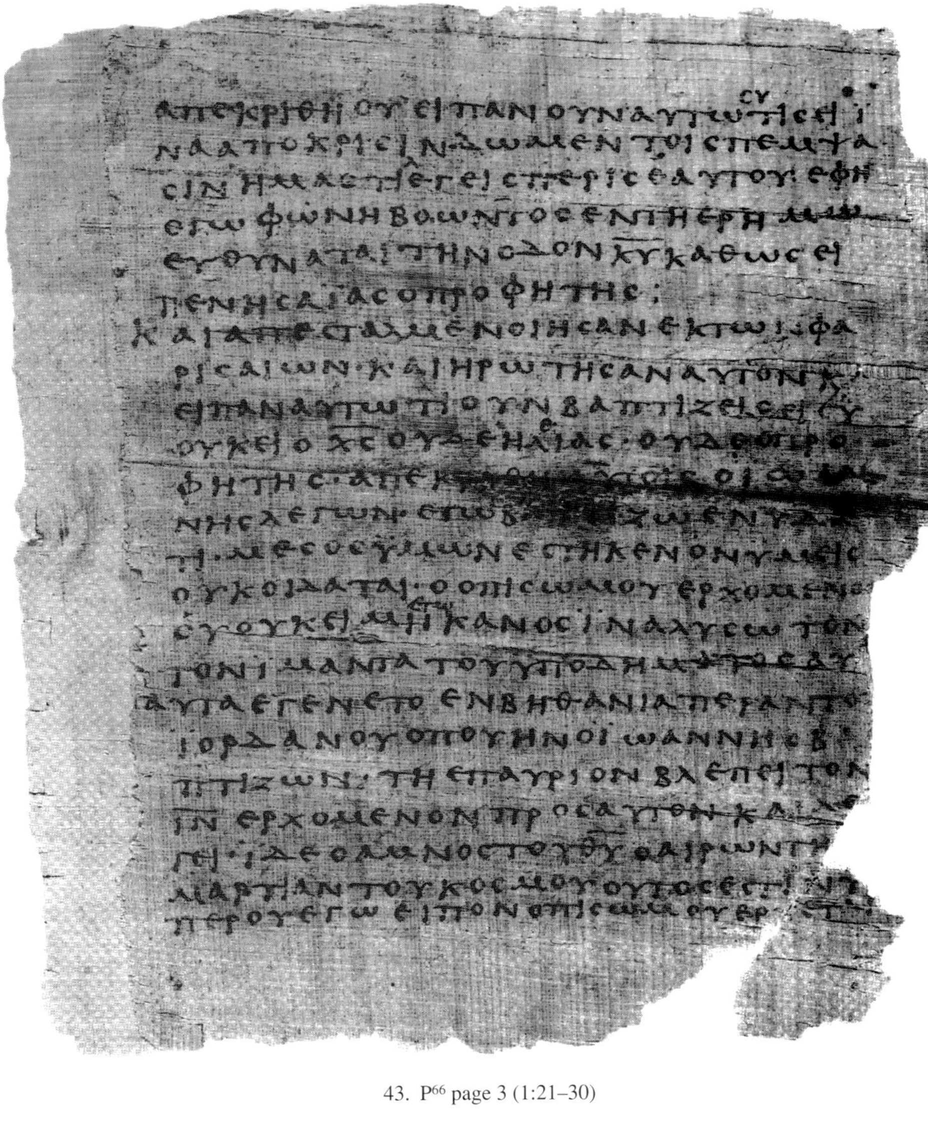

43. P[66] page 3 (1:21–30)

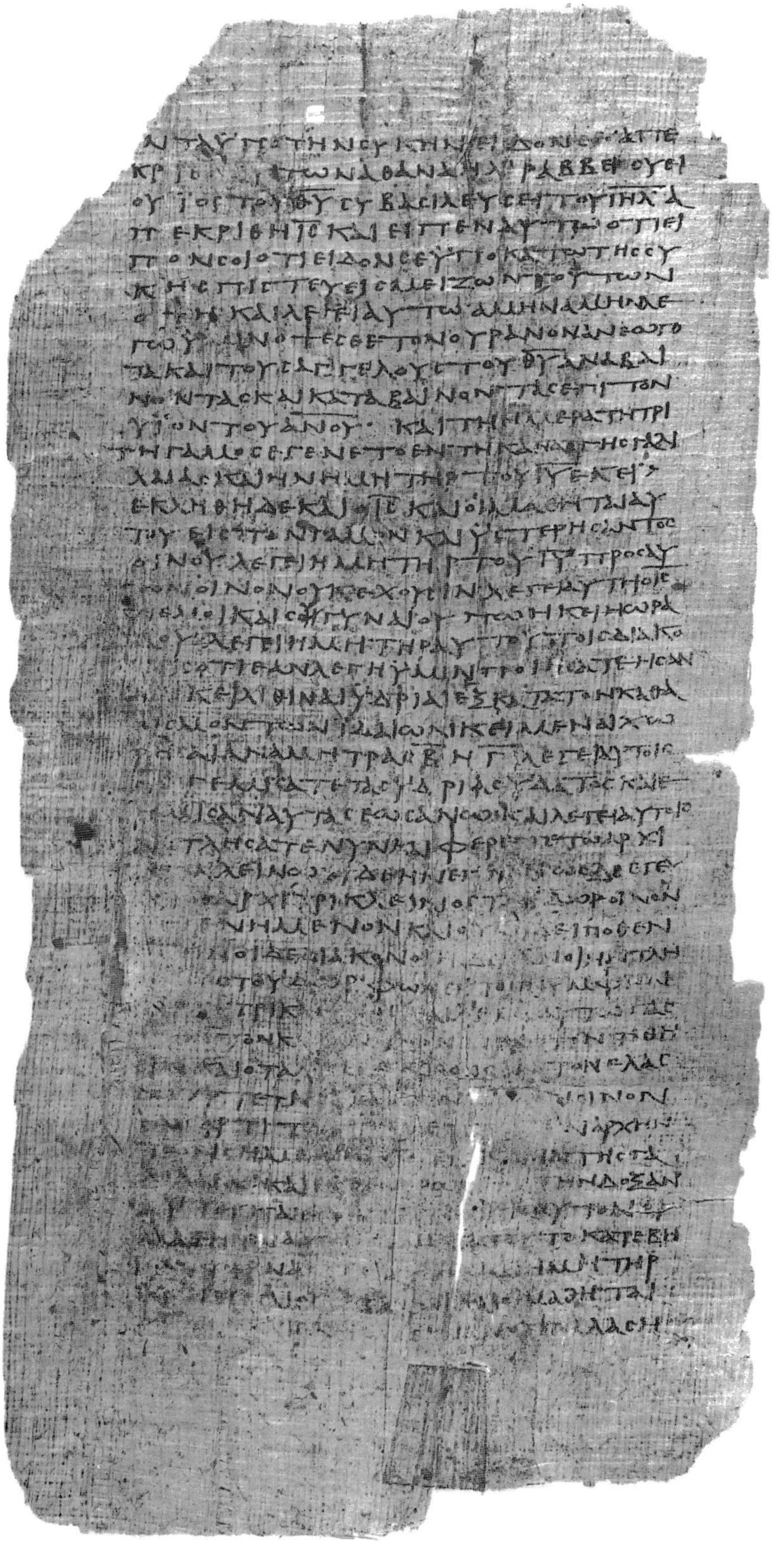

44. P^{75} page 64 (1:48–2:12)

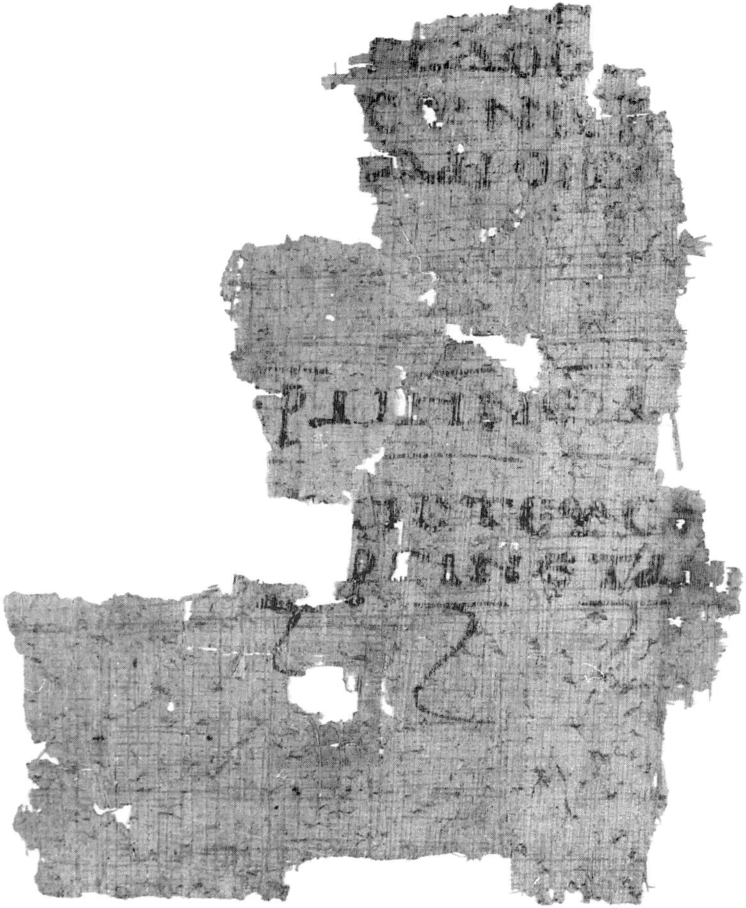

45.(a) P[76] ↓ (4:9 and hermeneia)

1 2 3 4 cm

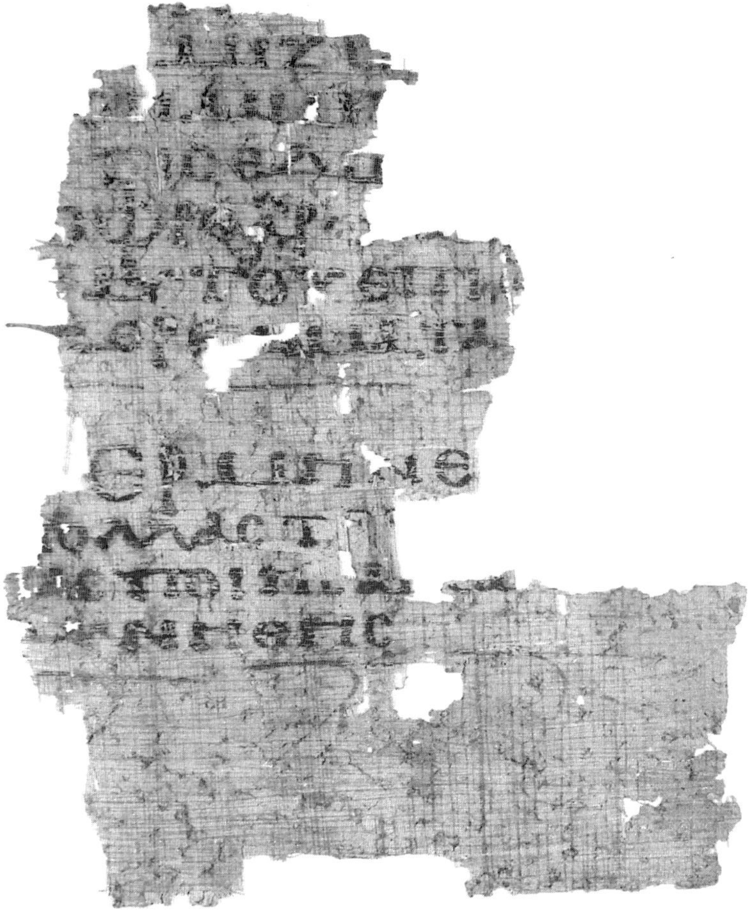

45.(b) P[76] → (4:12 and hermeneia)

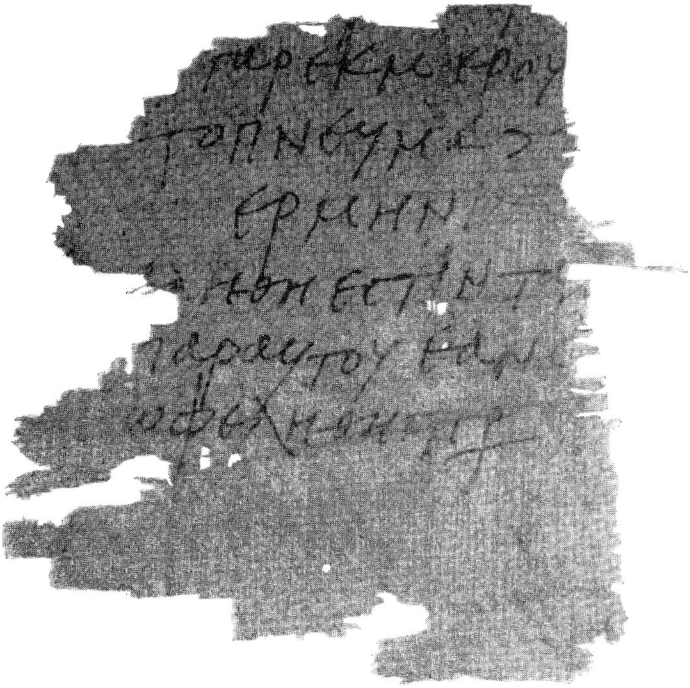

46.(a) P[80] ↓ (3:34 and hermeneia)

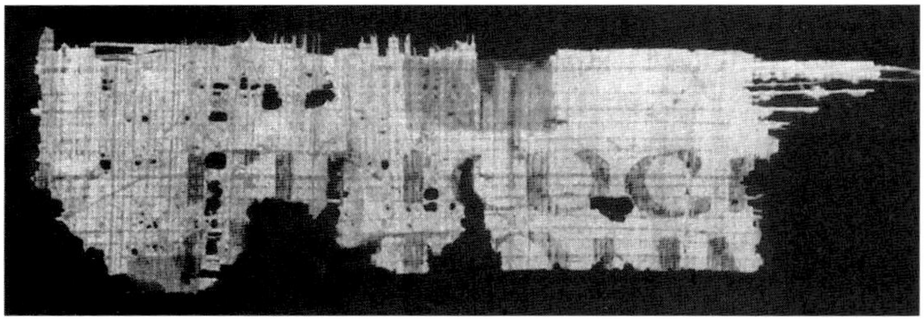

46.(b) P[84] second fragment → (17:3)

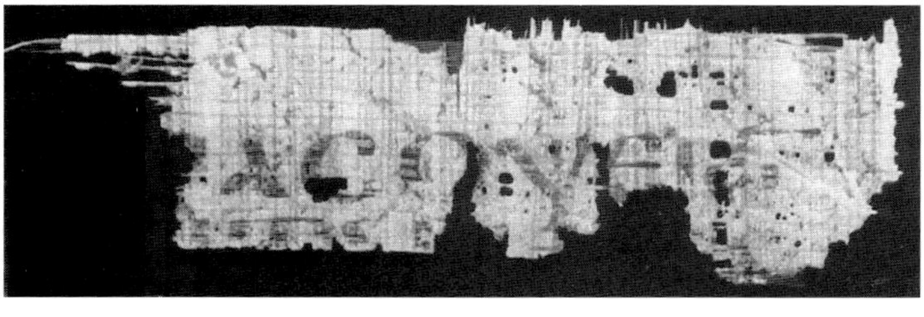

46.(c) P[84] third fragment ↓ (17:7–8)

1 2 3 4 cm

47.(a) P⁹⁰ → (18:36–19:1)

47.(b) P⁹⁰ ↓ (19:1–7)

48.(a) P[93] → (13:15–17)

1 2 3 4 cm

48.(b) P[95] → (5:26–29)

48.(c) P[95] ↓ (5:36–38)